Population Policymaking
in the American States

Population Policymaking in the American States

Issues and Processes

Edited by

Elihu Bergman
David N. Carter
Rebecca J. Cook
Richard D. Tabors
David R. Weir, Jr.
Mary Ellen Urann

Center for Population Studies
Harvard University

Lexington Books
D.C. Heath and Company
Lexington, Massachusetts
Toronto   London

Library of Congress Cataloging in Publication Data

Main entry under title:

Population policymaking in the American states.

1. United States—Population—Addresses, essays, lectures. I. Bergman, Elihu.
HB3505.P66   301.31   73-22248
ISBN 0-699-92973-5

Published simultaneously in Canada.

Printed in the United States of America.

International Standard Book Number: 0-669-92973-5

Library of Congress Catalog Card Number: 73-22248

Contents

Preface

This volume emerged from the common interests of participants in a state policy study group that met at the Harvard Center for Population Studies during the academic year 1972-73. The study group provided a forum for the exchange of interests, ideas, research enterprises, and written material on how the American states were dealing with policy issues generated by population change within their jurisdictions.

As its major project for the year, the group undertook to identify significant issues involving the substance and structure of population policymaking that were emerging at the state level, and to assemble material written about them in an organized sequence of readings.

For their contribution to this enterprise, we are indebted to many, but we should like to single out one individual for special mention. Roger Revelle, Director of the Harvard Center for Population Studies, encouraged our enterprise and provided us with a compatible environment in which to do our work. We are grateful to him for his professional and intellectual companionship.

Part I:
Introduction

1

American Population Policymaking: A Shift to the States

Elihu Bergman*

It could be said that interest in population matters at the federal level of the American government crested in 1970. This high water mark was symbolized in the enactment of two pieces of legislation by the 91st Congress: the Family Planning Services and Population Research Act (Public Law 91-572) and an Act to Establish a Commission on Population Growth and the American Future (Public Law 91-213).[1]

Two years later, the tide of interest had substantially receded. President Nixon greeted the completed report of the Commission on Population Growth and the American Future, when it was presented in April 1972, with instant sharp criticism of the recommendations on sex education and abortion, and then proceeded to ignore the balance of the comprehensive document. When the Family Planning Act came up for renewal in early 1973, the Administration opposed the legislation, and the Congress half-heartedly renewed authorizations for family planning services for only a single year (Public Law 93-45, approved June 18, 1973).

What transpired during the short flow and ebb on the national level provides a rationale for this volume, which deals with the emergence of interest in population phenomena in the American states. Much of the scientific and programmatic activity associated with the buildup at the federal level during the late 1960s created a base for the population activities evolving at the state level in the early 1970s. This volume inventories a number of these activities and how they happen within a framework that organizes them as political phenomena.

When President Nixon signed the act creating the Commission on Population Growth and the American Future in 1970, his then Counselor Daniel Patrick Moynihan characterized the significance of the occasion by observing:

Or to put it another way, how long do we want to stand in line to go to a movie?[2]

This characterization reflected the principal concern of the day, and the one most responsible for creating the scenario in which Moynihan was a major actor—anxiety about the consequences of population size and its rate of growth in America.

*Assistant Director, Harvard Center for Population Studies.

3

Until the mid-1960s American concern over population growth and the human behavior associated with it was focused outside the United States, where the major anxiety was not longer lines for movies, but longer lines for something to eat. This external focus of American interest had to do not only with the more ominous consequences of population growth abroad, but equally with official unwillingness to consider the fertility behavior of Americans as a legitimate object of public policy. The career of Margaret Sanger and the organization she founded, Planned Parenthood, provides vivid testimony to the substance and impact of American attitudes toward fertility matters.[3]

Accordingly, the related subjects of human fertility and population growth were effectively excluded from the public arena and consigned to the domain of private institutions. This particular distribution was determined by the inhibitions, based both in reality and illusion, that determine the entry of issues into the public arena. These reservations also determined the institutional structure that evolved in response to population concerns in the United States. Thus in the programmatic area the Planned Parenthood Federation of America continued its central role in providing family planning services to Americans in need. In the scientific area the major foundations, Rockefeller and Ford, recognizing the need, but still hesitant to make a direct institutional commitment in 1972, created a new institution—The Population Council—to deal exclusively with population matters. Consistent with the prevailing priorities and focus of activity, The Population Council addressed itself almost exclusively to problems and issues outside the United States.

The expanding store of knowledge about population phenomena created by the scientific enterprise and programmatic experience that had been moving forward under private auspices, primarily Rockefeller, Ford, and The Population Council, effectively penetrated the public sector by the mid-1960s and initiated a sequence of discourse and activity by the federal government. Entry of the U.S. government into this hitherto off-limits area was signified early in 1965 when President Johnson announced in his State of the Union Message: "I will seek new ways to use our knowledge to help deal with the explosion in world population."

Johnson was talking about problems abroad, but he was committing American public resources to their amelioration. A similar commitment on the domestic scene followed later the same year, when the Surgeon General issued a memorandum encouraging the Public Health Service to utilize its resources for the provision of family planning services. As in other areas of public concern during the mid-1960s, for example civil rights, the boundaries of what the American system would tolerate in the way of intervention by the federal government were being expanded in the population area.

Following the initial Johnson Administration signals, the sequence of events at the federal level moved rapidly. To provide the institutional base for domestic activities, a Center for Population Research was created in the National Institute of Child Health and Human Development (NICHD) in 1966, and a Center for Family Planning Services in the Health Services and Mental Health Administration (HSMHA) in 1969. A major study of how the federal government should organize and equip itself to discharge the newly-assumed responsibilities in population matters was performed in 1967 by Oscar Harkavy of the Ford Foundation, Frederick Jaffe of Planned Parenthood, and Samuel Wishik of Columbia University ("Implementing DHEW Policy on Family Planning and Population," September 1967).[4] This report not only pointed the way, but served as a base against which to measure DHEW performance in domestic population activities during succeeding years.

In 1966 the Office of Economic Opportunity was authorized to include family planning services as a component in its community action programs. To administer the activities, a population unit was established in OEO's Office of Health Affairs. And in 1968 President Johnson appointed a President's Committee on Population and Family Planning composed of specialists from the universities, foundations, and the government, to develop specific recommendations on the federal government's role in the population field. Among the major recommendations of this body was one to create a public commission to explore the causes and consequences of population growth in the United States.[5] This recommendation was realized by the establishment in 1970 of the Commission on Population Growth and the American Future. Other key recommendations called for major federal commitments to expand population research and to assure access to family planning services opportunities for all Americans. The Family Planning and Population Research Act was addressed to these targets.

Both pieces of population legislation enacted by the Congress in 1970 were ambitious in scope and represented a coming of age in both the willingness and capacity to confront population issues at the federal level. Though it was only an authorization to create and finance a national commission, the act establishing the Commission on Population Growth and the American Future envisioned a broad mandate for the inquiry, which would:

. . . provide information and education to all levels of government in the United States, and to our people, regarding a broad range of problems associated with population growth and their implications for America's future.[6]

And in so doing, the Commission was authorized to examine a wide range of subject matter:

. . . aspects of population growth in the United States and its forseeable social consequences:
(1) the probable course of population growth, internal migration, and related demographic developments between now and the year 2000;
(2) the resources in the public sector of the economy that will be required to deal with the anticipated growth in population;
(3) the ways in which population growth may affect the activities of federal, state, and local government;

(4) the impact of population growth on environmental pollution and on the depletion of natural resources; and
(5) the various means appropriate to the ethical values and principles of this society by which our Nation can achieve a population level properly suited for its environmental, natural resources, and other needs.[7]

With comparable breadth of design, the Family Planning and Population Research Act staked out the federal government's responsibility for assuring the opportunity to plan families to all Americans. This objective was envisioned in programmatic authorizations for the expenditure of $382.0 million over a period of three years to:

... promote public health and welfare by expanding, improving, and better coordinating the family planning services and population research activities of the Federal Government ...[8]

The rationale for federal action in this field was stated in the preamble of the Act:

... unwanted births impair the stability and well-being of the individual family and severely limit the opportunity of each child within the family ...

... over five million American women are denied access to modern, effective, medically safe family planning services due to financial need. ...

... family planning has been recognized nationally and internationally as a universal human right ...

... it is the policy of Congress to foster the integrity of the family and the opportunity for each child; to guarantee the right of the family to freely determine the number and spacing of its children within the dictates of its individual conscience; to extend family planning services, on a voluntary basis, to all who desire such services ...[9]

Though the Family Planning and Commission authorizations were the only legislative proposals actually enacted, keen interest in population issues was expressed in the Ninety-First Congress (1969-71) in the form of sponsorship of legislation, the variety of legislation proposals, and congressional hearings. Thirty-three Senators and 126 members of the House were involved in sponsorship of the Family Planning and Commission bills. In addition, thirty Senators and thirty-eight members of the House sponsored another thirty-four bills with population objectives involving statements of position, creation of commissions and conferences, manipulation of the tax structure, legislative and executive branch reorganizations, Congressional investigations, and authorizations and earmarking of expenditures. Supplementing the routine authorization and appropriations hearings for funding of domestic and foreign population activities, there were hearings in both the Senate and House on the Family Planning and Commission legislation, and another four sets of hearings which explored issues of population change related to urban growth, environmental conservation, and contraceptive technology.[10]

The two population enactments of the 91st Congress expressed certain expectations about the requirements for handling population issues in the U.S. Creation of the Commission suggested the need for a national inventory and analysis of the complex associations between population change and how Americans managed their lives, individual and communal. There was a hope that the output of the Commission might be put to some systematic use by the federal government in the planning of national priorities. The Family Planning Act established a goal, on a minimal financial base, of delivering the family planning opportunity to all Americans. In the case of both enactments and the objectives associated with them, expectations have remained largely unfulfilled.

The Commission on Population Growth and the American Future issued its report in March 1972 in the form of a comprehensive treatment of population change in the United States and its impact on all areas of national life.[11] The Commission report contained a series of policy recommendations in the fields of civil rights, housing, education, transportation, and economic development— developed after two years of deliberation, public testimony, and contributions from a wide range of specialists, scientists, and scholars. Though it was an enterprise deserving of serious response, if not consideration, at the federal level, the Commission report elicited no more than an angry rejoinder from the President confined to the recommendations on abortion and sex education.[12] Since the presidential reaction of April 1972, there has been no serious federal response to the Commission, neither to the substance of what it said, nor to how what it said might be usefully employed in the development of national priorities.

Federal disposition of the Family Planning Act is most vividly depicted in Table 1-1. Table 1-1a reflects the money actually appropriated to meet the authorizations set in the Act. To further illustrate the gap between requirements and realities in furnishing the family planning opportunity to all Americans, which the Act established as a national goal, Table 1-1b adds the amounts deemed necessary by the Department of HEW to fulfill the goal. These requirements as estimated by the Department, though above those authorized in the Act, were considerably below the financial levels recommended to HEW by a panel of experts called in to make the estimate.[13] In any event the Department failed to seek Congressional appropriation even at the levels it established as minimal requirements.

When the Family Planning Act came up for renewal in 1973, the Administration opposed its extension. In the face of a Presidential veto, the Congress enacted a single year extension. (At the time of writing, the President had reluctantly approved the extension, which was incorporated in other health legislation. The President's retreat from a threat to veto legislation which did not conform to his legislative recommendations has been interpreted as a gesture to placate a restive Congress.)

By themselves, the fate of the Commission Report and the Family Planning Act do not conclusively demonstrate the erosion of a concern for population

Table 1-1a

Federal Commitment to Family Planning, Fiscal Years 1971-73 (In Millions)[a]

		FY 1971	FY 1972	FY 1973	Totals
Research	Authorized	30	50	65	145.0
	Appropriated	28	38	38	104.0
Family Planning Service	Authorized	40	75	110	225.0
	Appropriated	6	61.5	79.5	147.0
Training	Authorized	2	3	4	9.0
	Appropriated	2	3	3	8.0
Information & Educational Materials	Authorized	0.75	1.0	1.25	3.0
	Appropriated	.5	0.9	0.6	2.0

Table 1-1b

		FY 1971	FY 1972	FY 1973	Totals
Research	HEW Proposal	28	37.7	75	140.7
	PL 91-572 Authorization	30	50	65	145.0
	Appropriation	28	38	38	104.0
Family Planning Services	HEW Proposal	86	134	190	410.0
	PL 91-572 Authorization	40	75	110	225.0
	Appropriation	6	61.5	79.5	147.0

[a]Figures derived as follows: (1) Authorizations from PL 91-752; (2) Appropriations from compilation of Washington Office of Planned Parenthood/World Population; (3) HEW Proposal from the Report of the Secretary of Health, Education, and Welfare Submitting Five-Year Plan For Family Planning Services and Population Research Programs, October 12, 1971.

matters which had peaked three years earlier at the federal level. But the Administration's neglect of what the Commission had to say, and the parsimonious treatment of family planning services and population research do provide visible evidence of a reduction in concern and priority. It is tempting to speculate on why, and in so doing to repeat some of the popular diagnoses of the concerns in American society of 1969, and the atmosphere in which they evolved, contrasted to comparable conditions four years later.

In 1969 there was a craving in America for relief from an anguish induced by the unpleasant realities of the Vietnam War, the apparent failures to dispose of these realities, and the pathologies in American society with which the realities, rightly or not, were associated. Many Americans sought more constructive and hopeful perspectives, and one such was provided by the emerging discourse on population, and a parallel one on the environment. Among the attractions of these relatively new and increasingly fashionable concerns was their optimistic perspective in which it was possible to visualize that individuals working alone and in groups enjoyed the capacity to realize immediate and tangible improvements in their own lives without damaging the lives of others. This was an attractive vision indeed at the time, and thus population subject matter commanded an increasingly prominent position on the attention span of mass publics, officials, and legislators, a quality of attention that was mobilized by skillful activities of population interest groups.[14] The euphoric attraction of the day may also have been a factor in creating some unrealistic expectations about the range of human and social problems that could be solved by influencing population characteristics, particularly growth. But in America of 1969 we were eager to solve problems, any we could lay our hands on, and we were groping for the means for so doing.

The reversal of some of the conditions and expectations of 1969 is a factor in the decline of interest in population matters at the federal level in 1973. Some of the problems no longer existed. The Vietnam War was terminated, and the resulting reduction of anxieties and anguish somewhat relieved the craving for involvement in constructive enterprises, such as the population and environment movements had become. The American birthrate had declined to a level, that if sustained, would terminate the natural increase of the American population in seventy years. Thus a major cause of anxieties about population growth was suddenly removed. Between 1969 and 1973 we also had learned more about national and international problemsolving, principally the limited value of instant elixers, unlimited amounts of money, and expert thinking. We had become more modest about the value of our resources and capacities in ameliorating major problems both at home and abroad. This modesty doubtlessly is a factor in prompting the national leadership to narrow the scope of its interests, activities, and willingness to commit public funds. Also, moved by various combinations of modesty, wisdom, experience, and ideology, these national leaders were increasingly inclined to eschew the responsibility for problems that might be handled equally or more effectively elsewhere, by states, cities, the private sector, and by other countries. And in the case of domestic problems, whatever the more sentimental rhetoric originating in Washington about New Federalism, there were sound reasons for the states and local units of government to assume a greater role in the management of the nation's affairs.

The federal commitment in population matters also suffered from the particular cast of characters and issues in the 1972 National Election. In the view of certain mass publics, for example among many voters in the state of Massachusetts, "population" is associated with "abortion." This association doubtlessly was reinforced by the increasing media coverage of the efforts to change abortion laws at both the federal and state levels during the previous four years. In the 1972 campaign, abortion—by then a recognizable issue—was transformed into an adversary issue with the Democratic challenger and Republican incumbent taking divergent positions on it. Thus Nixon stalked McGovern before the summer convention, and on one occasion employed the report of the Commission on Population Growth and the American Future for so doing by publicly attacking the proposal for abortion reform. Following McGovern's nomination, the abortion issue became part of his enlarged achilles heel, as his antagonists fastened on to it and used it to symbolize a whole cluster of social policy positions for which McGovern was incurring hostility among much of the electorate.

It could not be said that interest in population matters at the state level automatically evolved as a reciprocal of diminishing commitment at the federal level. Interest in the states was selective, that is, confined to individual population issues that for one reason or other had claimed a position on the policymaking agenda of individual states for reasons peculiar to each of them. The selection of issues frequently was determined by the particular concerns and organizational coalitions within the state—consisting of public officials, legislators, and private citizens. There was no standard pattern or rationale for the priorities. Thus abortion reform emerged as the prominent issue in several states, and land use provided the focus in several others. Surprisingly, a systematic response to the need for family planning services did not rank high on the agendas of most states, despite the availability of federal resources, however parsimonious, in support of initiatives by the states in this area.[15]

Though it was shelved by the federal authorities, the report of the Commission on Population Growth and the American Future provided the grounds for private support of policy initiatives at the state level. The Ford Foundation's support of efforts to disseminate and utilize the Commission report was directed in part toward creating an awareness of population issues which might be best handled in the states. An organization that enjoyed Ford support—the Citizens Committee for Population and the American Future—directed much of its organizational and educational efforts on the regional and state levels during 1973. And the Population Council conducted its first venture in the domestic policymaking area by sponsoring a New England regional conference on population issues in December 1972.

And at the federal level, though commitments in support of the universal family planning norm had diminished by decision of the executive branch, legislative action was underway that would provide incentive for state level initiatives in another population area. Thus in June 1973 the Senate enacted a Land Use Policy and Planning Assistance Act providing for grants to the states for land use planning.

Though the particular interests and objectives that it creates do not conform to a uniform pattern of priorities, the dynamics of population change provide a perspective in which to visualize and confront issues and problems that are more intimately experienced at the levels of community, locality, and state. The proximity of cause to consequence, and in many cases the capacity actually to see the relationships happen, is a powerful incentive for the growing concern with population policymaking at the state level. It is one thing to read aggregate statistics that suggest crowding in fifty states; it is quite another matter to see conservation land across the street being subdivided for condominiums, to experience a thirty-minute commute that took fifteen minutes two years ago, and to wait in line for accommodations at state parks, and even seats in movies. These proximate and physical experiences provide more incentive to think about population change than do remote Census Bureau reports on changes in birthrates. And the anxieties that emerge from these experiences in the first instance tend to be expressed in the neighborhood, and in meetings of towns, zoning boards, city councils, county commissioners, and at the state house.

Population policy has been most commonly characterized as policy designed to limit population size and growth rates. This is too limited a concept of population policy; it unduly restricts policy discourse, sometimes subjects it to spurious associations (i.e. the population/abortion linkage), and is increasingly out of step with priorities involving population distribution and composition that are of major concern in the American states, and in the nation as a whole. It is more realistic to visualize population policy in a broader perspective, involving the associations between group characteristics (including size and growth) and how groups live. This concept is depicted in the following diagram.

Population policy, accordingly, can be defined as *government action toward objectives which involve the influencing of population characteristics.* Thus

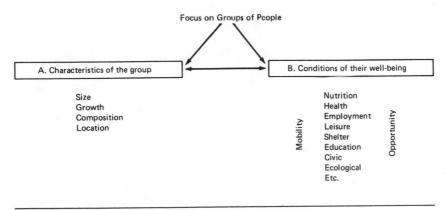

Population policy influences the reciprocal relationships between "A" and "B"

Figure 1-1. Perspective for Population Policy-making. Source: Reprinted from Peter Bachrach and Elihu Bergman, *Power and Choice: The Formulation of American Population Policy* (Lexington Books, D.C. Heath and Company, 1973), p. 103.

population policy might be visualized as government actions which influence population characteristics influencing size, composition, distribution, and rates of growth. However, these steps are not taken in a vacuum or exclusively to influence population characteristics merely for the sake of changing them alone. Rather they are taken with reference to other characteristics or conditions of a community or society in which change is sought, such as the expansion of opportunities for employment, education, shelter, health; or the contradiction of these opportunities; or the security of the community, internal or external; or other priorities envisioned by a society and its government. And these actions can be taken either to the advantage or to the disadvantage of a certain population group such as the young, the old, the rich, the poor, ethnic majorities, religious minorities, and the like. Moreover, deliberate action to influence a population characteristic might not involve the direct manipulation of the population characteristic itself, but rather its indirect manipulation through the influencing of another condition or characteristic, as for example in the case of fertility reduction through emphasis either on contraceptive programs (direct) or programs to expand female educational and employment opportunities (indirect).

Accordingly, population policy operates in an area involving a series of reciprocal relationships between individuals aggregated in various ways (population characteristics) and the conditions in which these groups are able to live in any given society, for better or worse. A definitive concept of population policy has not yet been evolved. At the best, the existing concepts in their broad versions are addressed to the ingredients that are employed in formulating population policy rather than to a standard package of objectives toward which population policy aims. But for present purposes this is an acceptable condition for population policy, because realistically its scope and targets will vary by region, country, society, and culture, in accordance with the particular requirements of those units. Accordingly, population policy is best identified by its ingredients, on which we may observe considerable consensus, rather than on a uniform set of policy targets in all places. To this extent population policy is a discrete and identifiable policy area.

It could be argued that this framework is so global as to render it meaningless as a distinctive area for population policy; that it is nothing less than a broad framework for social policy. Such an argument is valid to the extent it suggests that many policy areas have social policy objectives. But social policy is a composite of many policy areas including health, education, welfare, natural resources, taxation, and population. Admittedly all of these policy areas dovetail at the margin, to greater or lesser degree, depending on the particular policy issue or objective. But each has a distinguishable focus and set of concerns. Thus in the respective relationships with social objectives, taxation policy is concerned primarily with economic institutions and behavior; resource policy with land, forests, minerals, and water; health primarily with medical institutions and behavior; and education with the techniques and procedures for learning. Naturally all these concerns relate to people. But as its *distinctive* concern, population policy emphasizes relationships to social objectives involving ways in which people are aggregated and configured.

The variety of material that follows illustrates the utility of a broad and flexible concept of population policy. Clearly there is no standard formula that determines what is appropriate for inclusion in the population policy area. But the chapters in this volume all have in common a focus on issues involving aggregates of people in qualitative, spatial, or quantitative dimensions. Though not exhaustive, the concerns about land use, family planning, housing, community health, education, and abortion discussed in the chapters that follow are representative of the population policy issues that have emerged in the American states.

In addition to the substance involved in the individual issues, each of them develops a particular policymaking structure which determines the fate of the issue in the political arena. The policymaking structure is a political phenomenon comprising ingredients of power, ideology, norms, and institutions—and the interaction of all these qualities in the process of policymaking. Several chapters discuss the process and one or more of its components as they are associated with the substantive policy issues.

What remains unexplored in this volume, but always lurking in the background as perhaps the most intriguing subject for political analysis in the population area, is the impact of changes in their population characteristics, and the efforts to influence these changes, on the political systems of the American states. A stationary population, for example, which is the eventual outcome of low birthrates, yields an older population. To the extent the political behavior of an aging population is different from a younger population, the political choices and the distribution of political power in the states are likely to be influenced. There can be changes in voting behavior, alignments of political parties, composition of state legislatures, and preferences in the issues that are legislated. Together all of these changes can exert a significant impact on the political system of a state or the states that experience them. Some of the policy choices now emerging in the population area can indeed exert a long-term influence on political behavior, whatever the other issues involved in making them. Certain choices about the allocation of land for specified objectives can influence the distribution and quality of a population in a state. Likewise, the choices affecting fertility limitation can exert an impact on the rate at which population grows in the state, and in the nation.

Clearly the population choices increasingly available to the American states involve consequences to their political structures, and in the aggregate to the political system of the nation. This volume initiates an exploration of the policy issues and political process involved in the related choices. Hopefully subsequent enterprises will undertake more systematic analysis of the political consequences that are only suggested here.

Notes

1. Efforts to renew this legislation, which was the major vehicle for federal support of domestic family planning services and related research, are chronicled in the memoranda of the Washington office of Planned Parenthood/World Population. See especially: "Summary of Current Status and Emerging Debate Over Family Planning and Population Research Legislation," June 12, 1973.

2. *The New York Times*, March 17, 1970.

3. The evolution of the planned parenthood movement in the United States is best recorded and evaluated in: David M. Kennedy, *Birth Control in America: The Career of Margaret Sanger*, (New Haven: Yale University Press, 1970). (Note particularly the comprehensive bibliographical essay.) See also the review of this volume: Alan F. Guttmacher "Margaret Sanger's New Look," *Family Planning Perspectives*, 2 (3), June 1970.

4. This report is reproduced, among other places, in: "Family Planning and Population Research, 1970," Hearings Before the Subcommittee on Health of the Committee on Labor and Public Welfare, United States Senate, 91st Congress, 1st and 2nd sessions, pp. 333-377.

5. The recommendations of this committee are summarized in *Studies in Family Planning*, no. 40, April 1969.

6. Public Law 91-213.

7. Ibid.

8. Public Law 91-572.

9. Ibid.

10. The legislative activities are inventoried in Elihu Bergman, *The Politics of Population USA: A Critique of the Policy Process*, Population Program and Policy Design Series: no. 5 (The Carolina Population Center, The University of North Carolina at Chapel Hill, 1972).

11. "Population and the American Future," The Report of The Commission on Population Growth and the American Future, (Washington, D.C.: U.S. Government Printing Office, 1972).

12. *The New York Times*, May 6, 1972, pp. 1, 8.

13. The panel recommendations are not available in published form. The departmental recommendations are published as: Report of the Secretary of Health, Education, and Welfare Submitting Five-Year Plan For Family Planning Services and Population Research Programs, October 12, 1971. Prepared for the Special Subcommittee on Human Resources of the Senate Committee on Labor and Public Welfare, October 1971.

14. For a description of these groups, see: Peter Bachrach and Elihu Bergman, *Power and Choice: The Formulation of American Population Policy* (Lexington, Mass.: Lexington Books, D.C. Heath, 1973), chapter 4, "The Anatomy of a Coalition."

15. For an analysis of the state level record in this area, see: David Weinberg, "State Administration and Financing of Family Planning Services," *Family Planning Perspectives*, 4 (2), April 1972, pp. 32-41.

2

Formulating Population Policy: A Case Study of the United States

Rebecca J. Cook*

Introduction

The objectives of this article are: (1) to describe how population policies are perceived, formulated and implemented in the United States and (2) to analyze how and why the definition of demographic trends by ten state commissions have a profound impact on how policies are developed and evaluated. Some of the demographic components of policy will be outlined for the law maker and some of the legal components of policy will be described for the demographer.

For the purposes of explanation, four analytical population policy models are developed: (1) the family planning model, (2) the motivation model, (3) the population distribution model and (4) the per capita consumption model. There is no one correct policy model but rather many policy models have and can be developed based on different social, economic, political and environmental conditions of a state. *The article's principal analytical utility lies in its challenge to state officials to develop their policy model based on the unique conditions and goals of their state.*

A legal systems model outlines the many facets of policymaking that should be taken into consideration in helping to determine which kinds of legal change should be used in implementing policy. Since the demographic effectiveness of legal change on a population policy is uncertain or unknown, subjecting alternative pieces of legislation—the "inputs"—to test hypothesizing a desired "output" might help to formulate and choose more effective policies. For example, compare the effectiveness of two pieces of legislation—one requiring the teaching of population education and the other instituting programs to raise the status of women. Determine which legal change would be more functional in implementing a policy of population reduction. The answer depends on many conditions within a state, some of which could be determined by projecting the probable feedback.

The effectiveness of any institution in implementing policy is determined in part by how well policies are defined and how well institutions are structured. It could be a relatively straight-forward matter to establish effective statutory

*Rebecca J. Cook received the M.P.A. from the John F. Kennedy School of Government, Harvard University.
Reprinted by permission of *Environmental Affairs*, vol. 3 no. 1.

policy. Most states have developed adequate statutory family planning policies and have created the agencies necessary to implement the family planning objectives. However, they are just beginning to articulate and develop three subsequent models—the motivation model, the distribution model and the per capita consumption model—to enable them to adequately develop institutions capable of implementing these models' objectives.

Once a policy is selected, the next institutional problem becomes the determination of the indicators needed to measure the policy's effectiveness. The search for criteria raise such issues as: (1) is the two child family an adequate policy indicator to measure the effectiveness of a stabilization policy? (2) do the given indicators ignore the other dimensions of the problem?; and (3) how are institutions best designed to evaluate policy?

This article asks more questions about policymaking than it answers. It is hoped, however, that the questions will be helpful in determining how, and at what points, the legal process can be used in formulating and implementing population policies.

Population Policy Formulation

Population policy is the direct and indirect result of legislative, judicial, executive and administrative actions directly and indirectly affecting many demographic components. These components include (1) the size of population; (2) the rate of increase or decrease of either birth, death, or growth rates; (3) the distribution of a populace within an area including both internal and international migration; (4) the age and racial composition of a population, and (5) the qualitative composition of a population in terms of *inter alia*, education, per capita consumption, and per capita income.

Population policies fall along a wide spectrum: on one end, the anti-natalists assert the advantages of lower growth rates; at the other end the pro-natalists assert the benefits of an increased population. Between these extremes are variations with anticipated and unanticipated consequences.[1]

There are four behavioral elements of population change: political, economic, social and environmental. The effects of population change can be diagramed by comparing these behavioral elements on a vertical axis and their determinants (size, rate, distribution, and composition) on a horizontal axis.[2]

State Population Commissions

In formulating population policy states are faced with the choice of whether to allow existing trends to shape the future size, rates of growth, composition, distribution and per capita consumption of its population or whether to alter these trends by adopting population policies. Either alternative, in effect, constitutes population policy.[3] Twelve states through special state commissions have issued reports recommending explicit policies either to stabilize growth rates or to locate the populace in better balance relative to resources and services. These policy recommendations agree with the following conclusion of the Report of the Commission on Population Growth and the American Future which states:

The Commission believes that the gradual stabilization of population—bringing births into balance with deaths—would contribute significantly to the nation's ability to solve its problems, although such problems would not be solved by population stabilization alone. It would, however, enable our society to shift its focus increasingly from quantity to quality.[4]

These commissions have been either special population commissions,[5] sub-committees of State Environmental Commission,[6] or Commissions on Land Use and Population Distribution.[7] Although the commissions have been appointed by the Governors and/or the state legislatures, the reports have been primarily the result of research by citizens and state officials interested in population matters. The commission members represent a broad spectrum of racial, economic, religious and academic backgrounds. The reports are based in large part upon citizen testimony, academic studies performed at state universities, and statements of state and local officials. As a result these reports are useful in educating the general public about state population policies.

Demographic Trends

Recognizing that demographic trends form the basis of population policy, the California, Colorado, Hawaii, Massachusetts and Michigan reports investigate the recent history and the projected future of population growth and change.[8] Each report distinguishes between (1) growth due to natural increase; (2) growth due to migration; and (3) differential growth rates between the urban and rural areas. Policies are recommended based on these three important distinctions.

For example, Colorado's population grew by 26 percent from 1,753,947 to 2,207,259 in the sixties. However, 49 percent of this increase was due to net migration.[9] California expanded by 28 percent in the sixties, with a present population of about 20 million. 51 percent of that increase is attributable to net migration, but this factor has begun to diminish—relatively and absolutely—in relation to natural growth.[10] California and Colorado were used as examples not only because they were among the fastest growing states in population, but because their population problems should be solved by two distinct policies, one aimed at net migration and the other aimed at the birthrate.

Differential growth rates between urban and rural areas within states present another challenge to policymakers. The California, Colorado and Texas reports made specific recommendations to equalize disproportionate growth rates. 79 percent of Colorado's population live in urban areas.[11] 80 percent of California's population live in the Los Angeles and San Francisco megalopolises.[12]

The demographic movement nationally is from north and east to south and west. Besides California and Colorado, the large growth rates during the sixties occurred in Alaska (33.6 percent), Nevada (71.3 percent), Arizona (36.1 percent), Maryland (26.5 percent) and Florida (37.1 percent).[13]

States not only examined the historical nature of population change but also cited future projections. Some projections were made by extrapolating the average annual growth rate of the past ten years. For example, given Colorado's 2.3 percent average annual growth rate over the last decade its population will double in 30.1 years giving Colorado a population of 4.4 million in 2000.[14] The California Report indicates that if the rate of growth of the past decade continues, California's population could double giving California a population of 40 million by 1990.[15]

However, making general projections based on average annual growth rates was not precise enough for Michigan state planning purposes. Therefore, the Michigan Governor's Report made 3 projections based on different assumptions.

Projection I assumes that both current age, specific morality, and fertility rates continue . . . Projection II assumes current mortality rates but fertility rates reduced proportionately to achieve replacement reproduction beginning in 1970 . . . Projection III assumes that current mortality and fertility levels continue until 1990 when zero population growth suddenly occurs.[16]

There were considerable variations among the three projections.

The age structure is another important demographic variable that has to be considered in making projections. The Michigan Governor's Report, the California Legislative Report, the Colorado Report and the Hawaii Reports indicate that because of the large proportion of young persons who will enter child bearing ages within the next ten years, the replacement level fertility (2.1 children per family in the U.S.) would need to be maintained for 70 years in order to achieve zero population growth. The number of female children born will increase from 42 million in 1970 to 60 million in 1990. Therefore even if a 2.1 children per family average is maintained, the population will continue to increase until at least 1990. Only when the proportional increase in women of childbearing age relative to the entire population ceases, does zero population growth (ZPG) become possible.

Population Policy Models

The state reports base their policy considerations on a mixture of four models: (1) the Family Planning Model; (2) the Motivation Model; (3) the

Population Distribution Model; and (4) the Per Capita Consumption Model. These models are discussed below.

The Family Planning Model assumes that family planning information and services are available on a voluntary basis to all those who need and request them regardless of age. The presumption is that such services will reduce unwanted and illegitimate births, with a resultant slight decline in the overall birthrate. According to the Michigan Governor's Report: "Successful family planning programs could reduce the birthrate in Michigan approximately 5 percent by 1974."[17] The objectives of the Family Planning Model are based on an estimate of the unmet need for contraceptive services and the cost of providing them. One such estimate is provided by a Colorado estimate that 47,445 of the 66,558 low income women in need of such services were unmet.[18]

A typical Family Planning Model would allocate the greatest percentage of its budget to preventive contraceptive measures, while allocating at least 10 percent of the budget to curative birth control measures such as morning after pills and abortion.

The *Motivation Model* begins with the premise that the Family Planning Model is not the most effective way of instituting a population policy designed to stabilize the population growth rate. Proponents of the Motivation Model argue:

Logically it does not make sense to use *family* planning to provide *national* population control or planning. The planning in family planning is that of each separate couple. The only control they exercise is control over the size of *their* family. Obviously, couples do not plan the size of the nation's population, any more than they plan the growth of the national income or form of the highway network. There is no reason to expect that the millions of decisions about family size made by couples in their own interest will automatically control population for the benefit of society. On the contrary, there are good reasons to think they will not do so. At most, family planning can reduce reproduction to the extent that unwanted births exceed wanted births.[19]

An implicit Motivation Model assumption is that the social goal of lowering overall population growth does not coincide with average private behavior. Since private motivation to have smaller families is lacking, motivation must be induced through government action. The reports contend that motivation is primarily lacking in the middle and upper income classes. This contention is based on these groups' proportionately greater birthrate.

The reports assume that the birthrate in groups will change as a result of a change in the social or economic motives for having children. However, rather than investigating the extent of the correlation between a change in motives and change in fertility patterns and trying to quantify the results, the reports suggest that the motivation policies be tried in order to determine their effectiveness. The recommended policies include implementation of population education programs, improvement of the status of woman, and equalization of income taxes between single and married persons.

The *Population Distribution Model* attributes an increasingly significant part of the population problem to the ever increasing concentration of people in metropolitan areas and the accompanying depopulation of rural areas. None of the states considers this nonuniform distribution of population the sole problem, but each indicates that it could be an increasingly significant problem during the seventies.

Suggested policies focus on different but interrelated areas: (1) improving land use, powers and functions; (2) revitalizing rural areas; (3) directing urban growth; and (4) altering migration patterns. One example of this focus is evidenced in the Colorado Report which, after recognizing that metropolitan Denver had possibly surpassed her optimum size and might surpass her ecological carrying capacity within some twenty or thirty years, stated that:

It is imperative, therefore, both from the viewpoint of the well being of metropolitan Denver and also of the economic stagnation of rural Colorado, that the necessary steps be taken now to develop the necessary consensus and understanding to plan for an eventual limitation in the size of metropolitan Denver.[20]

The California State Office of Planning and the Department of Water Study provides another example. It developed three different models of future population distribution throughout the State's regions and analyzed the possible impact of each model for water management. It concluded that:

The results . . . vindicate the viewpoint that substantial benefits might accrue from a population and urbanization policy which would seek variations in the magnitude and spatial distribution of regional growth from that otherwise anticipated by an extrapolation of existing trends.[21]

Despite the fledgling nature of population distribution policy formation and the arguable question of how amenable such policies are to government action, the California, Hawaii, Colorado, Texas, Wisconsin and New York reports strongly support the implementation of such distribution policies in order that the ecological carrying capacity of certain metropolitan areas not be surpassed. Some reports state that such distribution policies are demographically limited because non-metropolitan areas will be able to absorb only a small percentage of the projected future natural growth of metropolitan areas.

The *Per Capita Consumption Model* attributes the problem of population not to numbers but to the individual demands of a populace on resources and services. While none of the state reports attributes depletion and pollution of natural resources to population growth *per se*, such conditions are recognized to result from many factors, among them per capita consumption rate and natural resources mismanagement.

Because the increasingly exorbitant consumption habits of individuals have been considered as a major source of the population resource dilemma, policies aimed at decreasing the demand for resources instead of policies to increase the supply of resources have been developed. The principle behind such policies are outlined in the Massachusetts Wetmore report:

The Committee feels strongly that the value system of the citizens of Massachusetts ought to be examined. America's emphasis on consumerism encourages waste and generates pollution. The American people often seem to measure their worth in material rather than humanistic terms. An adequate state population policy must eventually lead the people of Massachusetts to reexamine their values.[22]

Increased uses of energy are one example of increasing depletion of resources which result more from per capita consumption increase than population growth. Hawaii reports that:

about 90% of the growth in power generation in the last 30 years has been caused by increased per capita income, while only 10% can be attributed to population growth.[23]

Similarly, California reports that although population in California is growing at slightly over 1 percent per year, per capita consumption of electric power is increasing at 8.5 percent per year.[24]

The impact of population growth becomes more complicated when specific ages are taken into account. Certain age groups have higher utilization rates of certain goods than other age groups.[25]

The "multiplier effect," due to the interaction of increases in population and per capita consumption, magnifies the impact of population on resources, as the Michigan report explains:

In general, overall increases in resources consumption, or utilization can be attributed to changes in population, changes in per capita consumption (including changes in taste, substitution, etc.) and changes in the two variables acting together. When populations increase 50% consumption increases 50%. The total increase is not 100% derived by adding the two factors together, but is instead actually an increase 125%. The extra 25% is created by the interaction of the two changes occurring together . . . the multiplier effect of population.[26]

The Legal Component of Population Policy: Voluntarism vs. Coercion

Human Rights: Voluntarism vs. Coercion

Population policy can be implemented by various legal means ranging from voluntarism to coercion. A voluntarist would maintain that:

... the right to decide whether and when to have a child is a basic civil liberty and by the free exercise of that right we determine the constituency and quality of the world of the future ... if we really make freedom of choice possible with respect to human reproduction there will be no need to resort to compulsion in this area.[27]

Mr. Justice Goldberg gave a compelling argument for voluntarism in his concurring opinion in *Griswold v. Connecticut*:

Surely the Government absent a showing of a compelling subordinating state interest, could not decree that all husbands and wives must be sterilized after two children have been born to them. ... Yet, if upon a showing of a slender basis of rationality, a law outlawing voluntary birth control by married persons is valid, then, by the same reasoning, a law requiring compulsory birth control also would seem to be valid. In my view, however, both types of law would unjustifiably intrude upon rights of marital privacy which are constitutionally protected.[28]

Advocates of coercion maintain that the elimination of unwanted births is not enough to solve the problem, since the average couple desires more than 2.1 children, the number needed for zero population growth. They propose indirect conditioning of choice through manipulation or inducement and suggest legislative provisions such as monetary compensation to reward and/or penalties to punish specific kinds of reproductive behavior.

The choice of either the voluntarist or coercive measures depends upon a country's perception of the nature of the problem.

At issue first is whether a policy which aimed to ensure complete freedom of choice for an individual couple deciding whether to have a child would result in an average fertility equalling the replacement goal. Second, there is the question whether and to what degree, we should be willing to sacrifice some individual freedom of choice by instituting manipulative or overtly coercive regulation of reproductive behavior.[29]

Population growth is one of the factors that can erode personal freedom and if continued could eliminate individual freedom of choice.[30] As population grows, there will be an increasing need for government intervention to protect individual freedom of choice and to affect individual behavior patterns. At issue here is how to formulate the most humane laws to implement a specified policy.

Legal Change

Before analyzing legal change, one has to consider whether or not legal change should be voluntary or coercive. There are three kinds of legal change, ranging from voluntarism to coercion, from which population policy makers can choose: (1) removal of pro-natalist policies; (2) creation of incentives and (3) development of disincentives or implementation of anti-natalist policies.

Removal of Pro-natalist Policies. Pro-natalist policies originally based on moral grounds have been modified on the basis of the protection of fundamental rights, in particular the right of privacy. The first means of removing pro-natalist policies is typified by the repeal of laws prohibiting the distribution of information on birth control services and methods and the advertising and display of prescription and non-prescription contraceptive devices.[31]

The next legal step would be to allow abortions " . . . to preserve a woman's mental or physical health and/or to avert the birth of defective offspring in cases of rape or incest."[32]

The final legal means of insuring the right of privacy was taken by the Supreme Court in the companion cases of *Roe v. Wade* and *Doe v. Bolton*.[33] The court held that a Texas statute[34] and a Georgia statute[35] which allowed abortions *only* where continued pregnancy would endanger a pregnant woman's life or endanger her health, was an unconstitutional infringement of privacy and personal liberty. The Court held that in the first trimester abortion would be a matter for the woman and her physician to decide; in the second trimester, the state may, if it chooses, regulate the procedures in ways that are reasonably related to maternal health; and only in the third trimester, subsequent to viability, may the states "regulate and even prescribe abortion except where necessary in appropriate medical judgment for the preservation of the life or health of the mother."[36]

Along with the repeal of the pro-natalist aspects of laws directly affecting fertility it is also necessary to consider the pro-natalist aspects of laws which indirectly affect births through social and economic processes.[37] In order to insure natal neutrality a change in tax laws would include the equalization of income taxes between single and married persons and the removal of tax deductions for children.

Creation of Incentives. The incentive stage would involve such legal changes as tax rebates for families of two or less children. Such incentives would be positive and would not jeopardize the human rights of an individual if he is a third or fourth child. Another example of an incentive measure is payments to those who voluntarily consent to sterilizations.

Development of Disincentives or the Implementation of Anti-Natalist Policies. The implementation of anti-natalist policies should include the development of measures requiring compulsory sterilization of persons with three or more children. There have been several unsuccessful legislative attempts to institute anti-natalist, or population control, policies for those on welfare,[38] and it would be a misrepresentation of state activity to avoid mentioning the attempts to institute such controversial measures. Among the examples of coercive legislative attempts are Tennessee and Ohio bills, making welfare payments conditional on the number of illegitimate children. If a woman has more than one illegitimate child, she would have been required by the Tennessee bill to be sterilized if she is eligible to receive welfare payments.[39] The Ohio bill would have required a woman to have injections of depo provera, the new shot contraceptive to qualify for aid.[40]

Despite official federal and state reports that the largest proportion of the population increase is attributable to the white middle class, some state legislators continue to introduce coercive legislation aimed against racial minorities under the auspices of population policy. These attempts to alter the racial composition of the population violate the equal protection clause of the Constitution and restrict the fundamental individual rights of one group.

Transformation of Policy into Law

The transformation of population policy into law through judicial or legislative action depends on two distinctive functions of the legal process.[41] First, the legal process outlines the limitations on the policy maker and defines the boundaries of permissible decision making. Second, the legal process shapes policy objectives as it transforms policy into principles of law.

Once the policy objectives (i.e., the stabilization of the population growth rate) "is incorporated as such into law, it takes on a life of its own and might well be expanded to cover a variety of circumstances"[42] never contemplated by the policy formulator. Option No. 1 in Figure 2-1 is the only viable alternative which can be transformed into a binding legal decision under the Griswold rationale. Whereas option No. 3 in Figure 2-1 can only be based on a policy objective of a decreased population growth, but not in a legal principle. Therefore great care must be taken both judicially and legislatively, in adopting the requisite legal standards.

Legal Systems for the Formulation of Population Policies[43]

One central issue in determining a population policy relates to the most effective use of scarce resources available to influence population growth. A systems approach to the examination of a comprehensive set of public policies to reduce rapid population growth can be a useful tool in assisting decision makers in gaining insight into the feasible alternatives available to them to directly and indirectly influence population growth (see Figure 2-2). The system could be conceptualized as those sets of public and private decisions which influence population growth and the interrelationship between the two sets. Assuming that the objective or output of the system is to reduce population growth to a level where a desirable balance between population and available resources is maintained, a logical approach would be to determine what kinds of decisions should be taken at the public and private levels to achieve said objective.

Voluntary ————————————————————————→ Coercive

Policy:	A/Removal of Pronatalist Policies.	B/Incentives for fewer children	C/Disincentives for more children
Legal Change:	1/Remove laws prohibiting contraceptives to unmarrieds	2/Change tax laws: i.e. tax rebates	3/Enact law compulsory sterilization after 3rd child

Figure 2-1.

The decision makers include (1) the couple who decide or do not decide to have another child, and (2) individuals in the judicial, legislative, and executive branches of municipal, state, regional and national government, who formulate, implement and administer policies.

The legal systems model is helpful in conceptualizing the problem, in order that all kinds of law, not just family planning and abortion laws, will be considered in formulating prescriptive population policies. In creating a population policy it is important to analyze pro-natalist laws which have but an indirect effect on a population policy. A change in these laws would also advance the objective of a decreased birthrate.

The legal systems model is particularly applicable to policy formation within the legislative process. The state legislatures have been an important forum in which prescriptive population policies have been debated, formulated and, often times, implemented. This interplay between prospective policy formulation and law is distinctively a legislative process. Legislators can outline existing laws, determine political and legal constraints on the policy and, based on available options, outline the necessary legal change.

The legislative process, while not always successful, has some distinct advantages over the judicial process in formulating general policy. The judicial approach is inductive, courts being constrained to decide the specific case before it. On the other hand, the legislative approach is deductive, and therefore the legislature is better able than the judiciary to consider overall policy based on all the facts and public opinion. The judiciary, however, does have the advantages of greater objectivity (through less public pressure) and expediency where necessary.

The legal systems model is useful in assessing the demographic effects that a change in one law might have on another law, an individual, a community, or a state. Consideration should be given to (1) the impact potential policy decisions would have on the direction and magnitude of population growth rates (both on the overall and on specific groups); (2) the political feasibility of adopting such measures; (3) the government action required to implement such policies and, finally, (4) the intended and unintended effects on other policies.[44]

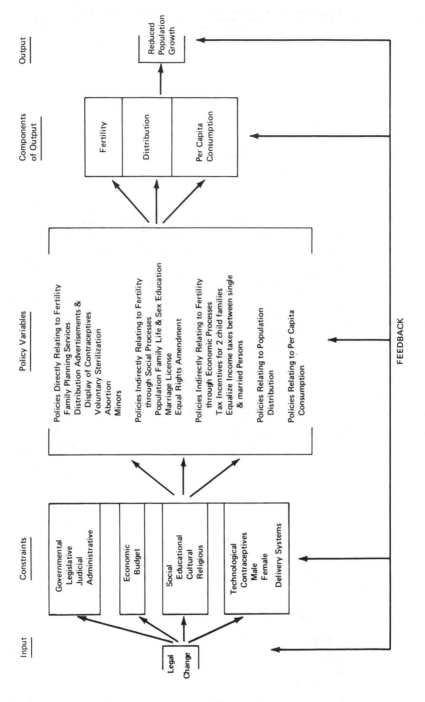

Figure 2-2. Legal Systems Model.

Although the legal systems model is crude, it provides a useful tool in creating a conceptual framework for analyzing the demographic effects of legal change on the population. It is not meant to be an implementing mechanism for the solution of the problem.

Legal Systems Model

A key element of any system is an identification of system output. Although different policy objectives determine different outputs, typical outputs include reduced birth rate and the reduced impact of population growth on state resources, services and environment. Some state legislatures have identified outputs by passing Population Stabilization Resolutions.[45] These resolutions are significant in that they establish a foundation on which further laws can be considered. They define the population problem, not in terms of numbers, but as a set of extremely complex social interactions between age structures, distribution and consumption patterns.

The elements of the legal systems model are discussed immediately below.

Inputs. The inputs consist of the different legal changes necessary for achieving the desired output. Foremost in choosing appropriate inputs is a knowledge and understanding of population dynamics, that is, the interrelationship among the determinants of population growth such as social attitudes and private behavior and the impact of population growth on resources and services. Such a sophisticated knowledge of population dynamics is necessary at all levels of decision making if the system is to function efficiently. Legislative inputs will refer to two types: (1) inputs necessary to either directly or indirectly affect policy variables; and (2) inputs necessary to establish administrative structures to assure the functioning of the system or the implementation of policies. (The latter will be dealt with in the last section of this article.)

Output. Outputs consist of the influences on population change of three interrelated determinants—fertility, distribution/migration, and per capita consumption.

Policy Variables. Policy variables could be altered by a given legal change. They can also be considered as intermediate outputs in themselves. (These variables and laws affecting them will be discussed in detail *infra*.)

Constraints. Many constraints are present which could interfere with the efficient attainments of the desired output. One such constraint is the legal system itself where it is not well organized, well manned, well funded and smoothly functioning. The laws themselves may be constraining forces in prohibiting certain actions. Another constraint might be society's perception of both the legal system and the laws enacted within that system. This is particularly true where individuals are uninformed about given laws and/or do not sanction them.

The political culture could act either as a constraint or as a facilitator. For example, the American political culture is based on the ideological tenets of Lockean democracy which advocate the natural right of the individual to work out his own destiny with minimal governmental intervention.[46] Such a political culture may inhibit the implementation of population solutions because they entail a degree of governmental control over individual autonomy. On the other hand, the classic liberalism of John Locke on the natural right of the individual may help facilitate population policy as evidenced in the Supreme Court's use of such doctrine in *Roe v. Wade*.[47]

Feedback

The input output and feedback within a legal system is a continual interplay of a society influencing law and law influencing society, its attitudes, behavior, administrative apparatus and, desires for legal modifications. Demographic surveys and information on population change are essential in evaluating the different kinds of demographic feedback in a legal systems model.[48] Among the demographic techniques used to evaluate a new law's effectiveness are (1) an analysis of the age specific fertility rates; (2) the decomposition techniques; and (3) parity level examination. While such techniques can be used with laws indirectly affecting fertility, they are more applicable for an analysis of laws directly affecting fertility. These techniques are discussed below.

Age Specific Fertility Rates. Age specific fertility rates (ASFR) are the number of births in a given year to women in a given age interval. The intervals are usually five years in duration. To determine a significant change in an ASFR interval with any degree of statistical reliability requires examination over a long term of at least fifteen to twenty years. Old laws should not be evaluated, nor new ones proposed, on the basis of short term fluctuations in the ASFR. One possible comparison would be between the ASFR with the legal change and an estimated ASFR assuming no change in the law. The estimate is obtained by considering the ASFRs before the change and extrapolating, taking great care to isolate the effect of the particular law in interest.[49]

Decomposition. This technique decomposes the change in the crude birth rate (CBR) (total births over total population at a given time) into 3 components: births due to changes in (1) age structure; (2) percent married; and (3) marital fertility. A sample chart is shown below.

State, Year Program Began, and Follow Up Year		CBR	Change in CBR	% of change in CBR due to change in:			
				All factors	Age Structure	% Married	Marital Fertility
State	1960	A		1960 – 1970			
	1965	B	– or +	100%	X%	Y%	Z%
	1970	C	– or +				

Figure 2-3.

This chart provides a clear indication as to which demographic factors one can attribute a change in the CBR. For example, if the greatest percentage of change in the CBR was attributable to the age structure, then the changes in law had little effect; but if it were attributable to the marital fertility then a change in law which legalized and made available free family planning services might have had some effect. The degree to which a change in marital fertility is attributable to such policy changes might not be easily quantified because of other social variables that would effect such a change, such as raising the status of women through better education. More detailed analysis can be performed by decomposing the change in age specific fertility rates instead of the crude birth rate and then comparing these with the data on the acceptance for family planning programs over the time period.

Parity Level. Because so many state reports emphasize the two child family, one useful demographic technique in evaluating the effect of a two child family policy is an analysis of the parity level. The parity level is the order of a particular birth, in other words, whether the child born is the first, second or third child within a family. Analysis of such data over time will indicate whether or not two child family policies have been effective. The parity order is also dependent upon the average age of the marriage and the average age of the first birth. It is therefore important to analyze these factors in order to determine whether women are actually having fewer children or the same number at older ages.

Policy Variables

To insure the desired system output, policy variables need to be examined for their potential in decreasing population growth. The five broad categories of policy variables are: (1) policies directly relating to fertility; (2) policies indirectly relating to fertility through social processes; (3) policies indirectly relating to fertility through taxes;[51] (4) policies directly and indirectly relating to population distribution; and finally, (5) those policies directly and indirectly relating to per capita consumption. The following discussion will encompass only those legislative proposals which deal with the above five categories of the policies. Judicial decisions will not be considered.

The systems model is designed to aid in determining which policies to choose. Since the effectiveness of legal change on population growth is uncertain or unknown, subjecting such inputs to a 'test' to determine a hypothetical output might help to choose and formulate more effective legislation. Thus, it might be useful to trace the effects and determine the outcome of the legislative categories considered below.

An example of this type of testing would be a theoretical comparison between the effects of legislation requiring (1) a population education curriculum and (2) instituting programs to raise the status of women. Which legal change would be more functional in implementing a policy of the reduction of population growth would depend on many conditions within a state, some of which could be determined by projecting probable system feedback. Budgetary considerations should be similarly analyzed.

Legislation Directly Affecting Fertility. Laws directly affecting fertility[52] are those that regulate family planning services, contraception, voluntary sterilization and abortion. They can also regulate distribution of information, advertising of contraceptive devices, eligibility and referral for family planning services and access to these services according to age and marital status.[53] Programs can be funded by state or federal appropriations or through health insurance coverage.

Family Planning Services. As of 1970 Colorado[54] and Tennessee[55] have enacted comprehensive family planning programs. The pertinent provisions provide that family planning is to be readily available to all persons regardless of sex, race, age, income, number of children, marital status, citizenship, or motive. Voluntary sterilization of a requesting and consenting patient over 18 years old is held to be consistent with public policy. Physicians may refuse to recommend any contraceptives for any medical reason and physicians, hospitals and program employees may refuse to participate for reasons of conscience or religion, provided appropriate referrals are made. The dissemination of contraceptive information in Colorado and Tennessee health and welfare agencies, schools, medical institutions, and other instrumentalities is allowed and encouraged by public policy.

Family planning must also be made available to the indigent free of charge and to others at a small fee that covers costs. The statutes also give authority to state health departments to receive funds from state and federal agencies which is provided on a matching basis ranging from 10 percent for Title X of the Public Health Service Act, the major federal resource, to 20 percent for Title II of the Economic Opportunity Act, to 25 percent for Titles V and IV-A of the Social

Securities Act.[56] In addition, the Tennessee law provides that health insurance covers voluntary sterilization, regardless of "the insured's reasons for sterilization."[57]

In general, however, contraception, voluntary sterilization, infertility and normal pediatric care are considered ambulatory care; and since health insurance covers little ambulatory care, such birth related and birth control services are not covered in most health insurance policies.[58] While there are currently several attempts to remedy this situation at the national level there have been no comprehensive attempts in the state legislatures to provide health insurance coverage for all ambulatory care. There have been unsuccessful state legislative attempts to provide health insurance coverage for specified care; Colorado bill on maternity care;[59] Michigan bill on voluntary sterilization;[60] California bill on abortion.[61] None of these bills, however, cover all ambulatory care relating to birth control services in general.

Advertising, Distribution, Display and Sale of Contraceptive Devices. The majority of states do not prohibit the advertisement, distribution and sale of nonprescriptive contraceptive devices. However, in some states, the sale must be made in a registered pharmacy and the seller must be a pharmacist. Furthermore, the person to whom contraceptives can be sold is limited by age and marital status.

A Colorado statute,[62] recently enacted, repealed state provisions prohibiting vending machine sale of prophylactics and restricting the sale of prophylactics to registered pharmacies, thus providing for retail sale through other stores and health clinics.

Voluntary Sterilization. Voluntary sterilization is legal in all states. Some states specifically require that the procedure be performed by a licensed physician or in a licensed hospital.

The state of Virginia has recently repealed their requirement that vasectomies upon persons 21 years and older be performed in a hospital,[63] thus allowing the procedure to be completed in a clinic or in a doctor's office.

Minors. There are a number of factors which influence the availability of medical care to minors without parental consent. Some of these are the age of majority, the general law governing medical treatment of minors, and specific statutes relating to family planning, contraception and venereal disease.[64] At least 14 states have recently reduced the age of majority from 21 to 18, thus allowing those 18 and older to obtain medical care without the consent of parents.

A recently enacted Georgia statute[65] provides for contraceptive services to be given to any female regardless of age and marital status and without parental consent. A 1972 Alabama Act[66] provides for such services to be given to minors fourteen years and older. However, there are some 25 states that do not allow for the provision of contraceptive care for minors without parental consent.

There has been a growing liberalizing trend in laws relating to family planning, general medical services to minors and contraception and venereal disease care to minors. In 47 states minors may now obtain examination and treatment for VD without parental consent.

Legislation Indirectly Affecting Fertility Through Regulation of Social Norms. *Population, Family Life and Sex Education.* State departments of education most often develop their own educational curricula. However, state legislators have often introduced resolutions recommending that certain courses be taught in the area of population, family live and sex education.[67]

Marriage Licenses. The Kentucky,[68] New Hampshire,[69] and Virginia[70] legislatures have recently required that a list of family planning clinics in the state be furnished to applicants for marriage licenses.

The Equal Rights Amendment. The proposed Equal Rights Amendment (ERA) states that "Equality of rights under the law shall not be denied or abridged by the United States or by any state on account of sex." The purpose of the ERA is to clarify the legal status of women, remove existing discrimination against women, and eliminate discrimination against women in the future. Three-fourths of the state legislatures must ratify it within seven years of the date of congressional acceptance for it to become the 27th amendment to the United States Constitution.

Legislation Indirectly Affecting Fertility Through Taxes. Legislation has been introduced in the United States Congress[71] and the California legislature[72] to equalize taxes between single and married persons. The bills extend to unmarried persons the tax benefits of income splitting now enforced by married persons filing joint returns. These bills, while they have not passed, represent important attempts to neutralize tax policy, so that couples are not given financial incentives to marry or not to marry.

Legislation Directly Affecting Population Distribution. Legislation specifically written to redistribute population is as yet not very developed.[73] Florida,[74] Maine[75] and Vermont[76] have enacted land use legislation. The Florida Act puts the state government in a position to exercise a limited degree of control over the growth and development of land within the state, while preserving the processes of local government agencies and rights of private landowners. The role of the state is focused on those land use decisions which will have a substantial impact outside the boundaries of the local government in which the land is located.[77]

Legislation Directly Affecting Per Capita Consumption. An increasing number of state legislators consider the exorbitant consumption habits of individuals as one of the sources of the population/resource dilemma and have therefore developed policies to decrease demand instead of increase the supply of resource.

Tax Proposals. One proposal which has yet to be translated into legislation is a suggestion put forth in *Ecologist* as follows:

A raw materials tax, scaled proportionately to the availability of certain raw materials, would favor labor intensive industries and discourage resource intensive industries. An amortization tax, scaled proportionately to the estimated life of a product would penalize short lived products and encourage the production of long lived products thus reducing resource utilization and the solid waste problem and pollution, particularly the solid waste problem. Plastics, for example, which are so remarkable for their durability would be used only in products where this quality is valued, and not for single trip purposes. This tax would also encourage craftsmanship and labor intensive industry.[78]

Rate Structure for Electricity. Other proposals deal more specifically with demand for gas and electricity. A Massachusetts bill[79] has been introduced to modify the rate structure for electricity. It proposes to alter present structures which charge less as you use more by creating separate rate structures for normal times and peak periods, the rates to be greater during peak periods such as summer.[80]

Conclusion. Hopefully by using a legal systems model the effects of legal changes on population policy can be approximately determined. Fundamental to this integrated systems approach is a population policy which takes account of fertility, distribution, and per capita consumption. The model is crude, but it is hoped that it can be practically used in determining a population policy for a particular state based on its resources, nature of its particular population problem and the desired output.

Institutional Design[81]

The structure of decision making for population policy depends in many respects on how the policy alternatives are designed. This in turn determines which options are chosen and how they are implemented. There are several general decision making designs that characterize some aspects of the process.

Decision Making Designs

Political Design. The political design is characterized by the dynamics of the political participants and deals with the issue of how to make the decision makers politically accountable to the public in the absence of any defined goal. In the case of population policy, states have avoided defining an optimum population goal[82] but rather have used the policy objective of "population stabilization." The more loosely defined population stabilization objective has allowed politicians to avoid value-laden judgments. It has also allowed them to avoid infringing on their constituent's individual right of deciding if and when to have a child.

Politicians and governmental reports have only pointed out the desirability demographically of a two child family in reaching a stabilized growth rate. While there are a few other politically acceptable alternatives to influence the personal component of the policy, such a predicament does pose problems for institutional design if decision makers are to be held politically accountable for population policy.

Common Law Design. To date, the courts have been the most significant institutional mechanism for generating a population policy, whether the objective has been a decrease or increase in the population. This is due in large measure to the political and emotional nature of the subject. Courts, according to Ackerman and Sawyer, have, and can, be significant mechanisms for complementing policy generally:

In theory at least the common law judge seems to have a good deal to recommend him: the ideal judge would strive to be impartial, seek to explicate the complex values of our legal tradition in an effort to formulate a sensitive response to the novel aspects of the ... problem ... respond to reasoned arguments advanced both by the lawyers in the case before him and by academic critics writing in the law reviews. It is true, of course, that the common law process will proceed slowly on a case by case basis, but in the absence of a satisfactory alternative, the Common Law Model at least seems to assure that these incremental decisions will be made in a conscientious, disinterested, and sensitive fashion.[83]

However, experience has shown that the courts are (1) an extremely expensive means of developing policy; (2) incapable of sustaining scientific inquiry beyond the time required for a decision and (3) restricted by the facts in the case before them.[84]

The Administrative Design. If a policy can be established statutorily it should be a relatively straight-forward matter to design an institution to implement that policy. The problem is, however, to establish the statutory policy. To date, there are at least four different ways states have defined the population problem.

Most states have developed adequate statutory family planning policies and established the agencies necessary to implement their objectives. However, states are just beginning to develop adequate definitions of policy alternatives based on the three other policy models—Motivation, Distribution and Per Capita consumption.

Once such policy alternatives are clearly defined, it will be necessary to establish standards "sufficiently clear and coherent to serve as an appropriate statutory basis for agency action."[85] Examples of such proposed standards or outputs are the stabilization of Hawaiian population growth,[86] an optimum limit on the Denver metropolitan area,[87] developing alternative patterns of distribution and settlement in rural areas of Texas,[88] and limiting per capita consumption of electricity by changing the rate structure of electricity in California.[89]

Massachusetts,[90] New Hampshire[91] and Hawaii[92] have recently enacted legislation to either establish a population study commission to formulate statutory policy or to organize a permanent commission with state appropriations to implement policy.

Policy Indicators and Evaluation

The next institutional problem is to decide what policy indicators institutions should use in order to measure the effectiveness of policy.[93] This raises such questions as: (1) is the two child family an adequate policy indicator to measure the effectiveness of a stabilization policy; (2) what policy indicators should states use to measure the effectiveness of an optimum population for a metropolitan area?; and (3) to what extent do these indicators ignore other dimensions of the problem?

Since facts are essential to this evaluation process, inquiry must be made into how these institutions are to be best designed to facilitate fact finding, determine reliability and adequacy of data, and expose possible bias in the data. Care must be taken to ensure that the assembled facts are used not only to prove the effectiveness of a given program but to determine the effectiveness of alternative policies as well. States must design institutional controls to induce administrators to reveal the errors in their predictions. Administrators and/or agencies should not be (1) "so committed to the efficacy of reform that they cannot afford honest evaluation";[94] or (2) so aware of the political utility in advocating specific reforms knowing that certain outcomes would be more politically acceptable than others that they become biased;[95] or (3) so committed to reform so as to justify "the reform on the basis of the importance of the problem, not the certainty of their answer."[96]

Several state reports[97] discuss ways in which data collection functions, research and planning functions, and program implementation functions of population policy could be improved by either centralizing them in the Governor's office or integrating them into the specific functions of each relevant agency of state government.

In regards to fact finding functions, Michigan recommends that various functional agencies should make their analysis on the basis of alternative trends in population growth, maintaining that the various costs and benefits of alternative fertility levels should be known and considered by different departments.[98]

In deciding on a choice between integrating the population component into all planning functions of each of the executive departments or creating a separate office of population, *California's Twenty Million* recommended the model of California's Office of Planning and Research in the Governor's Office. The rationale for placing the state's planning operation in the Governor's office was that the functional planning within each of the existing departments (whether it be health, transportation, housing, etc.) become tools for implementing a set of deliberately determined objectives for state wide developments, rather than a means of assessing, in an unbiased manner, the passive determinants of development.[99]

Conclusion

This article has attempted to explain to the lawmaker the demographic dimensions of population policy. It has not attempted, as most articles do, to criticize the rationality of legal opinions but rather to show how and at what points the legal process can be used in formulating and implementing population policies. It has discussed how the demographic dimensions of policies are and can be used beneficially or detrimentally in evaluating the effectiveness of policy and pointed out the potential for error in using only certain policy indicators without regard to other indicators.

For the demographer and for the quantitative technician it has attempted to outline the legal dimensions that need to be considered in transforming policy into law.

A thorough understanding of both the demographic and legal components is essential if the formulation and implementation of policies are to be successful.

Notes

1. Sills, D., Unanticipated Consequences of Population Policies, *Concerned Demography*, 2:4:63, (March, 1971).

2. Such an outline is a variation of one created by Berelson, B., *Population Policy: Personal Notes*, 25 *Population Studies* 175-6 (1971). The reader should also be aware of the fact that there are internal relationships among demographic variables, for example the effect of declining mortality on fertility. The policy implication of such an internal relationship is that programs affecting mortality can indirectly affect fertility.

3. Davis, K. and F. Styles, *California's Twenty Million: Research Contributors to Population Policy*, at 6, (Population Monograph Series No. 10, Univ. of Cal., Berkeley, 1971). (Hereinafter cited as *California's Twenty Million.*)

4. *Report of the Commission on Population Growth and the American Future*, (Mar. 1972), available from the Superintendent of Documents, U.S. Government Printing Office, Washington, D.C. 20402.

5. *California Population Problems and State Policy*, (California State Assembly Science and Technology Advisory Council, Dec. 1971). (Hereinafter cited as *California Report*); *Report of the Temporary Commission on Population Stabilization* (Hawaii State Legislatures, 1971), (hereinafter cited as *Hawaii Report*); *Final Report of the House Special Committee Investigating the Trend and Impact of Population Growth in the Commonwealth of Massachusetts*, (Massachusetts State Legislature, Dec. 1971) (hereinafter cited as *Massachusetts Report*). *Hearings of the Michigan State Senate Special Committee on Impacts and Trends of Population Growth in the State of Michigan*, (Michigan State Legislature, Oct. 15, 1970); *Report of the Pennsylvania Abortion Law Commission*, (Pennsylvania Exec. Dept. June 1972); *Population Distribution in Texas* (Texas State Legislators Senate Interim Committee on Population Distribution, Dec. 1972), (hereinafter cited as *Texas Report*).

6. *Colorado Options for the Future*, (Colorado Environmental Commission, 1972), (hereinafter cited as *Colorado Report*); *An Environmental Policy for Connecticut*, (Governor's Committee on Environmental Policy, June 1970); Oakley D. and L. Corsa, *Population Policy for the State of Michigan*, (prepared for the Michigan Governor's Council Population Committee, March 1973), hereinafter cited as *Michigan Report*).

7. *Co-ordinating Governments Through Regionalism and Reform*, Vol. 1, *Land Use Control: Modern Techniques for Modern Problems,* and Vol. 2, *Fiscal Crisis and Municipal Manpower Opportunities: Letting Necessity Mother Invention*, (New York State Legislature Committee on Metropolitan Regional Areas Legislative Document No. 18, 1969-71); *Final Report of the Wisconsin Land Resources Committee*, (Wisconsin State Legislature, Feb. 1973).

8. *California's Twenty Million*, supra, n. 3 at 6.

9. *Colorado Report*, supra, n. 6, at 7.

10. *California's Twenty Million*, supra, n. 3, at 262.

11. *Colorado Report*, supra, n. 6, at 7.

12. *California's Twenty Million*, supra, n. 3, at 272.

13. Hauser, P., "The Census of 1970," *Scientific American*, 225:1:17-25 (July 1971).

14. *Colorado Report*, supra, n. 6, at 7.

15. *California Report*, supra, n. 5, at 6.

16. *Michigan Report*, supra, n. 6, at 33.

17. Id. at 19.

18. *Colorado Report*, supra, n. 6, at 55.

19. Davis, Kingsley, "Population Policy: Will Current Programs Succeed?" *Science*, 158:3802 732, (Nov. 1967). Copyright 1967 by the American Association for the Advancement of Science.

20. *Colorado Report*, supra, n. 6, at 53.

38

21. *California's Twenty Million*, supra, n. 3, at 298.

22. *Massachusetts Report*, supra, n. 5, at 12.

23. *Hawaii Report*, supra, n. 5 at 40.

24. *California Report*, supra, n. 5, at 18.

25. *Michigan Report*, supra, n. 6, at 42. The report elaborated by the following examples:

When there is a marginal increase in age groups having high utilization rates then consumption rates are magnified. Thus for constant ratios of car registrations, when the population aged 20-75 increases more rapidly than the total population no matter what the fertility projection, the impact on miles of highway needed is greater than the increase in total population size. Using the three population projections, by 2040 total population will grow by 91%, 33%, 25%, as compared with 1970 miles of highway needed to maintain current load factors will increase even with no change in registrations per person 20-75, by 112%, 57% or 50%. If age specific utilization rates are increased, the magnifying effect of growth by group will be even greater.

26. *Michigan Report*, supra, n. 6, at 42.

27. Pilpel, H., "Limiting Population: The Voluntary Approach," *Civil Liberties*, No. 281 (Nov. 1971). See also Lee, L., *Law, Human Rights and Population: A Strategy For Action*, (Law and Population Monograph Series, No. 6 (Fletcher School of Law and Diplomacy, Tufts University).

28. *Griswold v. Connecticut*. 381 U.S. 479, at 496-97 (1965).

29. Marks, J., "Legal Analysis and Population Control: The Problem of Coercion," 84 *Harv. L. Rev.*, at 1869-70 (1971).

30. Miller, A., "Some Observations on the Political Economy of Population Growth," *Law and Contemporary Problems*, at 614, (Duke School of Law, 1960).

31. Pilpel, H., *Brief Survey of U.S. Population Law*, (Law and Population Monograph series, No. 2, The Fletcher School of Law and Diplomacy, Tufts University).

32. Model Penal Code § 230.3 (American Law Institute, Proposed Official Draft, Phila. Pa. 1962).

33. *Roe v. Wade*, 410 U.S. 133 (1973); *Doe v. Bolton*, 410 U.S. 179 (1973).

34. *Vernon's Texas Stat.* §§ 1191-1194, 1196 (1948).

35. *Georgia Code.* §§ 26-1201-03.

36. *Doe v. Bolton*, 410 U.S. 179 (1973). For a more thorough analysis of Roe and Doe, see Gittelman, J., and D. Licht, *What the Supreme Court Said: An Examination of the Effect of Roe v. Wade and Doe v. Bolton on Existing Abortion Law* (Unpublished report, Harvard Law School, May 1973).

37. See Blake J., "Population Policy for Americans: Is the Government Being Misled?" *Science* 164:3879:522-529 (May 1969).

38. For a more thorough analysis of coercive measures see Paul, J., "The Return of Punitive Sterilization Proposals," *Law and Society Review* 3:1:9

(Aug. 1968) and Ferster, E., "Eliminating the Unfit—Is Sterilization the Answer?" 27 *Ohio St. L.J.* 591 (1966).

39. Tennessee H.B. No. 20 (1971) introduced by Representative Larry Bates. A segment of the Bill reads: "Before such female person, girl or woman, shall be eligible to receive such monthly welfare assistance, or benefits when it appears that she is presently the mother of more than one (1) illegitimate child, that such female person, girl or woman, shall first submit herself and agree that a sterilization operation may and shall be performed on her by competent medical personnel."

40. H.B. No. 512 (1971-1972) (109th General Assembly, Reg. Sess.) by Representative Robert E. Netzley. A segment of the Bill reads: "Unless free injections of depo provera on an every third month treatment basis are otherwise available to any person in a city or general health district who requests this treatment in order to qualify for aid under chapter 5107 of the revised code. . . ."

41. Katz, M., "Legal Dimensions of Population Policy," 50 *Social Sci. Q.* 732 (1969).

42. Id. at 733.

43. The fourth part of this paper is based upon an unpublished paper, Marson, W., *The Use of the Family Planning Model for the Reduction of Population Growth in Developing Countries* (Kennedy School of Gov't., Harvard University, 1970). See also McLaughlin, C. and E. Trainer, *Qualitative Evaluation of Family Planning Proposals and Programs: A Systems Approach* (Carolina Population Center, Monograph 12, University of North Carolina).

44. *Michigan Report*, supra, n. 6, at 76.

45. See, i.e., the following proposals: Massachusetts, H.B. 5012 (1972); Michigan S.R. 251 (1972); California H.R. 110 (1972); Colorado S.R. 11 (1972).

46. Nash, A., *Going Beyond John Locke? Influencing American Population Growth*, (Millbank Memorial Fund 14 1971).

47. Id. at 25.

48. See, Reynolds, J., "Measuring the Demographic Effectiveness of Anti-natalist Policies," *Proceedings of the General Conference of the Inter. Union for the Scientific Study of Population*, at 343-58, (Liege, Belgium, 1973).

49. Tanner, J., and F. Mosteller eds., *Statistics: A Guide to the Unknown*, at 304 (1972).

50. *Reports on Population and Family Planning* at 8 (Population Council, New York City, Oct. 1972).

51. Hoogenboom, H., "Population Policy and Law," at 94, *Concerned Demography*, (Mar. 1972).

52. For an ongoing report of state population legislation see, *Family Planning/Population Reporter*, (A review of state laws and policies published bimonthly by the Center for Family Planning Program Development, The

Technical Assistance Division of Planned Parenthood World Population, 1660 L Street N.W., Washington, D.C. 20036).

53. For a thorough analysis of state laws and administration see forthcoming report, *Information Summary and Analysis of State and Federal Laws Applicable to the Development of Family Planning Programs* prepared by the Center for Family Planning Program Development of Planned Parenthood World Population under the direction of Harriet F. Pilpel for the Department of Health, Education and Welfare, available from Government Printing Office.

54. Colorado S.B. 230 (1971), introduced by Senator John R. Bermingham. For a discussion of legislation providing family planning services as well as legislation in each of the categories subsequently discussed in this article, see Cook R., *State Population Legislation*. Baldwin, C. ed., *The New England Regional Conference of Population*, (N.Y. Population Council, June 1973).

55. Tennessee S.B. 871 (1971).

56. Weinberg, D., "What State Governments Can Do," *Family Planning Perspectives*, Vol. II, No. 2 (Mar. 1970); Weinberg D., "State Administration and Financing of Family Planning Services," *Family Planning Perspectives*, Vol. 4, No. 2 (April 1972).

57. Tennessee, S.B. 871 (1971).

58. Muller, C. and F. Jaffe, "Financing Fertility—Related Health Services in the United States 1972-1978: a Preliminary Projection," *Family Planning Perspectives*, 4:2:37, (Jan. 1972). The basic premise of this study is that underfinancing tends to create disincentives to birth control services for both providers and patients.

59. Colorado S.B. 417 (1973), introduced by Senator John R. Bermingham.

60. Michigan S.B. 1442 (1972); introduced by Senator Gilbert E. Bursley.

61. California, S.B. 283 (1972), introduced by Senator Anthony C. Beilenson.

62. Colorado S.B. 257, (1973) introduced by Senator John R. Bermingham et al. This law provides for wider distribution of condoms while insuring a safe product. The statute further requires that:

every unit package shall bear notation, printed in both English and Spanish, that the product should not be used more than 3 years after date of manufacture as shown on the package. Prophylactic vending machines shall contain only written advertising thereon in Spanish and English which shall only indicate the materials to be purchased, the price of said merchandise and the notice directing the purchaser to local venereal disease prevention services or clinics.

S.B. 257, § 3 source L.47, § 8 at 521; C SA C.78 § 170(11) CRS 53 § 66-10-2, 3, 4, 5, 6. For a more thorough analysis of laws and legislation affecting the sale, distribution and advertisement of non prescriptive contraceptive devices see Redford, M. and D. Praeger, *The Batelle Conference Proceedings on the Condom*, (forthcoming).

63. Virginia H.B. 69, (1972) introduced by Delegate Calvin W. Fowler et al.

64. Pilpel, H. and N. Weshsler, "Birth Control, Teenagers and the Law: A New Look," *Family Planning Perspectives*, Vol. 3, (July 1971). See also Pilpel, H. and J. Zuckerman, *Abortion and the Rights of Minors*, 23 *Case W. Res. L. Rev.* 979 (1972).

65. Georgia H.B. 2072 (1972), introduced by Representative George Busbee, et al.

66. Alabama S.B. 664 (1972), introduced by Senator Cooper.

67. Washington S.R. 12, (1972) introduced by State Senator Peter Francis.

68. Kentucky S.B. 106 (1972) introduced by Senator C. Gibson Downing.

69. New Hampshire H.B. 95, (1973) introduced by Representative Elizabeth Greene.

70. Virginia H.B. 1095 (1972) introduced by Delegate William F. Reid.

71. United States B. 898, (February 1971) introduced by Senator Abraham Ribicoff.

72. California Assembly Bill 555, (Feb. 1972) introduced by Assemblyman Robert Cline.

73. For a more thorough analysis of land use and population see Lamm, R. and S. Davison, "The Legal Control of Population Growth and Distribution in a Quality Environment: The Land Use Alternative," 49 *Denver L.J.* 1 (1972). See also *The Use of Land: A Citizen's Guide to Urban Growth* (The Lawrence Rockefeller 1972). For an ongoing review of state land use legislation see *Land Use Planning Reports*, published bi-weekly.

74. Florida S.R. 629 (Feb. 1972) introduced by Senator Robert Grahm, et al.

75. *Maine Revised Stat. Ann.*, Tit. 38, C.3, Art. 1, 6.

76. Land Use and Development Act, Vermont Legislature Act 250 (1970).

77. Under the Florida Law, the Governor and Cabinet are empowered to designate specific geographical areas as 'areas of critical state concern' and to establish principles to guide the development of each of those areas. To be an area of critical state concern, the area must (1) have environmental, historical, natural or archeological value of regional or statewide importance; (2) be an area where an existing or proposed major public facility will be located or major public investment made; or (3) be a proposed area of major development potential, such as a new community.

78. "Blueprint for Survival," *The Ecologist*, (Jan. 1972).

79. Mass. (1973) H.B. 1901.

80. Doctor et al, *California's Electricity Quandry: III Slowing the Growth Rate*, (Rand Study R-1116-NSF/CSA Santa Monica, California, Sept. 1972).

81. This section on Institutional Design is based in part on Ackerman B. and J. Sawyer, "The Uncertain Search for Environmental Policy: Scientific Factfinding and Rational Decisionmaking Along the Delaware River," 120 *U.Pa. L.Rev.* 419 (1972).

82. An argument to establish an optimum population size is made in *Size Can*

Make a Difference (1970), written by the Advisory Commission on Intergovernmental Relations, Washington, D.C. The Report argued that after a certain size, it is probable that an urban area suffers diminishing returns to scale, making further increments in population inefficient. The report indicated the diseconomies of scale set in after population passes 250,000.

83. *California's Twenty Million*, supra, n. 3, at 427.

84. *Id.*, at 428.

85. *Id.*, at 426.

86. Hawaii S.R. 303 (1972).

87. *Colorado Report*, supra, n. 6, at 11.

88. *Texas Report*, supra, n. 5, at 8.

89. Doctor et al., supra, n. 80.

90. Massachusetts House Bill 4420 introduced by Representative Robert D. Wetmore et al. (1973).

91. New Hampshire Senate Joint Resolution introduced by Senator Eileen Foley (1973).

92. Hawaii SB 37 introduced by Senator Kenneth F. Brown et al. (1973).

93. See: Elihu Bergman, "The Evaluation of Population Policy: Some Missing Links," prepared for the Rahovot Conference in Economic Growth in Developing Countries, Weizmann Institute of Science, Rehovot, Israel, September, 1973.

94. Donald T. Campbell, "Reforms as Experiments," *American Psychologist*, Vol. 24, No. 4, April 1969.

95. Id., p. 1.

96. Id., p. 248.

97. *Michigan Report*, supra, n. 6, and W.P. Hollman, Isabel Hanibright and W. Nelson Rasmussen, "Population Research in the Department of Finance," in *California's Twenty Million*, supra, n. 3, at 336.

98. *Michigan Report*, supra, n. 6, at 86.

99. R.E. Greenwald, supra, p. 298.

3

Framework for the Analysis of State and Local Population Policy

Richard D. Tabors*

Introduction

At the local, the state, or the national level, a population policy is most frequently envisioned as one which directly influences the rate of growth or the distribution of population within a given geographical area, or a policy which is responsive to the demands placed upon the social system by a change, generally a growth, in the size or composition of the population in a given locale. Fertility control programs are usually considered to be *population-influencing* policies. While such programs frequently are conducted on a national basis, a state legislature's orientation on abortion or a local family planning program may also have a dramatic effect. *Population-responsive* policies are those most often undertaken within the state and local decision-making structure. These policies are typically responses to population growth in a given community—i.e., the construction of additional classroom space, the exclusion of development housing, the funding of additional bonding for metropolitan sewerage facilities or the opening of a new sanitary landfill.

Both the influencing and the responsive policies listed above are explicit. They attempt directly to influence or respond to a change in the size of the population. Can a population-responsive policy work to influence the size or composition of the population? Does the decision to construct more low or moderate income housing merely respond to the local demand, or does it influence the population structure at the micro level by encouraging the immigration of families seeking this type of housing?

The purpose of this chapter is to introduce two concepts into the analysis of the impact of population-related policy at the urban and regional level. The first is a broadened concept of population distribution; the second, a systems framework for urban and regional policy-impact analysis and assessment. The distribution of population is defined within three conceptual dimensions, that of the distribution of people over geographic space, population distributed along the axis of income, and the distribution of population by age and sex. Along these three conceptual dimensions, it will be argued that, within the systems framework, it is possible to analyze the impact of any given policy upon the

*Lecturer in City and Regional Planning and Research Associate in Population Studies, Harvard University.

distribution of population. It is further suggested that the framework will allow the researcher to analyze the likely outcomes or repercusssions of any given policy upon the social and physical service demands of the populace.

To do this, this chapter is divided into three sections. The first is a discussion of the more traditional dimensions (or axes) of urban and regional social policy analysis. The second section argues for the addition of a new dimension to the analysis of urban social policy—population (demographic) distribution. The third section introduces and discusses the framework for population policy analysis. The framework as it is presented in this chapter is in its early stages of development. Additional research is required into the efficacy of the consideration of demographic distribution in the analysis of urban population policy.

Traditional Dimensions of Urban and Regional Policy Research

Within the general fields of urban and regional studies, the role of the academic researcher, as in so many of his endeavors, sacrifices purity for pragmatism. Whether one accepts or rejects the role of academics as experts or consultants, one cannot deny that the increasing degree of interaction between decision-makers and professionals has forced the university-based urban researcher toward a posture which, for lack of more precise definition, one may call policy relevance. Federal, state, and local policies in economic and social development influence and alter what we as academics study. Our studies, on the other hand, either directly or indirectly affect at least the rationale for public policy based frequently on our evaluation of past policies.

Traditional policy research in urban areas is primarily economic, with inputs from political science, geography, and sociology. Population analysis enters only as an aggregate for projection of future demand. Very seldom is there an interest in the age or income distribution of the population.

In an oversimplified description, one may say that economists, when dealing with questions of population, tend toward high levels of aggregation. An aggregate group may be simply the total population, or a subgroup of that population defined by income or other economic characteristics. "They," as a group, demand goods and services and supply capital and labor. Income, goods, and services most frequently are seen as being distributed unequally between groups within the economy. These highly aggregated groups frequently do not take into consideration space, age, or social characteristics. In economics, population is seen as being distributed in "economic space" or "space-less" space. In the three dimensional structure under consideration, the first dimension is economic distribution, composed of two real axes, income and people. (See Figure 3-1a.)

The second conceptual dimension of urban and regional population analysis is

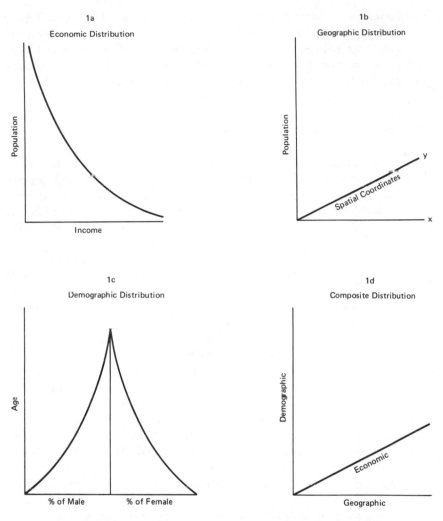

Figure 3-1. Three Dimensions and Population Distribution.

that of geographic space. Geographers recognize that people not only have demands, but that they express these demands in terms of their patterns of life. Demands for living space, for example, are generally localized to neighborhoods or suburbs which more than likely are not the areas in which the particular individuals are employed. People flow from home to job, from urban center to urban center, from exurbia or suburbia to the central city. Goods and services flow to geographic points of demand which are a function of location of home, of business, or of economic activities. This second conceptual axis is itself made up of a set of axes, of which the first is, in general, population; a second and third axis being required to describe residential location; a fourth and fifth, employment location; and further axes to describe other locations of economic and social activity within the urban or regional system. (See Figure 3-1b.)

Demographic Distribution of Population

The third conceptual axis, the demographic axis, is the one which this writer argues has been ignored in most of the research on urban and regional development policy. The people within a region are not all alike; they are black or white, rich or poor, urban or suburban. These "population" characteristics are frequently considered in the analysis. What has been missing is an explicit concern for the age distribution of the population. (See Figure 3-1c.)

The consideration of demographic distribution parameters in our present urban policy research concentrates explicitly on two age groups, the schoolaged and the elderly. We recognize the need to provide for children within our society. We make the effort to provide them with some guarantee of health and education, though we do not always succeed in providing the quantity or quality required at a specific point in time or space. Also, we are now recognizing a societal responsibility to the elderly through more general welfare operations such as social security. What of the group that lies between the very young and the elderly? In our society today, our most productive years are between ages twenty and sixty-five. In analyzing the growth of urban America we have seen an historical shift of the middle-aged, middle class away from the central city towards the suburb. We have heard the comment that the city has become the home of the poor, the black, the indigent, and the old. What do these patterns mean to an economist, a geographer, an urbanist?

The age and stage in life cycle determines the individual's relative level and pattern of consumption. One can hardly imagine the single, twenty-four-year old female executive being a heavy consumer of disposable diapers or single unit suburban housing. The same consumption pattern may hold for the recent retiree, though his historic consumption patterns may leave him with housing space in excess of his requirements. The question then becomes: What if any, insights into the process of urbanization, urban development, or urban change does a concern with population distribution (other than race) give to the individual urban researcher or interdisciplinary research team?[1]

In summary, this portion of the chapter has presented the first step in the argument for including population or demography, along with economics and geography, as a conceptual axis in a three-dimensional population distribution which may be incorporated into a framework for the analysis of urban and regional development. (See Figure 3-1d.) Any individual at a point in time will be a part of a population distribution defined in terms of this conceptual three-dimensional matrix. On the economic dimension he forms a part of an income group; on the geographic dimension he finds his home in an urban or suburban area and his work either there or in another portion of the geographic system; within the demographic dimension an individual is a member of a racial and ethnic grouping from which he never removes himself and is, over time, a member of an aging cohort. It is suggested here that the understanding of the interrelationships contained in this three-dimensional schematic model may offer a valuable tool to further urban research. For the remainder of this chapter, when referring to a population distribution this author will mean the three-dimensional distribution of economics, geography and demography.

A Framework for Policy Analysis

The section which follows attempts to place these three policy dimensions into a framework within which the researcher or decision-maker may analyze the impact of individual policy decisions upon the population structure. Implicit in this discussion is a broadening of the definition of a population-related policy decision beyond the concept of family planning. Figure 3-2 presents a simplified schematic diagram of a proposed analytic framework. The framework can be divided into four sets or sections: (1) a partial listing of urban and regional policy areas; (2) a taxonomy of the types of influences which individual urban and regional policy decisions can and do have upon the distribution of population; (3) a restatement of the three conceptual dimensions or axes of population distribution; (4) a feedback step in which the impact of an altered population distribution may be analyzed.

Step one of Figure 3-2 is the beginning of the analytic framework as it is presented in this example. It should be noted, however, that urban and regional policy decisions do not begin in a vacuum. It is the demands placed upon the social/governmental structure by the population which initiate any policy decision. Hence, the areas of policy analysis listed are only suggestive of the range of decisions made at this level, and the list is not intended to be exhaustive. Step one becomes, then, merely the statement of the policy decision which becomes the point of initiation of the analysis.

In many ways the core of this framework is contained in step two and three. Step two contains a taxonomy of policy decisions that corresponds to the impact of any given decision on the three axes of distribution of population discussed in the previous two sections of this chapter.

Decision-makers and academics as well have tended to recognize that population policy or population analysis was limited to what appears on Figure 3-2 as "direct" and "explicit" population-influencing policies (a family

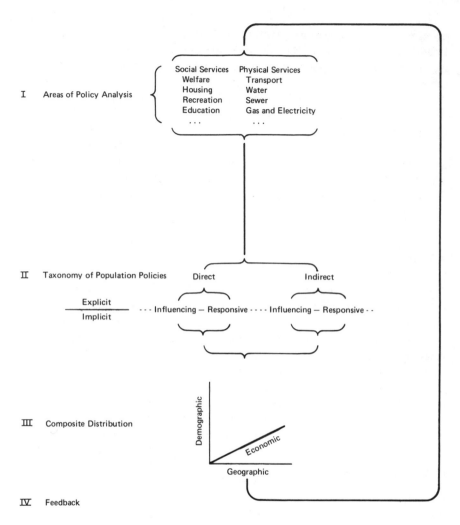

Figure 3-2. Analytical Framework.

planning program with goals to reduce fertility) or population-responsive policies (an education program to respond to increased demand for elementary school classrooms caused by the "baby boom"). In each of these instances policy decisions are made which will directly affect or are a direct effect of population change. Other examples of direct and explicit population policies are teaching population education in the schools (influencing), legalization of abortion (influencing and responsive), increased housing for the elderly (responsive).

What then would be the characteristics of a direct and implicit policy as opposed to a direct, explicit policy, within this taxonomy? An implicit policy decision is one which "happens," one which is never articulated but becomes established by precedence. An example of an implicit population-influencing policy in Massachusetts over the past several years has been the ability of single females to receive birth control information, despite a law on the books preventing such action. An implicit population-responsive policy may be seen in the education systems of older cities. We actively increased our classroom space during the baby boom; at present, our primary enrollments are going down. In the process we are consolidating the older buildings with the new, eliminating one or two classrooms, shifting rooms within schools to special use as classroom demands go down. We now imply quality as our demand rather than quantity and at the same time make marginal shifts in utilization of physical space.

Less obvious though possibly far more significant in impact on overall population distribution are indirect policy decisions. Indirect population policies have a measurable effect upon the distribution of population, though this is not the stated goal and frequently is not a recognized result of a given policy. Indirect policies like direct policies may be either population-influencing or responsive, explicit or implicit. One seldom if ever analyzes a housing policy or health and welfare policy to determine its effect on distribution of population. More often we see these policies, if we see them affecting population at all, as being direct and population-responsive.

Housing and land use policy in an urban area does not have a change in the distribution of population as one of its articulated goals. These policies do, however, have a measurable indirect effect on the distribution. As an example of the indirect population-influencing nature of a policy in an area such as land use or housing, one may consider the case of urban zoning, particularly as it is applied in the central city areas of many of our older cities. Zoning ordinances were put into effect after much of the central city development had been completed. As a result, current land use frequently does not conform to regulations, and any demolition for reconstruction or alteration of structure is likely to require zoning exception.

Explicitly, a city has the ability to encourage the redevelopment of areas in a manner which will increase the tax base while minimizing the demand for services. Within the inner ring cities of Boston, for instance, a zoning policy which encourages high density (particularly when done in the private sector) encourages the development of studio and one bedroom apartments which can bring the largest return on the investment (especially since the present demand for such housing units is high).

Implicitly, the appeals board may set either its own policy for housing or may liberalize or tighten the policy articulated through the zoning process by allowing those exceptions which follow a particular pattern of development for a city as a whole or for individual wards, precincts, or neighborhoods of a city. An example of this type of implicit policy is again the encouragement of privately developed high density units through exceptions in the zoning process by squeezing lot lines, by minimizing open space, and possibly also by granting parking exceptions.

It is either the planning board, the board of aldermen, or the city council which sets the explicit land use policy. The board of appeals interprets either strictly or loosely the allowable exceptions from the stated land use policy. The board of appeals decisions, through the setting of precedents, become an implicit policy covering land use exceptions for a city, ward, or neighborhood.

Assuming that these explicit and implicit policies have a long term viability in the urban area, what is the effect on the distribution of population? In the case of housing the effect on population is quite clear. Whether in terms of initial development or in terms of redevelopment, a policy which encourages private entrepreneurs to construct high density housing will encourage the development of small rather than large living units. These smaller units are principally consumed by fixed portions of the age distribution of the population; young adults—either singles or young couples with one or no children—who have a moderate income and see convenience to work or more traditionally closeness to the activities of the urban center as a desirable attribute. The same applies to individuals past child rearing who look upon the urban location again as a convenience to their point of occupation and as an opportunity to avail themselves of the urban amenities which may include closeness to transportation, cultural events, or in some instances shopping.

The final category within the framework is that of population-responsive policies, which are indirect in nature and may be either explicit or implicit. This, of the four basic groupings, is the least easily defined. These are policies which respond to demands, which themselves are only tangentially related to population growth. An increase in quality and quantity of social services is generally a direct result of social pressures to guarantee benefits, though indirectly the policy responds to an increase in the size and distribution of the population.

It is interesting to speculate on the role of welfare as an indirect population-influencing policy as well. One might argue that in a system in which there is a high level of information availability and high geographic mobility, individuals who are eligible for welfare would choose to live in that community whose benefits were the most attractive, that welfare recipients "vote with their feet." It is unlikely, however, that in the real world either the information system or individual mobility would be sufficient to allow more than the marginal instance of a choice between habitation in one of two adjoining counties.[2]

The third step or part of the framework is, as has been suggested earlier, the analysis of the impact of the policy or decision upon the distribution of the population. In this step we refer to the three-dimensional distribution discussed in the early portion of this chapter. In this the researcher attempts to analyze the impact of a given policy upon the distribution of population along the axis of geographic, economic, and demographic distribution. The altered distribution of population along these three conceptual axes is then used as an input into the framework for a second iteration in which the subsequent question is asked: Given this change in the distribution of population, what will be the resultant shifts in demand for urban or regional services? A feedback mechanism is suggested in which there would be several iterations during which to assess the impact of any given urban or regional social or physical policy.

The Framework: An Overview

Using the proposed framework it is possible to analyze the impact of a change in housing policy for a given community. The conscious choice of the urban leadership is for higher density housing in a core urban area which has traditionally had two and three family homes. *Ceteris paribus*, what would be the impact of such a policy? The lot sizes are not sufficient to allow for higher density housing if the builders must conform to the zoning regulations requiring a certain distance from lot lines and provision of one parking space for each apartment. The zoning board, aware of the explicit land use plan, but also aware of the need or desire for increased rehabilitation and replacement of housing units, allows exceptions which squeeze lot lines and allow builders to provide parking for only a fixed percentage of the units. This policy encourages a shift in the geographic distribution of the population toward that community as densities increase. The demographic distribution of the population will shift away from families who require living space and prefer the relatively spacious two and three family homes in favor of either singles, young couples, or couples past child rearing. The economic distribution is equally likely to shift as singles and young couples have a moderate income but no dependents and thus a relatively high income density, i.e., the per capita income of a working husband and wife each earning $12,000 per year would be far greater than the per capita income of a family of four with only the father working at a salary of $35,000.

In this scenario, what then would be the impact of this change in population distribution on the demands upon the urban center for further services–i.e., what would be the secondary effect in changed demands for urban services? Fewer families would mean fewer children and less expenditure on schools. It would also mean less expenditures on specific types of recreational activities such as large ball fields, etc. On the other hand, the increase in numbers of older people would require that there be additional park and recreational facilities for the elderly. While the singles and young couples would probably place few if any demands upon the social welfare services of the community, the shift away from families toward a larger proportion of elderly people would require a shift from teenage drop-in centers to elderly drop-in centers, from a preoccupation with drug abuse to a preoccupation with podiatrists.

One can foresee in this scenario that the city under discussion might find itself relatively well off in terms of demands upon its tax base, as the function of education would be curtailed in favor of other less costly services. What would be its disadvantages? Probably the most significant would concern the one consumption item of singles and young couples, the automobile. Combined with the assumed implicit policy of allowing exceptions to the zoning rule of one apartment requiring one off street parking place, on and off street parking densities could become an administrative menace. Certainly the demand for overnight parking in residential zones of major urban centers has been severe and is likely to require the attention of the decision-makers over time should this type of housing policy continue. Considered within this analytic framework, however, it is possible to see that the implicit policy of allowing zoning exceptions for parking could be foreseen and changed on a subsequent iteration of the analysis. Other examples may be seen in housing in suburbia, where we know that the provision of, or guarantee of, sewerage services will encourage the growth of housing. Zoning for single units further encourages the immigration of families into a suburban area. This in turn places a heavy demand upon the education, transportation, and health facilities of the community, which are a response to, among other forces, the increased significance of the child rearing age groups and the children that go with them.

The examples given in this scenario are only suggestive of the type of policy areas which are involved in a full analysis of urban and regional decision-making as it impinges on population and on the distribution of that population. The examples have been relatively clean and give the reader the opportunity of interpreting the results in light of his own experience in the shifting of population distribution along the three conceptual axes suggested. It is not difficult to discuss other policies such as those dealing with the provision of physical services in gas, water, and sewerage to see the manner in which these functions are also affected by alterations in the overall distribution of the population.

Only academics are allowed to operate in a system in which the term *ceteris paribus* may be used. When one begins to work in the real world and to interact with the decision-makers who are an integral portion of it, one becomes increasingly aware that decisions are made with all dimensions in relative disequlibrium. Individual policies do not, it would seem, affect only one dimension of distribution, but rather all dimensions. A housing policy is at one and the same time an influence on the economic, geographic, and demographic distribution of population in a given city, urban area or metropolitan region. In this chapter an argument has been made in favor of adding a dimension of demography to *all* urban and regional analysis. Neither academics nor decision makers have totally ignored this dimension. Policy decisions within the urban system impinge upon population. Only through a careful analysis of the effects upon the demographic distribution of population combined with economic and geographic distribution is it possible to understand many of the complex interrelationships which make urban systems often appear to move away from, rather than toward a state that one might refer to as dynamic equilibrium.

Summary

In this chapter, two concepts have been introduced into the analysis of the impact of population-related policy at the urban and regional level—a broadened concept of population distribution and a systems framework for urban and regional policy impact analysis and assessment. The distribution of population was defined within three conceptual dimensions: geographic, economic and demographic distribution. Along these three conceptual dimensions, it has been argued, it is possible to analyze the impact of any given policy upon the population of a given area and hence to analyze the likely further outcome or repercussions of this policy upon the social and physical service demands of the populace. This analytic framework at its most elementary level allows the policymaker or the academic the ability to assess the likely outcomes of particular policy decisions when viewed in the context of changes in the demand structure of the population. At its highest level, it is possible that the framework *could* be translated to an econometric model with appropriate transfer coefficients associated with each of the interrelationships between change in distribution and further change in the demand structure of the population. Such ambitious modeling can not be more than suggested here. The analytic framework as it has been presented does offer, this author would argue, the first step in bringing the three dimensions of population distribution into focus on the analysis of public policy decisions.

Notes

1. For a summary analysis of studies in which demographic distribution is taken into consideration see: Peter A. Morrison, "Dimensions of the Population Problem in the United States," in Commission on Population Growth and the American Future Research Reports, Vol. 5, *Population Distribution and Policy*, ed. Sara Mills Mazie (Washington, D.C.: U.S. Government Printing Office, 1973), pp. 3-30.

2. For an excellent discussion of distribution and income disparities see Roy W. Bahl, "Metropolitan Fiscal Structures and the Distribution of Population within Metropolitan Areas," in Commission on Population Growth and the American Future Research Reports, op. cit., pp. 423-439.

Part II:
The Substance of Policymaking

4

Population Trends in Massachusetts: An Overview of the Problem

Constantine Constantinides*

Changes in population growth and distribution in Massachusetts during the past several decades have precipitated many problems in land use and resource management which are among the most serious confronting public decision-makers at all levels of government.

Massachusetts is one of the most densely populated states in the nation. In 1970 there were over 5.7 million people settled in an area of about 8,000 square miles, a population density of 750 persons per square mile. Since the turn of the century, the population in Massachusetts has more than doubled in size, growing from 2.8 million people in 1900 to about 5.7 million in 1970, at an average rate of 45,000 per year. Between 1950 and 1970 Massachusetts gained a total of approximately one million new residents—equivalent to five new cities the size of Worcester or ten times the population of Barnstable County. What seems to be crucial about these trends in population increase is the fact that much of the growth has taken place within metropolitan regions. Today, more than 80 percent of the state's population is located in ten metropolitan areas, with Boston metropolis embracing more than 50 percent of the population.

Perhaps the greatest visible change that has occurred over the years has been the continuing decline in the number of small communities. In 1930 there was a total of 233 communities, or approximately two-thirds of the state's communities, with populations under 5,000. By 1970 the number of localities of that size was estimated to have declined to 148. Of major significance is the rate of increase in the number of communities with populations ranging between 10,000 and 30,000. In 1930 there were a total of 44 communities with populations between 10,000 and 30,000, and in 1970 there were about 100.

While most of the communities, except the cities, have experienced sharp population increases, the fastest rate of increase between 1950 and 1970 has occurred in localities within Boston and Springfield SMSAs. Conversely, of the three non-metropolitan regions in the state, Barnstable County experienced similar trends in population growth during the same period. (See Figures 4-1 through 4-6, pp. 63-68.)

As for the future,[1] the population in Massachusetts is projected to grow at the same rate as in previous years. (See Figures 4-7 through 4-12, pp. 69-74.)

---

*Chief Planner, Bureau of Regional Planning, Massachusetts Department of Community Affairs; Technical Advisor, Governor's Resource Management Policy Council.

However, many of these communities in the Boston and Springfield metropolitan areas that have doubled or tripled their populations between 1950 and 1970 are expected to level off during the next twenty to thirty years. On the other hand, communities in Barnstable County will experience sharp population increases in the future. This is particularly true in the case of Mashpee, Dennis, Brewster, Chatham, Orleans, Wellfleet, and Provincetown, where in most cases the population has more than doubled in the last twenty years and will more than triple during the next thirty years.

Expanding population in any area generates an almost insatiable demand for more land—for housing, industry, commerce, schools, recreation, transportation, waste disposal, and other resources vital to an urban environment. Land, unlike people, is a fixed and finite entity, and in many parts of the Commonwealth the supply of this resource is being depleted at an alarming rate with each passing year. For example, between 1952 and 1963 about 95,000 acres or 6.1 percent of the total land area in 152 communities in the eastern part of Massachusetts had been used up for various urban uses.[2] According to the Metropolitan Area Planning Council's 1968 report, "Guide for Progress," some 444,000 acres, or more than 50 percent of the area's vacant land, will be developed in some form or another by the year 1990.

Urban growth and its attendant impact on land resources is an experience shared not only by the Boston metropolitan region but also by the other metropolitan regions in the state. In the Lower Pioneer Valley Region, it is estimated that by the year 1990 about 60,000 acres or little over 20 percent of the area's vacant land will be used up by the projected increase in residential and economic development. According to estimates prepared by the regional planning commission, over half of the land projected to be developed will be used up by residential, commercial, and industrial users alone, with the remainder to be used for transportation, recreation open space, and public facilities.

The principal forces which determine the course and magnitude of local and metropolitan development in Massachusetts include highways and local zoning policies. Highways, in effect, have created urban land where none has existed before by extending the commuting distance from core cities. Suburbanization and the decline of the cities during the postwar years would not have accelerated both in speed and scope if it had not been for the metropolitan highway systems. Highways do not stop at the metropolitan fringes, and in recent years their effect upon built up areas (i.e. inside and outside Route 128) has understandably received greater attention than their impact in the rural areas of the state.

An equally significant force influencing the rate of growth and development at the local and regional levels is local land use policies or what is more commonly known as zoning.

Zoning, the principal land use regulatory device available to localities under the State Zoning Enabling Law (40 A) has been adopted by about 310 of 351

Table 4-1
Population Trends and Projections for Massachusetts Counties: 1950-2000

County	1950	1960	1970	1990	2000
Barnstable	46,805	70,286	97,393	217,687	239,803
Berkshire	132,966	142,135	149,867	169,148	179,548
Bristol	381,569	398,488	444,301	569,177	605,199
Dukes	5,633	5,829	6,117	8,765	9,997
Essex	522,384	568,831	737,887	844,724	1,052,333
Franklin	52,747	54,864	59,314	79,984	82,464
Hampden	367,971	429,353	459,050	550,450	580,218
Hampshire	87,594	103,229	128,657	166,210	179,762
Middlesex	1,064,569	1,238,742	1,400,155	1,667,419	1,762,747
Nantucket	3,484	3,559	3,774	5,137	5,865
Norfolk	392,308	510,256	596,523	841,800	911,275
Plymouth	189,468	248,449	334,069	571,544	632,063
Suffolk	896,615	791,329	735,190	690,834	718,079
Worcester	546,401	583,228	640,254	786,325	847,100
Total	4,690,514	5,148,578	5,689,170	7,169,204	7,806,271

Source: U.S. Bureau of the Census, 1950-1970; 1990 and 2000 Population Projections based on Massachusetts Department of Public Works "Massachusetts Solid Waste Management Report" (1972).

Table 4-2
Distribution of Communities by Population Size: 1930-2000

Size	1930	1940	1950	1960	1970	1980	1990	2000
Under 2,500	178	164	133	111	94	80	70	64
2,500-4,999	55	62	79	60	54	44	39	35
5,000-9,999	49	47	51	59	60	66	59	61
10,000-19,999	32	36	41	66	73	63	71	72
20,000-29,999	12	13	17	19	25	42	38	40
30,000-39,999	5	3	4	8	15	19	33	28
40,000-49,999	8	10	8	8	7	14	14	21
50,000-74,999	6	5	6	9	11	10	13	16
75,000-99,999	1	3	5	6	7	8	7	7
10,000-149,999	7	6	4	2	2	2	4	4
150,000-200,000	1	1	1	2	2	2	2	2
Over 200,000	1	1	2	1	1	1	1	1
Total	355	351	351	351	351	351	351	351

Sources: U.S. Census on Population, 1930-1970; Population Projection based on Massachusetts Department of Public Works "Massachusetts Solid Waste Management Report" (1972).

cities and towns in the state, embracing almost 98 percent of the state's total population. (See Tables 4-3, 4-4.) Zoning has had and will continue to have a significant effect on the allocation, distribution, and development of the Commonwealth's vital land resources. Clearly, zoning determines the rate of population growth and economic development in a community. In fact, zoning as practiced in a number of communities in Massachusetts and in other states often acts to reinforce racial and economic segregation, raises the costs of land and housing, and creates uneven distribution in population growth.

Because communities are forced to rely heavily on local property tax to meet escalating demands for services from constituents, they tend to lean inordinately on their splintered zoning power in order to bolster their tax base. The result of such practices is an oft-repeated story: fiscal crisis, serious economic and social dislocations, and inequalities among communities as to who bears the burden for the desired increased educational, health, police and other necessary services. How land within a community's borders is used becomes not merely an issue of aesthetic and social sensitivity but a matter of economic and fiscal solvency.

Frequently, the response of local governments to population and economic development pressures runs counter to regional and state interests. This is particularly true in the case of housing. The apartment exclusion policy—or moratorium on apartment development—adopted by a number of suburban communities in recent years will increase the pressure to develop such uses in other areas. Similarly, suburbs with large-lot zoning laws have succeeded in

Table 4-3

Number and Percent Distribution of Communities with Zoning by Year of Adoption

Year	Number of Communities with Zoning	Percent
1920	1	0.3%
1925	31	8.8%
1930	67	19.1%
1935	79	22.5%
1940	96	27.4%
1945	120	34.2%
1950	141	40.2%
1955	188	53.6%
1960	239	68.1%
1965	256	72.9%
1968	277	78.9%
1973	310	88.0%

Source: Massachusetts Department of Community Affairs, "The Status of Planning, Subdivision Control and Zoning in Massachusetts" (Commonwealth of Massachusetts, 1973).

Table 4-4
Number of Communities with Zoning by Community Size

Population Groups	Number of Cities and Towns in Each Population Group	Number of Cities and Towns with Zoning	Percentage of Cities and Towns Having Zoning
100,000 and over	4	4	100.0%
50,000 to 99,999	18	18	100.0%
25,000 to 49,999	37	37	100.0%
15,000 to 24,999	40	40	100.0%
10,000 to 14,999	45	44	95.6%
5,000 to 9,999	58	55	90.0%
2,500 to 4,999	54	49	88.9%
1,500 to 2,499	27	23	81.5%
1,000 to 1,499	19	17	89.5%
500 to 999	23	12	52.2%
250 to 499	18	9	50.0%
0 to 249	8	2	25.0%
Totals	351	310	86.6%

Source: Massachusetts Department of Community Affairs, "The Status of Planning, Subdivision Control and Zoning in Massachusetts" (Commonwealth of Massachusetts, 1973).

reducing the total amount of housing in their area, thus shifting the burden for residential development to communities with less restrictive zoning laws. Although this situation is particularly characteristic today in suburban communities within the Boston Metropolitan area, the idea is rapidly catching on in other communities across the state. While zoning was originally conceived and used by localities as an appropriate tool for regulating and directing growth and development in a positive way, today it is principally employed by a large number of municipalities as a means for excluding residential and economic opportunities. By the year 2000, a period less than thirty years from now, the population in Massachusetts is projected to grow by approximately 2.1 million; this will average about 75,000 new residents per year. This expanding population with its associated demand for increased residential, economic, and recreational opportunities will certainly put a serious strain on state land resources.

Clearly, the need to develop effective land use and population settlement policies in the Commonwealth is becoming more and more crucial with each passing year. Many localities are inept or unable to cope with increasing pressures of new development. New approaches must be developed to direct in a positive way the location, magnitude, timing, and characteristics of new development demanded by the state's growing population. The state must assume a greater role in the years ahead to guide and direct population growth. Clearly the future well-being of the people of the Commonwealth of Massachusetts, as well as other urban states, will be determined principally by our actions today.

Notes

1. See Massachusetts Department of Public Works, "Solid Waste Management Study Report," Vol. 2 (Commonwealth of Massachusetts, 1972).
2. Eastern Massachusetts Regional Planning Project, "Comprehensive Land Use Inventory Report" (Commonwealth of Massachusetts, 1967).

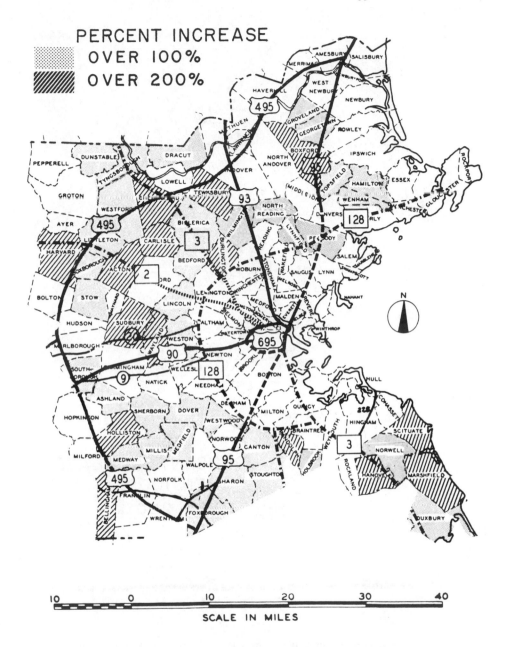

Figure 4-1. Population Projections (1950-1970) and Major Highways: Eastern Massachusetts Region. Source: The Commonwealth of Massachusetts Department of Community Affairs.

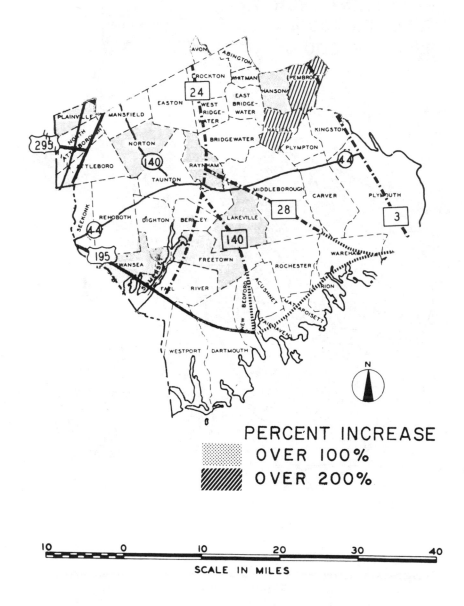

PERCENT INCREASE
OVER 100%
OVER 200%

10   0   10   20   30   40
SCALE IN MILES

Figure 4-2. Population Projections (1950-1970) and Major Highways: Southeastern Massachusetts Region. Source: The Commonwealth of Massachusetts Department of Community Affairs.

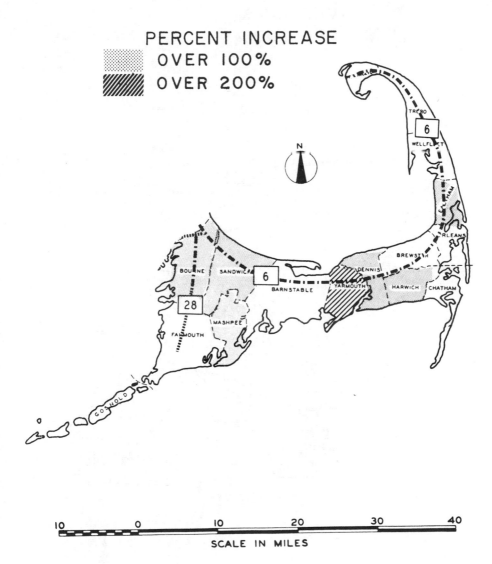

PERCENT INCREASE
OVER 100%
OVER 200%

Figure 4-3. Population Projections (1950-1970) and Major Highways: Barnstable County. Source: The Commonwealth of Massachusetts Department of Community Affairs.

PERCENT INCREASE
OVER 100%
OVER 200%

Figure 4-4. Population Projections (1950-1970) and Major Highways: Montachusetts and Worcester Area. Source: The Commonwealth of Massachusetts Department of Community Affairs.

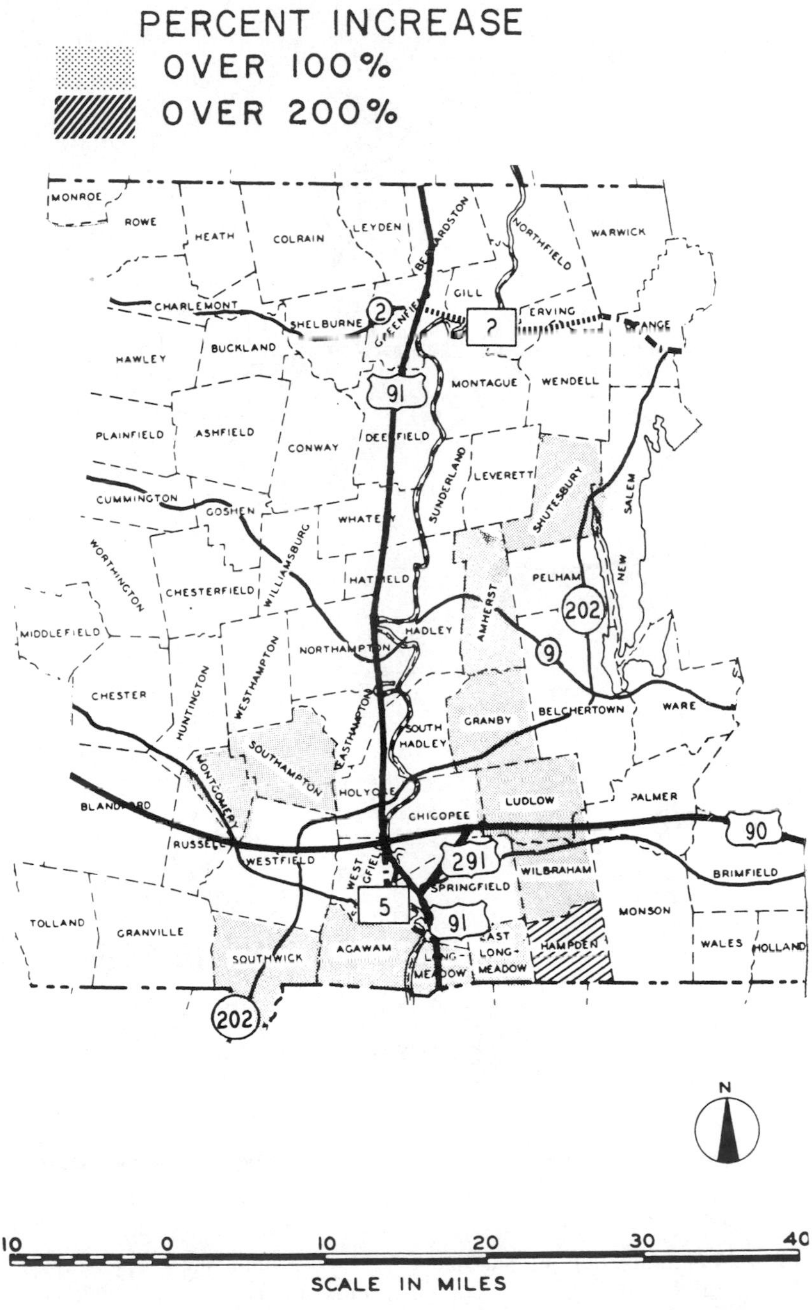

PERCENT INCREASE
OVER 100%
OVER 200%

Figure 4-5. Population Projections (1950-1970) and Major Highways: Franklin County and Lower Pioneer Valley Districts. Source: The Commonwealth of Massachusetts Department of Community Affairs.

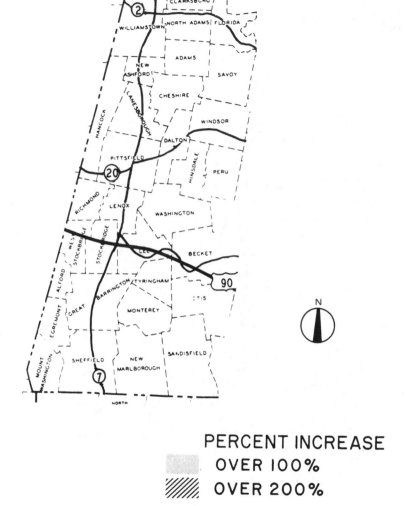

PERCENT INCREASE

OVER 100%

OVER 200%

SCALE IN MILES

Figure 4-6. Population Projections (1950-1970) and Major Highways: Berkshire Region. Source: The Commonwealth of Massachusetts Department of Community Affairs, Division of Planning.

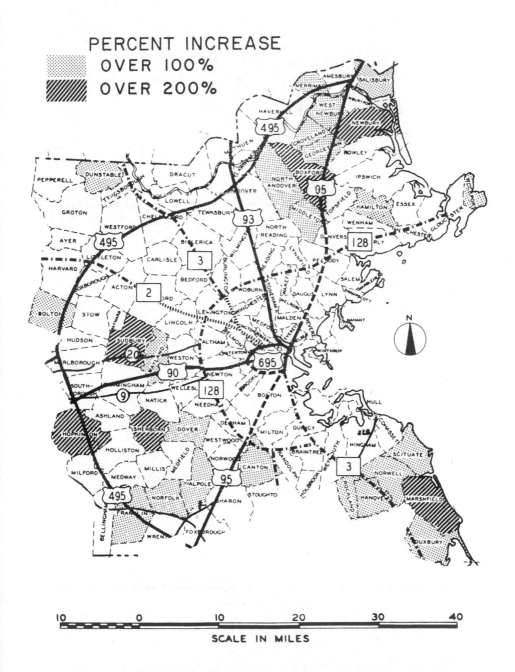

Figure 4-7. Population Projections (1970-2000) and Major Highways: Eastern Massachusetts Region. Source: The Commonwealth of Massachusetts Department of Community Affairs, Division of Planning.

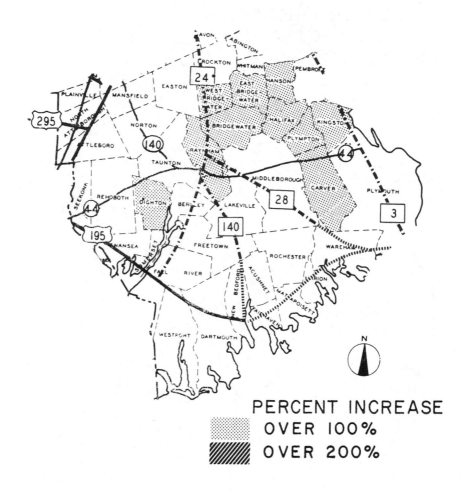

PERCENT INCREASE
OVER 100%
OVER 200%

10	0	10	20	30	40

SCALE IN MILES

Figure 4-8. Population Projections (1970-2000) and Major Highways: Southeastern Massachusetts Region. Source: The Commonwealth of Massachusetts Department of Community Affairs, Division of Planning.

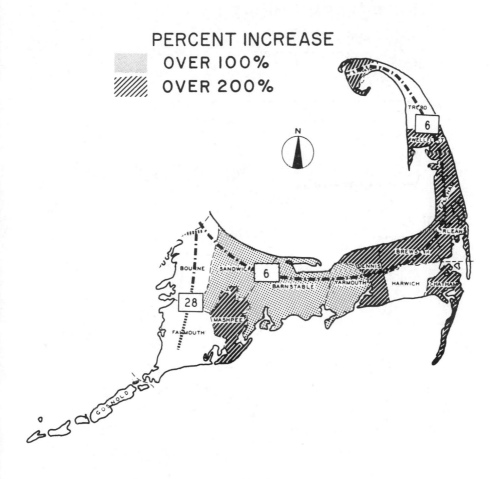

PERCENT INCREASE
OVER 100%
OVER 200%

Figure 4-9. Population Projections (1970-2000) and Major Highways: Barnstable County. Source: The Commonwealth of Massachusetts Department of Community Affairs, Division of Planning.

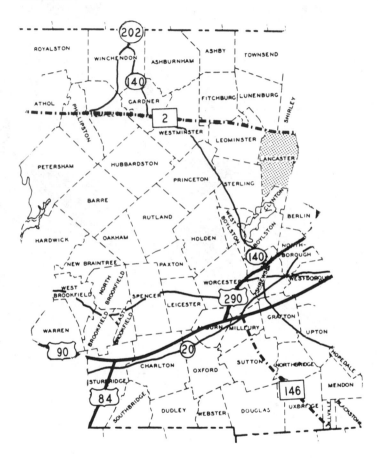

PERCENT INCREASE
OVER 100%
OVER 200%

SCALE IN MILES

Figure 4-10. Population Projections (1970-2000) and Major Highways: Montachusetts and Worcester Area. Source: The Commonwealth of Massachusetts Department of Community Affairs, Division of Planning.

PERCENT INCREASE
OVER 100%
OVER 200%

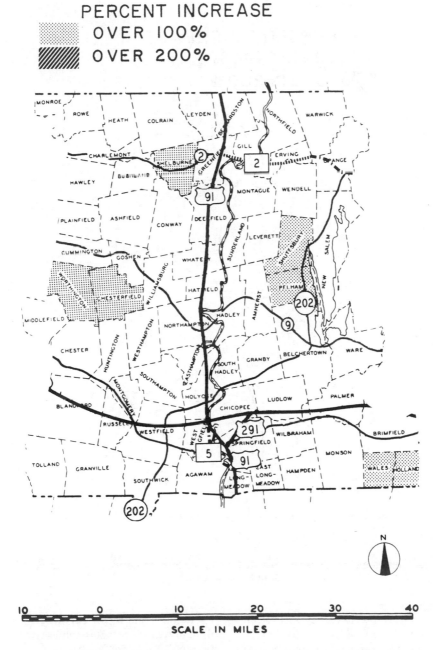

Figure 4-11. Population Projections (1970-2000) and Major Highways: Franklin County and Lower Pioneer Valley Districts. Source: The Commonwealth of Massachusetts Department of Community Affairs, Division of Planning.

PERCENT INCREASE
OVER 100%
OVER 200%

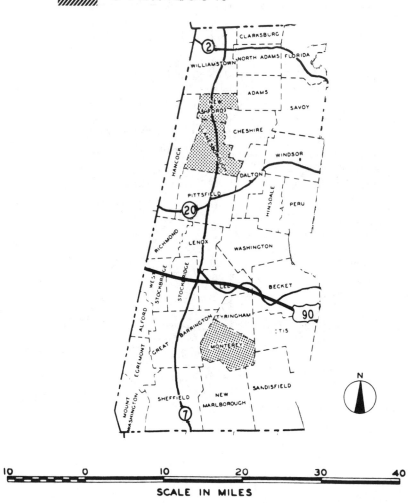

Figure 4-12. Population Projections (1970-2000) and Major Highways: Berkshire Region. Source: The Commonwealth of Massachusetts Department of Community Affairs, Division of Planning.

5 Family Planning in the American States

David Weinberg*

In the section on unwanted fertility in its report to the President, the Commission on Population Growth and the American Future stressed the role of states in removing legal barriers to fertility control information and medical services and urged states to enact affirmative legislation and agency policies in these areas.[1] The following is a review of state efforts to finance and administer family planning (contraceptive) services programs and an evaluation of the prospects for future state participation in family planning program development.

Two Approaches to State Participation

The development of the family planning field since the mid-1960s features the establishment of national objectives and the provision of substantial federal support for the expansion of family planning services for low-income persons. The underlying thought, the practical experience, and the political forces which have moved and shaped the field along these lines are complex. It may be useful to provide a generalized description of this development for purposes of comparison with another important, though less defined, approach to program development. This second approach, which has been given considerable impetus by the Nixon Administration's proposals for health services financing and administration, places considerable weight on state initiative and administrative capability in achieving the desired expansion of services. It relies heavily on existing general financing mechanisms, such as the state-administered Medicaid and social services programs (Social Security Act Titles XIX and IV-A), and on such widely discussed financing schemes as national health insurance, block grants, and special health revenue sharing. For the sake of convenience, the first approach to family planning program development will be called the "national program," the second, the "New Federalism." (The two approaches are summarized in Table 5-1.)

In his July 1969 Message to Congress on population, President Nixon set as a "national goal the provision of adequate family planning services within the next

*Senior Policy Analyst, Center for Family Planning Program Development, Planned Parenthood-World Population; Associate Editor, *Family Planning/Population Reporter*.

Table 5-1
Family Planning Program Development: Two Approaches to Federal and State Participation

	National Program	"New Federalism"
National Goal	The goal is established by Congress and the President: Provide family planning services within five years to all those who want and need them but cannot afford them.	The goal consists of the aggregate of state goals and priorities.
National Objectives	Specific services objectives and related financial and manpower requirements are established in the DHEW Five-Year Plan for each year from FY 1971 to FY 1975. The objectives are based on a national standard of medical indigency for family planning.	(See above.)
National Planning	DHEW has responsibility for maintenance of the Five-Year Plan authorized by Title X and for other studies of national and regional need and services.	(See above.)
Target Population	All persons who need and want family planning services are eligible with priority for low-income persons.	Eligibility is determined largely by the states and is tied closely to the income and social characteristics criteria of the public assistance program.
Financing		
Major Resources	Federal family planning project grants are the main source of funds for development of *new* services and, until other sources become available, for program maintenance. Other sources such as national health insurance and state-administered Title IV-A, Title XIX, and health revenue sharing funds may be utilized *as they become available* for maintenance of *existing programs.*	Federal family planning project grants remain at current levels or diminish; national health insurance and/or state-administered mechanisms such as Title XIX, health revenue sharing and block grants are emphasized. (Note: national health insurance, block grants and health revenue sharing have not been enacted.)
Overall Funding Level	Funding level is determined by congressional appropriations based on need, program performance and balance of national priorities.	Funding levels are not directly subject to congressional control; financing under Title IV-A, Title XIX and other mechanisms is subject to state administrative policies and eligibility limitations.
Resource Allocation	DHEW, through its national and regional offices, allocates family planning project grant funds among Federal Regions on the basis of the national goal and objectives.	(See above.)

five years to all those who want them but cannot afford them." An underlying premise of the national program is that need for family planning services is an objective phenomenon which lends itself to quantification and analysis and, ultimately, to translation into definable units of program effort. The publication in 1969 and 1970 of two government-sponsored studies of family planning need and services provided a baseline for future program development.[2]

The Family Planning Services and Population Research Act of 1970 (Title X of the Public Health Services Act) represents both a response and a further impetus to this systematic approach to program development. The Act provides for specific funding in the Department of Health, Education, and Welfare (DHEW) for designated activities including "categorical" project grants for development and maintenance of service programs; formula grants to states for planning, operation, coordination, and evaluation of family planning programs (appropriations for state formula grants have never been requested by the Administration); and grants and contracts for training, research, and development of informational and educational materials. The Act also authorizes a Deputy Assistant Secretary for Population Affairs in DHEW and requires DHEW to submit and maintain a five-year plan for implementation of family planning services and population research programs. Partially in anticipation of congressional intent to establish a specialized unit in DHEW to administer and coordinate family planning and population activities, DHEW created the National Center for Family Planning Services (NCFPS) in the Health Services and Mental Health Administration. (NCFPS was disbanded as part of a major reorganization of DHEW health services agencies in July 1973.) Although the scope of NCFPS activity did not include populations research (this function was assigned to the Center for Population Research, National Institute of Child Health and Human Development of the National Institutes of Health), the agency did constitute a specialized staff for the administration of family planning programs at the national level.

The DHEW Five-Year Plan for Family Planning Services and Population Research Programs, required by the Family Planning Services and Population Research Act of 1970, provides a blueprint for the phased expansion of family planning services over a period of five years. The plan describes a family planning services network in which program planning, evaluation, and resource allocating functions would be shared between the federal family planning agency, NCFPS, and "coordinating mechanisms" located in large cities, non-metropolitan multi-county areas, and at the state level:

Coordinating mechanisms will . . . be needed at the state level. These staffs will most likely monitor family planning activities within the state, manage state family planning funds and assure that services reach all areas of the state. Such an administrative body may be located in the maternal and child health section or other division of the Department of Health, or it might be placed directly under the Health Commissioner. It could also operate out of a Human Resources

Division or from the Governor's office. The state administrative agency might also be organized separately from state government as, for example, a private non-profit corporation.[3]

In some states, particularly where local medical resources are undeveloped, the plan envisions an additional role for states: the direct provision of family planning services. Depending on the functions to be performed, the plan recommends typical staffing patterns.

A contrasting strategy for family planning program development appears to be indicated in recent Administration actions and proposals regarding health services financing and administration. This strategy depends greatly on the ability of states to devise and implement policies which would increase the availability of funds for family planning under various state administered financing programs, eliminate barriers to such funding, and provide guidance and direction to local program efforts. At the same time, this strategy diminishes considerably federal resources and capability to provide support and overall direction to the national family planning effort. In fact, this "New Federalism" approach would largely replace the national family planning policy and program with individual state policies and programs.

Early in 1973 in congressional testimony on the budget, the Administration indicated that future increases in family planning funding would occur through Social Security Act Titles IV-A and XIX. Subsequent Administration opposition to the continuation of family planning project grant programs has confirmed the impression that it intends to reduce or eliminate the specific, flexible funding provided by these sources and to rely on Medicaid as the primary funding source. In Senate hearings on the extension of the Family Planning Services and Population Research Act held in May 1973, the Administration representative said: "The Department of Health, Education, and Welfare is encouraging the states to make use of the Social Security Act Title XIX mechanism as the principal source of financial support for family planning services."[4] Acknowledging that inadequacies in the state Medicaid programs in the past had necessitated categorical family planning project grants, he argued that improvements in Medicaid and Title IV-A brought about by the Social Security Act Amendments of 1972[5] meant that project grants were no longer required. Furthermore, he said:

The individual state [Medicaid] plans will determine the goals and priorities for family planning services within each of the states and the aggregates of these goals and priorities will constitute the national program.[6]

Later in May, the Administration proposed regulations requiring all applicants for family planning project grant funds to indicate how they would "eventually become self-sustaining" by securing alternate means of funding, such as Medicaid reimbursements.[7] Following a barrage of objections from national and local organizations, these proposed regulations were abandoned.

In July 1973, the Administration announced a reorganization of the health side of DHEW which included the dismantling of NCFPS, the Maternal and Child Health Service, and other specific program units and the establishment of a single Bureau of Community Health Services to administer these programs.[8] This reorganization drastically reduced the number of federal staff assigned specifically to "categorical" programs, such as family planning and maternal and child health. Instead, it favors the assignment of staff along broad functional lines which presumably relate to all types of health programs. In explanation of the impending reorganization prior to its announcement, the DHEW Assistant Secretary of Health, Dr. Charles Edwards, insisted that each program area, such as family planning, could be administered effectively by a specialized staff of five or six persons assigned to an Associate Bureau Director and by "at least" one such specialized person in each of the DHEW regional offices.[9] (NCFPS has had 100 or more staff assigned to headquarters and regional offices.)

The implications of this "New Federalism" approach to family planning program development appear to constitute a reversal of the "national program" approach. Prior to the emergence of the national family planning program in the mid-1960s, the availability of subsidized family planning services for low-income persons depended primarily on the policies of individual states and localities regarding eligibility for services and financing. Some of the earliest state activity consisted of small programs located in the southeastern states, where public health departments had traditionally been responsible for the delivery of some health services to the poor. For example, in North Carolina a limited program of contraceptive services provided through county health departments had been in existence since 1937.[10] By 1965, the American Public Health Association found that thirty states were providing some form of family planning service, including medical services and supplies and/or educational and referral services.[11] Nevertheless, the record of the nation as a whole in 1968 indicated that additional family planning services were needed for an estimated 4.6 million women who could not afford them.[12] Furthermore, it was found that in almost half the states family planning services had been provided to less than ten percent of the low-income women estimated to be in need of such services in each state, that less than 20 percent of the needed services had been provided in eighteen states, and that no state had served more than 37 percent of its population in need.[13]

The national program has replaced local policies with a national policy and has provided substantial federal financing, primarily in the form of project grants, in order to make family planning services available to anyone who wants them, with primary emphasis on low-income persons. The "New Federalism" approach, on the other hand, would dismantle the national policy, restrict eligibility for family planning services based on widely varying state welfare policies, reduce drastically the amount of specific, flexible funding available through the project grant mechanism, and eliminate the specialized technical support and guidance available from DHEW. It would relinquish financing to the state appropriations process and to state-administered programs such as Medicaid and place the burden of planning and developing new programs almost entirely on state and local agencies.

Having described two fundamentally different approaches to federal and state participation in family planning program development, it will be useful to examine some indicators of current performance by states and to explore some of the possible explanations for this showing. Then it may be possible to evaluate the feasibility of the two strategies.

Legislative Appropriations

State health and welfare agencies can commit state funds to family planning programs either by seeking specific legislative appropriations or by setting aside portions of their general budgets. In either case, these state funds can be used to hire administrative and/or technical staff, develop data systems, and carry out other functions not ordinarily covered by federal family planning funds, or they can be used to match federal funds applicable to family planning service costs, thereby increasing significantly the total amounts available for family planning services.

Recent surveys indicate, however, that state legislatures have provided little financial support for family planning services through specific appropriations, and that few state agencies request such appropriations.[14] In FY 1972, total state appropriations for family planning were $4.3 million (see Table 5-2), compared with an estimated total federal family planning budget of $150 million. Twenty state legislatures appropriated funds for family planning services in FY 1972. In FY 1971, fifteen state legislatures appropriated $1.6 million for family planning. Most of the FY 1972 funds, $3.5 million, went to seventeen state health departments and the remainder, $800,000, went to three state welfare agencies. Eighteen health agencies had requested such appropriations; none were requested by welfare agencies. Most state-appropriated funds were used directly to match federal project grants for services rather than to hire staff or otherwise develop state administrative capability.

Maternal and Child Health

The primary federal authority for financing family planning services by state health departments is contained in Title V of the Social Security Act. Title V authorizes the Secretary of DHEW to allocate to the states Maternal and Child Health (MCH) formula grants, which may be utilized for family planning services, in addition to other services for mothers and children. These funds, which constitute one of the major sources of financing for personal health services by state health departments, are allocated on the basis of a formula

Table 5-2

Legislative Appropriations for Family Planning Services to State Health and Welfare Departments in FY 1971 and FY 1972

State	Health		Welfare	
	FY 1971	FY 1972	FY 1971	FY 1972
Alaska	24,600	26,000		
Arizona			35,000	35,000
California		400,000		
Colorado	46,667	77,000		
Delaware	100,024	100,000		
Florida	200,000	142,000		
Georgia		417,000		
Kansas	70,000	70,000		
Kentucky	29,000			
Louisiana			250,000	700,000
Maryland		593,111		
Michigan		100,000		(2,022,350)*
Nevada		35,000		
New Hampshire		10,000		
New Jersey	100,000	100,000		
New York		500,000		(3,700,000)*
North Carolina			93,750	93,000
Oklahoma	200,000	270,000		
Oregon	29,880			
Rhode Island	56,000	56,000		
South Carolina		75,000		
South Dakota			10,000	
Tennessee	400,000	549,860		
Total	$1,256,171	$3,520,971	$388,750	$828,000

*Funds have been administratively withheld.

Source: "State Legislatures Provide Limited Family Planning Funds," *Family Planning/Population Reporter*, vol. 2, no. 2, April 1973, pp. 32-33. Reprinted with the permission of *Family Planning/Population Reporter*.

which takes into account urban and rural birth rates and per capita income. Allocations of formula grants to state health departments totaled $49.2 million in each of the fiscal years 1971 and 1972 and about $40 million in each of the fiscal years 1968, 1969, and 1970.[15]

As far back as 1942, a policy statement of the U.S. Surgeon General gave states the option of using federal MCH funds for family planning services.[16] In 1967, Congress amended Title V to require states to establish demonstration projects in family planning for low-income persons and to show that family planning services were being extended throughout the state. Since FY 1971, a portion of the total allocation of MCH formula grant funds, $8.25 million, has been earmarked each year for family planning services by DHEW.[17] In FY 1971, the first year of the earmarking policy, DHEW indicated that these new funds were to be spent "in addition to that expended during fiscal year 1970 for Family Planning Services."[18]

Yet, in each of the fiscal years 1968, 1969, and 1970, DHEW estimated that state health agencies expended only $3.5 million in MCH formula grant funds for family planning.[19] The 1971 earmarking policy required the states to expend an additional $8.25 million for family planning. Since the policy required the states to maintain the $3.5 million level of expenditures from previous years, total formula grant expenditures for family planning in FY 1971 should have been about $11.75 million. In fact, the states estimated that their family planning expenditures totaled only $8.3 million in FY 1971 and $9.4 million in FY 1972.[20]

Table 5-3 indicates the distribution of state MCH formula grant expenditures in fiscal years 1971 and 1972. Although there was little overall change over the period, individual states reveal a pattern of instability which may result from the generally low level of expenditures, the small staffs administering these funds, and difficulties of obtaining accurate reports. Taken together, these factors would appear to indicate that MCH funded family planning programs are small and are not administered systematically.

Medicaid and Title IV-A

Authority for the financing of family planning services by state welfare agencies is contained in Title IV-A and Title XIX of the Social Security Act. Title XIX is the authority under which the state Medicaid programs are established. These programs reimburse providers of medical care, primarily private doctors, for the provision of medical services to current welfare recipients and to very limited numbers of other people with similar characteristics. All current welfare recipients are eligible for a stated range of medical benefits, some required by federal law, others provided at the states' option. The federal government reimburses the states for a portion of their expenditures under Medicaid, 50 to 83 percent, depending on the state's per capita income, for all services except family planning. The 1972 amendments to Title XIX made family planning a required service (it had previously been optional), and federal matching for family planning expenditures under Medicaid was increased to 90 percent.

Surveys of state Medicaid programs in 1967, 1969, and 1970 indicated that few medically indigent women in general, and not even a substantial number of welfare recipients, had received family planning services and supplies paid for by Medicaid.[21] Because eligibility for Medicaid is limited almost entirely to welfare

Table 5-3
Maternal and Child Health Formula Grants to Health Agencies of the 50 States and the District of Columbia, FY 1971-1972

State	Total Allocation in FY 1972*	Federally Earmarked for Family Planning in FY 1971-1972†	State Expenditures for Family Planning‡ FY 1971	FY 1972	Change, FY 1971-1972
Alabama	1,238,285	212,556	293,203	NA	
Alaska	186,495	8,615	10,600	8,900	−1,700
Arizona	434,434	70,444	97,744	84,444	−13,300
Arkansas	694,603	117,345	294,493	154,000	−140,493
California	2,828,154	488,349	680,959	600,000	−80,959
Colorado	469,248	92,348	40,000	123,791	83,791
Connecticut	494,721	54,511	70,000	54,511	−15,489
Delaware	211,196	10,737	8,500	NA	
Dist. of Columbia	247,944	12,737	12,737	NA	
Florida	1,659,093	299,169	168,794	398,714	229,920
Georgia	1,635,785	316,201	501,608	536,201	34,593
Hawaii	245,080	16,103	28,250	20,103	−8,147
Idaho	234,870	17,825	34,000	59,900	25,900
Illinois	1,624,459	271,296	343,000	434,235	91,235
Indiana	1,258,011	222,464	144,000	277,464	133,464
Iowa	691,122	114,358	81,799	100,345	18,546
Kansas	479,770	87,789	123,395	87,789	−35,606
Kentucky	1,149,085	217,087	249,780	237,507	−12,273
Louisiana	1,336,337	236,572	NA††	462,882	
Maine	330,076	43,589	100,000	154,000	54,000
Maryland	1,063,730	255,368	255,368	250,000	−5,368
Massachusetts	847,061	128,180	128,180	NA	
Michigan	1,884,356	338,843	254,000	306,000	52,000
Minnesota	910,103	157,993	281,655	203,991	−77,664
Mississippi	1,052,599	174,528	NA	174,528	
Missouri	1,074,037	208,733	80,000	90,000	10,000
Montana	226,685	14,070	39,262	28,000	−11,262
Nebraska	346,379	57,018	41,494	53,665	12,171
Nevada	202,707	11,127	67,627	65,000	−2,627
New Hampshire	229,881	14,417	15,000	16,000	1,000
New Jersey	1,061,487	186,858	300,000	368,000	68,000
New Mexico	325,026	43,483	NA	43,483	
New York	2,651,940	452,236	572,236	549,505	−22,731
North Carolina	1,887,202	341,461	145,052	206,105	61,053
North Dakota	216,561	11,431	27,275	13,669	−13,606

Table 5-3 (cont.)

State	Total Allocation in FY 1972*	Federally Earmarked for Family Planning in FY 1971-1972†	State Expenditures for Family Planning‡ FY 1971	FY 1972	Change, FY 1971-1972
Ohio	2,260,887	393,156	383,000	390,711	7,711
Oklahoma	606,840	112,783	144,897	180,883	35,986
Oregon	534,555	100,047	51,328	166,000	114,672
Pennsylvania	2,522,102	419,405	349,777	419,405	69,628
Rhode Island	250,431	15,461	45,245	50,712	5,467
South Carolina	1,127,632	195,728	382,222	331,953	−50,269
South Dakota	223,592	14,715	30,000	37,751	7,751
Tennessee	1,214,192	215,866	148,968	395,503	246,535
Texas	2,584,320	476,029	596,970	469,970	−127,000
Utah	404,862	70,838	88,000	105,000	17,000
Vermont	195,331	9,030	53,350	27,000	−26,350
Virginia	1,325,581	224,501	216,150	215,000	−1,150
Washington	794,386	171,385	NA	171,385	
West Virginia	624,050	108,366	148,431	98,450	−49,981
Wisconsin	997,099	144,294	208,869	144,294	−64,575
Wyoming	181,723	7,815	7,815	6,000	−1,815
Total	47,276,105‡‡	7,985,260‡‡	8,345,033#	9,372,749	

Departments of Labor and Health, Education and Welfare Appropriations for 1973 (Hearing Before a Subcommittee of the Committee on Appropriations, U.S. House of Representatives) Part 3, March 7, 1972.

†Maternal and Child Health Service, DHEW, Director's Letter, MCH-71-1, January 22, 1971.

‡Estimates derived from data reported by state health agencies in 1971 and 1972 CFPPD surveys.

‡‡Allocations to Guam, Puerto Rico and the Virgin Islands raise these totals to $49.2 million and $8.25 million, respectively.

††Not Available.

#State expenditures for FY 1971 may differ from previously published figures due to corrected estimates provided by some state agencies.

Source: Reprinted with the permission of *Family Planning/Population Reporter*, vol. 2, no. 1, February 1973, pp. 12-13.

recipients, it is not surprising that few poor non-welfare women are assisted through this mechanism. However, the failure to aid substantial numbers of welfare women points to a basic flaw in the program: while Medicaid is designed primarily to reimburse private physicians, few poor women have access to them for routine preventive services such as family planning. Instead they obtain such services primarily from health departments, independent clinics, and some hospitals. However, Medicaid programs frequently have policies which exclude public agencies from reimbursement. Thus, public health departments (and frequently others who provide free services) are unable to claim reimbursement for services provided to Medicaid-eligible patients. This limits the amount of funds available to service providers and restricts the flow of funds to those particular providers which may be most convenient to patients. A recent survey of family planning service agencies indicated that less than one in four agencies received *any* Medicaid reimbursement, that such payments were generally inadequate to cover operating costs (average payments amounted to 36 percent of average costs), and that most state Medicaid agencies base their family planning payments exclusively on the costs of the medical examination and without consideration of the other supportive services which characterize organized family planning services.[22] Furthermore, the survey indicated that some service agencies lack experience in dealing with the administrative and fiscal complexities of the Medicaid mechanism, and that Medicaid agencies themselves are ignorant of, or uninterested in, the specialized nature of organized family planning care.

Title IV-A authorizes the state social services programs administered by state and local welfare departments. Since 1967, states have been required by Title IV-A to secure family planning services on behalf of current Aid to Families with Dependent Children (AFDC) recipients. Amendments to Title IV-A adopted in 1972 require states to ensure that family planning services are "provided promptly" to former and potential recipients of AFDC, as well as to current recipients, and encourage provision of family planning to sexually active minors. (Under the 1967 amendments, states were authorized to provide family planning services to former and potential recipients at their own option.) Where free public or private family planning services are inadequate to meet the needs of eligible persons, the welfare agency is authorized to provide these services through purchase of service contracts or other arrangements with providers of family planning services. Federal financing is available to cover up to 90 percent of the administrative and service costs. (The federal matching rate had been 75 percent under the 1967 amendments.) A penalty provision is established whereby states which fail to provide services for current AFDC recipients will be penalized 1 percent of their total federal AFDC payments.

Although there has been little experience with state Title IV-A family planning programs under the 1972 Social Security Act amendments (final regulations for Title IV-A were not issued until April 1973 and were promptly suspended by Congress), some earlier Title IV-A programs indicate the scope of state efforts and some shortcomings of the programs. As of October 1972, information was available on such programs in nine states.[23] The limited distribution of such programs four years after the enactment of the 1967 Social Security Act amendments indicates that welfare agencies were less than aggressive in utilizing this authority and financial resource. Problems observed in individual state programs included restrictions on the types of providers eligible for payment (only two states had made serious efforts to involve hospitals and non-health department clinics), a critical shortage of program staff, a lack of clear plans and strategies for utilization of various funding sources, and a conspicuous absence of program standards.

Administration and Staffing

Administrative responsibility for family planning programs in state health departments is characteristically assigned to MCH units. These units generally have responsibility for interpreting regulations regarding MCH and related programs authorized by Title V of the Social Security Act and for general policy guidance to local health agencies. Where staff are assigned to family planning administrative duties in state welfare agencies, they are frequently located in the unit administering the state's social services program.

The DHEW Five-Year Plan cited earlier estimated manpower requirements for state-level agencies: 228 full-time staff for "coordinating" (non-service) functions and 120 full-time staff for administration of "direct services." The estimates were projected on the basis of a staffing pattern calling for six to ten full-time professional staff in each state, depending on local health delivery capabilities.

Recent surveys of state agency staffing for family planning services indicate that the number of personnel assigned is well below that recommended by DHEW, and that there is considerable variability in staffing from year to year, even among those agencies with larger staffs.[24] Overall, the total number of full-time family planning staff assigned to administrative (non-clinical) responsibilities in state health agencies grew from eighty-five in 1971 to 124 in 1972, while part-time staff dropped from 160 to 130. (See Table 5-4.) Only nine full-time administrative staff were reported by state welfare agencies in both years, though part-time staff increased from fifty-six to seventy-nine. The data suggest that while state health agencies may be laying the groundwork for the type of administrative capability recommended by DHEW, at least in terms of numbers of staff assigned, welfare agencies have hardly begun.

By all indications, states have shown less initiative in encouraging and guiding family planning program development and have provided less sustained support of family planning services than might have been expected by the proponents of state participation. Although there has been little or no systematic study of the causes of this restraint, it may be useful to examine some of the factors underlying state policymaking which could influence state behavior in this regard.

Increasing financial pressure on states, generated at least in part by rising welfare costs, undoubtedly has had a braking effect on state investment in health and social services programs. State legislators tend to be sensitive to the penalties associated with rapidly expanding state budgets and the necessary corollary to such expansion, tax increases. They, in turn, communicate these political

Table 5-4

Family Planning Administrative Staff in Health and Welfare Agencies of 50 States

	Health Agency				Welfare Agency			
	September 1, 1971		June 30, 1972		September 1, 1971		June 30, 1972	
	F/T	P/T	F/T	P/T	F/T	P/T	F/T	P/T
State								
United States	85	160	124	130	9	56	9	79
Alabama	1	2		2				
Alaska	1	1	1	3				
Arizona		3		1		1		1
Arkansas	4	3	2	8				
California	2	12	5	2	1		1	
Colorado		8	2	5		1		2
Connecticut		6	1	9				4
Delaware	1	4	5					
Florida	5		5	7				
Georgia	5		4	5	4		4	
Hawaii	1			3		5		1
Idaho		3	1	1				2
Illinois		7		3				
Indiana		10		2		6		
Iowa	1	2	1	1	1			1
Kansas	2	6	2	4				
Kentucky	3	1	5	1				1
Louisiana	NA	NA	1	8				
Maine	1	1	1	1		2		
Maryland	4	5	9	4		2		1
Massachusetts	7	4	1	NA		3		7
Michigan	4	5	7	6		1		10
Minnesota	1	2	1	1	1		1	
Mississippi	NA	NA	4	0		1		2
Missouri		3		3			NA	NA
Montana		6	2	2				
Nebraska		2		5		2		2
Nevada		1		4		3		1
New Hampshire	4	3	3	3		3		3
New Jersey	4	2	5	1				
New Mexico		3		2				
New York	3	2	2	5		3		1
North Carolina	1	4	5	1	1	1		11
North Dakota		1						1
Ohio	2		3	1		3		1

Table 5-4 (cont.)

State	Health Agency September 1, 1971 F/T	P/T	June 30, 1972 F/T	P/T	Welfare Agency September 1, 1971 F/T	P/T	June 30, 1972 F/T	P/T
Oklahoma	2	7	8	2		2		1
Oregon	2	6	2	3				4
Pennsylvania	2	2	2	1	1		1	2
Rhode Island		4	2	2				
South Carolina	2	9	10	2		8		7
South Dakota	2	1	3	1				
Tennessee	5		9		1			1
Texas	2	2		2				6
Utah	1	4		4				1
Vermont		1	NA	NA				
Virginia	2		3	1	1			1
Washington		5	1	3	2			2
West Virginia	5	3	4	1	1		2	
Wisconsin	3	2	2	2	3			1
Wyoming		2	1		1			1

Full-time (F/T)   Part-time (P/T)   Not Available (NA)

Source: Reprinted with the permission of *Family Planning/Population Reporter*, vol. 2, no. 1, February 1973, pp. 20-21.

priorities to the officials responsible for administering the states' expenditure mechanisms. The effect is to discourage new initiatives which may appear to involve future unknown financial commitments, particularly where there is no substantial political support for such initiatives.

One possible response to rising welfare costs might be to concentrate investment of scarce resources in those preventive services, such as family planning, which tend to ameliorate the causes of economic dependency. Instead of investing in preventive services, however, state efforts to combat this financial squeeze generally have taken the form of attempts to restrict eligibility for welfare and medical assistance and to limit or cut back on benefits. One explanation of this choice is that state legislators tend to be more concerned about the immediate political liabilities associated with additional expenditures for preventive services than they are with possible future savings which may result from these programs. Although family planning as a political issue has been increasing steadily in acceptability and popularity in Congress and state legislatures, there is some reason to believe that the recent surge of controversy regarding abortion has temporarily dampened the enthusiasm of legislators, at least at the state level. Most observers believe that the political support for family planning services is very broad, and that it runs to quite fundamental convictions regarding the importance of fertility control for preserving family solidarity, increasing maternal and child health, preventing poverty, and limiting population growth. Until the abortion controversy begins to subside, however, it may be difficult to determine whether this has been simply an interlude for family planning before state legislative support will soon grow to unprecedented levels, whether the abortion issue has been a setback, or whether legislatures will continue to provide only limited support.

The balkanization frequently observed among public and private health and welfare agencies is another factor which appears to inhibit state participation in family planning programs. For example, in some states which have demonstrably high levels of need for family planning services and in which the state health departments have been awarded large federal family planning project grants, these agencies have had considerable difficulty expending program funds. At the same time, it has been observed by family planning workers that these state health agencies have been hesitant to allocate such funds to non-health department agencies, such as hospitals and independent clinics, which could provide family planning services and thereby aid the state program in its objective of expanding services. This general problem has also been exemplified by the slowness with which state welfare agencies have sought cooperation from public and private health providers in implementing Title IV-A programs.

These general explanations, while pertinent, do not fully explain state inaction in the family planning field. It is still reasonable to ask, for example, why those state agencies without *any* appropriations for family planning in FY 1972 did not at least request them (only two did), why several state health agencies which reported sizable staffs in 1971 apparently lost personnel the following year, why state welfare agencies failed to respond to the congressional mandate to provide family planning to welfare recipients and claim generous federal matching, and why, at the very least, *states have not seriously studied family planning service requirements or planned for the expansion of such services.* Without attempting a complete explanation of these occurrences, more insight can be gained by an examination, very brief here, of the development of the public health and welfare fields and of some of the ideas which underlie the field of social services.

Public Health

The development of the public health field in the United States, particularly with respect to the issue of health department involvement in the delivery of medical services to individual patients, sheds some light on the nature of current health department participation in family planning. The public health field originally grew out of a concern in the 1870s with the issue of "sanitary administration" and the prevention of disease through the elimination of conditions which bred disease.[25] Interest in sanitation expanded in the next thirty years to include communicable diseases, hygiene, water pollution, and vital statistics. By the 1920s, however, public health advocates began to turn their attention to the provision of medical care and to the inadequacy of care for some people. Nevertheless, "cooperation" was a watchword of the time, and it was suggested by some members of the American Public Health Association that private physicians should be reassured that public health programs would not threaten their incomes.[26] The economic depression of the 1930s did threaten and diminish private physician income, however, which apparently led to charges that "state medicine has already gone too far . . . " with respect to providing health services to the poor.[27] The passage and subsequent implementation of the Social Security Act of 1935 stimulated sharper debate of the issue, with opponents of government involvement condemning federal aid to local agencies for personal health services as an infringement on the prerogatives of local communities and on the practice of medicine.

If the passage of the Social Security Act raised the issue of public support of medical care, it also crystallized it. Title V of the Act, as approved in 1935, provided for very limited annual appropriations, $3.8 million and $2.8 million, respectively, for maternal and child health services and for services to crippled children.[28] The maternal and child health appropriation was (and still is) "for the purpose of enabling each state to extend and improve, as far as practicable . . . services for promoting the health of mothers and children, especially in rural areas and in areas suffering from severe economic distress. . . . "[29] Furthermore, the law mandated "cooperation" with interested parties, notably "medical . . . organizations." The result of the legislation was that government support of medical care would be quite limited, overall, because appropriations were small. It would also be channeled along very specific lines of health care and for people of little means. It did not provide a substantial threat either to the current practice of medicine or to private incomes.

Although public health responsibilities have broadened since the passage of the Social Security Act, they have followed the pattern established at the time. Little is known about the actual conduct of public health functions by local agencies, although an inference regarding the limits of such activity can be drawn from statements of policy or principle in the public health field. For instance, in a 1963 American Public Health Association policy statement, local health department activity in "community health" is limited to "promotion of community health through leadership in planning and community organiza-tion."[30] Regarding the actual operation of service facilities by local health agencies, the policy emphasizes the provision of care to the poor rather than to the general population. The policy contains no specific recommendations regarding maternal and child health services, except to list them among "traditional services" and to urge greater efficiency in their delivery.[31]

The relationship between the local health department and local private practitioners clearly has an impact on the health department's role in providing medical services, though the relationship and the impact obviously vary from urban to rural areas and from one region to another. The position of the local health officer has been described as a lonely one subject to lay leadership from the local governing authority, to political pressure through the governing authority and directly, and to peer pressure through the health officer's membership in the local medical society.[32] In large cities or urbanized counties, where the health officer has the support of a well established bureaucracy behind him, particularly where the health agency provides a substantial amount of medical services, the effects of medical society pressure are unlikely to be as great as they would be in less developed areas. Also, where the local health agency has traditionally provided at least some medical services to the poor, as in the southeastern states, resistance to such activity may be less. However, as one writer has noted about North Carolina: "Significant opposition [to public family planning programs] did come from the medical profession as a result of disapproval of the *means*, although not the *goals*, of the program. That is, they favored publicly funded birth control services for the poor, but wanted them to be provided in private doctors' offices on a fee-for-services basis."[33] Not surprisingly, it was found that the response of local health officers to physician resistance depended on their status as full-time or part-time officers. Part-time health officers, "affiliated with their colleagues in full-time practice in a social and professional system centered around the local medical society . . . expressed concern that private patients might take advantage of the [health department] family planning program. . . . "[34] Full-time officers apparently did not express such opinions.

The picture which emerges is that of a public health system equipped to play only a circumscribed role in the provision of medical services. That role is to *complement* the private medical care system where it is not possible or profitable for it to operate. This includes, for example, the provision of medical care to large groups of patients, as in the immunization of school children, and the provision of services to the poor, particularly in rural areas with insufficient numbers of private doctors. The vulnerability of the health officer to political and peer group pressure makes it unlikely that he will stray too far outside recognized boundaries unless, of course, he receives substantial pressure and/or support either from within or outside the public health care system.

State or local health departments are in a difficult position, therefore, to undertake the most basic positive steps towards design and implementation of a full-scale subsidized family planning program to reach all persons in need. A logical first step, for example, would be to produce a phased plan for expansion of family planning services in the state. This would involve a detailed assessment of the amount and location of need for family planning services, of existing sources of family planning services, and of potential sources. Relevant state policies and administrative practices would have to be carefully studied and explicated and an administrative plan for guidance and support of local service programs prepared. Finally, financial, manpower, and other resource requirements would have to be estimated. Indeed, it is difficult to imagine that many public health agencies would have either the capability or the appetite to undertake such a systematic, detailed evaluation of the performance of private physicians, hospitals, and voluntary agencies. It is even less likely that they would propose to seek or to allocate the substantial amounts of public funds necessary to compensate for the shortcomings of the private health care system in meeting the needs of the community.

Public Welfare

The development of public welfare agency functions provides some insight into the record of limited support and initiative demonstrated by these agencies in the implementation of family planning medical services. State welfare agencies are primarily responsible for the administration of money payments to individuals and families which meet specific economic and social eligibility standards defined in federal and state law. Consequently, "means tests" are a central feature of state-administered welfare programs and accountability for the distribution of cash assistance is a vital concern, if not a preoccupation, of welfare agencies. An expanding welfare population and rising costs have increased the pressure on state welfare agencies to enforce eligibility standards strictly and to demonstrate accountability.

A more recent function of state welfare agencies is the administration of social services programs designed to prevent or reduce economic dependency. As envisioned by their proponents, these programs consist of specialized diagnostic, counseling, and referral services provided by highly trained and motivated caseworkers. Where the medical or social services needed by a client are not available within the welfare agency, the caseworker typically acts as an intermediary between the client and outside service providers, determining the needs of the client through counseling and casework and making the necessary referrals to providers. For the most part, welfare agencies have relied on available free community resources for such services. Since the passage of the 1967 Social Security Act amendments, however, state welfare departments have been required to *purchase* certain social and medical services, including family planning services, for current welfare recipients where there are no free community services or where they are inadequate.

Eligibility requirements for social services provided by the welfare agency (counseling and referral) are generally quite distinct from the requirements for social and medical services purchased by the agency (including those required by the Social Security Act). Eligibility for provided services is ordinarily defined broadly, reflecting the intent to prevent dependency. However, eligibility for purchased services is generally defined in terms of the strict categories of eligibility for cash assistance and is frequently limited to current recipients of such assistance. (The same is true of eligibility for Medicaid.) Thus, in order to receive purchased medical or social services, the potential recipient is necessarily subjected to the rigorous eligibility determination procedures associated with cash assistance. Similarly, the reticence of welfare agencies to purchase services is conditioned by their preoccupation with accountability and cost-cutting.

Whatever the merits of casework activity in preventing or reducing economic dependency, the level of dependency on public welfare assistance has increased immensely since social services programs began receiving generous federal support under the Public Welfare Amendments of 1962 (P.L. 87-543). Partly as a result of growing welfare dependency and the consequent need for welfare staff to carry out eligibility determination activity, welfare agencies virtually have never obtained the number or quality of casework staff required to cope with a mushrooming clientele.[35] Without enough caseworkers to serve even the current welfare population, social services have hardly been available to low-income people not dependent on welfare but in danger of becoming so. Added to the fact that low-income people who are not public assistance recipients are often reluctant to seek welfare-related services, the shortage of caseworkers has severely limited even the possibility of preventing welfare dependency through social services.

Current social services thinking about the causes and cures of economic dependency provides additional insight into state welfare agency resistance to the development of family planning medical services. Piven and Cloward indicate a transition in welfare thinking regarding the causes of poverty from a sort of Calvinistic "philanthropic doctrine" to modern "casework doctrine":

Where philanthropic doctrine traced the cause of poverty to moral defects, casework doctrine traces it to psychological defects. The older philanthropic treatment consisted of a strict regimen of individual surveillance and discipline, the contention being that poverty proved the existence of moral weakness; casework prescribes modern procedures of psychosocial diagnosis, "individualization," and counseling, as if by being poor the client proves his personality weakness and his need for professional treatment.[36]

The idea that psychological or motivational defects constitute a major cause or explanation of economic dependency seems to pervade the social services field. In a recent critique of reform in social services, the author says that " 'social services' deals with the question: What should be done to handle these problems of social and personal disorganization that are believed to create . . . economic dependencies . . . ?"[37] The aim of social services is to enable individuals to achieve "functional independence," which means "the capacity to take care of one's own affairs to the extent that physical . . . and . . . economic conditions permit."[38] Given adequate economic opportunities, such as jobs, functional independence may lead to economic independence. However, without economic opportunities, "functional independence results in a *socially unhealthy* individual." [Emphasis added.] [39]

The major implication of this thinking for social services programming seems to be that since the poor, or whatever groups are defined as the target for social services, are, by definition, "socially unhealthy," then efforts to provide economic opportunities, at least without substantial social services, are fundamentally without purpose, since such people are not able or "qualified" to benefit from them. In Morris's terms, one must be "socially healthy" ("functionally independent") before he can take advantage of opportunities to become economically independent.

As applied to the major questions of family planning program development, the social services approach provides some sharp contrasts with the approach embodied in the national family planning program. According to Jaffe and Polgar, the social services approach (the "cultural motivational" approach, in their terminology) has fixed on a view of the poor which regards them as being insufficiently motivated or sincere about adopting effective family planning methods to justify a concerted effort to make such services available.[40] Instead, this approach requires emphasis on the treatment of factors in the psyches of the poor which prevent their using, or wanting to use, fertility control services which are more or less available. From the viewpoint of family planning program development, short shrift is given to the supply side of the health care system, and an inordinate amount of attention is given to the demand side. Whereas the national family planning program (the "accessibility" approach, in Jaffe and Polgar's terminology) aims at creating a network of accessible, efficient, free or partially subsidized family planning services, the aim of the "cultural-motivational" approach is to " 'instill' stronger motivation for fertility control by intensive counseling and by family life and sex education programs designed to bring about less 'maladaptive' values and behavior."[41] Whereas the accessibility approach proposes to develop medical family planning services in existing facilities such as hospitals, health departments, and independent clinics, and to provide supplementary outreach/educational services to inform patients of the content, location, and scheduling of services, the cultural-motivational approach urges that family planning services be developed "*only* as part of more 'comprehensive' health or welfare programs which include educational, economic, social, and psychological counseling and services."[42] Whereas the accessibility approach implies a reordering of public and private agency priorities and the allocation of substantial resources for the development of medical services, the "cultural-motivational" approach emphasizes "familiarization and orientation programs for health and welfare professionals, particularly sensitivity training in 'life styles' of the poor."[43]

The conceptualization of social services by function offered by Morris tends to reinforce Jaffe and Polgar's characterization of the "cultural-motivational" orientation in social services.[44] Morris organizes social services under several broad headings. He lists family planning services under two of these headings, "assessment and counseling" and "training, education and equipment." Even more revealing, however, is the *exclusion* of certain services from Morris's conceptualization:

[This] formulation excludes certain services: for example, programs to prevent a recurrence of disabling conditions at the source are omitted, primarily because too little is known about preventive measures. Medical treatment, income maintenance, and fundamental education have been omitted because these have substantial and well-established service systems of their own.[45]

By excluding "preventive measures," the scheme rules out the central tenet of the accessibility strategy which is to make available a medical service which enables individuals to *prevent* unwanted or ill-timed pregnancies. Morris's inclusion of family planning under the two headings above only retains the "cultural-motivational" premise that the poor must be treated to *cure* the personal deficiencies which prevent their use of family planning services. (The idea that too little is known about family planning to implement an effective public program is curious in light of DHEW's estimate that organized family planning programs had reached 2.6 million patients in 1972.) The notion that "medical treatment" has a "well-established" service system reinforces the impression that in the social services view, medical services for the poor, including family planning services, are more or less adequate.

To the extent that the social services field, as portrayed here, represents the outlook of welfare agency officials and staff, it helps explain why welfare agencies stress counseling over the provision of medical family planning services. Since the accessibility approach to program development requires state health and welfare agencies to reorder their priorities and increase substantially their allocations of staff and budget resources to family planning, it is not surprising that, in the absence of strong pressure to support family planning services development, very few state agencies have done so.

Prospects for Program Development

The two approaches to federal and state participation in family planning programs outlined earlier would result in vastly different family planning programs in the United States and would place contrasting demands on states. The "national program" would result in an extensive network of family planning services provided in hospitals, health departments, independent clinics, and private doctors' offices. Federal subsidy through project grants, Medicaid, Title IV-A, and formula grant funds, while directed primarily towards the development of family planning services for low-income persons, would aid in the extension of services to everyone who wanted and needed them, including minors, persons without convenient access to private medical care, and those who prefer organized clinical services to private physician services. States, with the benefit of considerable federal direction and financial support, would be expected to develop the capability to manage state and some federal family planning funds, to provide technical assistance to local family planning funds, to provide technical assistance to local family planning programs, and to provide some family planning services directly. The "New Federalism" approach, on the other hand, would dispense with the broad eligibility standards established under the "national program" and substitute individual state eligibility standards by shifting financing from federal project grants to state welfare-administered programs, such as Medicaid and Title IV-A. Therefore, the "New Federalism" approach would result in a state-administered program of subsidized services limited essentially to welfare recipients.

Full state participation under the "national program" model would be feasible under certain conditions: First, states would need federal financing, policy guidance, and technical assistance in order to develop the capability to manage family planning programs. Second, governors and state legislators would need to establish family planning as a high priority in order to stimulate state agency action. Finally, state agencies themselves, in order to be equipped to administer family planning programs, would need to seek legislative appropriations for family planning, establish specialized family planning administrative units, and assign substantial numbers of family planning staff. DHEW could provide financing for state family planning programs through the formula grant authority in Title X of the Public Health Service Act and could provide policy guidance and technical assistance to state agencies through a specialized family planning agency of the sort once represented by NCFPS. State legislatures could appropriate funds which would enable state health and welfare agencies to hire staff to manage family planning programs and to match federal funds to expand services. They could also enact comprehensive family planning services laws which would establish an overall framework for statewide program development efforts. Legislatures and governors could establish family planning councils to investigate service needs and resources, recommend specific policies to promote broad state action, and to coordinate public and private family planning programs. Although initiatives such as these have not occurred widely, they have been observed in several states, including California,[46] Florida,[47] Georgia,[48] and Tennessee.[49] Assuming continued and even increased federal direction and support for such initiatives, it appears likely that states could broaden their contribution to program development.

Under the "New Federalism" approach, the future of United States family planning progams would be bound inextricably to the policies and to the actual willingness and capability of states to support family planning services *without substantial federal intervention.* The success of this approach turns almost entirely on the assumption that the agencies, primarily welfare agencies, will make unprecedented progress in improving their management capability, assigning family planning staff, and increasing their financial support of family planning services—with little specific federal guidance or technical assistance beyond the customary controls on expenditures of federal funds. Given the encumbrances of traditional health and welfare policy and practice, the prospects for establishing even a minimal family planning program under the "New Federalism" approach do not appear good.

Notes

1. The Commission on Population Growth and the American Future, *Population and the American Future* (New York: New American Library, 1972), p. 167 ff.

2. Office of Economic Opportunity, *Need for Subsidized Family Planning Services: United States, Each State and County, 1968* and Office of Economic Opportunity, *Need for Subsidized Family Planning Services: United States, Each State and County, 1969.* Washington, D.C.: U.S. Government Printing Office, 1973.

3. *Report of the Secretary of Health, Education and Welfare Submitting Five-Year Plan for Family Planning Services and Population Research Programs,* (Washington, D.C.: U.S. Government Printing Office, 1971), pp. 434-435.

4. "Statement of Dr. Henry E. Simmons, Deputy Assistant Secretary for Health and Scientific Affairs Before the Special Subcommittee on Human Resources, Committee on Labor and Public Welfare, U.S. Senate, May 8, 1973," p. 10.

5. See later section on "Medicaid and Title IV-A," p. 10.

6. Simmons, op. cit., p. 11.

7. *Federal Register,* Vol. 38, No. 97, May 21, 1973, p. 13418.

8. *Federal Register,* Vol. 38, No. 130, July 9, 1973, p. 18262.

9. Planned Parenthood-World Population, "Washington Office Memorandum," W-13, 7-73, July 11, 1973.

10. Anthony R. Measham, M.D., "Family Planning Policy Development in North Carolina: Weak Tea," *Family Planning Perspectives,* Vol. 4, No. 2, April 1972, p. 47.

11. Frederick S. Jaffe, "Family Planning, Public Policy and Intervention Strategy," *Journal of Social Issues,* reprint by Planned Parenthood-World Population (New York, February 1966), p. 4.

12. Office of Economic Opportunity, *Need for Subsidized Family Planning Services, United States, Each State and County, 1968,* p. 12.

13. Ibid., p. 11.

14. "State Legislatures Provide Limited Family Planning Funds," *Family Planning/Population Reporter*, Vol. 2, No. 2, April 1973, p. 32.

15. "State MCH Expenditures for Family Planning Show Slight Increase," *Family Planning/Population Reporter*, Vol. 2, No. 1, February 1973, pp. 12-13.

16. Memorandum from Surgeon General Parran to State Health Departments, 1942.

17. Maternal and Child Health Service, DHEW, Director's Letter MCH-71-1, January 22, 1971, and additional communications.

18. Ibid.

19. "State MCH Expenditures . . . " op. cit.

20. Ibid.

21. J.I. Rosoff, "Medicaid, Past and Future," *Family Planning Perspectives*, Vol. 4, No. 3, July 1972, p. 26.

22. Russell H. Richardson, "Local Outlook on Growth of Family Planning Services," *Family Planning/Population Reporter*, Vol. 2, No. 2, April 1973, pp. 30-32.

23. D. Fisher and J.I. Rosoff, "How States Are Using Title IV-A to Finance Family Planning Services," *Family Planning Perspectives*, Vol. 4, No. 4, October 1972, pp. 31-43.

24. "State Family Planning Staff Still Below HEW Recommendations," *Family Planning/Population Reporter*, Vol. 2, No. 1, February 1973, pp. 20-21.

25. N.R. Bernstein, *The First One Hundred Years: Essays on the History of the American Public Health Association* (Washington, D.C.: American Public Health Association, 1972), p. 2 ff.

26. Ibid., p. 52.

27. Ibid., p. 57.

28. G.G. Udell, *Laws Relating to Social Security and Unemployment Compensation*, (Washington, D.C.: U.S. Government Printing Office, 1968), p. 11.

29. Ibid., p. 12.

30. "The Local Health Department—Services and Responsibilities," *American Journal of Public Health*, Vol. 54, No. 1, January 1964, p. 136.

31. Ibid., p. 133.

32. Ellis D. Sox, M.D., "The Local Health Officer—His Job," *American Journal of Public Health*, Vol. 54, No. 2, February 1964, p. 249.

33. Measham, op. cit., p. 54. Reprinted with the permission of *Family Planning Perspectives*.

34. Ibid., p. 55. Reprinted with the permission of *Family Planning Perspectives*.

35. G.Y. Steiner, *The State of Welfare* (Washington, D.C.: The Brookings Institution, 1971), p. 39.

36. F.F. Piven and R.A. Cloward, *Regulating the Poor* (New York: Pantheon Books, 1971), p. 177.

37. R. Morris, "Welfare Reform 1973: The Social Services Dimension," *Science*, Vol. 181, 10 August 1973, p. 515.

38. Ibid., p. 519.

39. Ibid.

While it would be inaccurate to ascribe to Morris the notion that being poor means being functionally dependent or socially unhealthy (he certainly acknowledges the importance of economic opportunity in achieving economic independence), his description of the target population for social services seems to contain virtually all welfare recipients. People in need of social services, according to Morris, are those "in conflict with the law..., those with educational or occupational disability..., those with physical or mental disability..., children living with families under severe social disability... and the aged." (pp. 519-520.) These correspond very closely to the categories of disabilities which qualify individuals for the federally-assisted welfare programs, Aid to the Blind, Aid to the Permanently and Totally Disabled, Aid to Families with Dependent Children, and Aid to the Aged. It is not difficult to draw the conclusion, therefore, that virtually all welfare recipients are socially unhealthy and in need of social services and that jobs and other economic opportunities would be wasted on them without prior social services.

40. F.S. Jaffe and S. Polgar, "Family Planning and Public Policy: Is the 'Culture of Poverty' the New Cop-out?," *Journal of Marriage and the Family*, Vol. 30, No. 2, May 1968, p. 228.

41. Ibid., p. 232.

42. Ibid.

43. Ibid.

44. Morris, op. cit., p. 520.

45. Ibid. Copyright 1973 by the American Association for the Advancement of Science.

46. D. Fisher and J.I. Rosoff, op. cit., p. 39.

47. "Florida: Comprehensive Family Planning Act Adopted," *Family Planning/Population Reporter*, Vol. 1, No. 1, December 1972, p. 1.

48. P. Donovan, "Georgia Governor Jimmy Carter," *Family Planning/Population Reporter*, Vol. 2, No. 3, June 1973, p. 58.

49. D. Fisher and J.I. Rosoff, op. cit., p. 40.

6

Preferences for Municipal Services of Citizens and Political Leaders: Somerville, Massachusetts, 1971

Richard D. Tabors*

Maris A. Vinovskis†

The purpose of the following article is to present a methodology for the analysis of preferences for municipal services. As a result it focuses more upon the manner in which the study was carried out and less upon the actual results of that study. The authors believe that the structure of this study is sufficiently unique as an analytical framework for comparing the response of political leaders to the preferences of their constituents to recommend it for replication on a larger scale in other decision–making situations.

This chapter is divided into five parts. The first is an introduction to the methodology employed in this study. In the next section there is a discussion of the survey that was administered in Somerville, Massachusetts in 1971. The third section presents a framework for analysis and the fourth a discussion of the results of this survey. The concluding section is a summary discussion of the manner in which a survey of this type could be improved to analyze more effectively the relationship between the perception of preferences for municipal services of political leaders and their constituents.

Introduction

One of the major problems in allocating resources within the government is to establish some set of priorities that take into account the preferences of the public. As there is no effective market mechanism operating in the government sector, it is very difficult for political decision-makers to ascertain the proper mixture or level of programs to satisfy the needs of their constituents.

We are particularly indebted to Professor Roger Revelle for his intellectual and personal guidance and stimulation throughout this project. Any errors of fact or interpretation are, however, solely the responsibility of the authors. We would further like to gratefully acknowledge financial assistance for computer time from the Harvard University Center for Population Studies and the Research Committee of the Graduate School of the University of Wisconsin.

*Lecturer in City and Regional Planning and Research Associate in Population Studies, Harvard University.

†Assistant Professor of History, University of Wisconsin, Rockefeller Fellow in the History of the Family Project, American Antiquarian Society and Clark University.

Public opinion pollsters have tried to deal with the problem of preferences for governmental services by asking people their desire for increases or decreases in programs in such broad areas as defense spending or improving of the environment. Most of these studies have found a high percentage of the public advocating more government expenditures on a wide variety of issues. However, when an additional question was asked on whether these same people would be willing to pay the increase in taxes necessary to finance these programs, there was a sizable drop in the desire for more services.[1] Most recent efforts to analyze public preferences for government services in relation to the political decision-makers have been handicapped by several methodological shortcomings:

1. The surveys usually ask the public whether they want increased government services without specifying exactly what level of the government should be or will be involved (i.e. federal, state, or local).
2. During the survey no attempt is made to inform the interviewee of the extent of present government activities in the issue under consideration. Though the results from such surveys may be a reflection of current public opinion toward government programs, they are not as useful to the decision-maker interested in the preferences of an informed public.
3. The surveys do not specify the particular government services being evaluated. Therefore, these studies can only measure general attitudes toward such large issues as assistance to the elderly or expansion of the existing medical facilities. As a result, many of the citizens interviewed respond to these questions on the basis of very different perceptions of what specific government programs are being considered.
4. The surveys do not attempt to specify the relative cost of the various alternatives. Instead, the questions simply ask the person if he would be willing to pay the increased taxes necessary to finance any additional expenditures. Furthermore, as there is no attempt to establish the monetary cost of these services, it is impossible for the public to determine how much increase in the present tax rate would be needed to finance these programs.
5. Finally, most of these surveys are only administered to the general public. Seldom is any effort made to poll the political decision-makers about their preferences. It is, therefore, impossible to analyze the relationship between the public's and the political leaders' preferences for government services.

In order to avoid many of the methodological problems mentioned above, we undertook a detailed survey of the preferences of municipal services of citizens and political leaders in one particular locality. Though we have not been able to resolve all of the difficulties in trying to compare the preferences of political leaders and their constituency, we do feel that many of our objections to the earlier efforts in this field have been met.

1971 Somerville Survey

The present study was designed to ascertain preferences for municipal services in one community—Somerville, Massachusetts. Somerville is a residential suburb of Boston with a population of 88,779 in 1970. Whereas the median years of school completed in the Boston Standard Metropolitan Statistical Area is 12.1 and the median family income is $6,687, the median education level of the Somerville population is only 10.8 years and the median family income only $6,024. Somerville's population is largely Catholic and, politically is heavily Democratic. During the period immediately prior to this study, the city elected a new mayor, board of aldermen, and school committee who were quite concerned with the problem of taking into consideration the preferences of the public in allocating municipal government funds among the various service sectors.[2]

A questionnaire on preferences for municipal services in Somerville was designed and administered to a random sample of 120 residents in that community.[3] In order to acquaint the citizens with the existing municipal services in each of the eighteen areas being investigated, a brief paragraph was read to them describing the extent of government activity in each category. The questionnaire developed is presented as Appendix 6A.[4]

The public was asked whether they wanted expenditures to increase, decrease, or be maintained at the same level for each of the municipal services under investigation. However, as we noted earlier, the responses to such a question exaggerate the extent of public support because they do not take into consideration the costs of these services to the taxpayer.

The earlier studies which introduced the tax consideration into the analysis did not attempt to measure the relative costs of the proposed programs. This is a major shortcoming of these studies because it does not permit the respondents to adjust their general preferences for these services on the basis of the relative tax burden of each proposal. In our study, we were able to estimate the cost of each of the municipal services by using the city budget and interviewing the department heads in each of the areas. Therefore we were able to calculate the resultant tax increase or decrease that would accompany any shift in the services being offered. In this way we were able to ascertain the relative costs of each of the proposed services as well as their impact upon the present tax rate.

Finally, in order to minimize the tendency of people to overestimate the sum of their preferences for municipal services when considered individually, we computed the overall change in the tax rate on the basis of each individual's choices. Then we asked each person if, overall, he was now satisfied with his previous choices. While no effort was made to redo the survey if the respondent expressed dissatisfaction, we feel very few of the interviewees would have shifted significantly their earlier preferences.[5]

As our analysis is concerned with the relationship between the preferences of citizens and political leaders, it was necessary to administer the same questionnaire to Somerville political leaders. We identified twenty-three individuals who were particularly important in the decision-making process in the city government—the mayor, four of his department heads, the eleven members of the board of aldermen, and the seven school committee members. Of these twenty-three individuals, it was possible to obtain interviews with seventeen.

Using the same questionnaire, the political leaders were asked their personal preferences for municipal services. In addition, we also asked them how they thought that the majority of their constituents would respond to these same issues. In this way we were able to compare the preferences for municipal services of the Somerville citizens, political leaders, and the perceptions of the political leaders of their constituents.[6]

Framework for Analysis

To compare the preferences for municipal services of Somerville citizens and political leaders, we have utilized first the following two by two matrix as an analytical framework.

	Citizens	Political Leaders
Citizens		
Political Leaders		

Figure 6-1. Service Preference Matrix.

Within this framework we can focus upon the preferences for specific municipal services as perceived by either the political leaders alone (lower right quadrant), by the citizens alone (upper left quadrant), or as a comparison of the preferences of the political leaders and the citizens (lower left hand quadrant).

It is generally argued by other scholars that the comparison of the preferences of citizens to those of political leaders offers a means of analyzing the degree of responsiveness of the political leaders to their constituency. Yet the political leaders may not be responding to the desires of the actual citizens, but rather to the preferences of the citizens as perceived by the political leaders themselves. One would like to know whether the preferences of the political leaders are more nearly identical to their perception of the preferences of their constituents or to the actual preferences of their constituents. Ideally, then, the analysis requires a three by three matrix rather than the two by two matrix traditionally used.

	Citizens	Political Leaders	Perceived Constituents
Citizens			
Political Leaders			
Perceived Constituents			

Figure 6-2. Perceived Service Preference Matrix.

By using the three by three matrix (Figure 6-2), the researcher is able to expand his analysis to evaluate political leaders' perceptions of the relative importance of specific municipal services to their constituents. The researcher may also compare the preferences of the political leaders with those of their constituents as perceived by these decision-makers. Finally, this new framework allows comparison between the actual preferences of the public and their preferences as perceived by the political leaders. As will be seen later in this analysis, this last step is the most difficult to accomplish within the scope of our survey.

Analysis of 1971 Survey Results

In this section we will discuss the results of our interviews with Somerville citizens and political leaders in 1971. We will rely upon the three by three matrix as a framework for our presentation of the data, though we will begin with an analysis of the three elements common to both matrices—the preferences of the citizens, the preferences of the political leaders, and a comparison of the two.

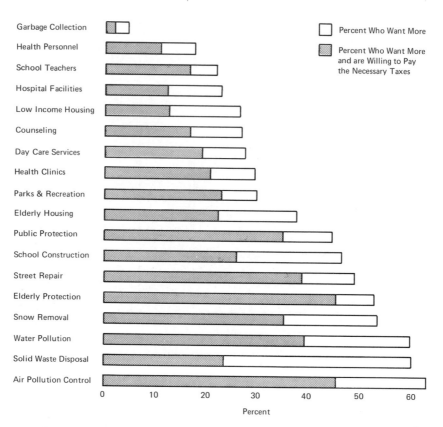

Figure 6-3. Municipal Service Preferences of Somerville Citizens, 1971.

The preferences of Somerville citizens for increased municipal services in each of the eighteen areas is presented in chart number one. The citizens interviewed were satisfied with the services provided by the city 61.2 percent of the time and wanted additional services 37.5 percent of the time (only 1 percent of the time did the citizens want less services). On five of the eighteen issues under investigation a majority of the public wanted more of a particular municipal service—elderly protection, snow removal, water pollution control, solid waste disposal, and air pollution control.

However, when the citizens were asked if they would be willing to pay the additional taxes necessary to finance the cost of the expanded municipal services, the percentage of persons now favoring an increase in services dropped from 37.5 percent to 24.6 percent. No longer were a majority of those interviewed willing to pay the necessary taxes to cover an increase in any of the services. The five most significant issues remain the same except that solid waste disposal is replaced by street repair when we take into consideration the actual cost of the services.

While there are important differences in the levels of support for many of the issues when the question of paying for the service is introduced, it is significant to note that overall the relative ordering of the issues does not change dramatically. There are, however, some shifts in the relative priorities—particularly in the area of solid waste disposal which decreases in importance with the addition of the consideration of the costs of the programs. Protection of the elderly, on the other hand, now increases in significance relative to the environmental issues which had the highest priorities initially.

The political leaders interviewed were in general less satisfied with the present level of municipal services than were the citizens—only 52.8 percent of the political leaders were satisfied compared to 61.2 percent of the general public. The services seen as most important by the political leaders were street repair, protection of the elderly, air pollution control, and public protection. It is interesting to observe that of the five highest preferences of the political leaders, two were in the area of improvement of the environment and two the protection of the citizens.

The political leaders showed marked variation in their preferences when the consideration of additional taxes was introduced. This was most apparent in the area of environmental protection as air and water pollution control become considerably less important. Reordering the preferences according to the willingness to pay leaves street repair, school construction, health personnel, public protection, and elderly protection as the five most important issues.

Though there was a sizable drop in support for most programs by the political leaders once the cost element was introduced, there were six issues in which there was no difference between the interest in gaining more of a given service and the willingness to pay for it—hospital facilities, health personnel, school teachers, counseling, snow removal, and street repair. In the area of street repair, all of the political leaders felt a need for higher level of municipal commitment and all were willing to pay the necessary taxes.

Now that we have examined the priorities of the citizens and the political leaders, we can ask whether the preferences of the political leaders are the same

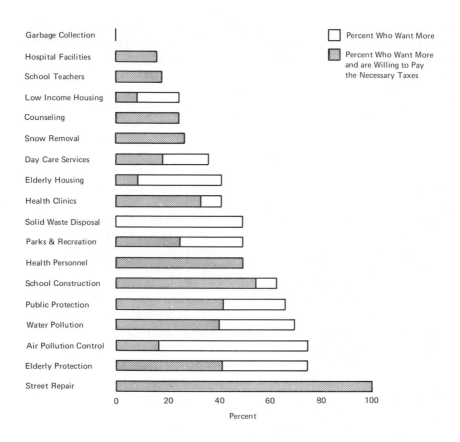

Figure 6-4. Municipal Service Preferences of Somerville Political Leaders, 1971.

as those of the citizens and, more significantly, whether the political leaders are willing to pay additional taxes for the same services as the citizens.

In general, political leaders wanted more services 46.2 percent of the time, while their constituents wanted additional services only 37.5 percent of the time. But the gap narrows when one considers the willingness to pay as only 29.1 percent of the political leaders were willing to pay for additional services while 24.6 percent of the public was willing to pay more.

Of the eighteen municipal service issues analyzed in this study, there was a greater than five percent higher preference for individual services on the part of

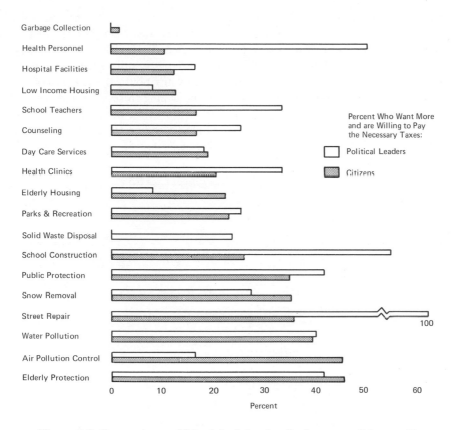

Figure 6-5. Comparison of Municipal Service Preferences of Somerville Citizens and Political Leaders, 1971.

the political leaders in six areas—health personnel, school teachers, counseling, health clinics, school construction, and street repair. A greater than five percent higher proportion of citizens than political leaders were willing to pay for additional services in four areas—elderly housing, snow removal, air pollution control, and solid waste disposal. Thus the political leadership reflected the preference pattern of the citizens for additional services within five percent for only half of the municipal services being analyzed. There are at least two explanations for the differences in preferences observed within the two groups. The first is that political leaders have admittedly different preferences from those of their constituents. The second is that political leaders are trying to reflect the preferences of their constituents but have perceived them incorrectly.

The information gathered about the political leaders' perception of the preferences of their constituents is not perfectly parallel to either that of the

110

preferences of the political leaders or of the citizens surveyed. The questions posed to political leaders about their constituents was: "Do you feel that a majority of your constituents would favor increased services?" and "Would they be willing to pay for those services?" The key difference is the word "majority." The responses do not represent the evaluation by the political leadership of the proportion of their constituents who would be willing to support and then to pay for additional services but rather the proportion of the political leaders who felt that a majority of their constituents would be willing to support and then pay for additional services in each of the eighteen areas.

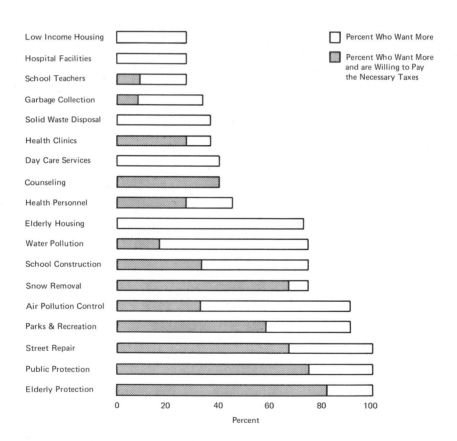

Figure 6-6. Constituent Preferences for Municipal Services as Perceived by Somerville Political Leaders, 1971.

Figure 6-6 shows constituent preferences as perceived by political leaders. On all of the issues taken together, the political leaders responded that they felt that a majority of their constituents wanted more services 60.8 percent of the time, that only 37.7 percent of the time did the majority want the same level of services and 1.5 percent of the time less services. Focusing on the individual issues, all of the political leaders felt that a majority of their constituents would favor additional protection for the elderly, protection for the public, and street repairs. More than half of the political leaders felt a majority of their constituents would wish additional services for parks and recreation, air pollution control, snow removal, school construction, water pollution, and elderly housing.

Whereas in the above nine issues the political leaders felt that a majority of their constituents wanted additional services, in only five of those areas did more than half of the political leaders believe that a majority of their constituents were willing to pay for the additional services—elderly protection, public protection, street repair, snow removal, and parks and recreation. In the areas of air pollution control, water pollution control, elderly housing, and school construction, political leaders perceived their constituents as wanting additional services but being unwilling to pay for them.

There were five issues on which none of the political leaders felt that a majority of their constituents were willing to pay additional taxes—elderly housing, day care services, solid waste disposal, hospital facilities, and low income housing.

Comparing the political leaders' preferences with their perception of the preferences of their constituents is not straightforward. It must be remembered that in the case of the political leaders we measured the proportion of leaders with a given preference while with their perceived constituency we measured the proportion of political leaders who felt that a majority of their constituents would prefer more of a given service. As a result, one must be cautious in interpreting Figure 6-7. Taking one example, that of street repair, it is possible to say that nearly 70 percent of the political leaders felt that a majority of their constituents would pay for increased street repair services. And as all of the political leaders who initially wanted increased street repairs were also willing to pay for it, at least 30 percent of the political leaders were willing to support street repairs believing that less than a majority of their constituents would support such an expenditure.

There were a number of issues in which some political leaders wanted increased services though none believed that a majority of his constituents would be willing to pay for them—solid waste disposal, elderly housing, low income housing, hospital facilities, and day care services. However, in six cases fewer political leaders were willing to pay for specific services than those who believed that a majority of their constituents wanted these services—air pollution control, counseling, parks and recreation, snow removal, elderly and public protection.

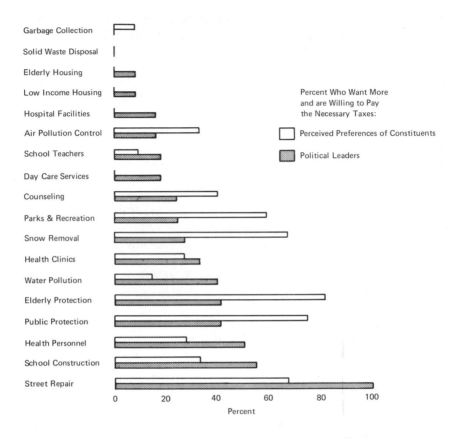

Figure 6-7. Comparison of Municipal Service Preferences of Somerville Political Leaders and Their Perception of the Preferences of Their Constituents, 1971.

The analysis of the relationship between the preferences of the political leaders and their perception of their constituents suggests that these leaders did deviate in their own eyes from the preferences of their constituents. However, we must not exaggerate the extent of disagreement between the political leader and his perception of his constituent. On the basis of the individual responses from the Somerville political leaders, we calculated that over seventy percent of the time the political leader wanted the same amount of services as his perceived constituency. Furthermore, in the remaining thirty percent of cases where the political leader felt he was disagreeing with his constituents, the political leader felt that the public was usually unwilling to pay the necessary taxes to finance the additional services.

The final area of analysis within the framework proposed is the relationship between the citizens' priorities for municipal services and the political leaders' perception of the priority of their constituents. It is necessary here to reiterate the caution presented above. The preferences of the citizens and the preferences of the citizens as perceived by the political leaders are not parallel. We are actually comparing the proportion of citizens who favored additional services in any given area with the proportion of the political leaders who felt that a majority of their constituents would favor additional services in that area.

In a number of areas there are relatively large discrepancies between the responses of the political leaders, their perception of their constituents and the actual preferences of the citizens. For example while 50 percent of the political leaders wanted additional health personnel and were willing to pay the necessary taxes, only 27 percent of them felt that a majority of their constituents would be willing to be taxed to provide additional health personnel, yet only 12 percent of the citizens were willing to be taxed to provide for this service. This position might be classed as one of greater social conscience on the part of the political leaders despite either the actual preferences of their constituents or their perception of their constituents' preference.

A pattern of responses similar to that for health personnel appears for three other social service issues—additional teachers, health clinics, and school construction. In each of these instances political leaders are more willing than citizens actually are, and more willing than political leaders think citizens are—to pay for the additional services. Though the political leaders demonstrated a larger concern for social services than either their perceived or actual constituencies, on other issues such as air pollution control and solid waste disposal the political leaders seriously underestimated the strength of the public's commitment to those areas.

Up to now we have focused our attention upon municipal service preferences of political leaders and their constituents. However, this same type of analysis should be applicable in other areas of decision-making. As another test of the usefulness of such an approach we included on our questionnaire three questions dealing with the issue of birth control. We were particularly interested in the response of both citizens and political leaders to this issue as we were dealing with a predominantly blue-collar, heavily Catholic community whose state representatives and senators have been generally very hostile to any liberalization of the birth control laws in the Commonwealth. The questions asked were:

1. If an additional neighborhood (health) clinic were built, do you think it should provide birth control information and devices as one of its services?
   yes _____   no _____   no opinion _____ .

2. Do you think any person who wants such information or devices should be able to get them?

    yes _____ no _____ no opinion _____ .

3. If you wanted such information or devices would you have access to them now?

    yes _____ no _____ no opinion _____ .

The preferences of the political leaders and their perception of the preferences of the majority of their constituents on the birth control issues are summarized in Table 6-1.

Of the political leaders expressing an opinion on the desirability of birth control services in neighborhood clinics, a large majority favored inclusion of that service (70 percent). On the issue of whether any person who wants such information or devices should be able to obtain them, an even larger percentage (88 percent) responded affirmatively. Yet when some local citizens attempted to solicit aid from their political leaders on the issues of liberalization of the birth control or abortion laws, they were unable to generate any appreciable support from among the political leaders. Many of the political leaders responded by saying that though they personally favored the liberalization of the present birth control laws, they were unwilling to risk the political consequences of openly supporting such a position in Somerville. This is partly reflected in the fact that many of these political leaders perceived their constituents as being less willing to support the availability of birth control information and services than they themselves yet it is interesting to note that one half of the political leaders felt that a majority of the citizens wanted birth control information and devices provided in the neighborhood health clinics and 70 percent of the leaders felt that the majority of Somerville's citizens favored the availability of birth control information or devices to anyone who desires them.

Focusing attention now upon the attitudes of the citizens on these same questions, we discover that a large majority of them favored both birth control information and devices in the neighborhood health clinics and availability of such information or devices to everyone. In fact the preferences of the citizens were almost identical to those of their political leaders.

Table 6-1
Birth Control Issues: Responses of Political Leaders

	Political Leaders			Perceived Constituents		
	Yes	No	No Opinion	Yes	No	No Opinion
Q, 1	58.3	25.0	16.6	41.6	41.6	16.6
Q, 2	66.6	8.3	25.0	58.3	25.0	16.6
Q, 3	91.6	–	8			

Table 6-2
Birth Control Issues: Responses of Citizens

	Citizens		
	Yes	No	No Opinion
Q, 1	56.7	19.2	24.2
Q, 2	76.0	12.5	10.8
Q, 3	63.3	17.5	19.2

But whereas all of the officials said they had access to such information and devices themselves, over 10 percent of the public acknowledged that they did not have access to either birth control information or devices. Thus political leaders underestimated the extent of public support for birth control information and devices and suffered less from the absence of governmental provision of information and devices than did their constituents.

Summary

The results of our study suggest the utility of attempting to be as specific as possible in designating the level of government involved, the type of service proposed, the extent of the specific existing government activities, the costs of providing each of the additional services, and the overall change in the current tax rate. In this way we feel we are better able to gauge the relative priorities of an informed public for any current set of alternative government expenditures.

In addition, we would argue, that it is necessary not only to poll the political leaders on their personal preferences for this same set of services but also to question them as to their perception of the preferences of their constituents. We have found marked differences in several instances between the actual priorities of citizens and their priorities as perceived by the political leaders. Particularly interesting to the analysis is the fact that there appears to be systematic biases on the part of the political leaders in areas such as social services and improvement of the environment. This would suggest that further research is required to explain the underlying factors affecting political leaders perceptions of the preferences of their constituents. What, for instance, is the role of the vocal minority in influencing the perception by the political leader of his constituent's needs? What role does the local or national press play in these perceptions? Only further research beginning with the proposed analytic framework will allow us to approach answers to questions such as these.

While our proposed analytic framework provides a more realistic means of ascertaining relative preferences of the public for government services, we feel that there are several points in our survey procedures which could and should be improved in further efforts of this nature. In measuring the individual's overall satisfaction with the change in the tax rate resultant from his set of preferences arrived at singly, we first calculate the overall tax increase and then ask the individual if he is satisfied with the cost of his choice of additional services. Should he not be satisfied with the results of his overall choices, the interviewer should then allow the individual to adjust his service preferences for any of the proposed services, totaling a second time to arrive at an acceptable overall tax level. Though this process will be more time consuming, it will reflect more accurately the individual's preference for and willingness to support his service preferences given his personal budget constraint as reflected in his inability to pay the required higher taxes for all of his preferred services.

Our analysis of political leaders is limited by the fact that we asked them only to state their personal preferences on issues. We should have included an additional question to ascertain their anticipated public position on each of these issues. Though in most instances the political leader's personal preferences and public position on any issue would be identical, in some controversial areas such as liberalization of birth control laws they are quite likely to diverge. Furthermore, instead of simply asking the political leader whether he felt that the majority of his constituents favored a particular program, we should have tried to devise a scale that would reflect more accurately the relative proportion of his constituents who would support increased services. This would make it easier to compare the political leaders perception of the references of their constituents with those of the citizens and the political leaders.

One major question remains to be solved. How useful is a method such as the one proposed when applied at the various levels of government? Is it realistic to expect the public to be able to make intelligent decisions about the allocation of funds for government services at the state or federal level? One of the major assumptions behind revenue sharing is that local political leaders perceive and are able to react more effectively to the needs of their constituency than are those at federal level. Despite this assumption very little effort has been made actually to test the responsiveness of the local political leaders to the perceived needs of their constituents. Even worse, no effort to date has been made to devise ways of allowing local leaders more accurately to ascertain the preferences of their constituency. We believe that the analytic framework put forward answers the majority of the criticisms presented and as such offers a more variable method for the analysis of public preference, both for the political decision-makers and the academic researcher.

Appendix 6A:
Questionnaire

I *SERVICES*

A. EDUCATION

    1.a. Do you have children of school age?   no   4:0

            If no, 2.   If yes, 1.b.   yes

      b. Do your children go to public school, private, school, or both?   private   4:1
                                              both   4:2
                                              public   4:3

    2.   School Construction

Somerville now has 22 elementary schools, three junior high schools, one high school, and one trade school. New elementary schools are being built in Ward 1 and Ward 7. Five new classrooms have been added to the Pope School in Ward 3.

      a. Do you think the Somerville city government should do the same as or more than it is now doing in the area of school construction?   same   5-6:0

            If same, 3.   If more, 2.b.   more

      b. At the present tax rate, for every $1000 that your house is assessed for, you pay $170. If Somerville were to construct another new elementary school, your tax rate would increase from $170 to $173.84 per $1000 for the next ten years. Would you be willing to pay this higher tax rate for this new school construction?   no   5-6:1
                                              yes   5-6:2

    3.   School Teachers

Somerville now has 640 teachers for the 13,000 students in its 27 public schools. There is an average of one teacher for every 25 students.

      a. Do you think the Somerville city government should do less than, the same as, or more than it is now doing in the area of school teachers per student?

	less	
	same	7-8:0
If less, 3.b. If same, B.1. If more, 3.c.	more	

b. If Somerville were to employ 60 fewer teachers than it does now, there would be 28 students for every one teacher, and your tax rate would decrease from $170 to $166.39 per $1000. Would you favor this lower tax rate as a result of fewer teachers?

	no	7-8:−1
	yes	7-8:−2

c. If Somerville were to employ 60 more teachers than it does now, there would be 23 students for every one teacher, and your tax rate would increase from $170 to $173.61 per $1000. Would you be willing to pay this higher tax rate for these additional teachers?

	no	7-8:1
	yes	7-8:2

B. PUBLIC WORKS

1. Garbage Collection

Somerville now spends $800,000 per year for the personnel and equipment that collect your garbage twice a week.

a. Do you think the Somerville city government should do less than, the same as, or more than it is now doing in the area of garbage collection?

	less	
	same	9-10:0
If less, 1.b. If same, 2. If more, 1.c.	more	

b. If Somerville were to decrease the frequency of its garbage collection to once a week, your tax rate would decrease from $170 to $168.40 per $1000. Would you favor this lower tax rate as a result of less frequent garbage collection?

	no	9-10:−1
	yes	9-10:−2

c. If Somerville were to increase the frequency of its garbage collection to three times a week, your tax rate would increase from $170 to $171.60 per $1000. Would you be willing to pay this higher tax rate for this more frequent garbage collection?

	no	9-10:1
	yes	9-10:2

2. Snow Removal

Somerville now spends $150,000 per year for the personnel and equipment that remove snow from the streets during the winter.

a. Do you think the Somerville city government should do less than, the same as, or more than it is now doing in the area of snow removal?

    less
    same   11-12:0
    more

    If less, 2.b.   If same, 3.   If more, 2.c.

b. If Somerville were to spend 10% less than it now does on snow removal, your tax rate would decrease from $170 to $169.88 per $1000. Would you favor this lower tax rate as a result of less snow removal service?

    no   11-12:−1
    yes   11-12:−2

c. If Somerville were to spend 10% more than it now does on snow removal, your tax rate would increase from $170 to $170.12 per $1000. Would you be willing to pay this higher tax rate for more snow removal service?

    no   11-12:1
    yes   11-12:2

3. Street Repair

Somerville now spends $1,000,000 per year for the personnel and equipment that repair the city's streets and sidewalks.

a. Do you think the Somerville city government should do less than, the same as, or more than it is now doing in the area of street and sidewalk repair?

    less
    same   13-14:0
    more

    If less, 3.b.   If same, C.1.   If more, 3.c.

b. If Somerville were to spend 10% less than it now does on street and sidewalk repair, your tax would decrease from $170 to $169.19 per $1000. Would you favor this lower tax rate as a result of less repair service?

    no   13-14:−1
    yes   13-14:−2

c. If Somerville were to spend 10% more than it now does on street and sidewalk repair, your tax rate would increase from $170 to $170.81 per $1000. Would you be willing to pay this higher tax rate for more repair service?

no	13-14:1
yes	13-14:2

C. SPECIAL SERVICES

1. Day Care

Somerville now has one center that provides free, full-time day care and educational activities for pre-school-age children of low-income working mothers. Several privately-operated centers provide part-time care for fixed fees. The one free center serves about 90 Somerville children.

a. Do you think the Somerville city government should do the same as or more than it is now doing in the area of day care?

same	15-16:0

       Is same, 2.   If more, 1.b.   more

b. If Somerville were to expand its day care services to cover 60 more children, your tax rate would increase from $170 to $171.01 per $1000. Would you be willing to pay this higher tax rate for this expansion of day care services?

no	15-16:1
yes	15-16:2

2. Counseling

Family and individual counseling services in Somerville are provided largely by private organizations such as the Catholic Charities, the Family Service Association, and the Somerville Guidance Center.

a. Do you think the Somerville city government should do the same as or more than it is now doing in the area or counseling?

same	17-18:0

       If same, 3.   If more, 2.b.   more

b. If Somerville were to build and staff a counseling center, your tax rate would increase from $170 to $170.81 per $1000. Would you be willing to pay this higher tax rate for this expansion of counseling services?

no	17-18:1
yes	17-18:2

3. Elderly Protection

Somerville today does not provide special police protection for the housing projects of elderly citizens over and above the normal number of patrolmen walking their beats or cruising in police cars.

    a. Do you think the Somerville city government should do the same as or more than it is now doing in the area of protection of the elderly?   same   19-20:0

        If same, D.1.   If more, 3.b.   more

    b. If Somerville were to assign one additional patrolman to each of the four elderly housing projects, your tax rate would increase from $170 to $170.28 per $1000. Would you be willing to pay this higher tax rate for this special protection service?   no   19-20:1
   yes   19-20:2

D. POLLUTION CONTROL

   1. Air

A major source of air pollution in Somerville today is the incinerator. The incinerator's budget at the present time does not include funds to be used to lower the amount of pollution produced by the incinerator.

    a. Do you think the Somerville city government should do the same as or more than it is now doing in the area of air pollution control?   same   21-22:0

        If same, 2.   If more, 1.b.   more

    b. If Somerville were to supply the funds needed to install anti-pollution devices so that the incinerator would meet Federal air pollution control standards, your tax rate would increase from $170 to $170.63 per $1000. Would you be willing to pay this higher tax rate for this improvement in air pollution control?   no   21-22:1
   yes   21-22:2

   2. Water

The Mystic River has become polluted by sewage and industrial waste from several communities along the River, including Somerville. A number of sewage pipes from Somerville which had been emptying into the River have been repaired and re-channeled in response to individual citizens' complaints.

    a. Do you think the Somerville city government

should do the same as or more than it is now
doing in the area of water pollution control? same 23-24:0

    If same, 3.   If more, 2.b. more

b. If Somerville were to re-channel its entire sewage
system in order to alleviate the pollution problem,
your tax rate would increase from $170 to
$171.46 per $1000 for the next ten years. Would
you be willing to pay this higher tax rate for this
decrease in the River's pollution level? no 23-23:1
yes 23-24:2

3. Solid

The trash, garbage, and other solid waste produced by
Somerville is brought to the incinerator for burning. At the
incinerator's present level of efficiency, the volume of the
substance left after incineration is one-half that of the
original solid waste.

a. Do you think the Somerville city government
should do the same as or more than it is now
doing in the area of solid waste disposal? same 25-26:0

    If same, E.   If more, 3.b. more

b. If Somerville were to supply the funds needed to
upgrade the incinerator's operation so that the
volume of the substance left after incineration
would be one-fifth of that of the original solid
waste, your tax rate would increase from $170 to
$173.25 per $1000. Would you be willing to pay
this higher tax rate for more efficient solid waste
disposal? no 25-26:1
yes 25-26:2

E. PARKS & RECREATION

Somerville now has six parks and 24 playgrounds. The city
uses these areas as sites for a variety of recreational
programs for all age groups, including the elderly, teenagers, and young children. Programs include arts and crafts,
sports, dramatics, and other activities.

a. Do you think the Somerville city government
should do less than, the same as, or more than it is
now doing in the area of parks and recreation? less
same 27-28:0

    If less, b.   If same, F.   I more, c. more

b. If Somerville were to employ ten fewer full-time group leaders and counselors, your tax rate would decrease from $170 to $169.51 per $1000. Would you favor this lower tax rate as a result of fewer recreational activities?

no   27-28:—1

yes   27-28:—2

c. If Somerville were to employ ten more full-time group leaders and counselors, your tax rate would increase from $170 to $170.49 per $1000. Would you be willing to pay this higher tax rate for more recreational activities?

no   27-28:1

yes   27-28:2

F. PUBLIC PROTECTION

There are now about 130 patrolmen on the Somerville police force, with an average of 15 assigned to each ward.

a. Do you think the Somerville city government should do less than, the same as, or more than it is now doing in the area of public protection?

less

same   29-30:0

If less, b.   If same, G.1.   If more, c.   more

b. If Somerville were to decrease the size of the police force by 20 men, your tax rate would decrease from $170 to $168.60 per $1000. Would you favor this lower tax rate as a result of this reduction in the number of policemen?

no   29-30:—1

yes   29-30:—2

c. If Somerville were to increase the size of the police force by 20 men, your tax rate would increase from $170 to $171.40 per $1000. Would you be willing to pay this higher tax rate for this additional number of policemen?

no   29-30:1

yes   29-30:2

G. HOUSING

1. The Elderly

Somerville now has four housing projects which provide homes for about 450 people 65 years of age or older with incomes of under $4800.

a. Do you think the Somerville city government

should do the same as or more than it is now
doing in the area of housing for the elderly? same   31-32:0

       If same, 2.   If more, 1.b.   more

b. If Somerville were to construct housing for 100
more elderly persons, your tax rate would increase
from $170 to $173.64 per $1000 for the next ten
years. Would you be willing to pay this higher tax
rate for this additional housing for the elderly?   no   31-32:1

    yes   31-32:2

  2. Low-Income Families

Somerville now has two housing projects which provide
homes for about 670 families with incomes equivalent to
$5200 or less for a four-member family.

a. Do you think the Somerville city government
should do the same as or more than it is now
doing in the area of housing for low-income
families?   same   33-34:0

       If same, H.1.   If more, 2.b.   more

b. If Somerville were to construct housing for 50
more low-income families, your tax rate would
increase from $170 to $172.62 per $1000 for the
next ten years. Would you be willing to pay this
higher tax rate for this additional housing for
low-income families?   no   33-34:1

    yes   33-34:2

H. MEDICAL CARE

  1. Hospital Facilities

Somerville Hospital is one of two hospitals located in the
city. It provides facilities and staff for performing surgery,
delivering babies, and dealing with various medical problems. The Hospital has 150 beds, of which about one-third
are modern, an X-ray service, and a 24-hour emergency
room. The Hospital is now seeking funds for a major
expansion and improvement of its services. A new facility
for physical therapy and rehabilitation, a more complete
laboratory, more and modernized beds, a larger walk-in
clinic, and an expanded emergency service are among the
improvements being planned.

a. Do you think the Somerville city government should help supply funds for this expansion of hospital facilities?   no   35-36:0

       If no, 2.   If yes, 1.b.   yes

b. If Somerville were to supply half of the funds needed for the planned expansion, your tax rate would increase from $170 to $176.18 per $1000 for the next ten years. Would you be willing to pay this higher tax rate for this improvement in hospital facilities?   no   35-36:1
                                                                                      yes   35-36:2

2. Health Personnel

Somerville now employs eight school nurses and three public health nurses. The eight school nurses give children innoculations, physical examinations, and medical care in case of accidents at school. The three public health nurses provide Somerville citizens with tuberculin tests and help operate the Mystic Health Center in Ward 2.

a. Do you think the Somerville city government should do less than, the same as, or more than it is now doing in the area of health personnel?

       less

       same   37-38:0

       If less, 2.b.   If same, 3.   If more, 2.c.   more

b. If Somerville were to employ five fewer school nurses and three fewer public health nurses, your tax rate would decrease from $170 to $169.56 per $1000. Would you favor this lower tax rate as a result of this reduction in the number of health personnel?   no   37-38:−1
                                                                      yes   37-38:−2

c. If Somerville were to employ five more school nurses and three more public health nurses, your tax rate would increase from $170 to $170.44 per $1000. Would you be willing to pay this higher tax rate for this additional health personnel?   no   37-38:1
                                                                      yes   37-38:2

3. Neighborhood Clinics

Somerville now has one full-time neighborhood health clinic, which is located at the Mystic River Housing Project.

The clinic provides speech therapy, dental care, personal guidance, treatment for pregnant women and young children, and family planning assistance.

a. Do you think the Somerville city government should do less than, the same as, or more than it is now doing in the area for neighborhood clinics?

less	
same	39-40:0
more	

If less, 3.b.   If same, 4.   If more, 3.c.

b. If Somerville were to close down the Mystic Health Center, your tax rate would decrease from $170 to $169.19 per $1000. Would you favor this lower tax rate as a result of this decrease in neighborhood health services?

no	39-40:−1
yes	39-40:−2

c. If Somerville were to build and staff a second full-time neighborhood clinic, your tax rate would increase from $170 to $170.81 per $1000. Would you be willing to pay this higher tax rate for an additional neighborhood clinic?

no	39-40:1
yes	39-40:2

4.a. If an additional neighborhood clinic were built, do you think it should provide birth control information and devices as one of its services?

no	41-42:−1
no opinion	41-42:0
yes	41-42:1

b. Do you think any person who wants such information or devices should be able to get them?

no	43-44:−1
no opinion	43-44:0
yes	43-44:1

c. If you wanted such information or devices, would you have access to them now?

no	45-46:−1
no opinion	45-46:0
yes	45-46:1

I.   TOTAL COST

1.   If all the increases and all the decreases in the tax rate that you have approved of in this questionnaire were to

take place, your new tax rate for next year would be
_____ rather than the present $170 per $1000.

$139.99 or less	47-48:—4
$140.00-$149.99	47-48:—3
$150.00-$159.99	47-48:—2
$160.00-$169.99	47-48:—1
$170.00	47-48:0
$170.01-$180.00	47-48:1
$180.01-$190.00	47-48:2
$190.01-$200.00	47-48:3
$200.01 or more	47-48:4

2.   Given the level and types of public services you
have indicated that you prefer, are you satisfied or dissatisfied with the tax rate that you have ended up with?

If dissatisfied, do you think this tax rate is too
high or too low?

dissatisfied (too high)	49-50:—1
satisfied	49-50:0
dissatisfied (too low)	49-50:1

To complete this questionnaire, we would like to get
some basic background information about such things as
age, education, length of residence, and income. This will
help us to make sure that our survey reaches all kinds of
Somerville citizens, old people as well as young people,
newcomers as well as lifetime residents, tenants as well as
homeowners, and so on.

II.   CHARACTERISTICS

A.   SEX

male	51:0
female	51:1

B.   AREA

Ward 1	52:0
Ward 2	52:1
Ward 3	52:2
Ward 4	52:3
Ward 5	52:4
Ward 6	52:5
Ward 7	52:6

C.   AGE

Within which of the following age groups are you?

less than 30 years old	53:0
30 to 39 years old	53:1
40 to 49 years old	53:2
50 to 59 years old	53:3
60 or more years old	53:4

D.   HOMEOWNER STATUS

Do you rent or own your home?

tenant	54:0
owner	54:1

E.   EDUCATION

What was the last grade in school that you completed?

8th grade or less	55:0
9th, 10th, or 11th grade	55:1
high school (12th grade)	55:2
some years of college	55:3

F.   LENGTH OF RESIDENCE

How many years have you lived in Somerville?

12 months or less	56:0
13 months to 5 years	56:1
6 to 15 years	56:2
more than 15 years	56:3
lifetime	56:4

G.   INCOME

Within which of the following income groups are you?

less than $3000 per year	57:0
between $3000 and $6000 per year	57:1
between $6000 and $10,000 per year	57:2
$10,000 or more per year	57:3

H.   MARITAL STATUS

Are you . . . ?

single	58:0
married	58:1
divorced/widowed	58:2

I.   ACTIVISM

Which of these community activities, if any, have you
been involved in lately?

no community activities 59:0
veterans' organization, Rotary Club,
  PTA, sports team, religious group 59:1
political party or campaign work, citizens' group 59:2
candidate for city office 59:3
officeholder 59:4

Appendix 6B

Table 6B-1
Municipal Service Preferences of Somerville Citizens, 1971

	Less	Same	More	More if Taxed
School construction	—	53.7	46.3	25.9
School teachers	2.7	75.7	21.6	16.2
Garbage collection	1.7	94.2	4.2	1.7
Snow removal	1.6	45.0	53.3	35.0
Street repair	.9	50.4	48.8	38.5
Day care services	—	71.4	28.5	19.0
Family & individual counseling	—	73.1	26.9	16.7
Elderly protection	—	47.2	52.8	45.3
Air pollution control	—	33.6	66.3	45.1
Water pollution control	—	40.2	59.8	39.3
Solid waste disposal	—	40.2	59.8	23.4
Parks and recreation	2.7	67.5	29.8	22.8
Public protection	.9	54.7	44.5	34.8
Elderly housing	—	62.5	37.5	22.1
Low income housing	—	68.3	26.1	12.6
Hospital facilities	—	77.2	22.8	12.3
Health personnel	1.9	80.8	17.3	10.6
Neighborhood health clinics	5.6	65.4	29.4	20.6

Table 6B-2
Municipal Service Preferences of Somerville Politicians, 1971

	Less	Same	More	More if Taxed
School construction	–	36.3	63.6	54.5
School teachers	0	81.8	18.1	18.1
Garbage collection	8.3	91.6	0	0
Snow removal	–	72.7	27.2	27.2
Street repair	–	0	100.0	100.0
Day care services	–	63.6	36.3	18.1
Family & individual counseling	–	75.0	25.0	25.0
Elderly protection	–	25.0	75.0	41.6
Air pollution control	–	25.0	75.0	16.6
Water pollution control	–	30.0	70.0	40.0
Solid waste disposal	–	50.0	50.0	0
Parks and recreation	0	50.0	50.0	25.0
Public protection	0	33.0	66.0	41.6
Elderly housing	–	58.3	41.6	8.3
Low income housing	–	75.0	25.0	8.3
Hospital facilities	–	83.3	16.6	16.6
Health personnel	0	50.0	50.0	50.0
Neighborhood health clinics	8.3	50.0	41.6	33.3

133

Table 6B-3

Constituent Preferences for Municipal Services as Perceived by Somerville Political Leaders, 1971

	Less	Same	More	More if Taxed
School construction	—	25.0	75.0	33.3
School teachers	18.1	54.5	27.2	9.0
Garbage collection	0	66.6	33.3	8.3
Snow removal	0	25.0	75.0	66.7
Street repair	0	0	100.0	66.7
Day care services	—	60.0	40.0	0
Family & individual counseling	—	60.0	40.0	40.0
Elderly protection	—	0	100.0	81.8
Air pollution control	—	8.3	91.6	33.3
Water pollution control	—	25.0	75.0	16.5
Solid waste disposal	—	63.6	36.3	0
Parks and recreation	0	8.3	91.6	58.3
Public protection	0	0	100.0	75.0
Elderly housing	—	27.2	72.7	0
Low income housing	—	72.7	27.2	0
Hospital facilities	—	72.7	27.2	0
Health personnel	0	54.5	45.4	27.2
Neighborhood health clinics	9.0	54.5	36.3	27.2

134

Notes

1. Aaron Wildowsky, "Aesthetic Power or the Triumph of the Sensitive Minority Over the Vulgar Mass: A Political Analysis of the New Economics," in *America's Changing Environment*, ed. Roger Revelle and Hans H. Landsberg (Boston: Houghton Mifflin Co., 1970), pp. 147-160.

Eva Mueller, "Public Attitudes Toward Fiscal Programs," *The Quarterly Journal of Economics*, Vol. 77 (May 1963), pp. 210-235.

Robert S. Eriksen and Norman R. Luttbeg, *American Public Opinion: Its Origins, Content and Impact* (New York: John Wiley & Sons, 1973).

Warren E. Miller and Donald E. Stokes, "Constituency Influences in Congress," *American Political Science Review*, Vol. 57 (March 1963), pp. 45-56.

2. For a discussion of the political background in Somerville, Mass., see Carl E. Schneider, *Patterns of Political Recruitment: Somerville, Massachusetts, 1963-1969* (unpublished Senior Honors Thesis, Department of History, Harvard University, June 1972).

3. As the sample was only 120 households, no attempt was made to cross-tabulate the preferences for municipal services by the personal characteristics of the respondents. In addition, the reader should be aware that the size of sampling error for a study of this size is approximately ±7% at the .9 confidence level.

4. We are indebted to the members of Harvard University's Natural Science 119, spring semester, 1971 who administered this questionnaire to the sample of citizens in Somerville. We would particularly like to thank Simeon M. Kriesberg, David Harman, and Thomas O'Neil, who undertook the major portion of this effort.

5. Unfortunately, the question about the reaction of the respondents to increased taxation as a result of their preferences was ambiguous. The question did not distinguish between being dissatisfied with the increment to the present tax rate or being dissatisfied with either the present or the resultant total tax rate.

6. It was essential to protect the confidentiality of the responses of the political leaders, as one of the authors was then actively involved in Somerville politics. Therefore, it was necessary to have someone else conduct the interviews with the political leaders and provide us only with the anonymous responses. It is to Ms. Pamela Clark, then a student at Suffolk University, that we owe a large debt, as it was only through her tireless efforts that the questionnaires for the political leaders was obtained.

As no survey research of this nature can be accomplished without active cooperation between the interviewer and those interviewed, we were particularly grateful for the cooperation of Mayor S. Lester Ralph, the members of the Somerville Board of Aldermen, and the Somerville School Committee who willingly took time from their busy schedules to participate in this survey.

7 Family Health Services

Paul B. Cornely*

Benedict J. Duffy, Jr.†

Population policymaking at state and national levels has been of concern to all of us in recent years due in part to the so-called population crisis. A Presidential Commission on Population Growth and the American Future was established in 1970, deliberated for two years, and made a rather comprehensive report with many recommendations and some six massive volumes of research data and reports of public hearings. In addition to this, a film was produced and subsequently a Citizen's Committee was established for a year for the purpose of publicizing the Commission's Report. Nevertheless, the official report was condemned by the President and has hardly made a dent in the consciousness of the American public. During the same period of time it has been amazing that the rate of growth has continued to decline and has gone below the zero population growth level of 2.11.

Demographers for quite some time have indicated that the fertility rate cannot be estimated with any precision. This generally depends entirely on the whims and fancies of the population. As McDermott[1] has indicated:

To reduce fertility requires a decision by an individual or by individual couples; for most birth-limiting techniques, that individual decision must be made over and over again throughout several decades of adult life. In this, as in so many other activities in which a change in habit is desired, it is not enough to know how to accomplish a particular result, it is equally essential to know why the effort should be made in the first place. Once the know-why has been personally accepted, the know-how usually becomes of quite secondary importance.

If determinations of family composition are to be made by individual families, one may then have to come to the realization that the most effective way to reach families must come from this social organism itself and not from above by a bureaucratic structure. This idea has been well expressed by Wyon and Gordon:

*Assistant to the Executive Medical Director, UMWA Welfare and Retirement Fund; Past President, American Public Health Association.

†Lecturer on Medicine, Harvard University Medical School; consultant on community health.

135

Programs in population control will more likely emerge consistently and progressively from the simpler family unit to the larger social complex, rather than through any hope that it can be successfully imposed from above through central authority.[2]

This chapter, then, is concerned with the family as the basic unit of society and the ways and means by which family life support services can be made available. And, further, it is concerned with how these family support services may provide the opportunity for each family to make the decision for family limitation or control on the basis of informed judgment in an environment which provides many options for the growth and development of every individual in the society in which he finds himself. This concept is certainly not new. It has been mentioned by many, but achievement has been minuscule because of many barriers.

One of the most important barriers to the wellness or well-being of families is the fragmentation in the human services being offered to families. This can be seen in education, health care, welfare housing, nutrition, and environmental sanitation. All of these contribute to the health totality of the family, yet all are given by disparate and separate individuals or agencies without any coordination and much duplication. Not only are the major human services units fragmented but each of the fragments is subdivided. Health services may be considered one of these and may be discussed as a prototype.

The lack of adequate health care for the American people has been repeatedly documented since the 1932 report on "Medical Care for the American People"[3] to the 1972 Presidential Message on Health which called attention to the "critical state" of health care in the United States.

Although over the past forty years a variety of blueprints have been offered, nevertheless, fragmentation and duplication have been rampant. At the level of the Federal government some twenty-five separate units are concerned with administering various legislative acts which total in the neighborhood of some thirty billion dollars. As one moves to the state and local levels conditions worsen. A family of four with one child with rheumatic heart disease, the other with dental malocclusion, the mother with hypertensive heart disease, and the father with low back pain may have to go to a variety of clinics, located at different facilities, on different days and hours and handled by multiple providers.

Family planning all too often has been part of this fragmentation. In a number of instances birth control clinics have been established as separate facilities in connection with Planned Parenthood Associations, in others it is located in the hospital or may be part of the maternal and child health clinic. Sometimes it is found in a neighborhood comprehensive clinic. Presently, abortion clinics have been set up also as separate units, and in many cities glaring signs with the location and telephone number of the facility are in evidence throughout the city.

Fragmentation of health services is not the only barrier. There are of course other obvious ones such as high cost, inaccessibility, and inadequate facilities. But there are also other barriers not quite as apparent, and these have been called the hidden enemies of health by one of the authors and may be briefly summarized: first, a national addiction to the abundant life or crass materialism; second, perversion of the democratic process by special interests and control of legislators by lobbyists; third, pollution of the mind and specifically, children's television dominated by an advertising industry whose basic ethic is sales; and finally, the root cause of our disarray, a prevailing and pervasive racism.[4]

The barriers will continue to exist and family wellness will deteriorate unless an effort is made to find ways and means whereby the integrity of the family is maintained by a coordinated program of life support services. It is not the purpose of this paper to consider each of the services necessary for the wellbeing of the family. Some of these are being considered in other chapters in this book. Our sole concern is family health and it is important because it is the one which has traditionally been used to introduce population policies within the family unit from above. Planning for family health should be related to other life support services in order that whatever population policy is developed will come from within the family and will be a voluntary choice and not a coercive or subtly oppressive force.

The model for family health then should not be the traditional clinical therapy model found in our medical centers, universities or community hospitals, public health clinics, school health programs, and all the others in which medical care is the product provided. If perchance tomorrow by a magic wand one could bring to every child medical care which he needs, the health status of our children, particularly those in the disadvantaged group, would continue to show deficits in health no matter the nature and type of their providers. The greatest myth which continues to pervade our society is that the provision of medical care no matter what its cost will make us a healthy nation. Thus we continue to pour untold millions into a bottomless pit with little avail.

Health has been defined as a favorable ecologic balance. In other words, health is a unity made up of many components which include the total environment of the individual and family. Medical care may be the least important of the variegated number of components. What gaineth a child to be screened, diagnosed, and treated in the most scientific and well-staffed hospital if he is sent back to the house from whence he came? Much of our marginal mental retardation is due not to genetic factors but rather to the low nutritional state of the pregnant mother. The lowest infant mortality rates in this country are to be found among the Japanese-Americans, and the factor which shows a positive correlation with this phenomenon appears to be the educational level of the Japanese-American. Thus it might be much more productive in achieving a lowered infant mortality rate if we spent our dollars for education.

We must then come to the conclusion that if the health of our children and for that matter that of this nation is to be improved, we must abandon the clinical services therapeutic model as the major thrust and turn our focus to a social services therapeutic model. Medical care would be included because medicine is a social science. This country needs a national health policy which would embody this concept.

What basic social service components would maximize the favorable ecologic balance of each of the members of the family? The authors wish to summarize succinctly the major components of one such possible model. No effort will be made to describe all of the components in detail because these are to be found in practically all of the blueprints which have been recommended to improve the nation's health during the past half century. Emphasis will be given to those which are not usually found in such catalogues. The reader should exercise his constitutional privilege in disagreeing with such emphases or use his imagination or experience in adding others which he deems more important. The components which should be packaged for every family include the following:

Environmental Services

This could include shelter, the immediate surrounding, land environment, and the work place. Housing and the land environment have already been emphasized in another chapter, but it bears repeating that family health is in jeopardy whenever human beings have to live in places where they are exposed to lead poisoning, defective heating, sewage contamination, vermin, and rat bites. Neighborhood pollution plagues all, but none more so than the disadvantaged living in inner cities, rural areas, or Indian reservations. Carbon monoxide poisoning among children who play near expressways may reach 100 ppm, inner city noise because of truck routes may reach levels of 100 decibels or more; and lead is the hidden environmental curse of the ghetto.[5] But in addition, one must not forget the other kinds of pollution which are indeed more subtle and damaging to young bodies and minds such as police brutality, assaults and battery, the high homicide rates among young Black males, and the numerous bars and liquor stores found in such neighborhoods—all due to the behavior and attitudes of the controlling bureaucracies. The employment condition of millions of workers has an impact on family health, and certainly the concern of the U.S. Government in the passage of the Federal Coal Mine Health and Safety Act of 1969 as well as the Occupational Health and Safety Act of 1970 attests to the importance of this problem area. But more is involved than physical injury and death. The boredom associated with repetitive work, the anxiety of the worker who engages in hazardous work, such as in the mines, farm, or construction work affect in no small manner the behavior of individual members of the family.

Food and Nutritional Services

An affluent society which includes in its population some 25 million persons who are overweight must see to it that all families have a minimum basic diet which will prevent undernutrition and malnutrition. Such deficiency diseases are more prevalent in families with large numbers of children. The distribution of foods and the availability of food stamps are measures which have been available but have not been well coordinated. Increased food availability must be enhanced by an educational program which will make it possible for each family to get the most out of its food dollars and to prepare well balanced diets in keeping with their ethnic, cultural, and economic considerations.

Employment, Underemployment, and Welfare Services

An adequate income is one of the most significant determinants of health. Yet in this country, the unemployment rate of certain segments of the population is staggering; and when added to the underemployed, the number is startling. Our welfare problem has been the subject of much discussion for many years yet no agreement has been reached concerning reform in this area. The families who find themselves adversely affected by economic disadvantage continue to have the worst health experiences, the most social pathology, and are least able to improve upon their level of existence. This country must develop a national policy of full employment for all of those who are able to work and an adequate income for those unable to do so.

Personal Health Services—A Minimum Quantum for Each Family

All health professionals, as well as all citizens in this country, should be concerned about the availability of health services to every individual and family. Whenever this is discussed it is generally stated rather glibly that health services must be comprehensive and of the highest quality. Yet it is obvious that this could not be done for each of the 200 million citizens in this country. It is our belief that the time has come for this country to consider as a policy a minimum quantum of personal health services for each family.

The idea of a minimum in reference to health is one which does not settle well with many people. It is said that the provision of care, unlike education, cannot be easily regulated because illness is unpredictable in terms of time, place, and severity. Therefore, health care cannot be put into a limited package—for when it is exhausted, the patient would be released from care. This, of course, is unthinkable. Other approaches to health care coverage have been suggested for those whose personal and financial resources are inadequate. One of the suggestions is that we limit services to particular age categories, or groups, and add to these as resources become available until the total population is covered. We have already made a start with Medicare for those over sixty-five years of age, we then could add Kiddie-Care for those under fifteen, subsequently for the working population not covered by the first two and, finally, to the remainder of the population. Each of these categories would receive comprehensive health care at the time it was brought into the system. There are others who believe that this should be done on an economic basis such as Medicaid. Thus, we could provide comprehensive care on a nationwide basis for those under $3,000, subsequently, for those under $7,500, and on upward until the total population was covered. But all of these suggestions would continue to leave large segments of the population without care for a long period until it was their turn.

We have no qualms about discussing minimum health services as a right for every individual. As long as a health crisis exists, as long as millions of people go without health care, there is need for some definition as to what is meant by President Nixon's statement in his State of the Union Message on January 20, 1972 that "no American is denied basic medical care because of inability to pay."[6]

Minimum health services cannot be considered in isolation, and therefore three ingredients must be present for whatever program of personal health services we establish: accessibility, acceptability, and continuity. Health services must be accessible to the individual and family at the time and place where they need them. Whatever health servcies are provided, personal acceptability is also of primary importance. Even with a very knowledgeable patient a compromise may be necessary when the individual perceives his needs differently from the provider and refuses to accept the professional recommendations for care. Continuity is extremely important if maximum benefit is to be obtained from the availability of minimum health services. The medical care process must treat the patient as a whole person and not just as a fragmented collection of separate cells, organs, or body systems.

What, then, would constitute minimum health services for all Americans? The spectrum of health care formulated by Leavall[7] may be used as a guide. Five levels of care are proposed: health promotion, specific health protection, early diagnosis and treatment, disability limitation, and rehabilitation.

The first important component in this concept of minimum health services is health promotion. As has already been indicated above, the provision of minimal personal health services is entirely wasteful unless such health services are intimately related to an adequate environmental situation. Therefore, every individual receiving basic health services must be provided with a diet which would meet the minimum standards for his age and condition of life; housing which adheres to minimum health standards; basic neighborhood sanitary services; and a healthful work environment.

Minimum health services would put major emphasis on specific health protection or the delivery of preventive health services adjusted for age groups in some fashion as listed below:

1. Pregnant woman

Prenatal care with emphasis on serology, measure of nutritional state; chest x-ray.

2. Infant and preschool child

Specific immunizations; dental prophylaxis; nutritional status; lead blood level screening.

3. School child and young adult, 6-24 years

Chest x-ray; blood serology; sickle cell screening; physical defects assessment.

4. Adult, 25-44 years

Screening examinations for hypertension, cancer of selected sites, glaucoma; chest x-ray; baseline electrocardiogram.

5. Adult, 45-64 years

Same as above including prostate examination for the male.

6. Adult, 65 years and over

Chronic disease evaluation and functional maintenance programs—nutrition, medication, and emotional support.

As one looks at this suggested list, it is to be noted that most of these procedures could easily be done by persons other than physicians.

The last three items in the spectrum of health care, early diagnosis and treatment, disability limitation, and rehabilitation, may be discussed together and briefly. There is no doubt that early diagnosis and prompt treatment would be a keystone in the concept of minimum health services. This would include emergency care for immediate and severe threat to life. Professional rehabilitation services would be part of the treatment only for those who can be returned to productive life within a reasonably short period of time. Medication selected from a national formulary of drugs according to generic names would be provided for all patients. Minimum health services would not include extensive and long-term rehabilitation.

A brief word should be included about the providers of minimum personal health services. It is hardly reasonable to suggest that in every nook and corner of the land, health services should be provided by a comprehensive neighborhood health center. If minimum health services are to be available to every American, they will not be rendered by the highly trained physicians coming out of our residency training programs but rather by new professionals who have had less training but have been specifically prepared for this purpose.[8] For instance, a neighborhood health care clinic housing a physician assistant or nurse practitioner, with a public health nurse, an environmentalist, and two or more community health workers specially trained for this purpose could very well meet this need. But even this might be more than could be developed in certain isolated communities, and we would need to resort to the training of indigenous persons living in those communities. It should be emphasized, at all times, that these modules of health care should always be part of a system, however rudimentary. This health care system should include primary care centers, group practice units, acute general hospitals, extended care facilities, and regional specialized hospitals.

Summarily, it would have to be said that if our affluent society made possible the provision of a minimum quantum of personal health services to all Americans, then the quality of life for a large segment of the population could be markedly improved.

Education for Health and Family
Counselling Services

This last component is made up of two facts which are closely interrelated but which should be discussed separately. The major diseases which strike our families are the chronic diseases, the etiology of which in many instances is presently unknown or appears to be associated with multiple factors. Since there are no specific measures of prevention or cure in most instances, personal responsibility for health based on adequate knowledge becomes the most important key to stem the tide of death and disability.

Education for health is then of major importance and constitutes half of the key to better health. The facets which must be emphasized are many, but five of the most important ones may be considered. The first has to do with education about personal hygiene, including nutrition, human sexuality, cleanliness, emotional development, dental care, and prevention of the common acute diseases. The second educational area concerns the care of the chronically ill patient in the home, as well as elements of first aid. There are many people in their own homes who are bedridden, who must have special diets, and who are on medications many of which have side effects. One of the family members should be well-informed in this area. A third and rather important consideration has to do with information about the health care delivery system and how to enter it, where to go and how to cope with various kinds of provider organizations. The competing non-systems of health care in this country are so fragmented that *all of us* are often confused as to the entry point. No educational effort would be complete without information about environmental sanitation and how best to maintain a high level of environmental health within and outside the home. Lastly, all families should have some knowledge about their health entitlements or rights. What are the responsibilities of the slum landlord to the tenants? To whom is a Headstart Program available? What about permission for operative procedures or experimentation? Families, especially the disadvantaged, are too often victimized by the health systems they use.

Family counselling is the other half of the key to better health. The complexities of our technologically advanced society place families at serious disadvantages which jeopardize their integrity and may cause untold damage. The counselling services which are being envisioned here would be concerned with all aspects of family life: information about finances, lending of money and credit rating, how best to find employment, rental and ownership of housing, career opportunities for the young and retirement arrangements for the elderly, the protection of the young who come in contact with the law, runaway adolescents, what to do in case of rape, behavioral problems of children, drug abuse, and thousands of other problems which daily threaten the health of the family. Family counselling is generally totally unavailable to those families most in need of such informational and support services.

As one reviews the concept which has been put forth, it should be emphasized that what is being proposed here is the "incorporation of all the elements involved into a comprehensive program of social and economic development reaching from the central government into local agencies employing a holistic approach to the problem of development of human resources, as well as, general social and economic development."[9] This concept has been expressed even more fundamentally by the Chairman of the President's Commission on Population Growth and the American Future:[10]

The chief purpose of an industrial society is industrial production. The chief purpose of the new society—a humanistic society—will be human growth, the creating of conditions which provide genuine opportunity for each member to develop his full human potential. Instead of having two sets of values in conflict, with the humanistic value subordinated to the materialistic ones, we need to turn the tables; we need to make the humanistic values dominant and operative at the same time preserving the benefits and successes that industrialism has brought us.

Notes

1. W. McDermott, in E. Kilbourne and W. Smillie (eds.), *Human Ecology and Public Health*, 4th ed. (New York: The Macmillan Co., 1969), pp. 21-22.

2. J. Wyon and J. Gordon, *The Khanna Study* (Cambridge: Harvard University Press, 1971), p. 256.

3. Final Report of the Committee on the Costs of Medical Care, *Medical Care for the American People* (Chicago: University of Chicago Press, 1932).

4. P. Cornely, "The Hidden Enemies of Health and the American Public Health Association," *American Journal of Public Health*, 61: 7-17, January 1971.

144

5. Conservation Foundation Letter, "The Environment of the Poor: Who Gives a Damn?," July 1973.

6. Richard M. Nixon, "The State of the Union—Address by the President of the United States," *Congressional Record*, 118: H-146-H-160, January 20, 1972.

7. H. Leavall and E. Clark, *Preventive Medicine for the Doctor in the Community* (New York: McGraw-Hill Book Co., Inc., 1958).

8. S. Proger, "The Education of Different Types of Physicians for Different Types of Health Care," *Pharos*, 35: 53-66, 1972.

9. P. Hauser, "On Non-Family Planning Methods of Population Control," *Proceedings of the International Conference on Family Planning, Dacca, Pakistan*, January 1969, p. 65.

10. John D. Rockefeller, III, *The Second American Revolution* (New York: Harper & Row, 1973), p. 38.

8

Population Policymaking: The Abortion Issue

Stephen J. Williams*

In attempting to understand the issues involved in population policymaking, the topic of abortion cannot be avoided. Women have sought abortions in many societies throughout history, often regardless of social taboos or legal constraints that have been raised as barriers in their paths. This chapter will examine considerations related to abortion that must be included in any approach to population policymaking.

Attitudes and practices toward abortion have rapidly changed not only in the United States, but throughout the world, in recent years. Yet, abortion as a method of fertility control has a history that goes back thousands of years.

This chapter will begin with the role of abortion in primitive and pre-industrial societies. The focus will then be turned toward more recent experiences with abortion in selected countries in modern times. With cross-cultural and temporal perspectives, the development of abortion policymaking at the state level in the United States will be traced to the January 1973 United States Supreme Court decision on abortion. The chapter will conclude with a discussion of the Court's far-reaching decision and its implications for population policymaking.

Abortion in Cross-cultural Perspective

Induced abortion has been used to limit population by many societies throughout the history of man. Tietze and Lewit have written:

The practice of abortion goes back to human traditions far older than the earliest written history. Abortion is still the most widespread, and the most clandestine, method of fertility control in the modern world.[1]

C.S. Ford has noted[2] that cross-cultural studies of abortion indicated that the practice is almost universally known; that in almost every society abortion has been practiced at some time. But the collection of data on abortion practices is quite difficult, since the practice was accepted only with some degree of

*Candidate for the Ph.D. in Population Sciences and Health Services Administration, Harvard University. Mr. Williams's research was supported by a grant (HS 00003-06) from the Health Services and Mental Health Administration to the Department of Health Services Administration, Harvard University School of Public Health.

ostracism.[3] It is known, however, that many societies established taboos to regulate abortion practices, often to avoid children outside of marriage.[4,5,6] Whether or not preindustrial societies induced abortion for the explicit purpose of limiting the size of their population or family size is a far more complex question.[7,8,9]

In recent years abortion has been practiced by many societies, and the focus of the discussion will now be directed toward international abortion practices in the twentieth century.

Abortion in International Perspective

Many writers have reviewed the use of abortion in modern times[10-14] so that the focus of this discussion will be on those countries with extensive experience in providing legal abortion services. Cross-cultural transfer of experiences is limited by differences between nations, both as to the extent to which abortion has been used and the response to the practice. But it is interesting to compare changes in United States laws to those of other nations. Abortion law reform in the United Kingdom has been extensively discussed.[15] Abortion was rarely considered in a criminal context before 1803, when the practice became punishable as a felony during the entire period of gestation. Before 1803, abortion in early pregnancy was not considered a crime, and after 1803 abortion in early pregnancy was still considered a less serious crime than abortion performed in late pregnancy. The Offenses Against the Person Act of 1861 established a maximum sentence of life in prison for the performance of an abortion without regard for the length of gestation of pregnancy when the abortion was performed. The act also held that the women involved, as well as the abortionist, was liable for prosecution.

Not until 1938, after the rape of a fourteen-year old, was there a substantial change in British law. The girl was aborted by an obstetrician, Aleck Bourne, who was subsequently prosecuted on the criminal offense of abortion. The judge in the Bourne case ruled that abortion was acceptable to preserve the life of the pregnant woman and liberalized British law by establishing health grounds for performing an abortion.[16] The judgment in the Bourne case was upheld in a subsequent case in 1948 in which two physicians accused of violating the abortion statutes were acquitted. In this case the judge "pointed out that it was not for the jury to attempt to determine whether the doctors were in fact correct in their diagnosis, merely whether they acted in good faith."[17]

The number of therapeutic abortions performed in Great Britain remained somewhat low, but steadily increased through the 1960s, reaching a rate of about 0.4 abortions per 1,000 population by 1966.[18] The estimated number of abortions performed in National Health Service hospitals and private offices before the revision of British law in 1967 ranged from slightly over 14,000 in 1961 to over 20,000 in 1966.[19]

The Abortion Act was passed by Parliament in 1967 and came into effect in April of 1968. The following grounds for legal abortion were specified in the Act:[20]

1. An abortion must be performed by a registered medical practitioner;
2. The abortion must be performed in a National Health Service Hospital or in a place specifically approved for such surgery, except in an emergency;
3. Two physicians must certify the necessity for the abortion on one or more of the following grounds:
   a) Continuing the pregnancy would involve a greater risk to the woman's life than would be involved in an abortion procedure;
   b) The continuance of the pregnancy would involve risk or injury to the physical or mental health of the women that exceeds the risk of the abortion;
   c) The continuance of the pregnancy would involve risks of injury to the physical or mental health of existing children that exceed the risk of the abortion;
   d) There is substantial risk of fetal abnormality, either physical or mental;
   e) To save the life of the pregnant women; or
   f) To prevent grave and permanent injury to the physical or mental health of the woman.

The Act required notification of the performance of the abortion for purposes of statistical recording and allowed the physician to take into account, in determining the appropriate indication, the pregnant women's present and reasonably foreseeable environment.

During 1969, the first full year of operation of the new law, nearly 55,000 legal abortions were performed in approved facilities of which slightly less than half were performed on single women; slightly less than half of the total number of abortions were performed on women with no previous live or stillborn children. Of the nearly 55,000 abortions, about 35,000 were performed under thirteen weeks gestation of pregnancy.[21] In England and Wales, for which these statistics were reported, the increase in the number of legal abortions was on the order of 30,000 abortions a year over the estimated number performed the year before the law was changed. The Act has been received in the United Kingdom with mixed reactions, and abortion in Great Britain, as in many other societies, has not met with complete acceptance.

While reform in Great Britain occurred somewhat earlier than in the United States, the national legislative approach in England and Wales provided a less complex avenue for debate than the consideration of abortion policy by the individual states in the United States, at least until the U.S. Supreme Court ruled on abortion.

Many other nations have faced the abortion issue. Japan, in particular, has received much attention from reform-minded individuals in the United States as an example of the use of abortion in population policymaking.

Japan substantially liberalized her abortion laws in 1948 with the passage of the Eugenic Protection Law. The number of reported legal abortions in Japan in the following year was 246,104, and by 1952 the number had reached 805,524.[22] The reported number of abortions exceeded 1,100,000 in 1955, but began to decline after 1955 reaching 748,000 by 1967.[23] The reason for the substantial increases in the number of abortions performed after the Law came into effect has been suggested as family economy, which is the aggregation on a national level of individual household economic decisions relating to family size.[24]

Abortion has been legally provided elsewhere in Asia, such as in Singapore which enacted legislation similar to the British Abortion Act of 1967, although approval from a Termination of Pregnancy Authorization Board is required before the abortion is performed for any indication except to preserve the life or health of the pregnant women.[25]

Many countries in Europe, especially those in Scandinavia, have had wide experience with providing abortion services. Eastern European countries have provided abortion services for many years.[26]

While a complete review of abortion laws in each country is beyond the scope of this book, these laws can be classified by their restrictiveness. Roemer has categorized the world wide abortion legislation as follows:[27]

1. Abortion at the insistence of the women—this category now would include the United States, Bulgaria, and some other Eastern European countries;
2. Abortion on social grounds—Finland, Denmark, and possibly Sweden fall into this category of relatively non-restrictive abortion laws;
3. Abortion on Sociomedical grounds—England and Wales, discussed previously, as well as Singapore, the state of South Australia, the German Democratic Republic, and India provide abortion for sociomedical reasons;
4. Abortion on medical grounds—this somewhat restrictive category includes the abortion laws of Canada and Peru.
5. Abortion only to save the life of the woman—this restrictive category has diminished in importance and in number of countries included as abortion laws have been revised throughout the world.

Worldwide experience with abortion is neither new nor limited to only a few countries. Abortion has been and continues to be provided in many countries, often on a highly non-restrictive basis. The United States, with the advent of the U.S. Supreme Court decision on abortion in 1973, joined a large and growing number of nations which have accepted the necessity for providing legal abortion services. The reform of abortion laws was often motivated by a concern for the effects on maternal health of illegal abortions; rarely was a concern for controlling the size of a nation's population the sole motivation for reform.

Not all nations, however, accepted the necessity or desirability of providing legal abortion services. Concern for the practice of abortion has been expressed in Latin America,[28] for example, and has led to efforts aimed at controlling abortion in Chile.[29] Yet even in the Soviet Union, which has strongly opposed the Malthusian approach to population pressures, abortion has been made available and incorporated into a national population policy.[30]

Throughout the world, abortion has been an important concern which was frequently dealt with by demographers, public health officials, and the medical community. Increasingly, it is of considerable concern to officials at the highest levels of government. As a result, many nations now have formulated official policy positions on abortion and have acted to implement such policies, ranging from providing abortion services to all who request them, as in Bulgaria, to working to reduce the number of abortions, as in Chile.

There was clearly considerable precedent throughout the world for policy-makers in the United States to consider in formulating, at the state level, an appropriate response to cries for reform. Clearly, also, abortion legislation must be viewed as a component of a dynamic, not static, population policy that can respond to changing national goals and needs. Japan, Hungary, and other nations have changed their abortion policies in response to changing national require-ments, and abortion policy has been used to implement population policies that consider many of the factors discussed elsewhere in this book.

The wide experience with abortion throughout the world and throughout history provides a perspective from which the focus of attention can now be directed at abortion policymaking in the United States.

The Evolution of Abortion Policymaking in the United States

The evolution of United States abortion laws can be divided into two time periods. The initial stages of development of abortion laws occurred between the early years of the nineteenth century and the middle 1960s. Widespread reform and increasingly non-restrictive legislation characterized the years from the middle 1960s through the early 1970s. While the discussion will be primarily directed toward the reform of recent years, a review of the historical precedents is also useful.

Abortion legislation in the United States was not passed until the first third of the nineteenth century.[31] Until then abortion was not a matter of legislation, although modern medical techniques were not available, and any attempt to terminate a pregnancy certainly must have been a dangerous and perhaps even life-threatening experience. Abortion has been practiced for thousands of years and some abortions most certainly were performed in the United States during the eighteenth and early nineteenth century, although the expansion of a young country into new territories fostered a pronatilist attitude. The belief that abortion legislation was needed to regulate or restrict the practice also indicates that abortions were performed, although the extent of the practice is speculative.

Abortion legislation was originally passed by various states in response to the prospects of women dying as a result of primitive surgical procedures in the years before asepsis. Perhaps other considerations also played a role in motivating the state legislatures to act. To some extent a pronatilist attitude may have been a factor. At the least, pressures of population were unknown in the American states.

The early abortion laws have been described as restrictive[32] compared to the laws that resulted from the abortion reform of more recent years. Thirty-one states are included in the more restrictive category based on laws that were in effect in 1971 (Table 8-1). Two additional states can be placed into this category. They are Massachusetts where the original legislation was passed in 1845 and modified by a court ruling in 1944, and Pennsylvania in which an abortion law was passed in 1860. However, both of these laws are vague and poorly defined. The Massachusetts law, for example, allows abortion to preserve the pregnant woman's life or health provided that the physician's judgment conforms to the average judgment of the other physicians in the area in which he

Table 8-1
Date of Enactment for Selected State Abortion Laws

State	Enactment Date	State	Enactment Date
Arizona	1865	Nevada	1861
Connecticut	1860	New Hampshire	1848
Florida	1868	New Jersey	1849
Idaho	1863	North Dakota	1943
Illinois	1874	Ohio	1841
Indiana	1838	Oklahoma	1910
Iowa	1843	Puerto Rico	1913
Kentucky	1910	Rhode Island	1896
Louisiana	1914	South Dakota	1929
Maine	1840	Tennessee	1883
Michigan	1846	Texas	1859
Minnesota	1851	Utah	1876
Missouri	1835	Vermont	1867
Montana	1864	West Virginia	1848
Nebraska	1873	Wisconsin	1858
		Wyoming	1869

Source: E.A. Duffy, *The Effects of Changes in the State Abortion Laws* (Washington, D.C.: U.S. Department of Health, Education and Welfare, Government Printing Office, 1971), PHS Publication no. 2165.

practices. Since abortions have, for a number of years, been performed under this law, it might be interpreted as allowing abortions for any indication that the general consensus of physicians in a community believe justifies an abortion, including socioeconomic indications. The Pennsylvania law prohibits unlawful abortions, a term which was not defined. Interpreting such a law is obviously difficult, and in Pennsylvania, as in Massachusetts, abortions were performed for various indications under the vague statute.

The incidence of abortion in the United States during most of the nation's history is largely unknown. The number of illegal abortions that were performed annually has been estimated at from 200,000 to 1,200,000.[33] No uniform reporting system for legal induced abortion existed at the state or national levels for these years, so that even estimates of legal abortion incidences remain obscure. By the 1950s and 1960s some reliable statistics on abortion incidences were being published, but these reports continued to leave unanswered the immense question of how many illegal abortions were being performed.

Perhaps the most reliable statistics on abortion before the middle 1960s were collected by the New York City Department of Health which has a long tradition of aggressively collecting health statistics. From 1943 through 1967 (Table 8-2), the reported number of therapeutic abortions actually declined, with the exception of 1964, when an increase occurred associated with the 1963-1964 epidemic of rubella. Of course, these are reported legal abortions and do not include statistics for non-reporting, illegally induced abortions, and women travelling outside of the city to obtain an abortion. The indications for

Table 8-2
Number of Reported Therapeutic Abortions and Ratio per 1,000 Live Births: New York City, 1943-67

Period	Number Total	Annual Average	Ratio per 1,000 Live Births
1943-47	3,592	718	5.1
1949	668	668	4.3
1951-53	1,698	566	3.5
1954-56	1,096	365	2.2
1957-59	1,034	345	2.1
1960-62*	875	292	1.8
1964	579	579	3.5
1965-67*	964	321	2.1

*Not adjusted for underreporting. Corresponding adjusted figures are 1,029, 343, and 2.1 for 1960-62; and 1,407,469, and 3.1 for 1965-67.
Source: C.L. Erhardt, C. Tietze and F.G. Nelson, "United States: Therapeutic Abortion in New York City," *Studies in Family Planning* 51 (1970).

performing most of these abortions were primarily medical, including such diseases as rubella, cardiovascular disease, and diabetes, and mental disorders which were not specifically defined.[34]

Hall[35] surveyed sixty-five major hospitals in the United States. The results indicated that abortions were more frequently performed for psychiatric indications on private patients than on ward patients, which might be an indication that abortion services were not equally accessible to all women. Among the hospitals participating, the number of abortions performed was relatively few, and this supports other estimates that about two abortions were performed for each 1,000 live births in the United States during the early and middle 1960s.[36]

From 1967 through 1972 a number of states revised their abortion laws or had laws that were declared unconstitutional by the courts. Before we discuss the development of abortion policymaking in selected individual states, an overview of the national situation until the U.S. Supreme Court decision is appropriate.

For many years, various legal and medical organizations have issued guidelines for the provision of abortion services. The American Law Institute Model Abortion Law was published in 1962[37] and subsequently adopted in various forms by Arkansas, California, Colorado, Delaware, Kansas, Maryland, New Mexico, North Carolina, South Carolina and Virginia. The model law states that a physician can perform an abortion under the following conditions:

1. Continuing the pregnancy would gravely impair the pregnant woman's physical or mental health;
2. The child would be born with grave mental or physical defects; or
3. The pregnancy resulted from rape, incest, or other felonious intercourse.

It should be apparent that there are significant difficulties in defining many of the terms in these and other abortion laws. How much evidence is sufficient to determine that a child would be born with grave mental or physical defects? What constitutes grave impairment of the woman's physical or mental health? What constitutes evidence that a rape actually was committed? Of course, laws based on the American Law Institute Model Law and those based on other model laws are considerably more precise than the 1860 Pennsylvania law which prohibited unlawful abortions. Yet the problems of definitions and of clearly specifying the intent of abortion laws remained.

In May 1968 the American College of Obstetricians and Gynecologists issued guidelines for abortion policy. These recommendations allowed abortion when the pregnancy was the result of felonious intercourse or when there was risk that the continuance of the pregnancy would impair the physical or mental health of the woman.[38] Oregon adopted a law based on these guidelines.

Other medical and public interest organizations issued statements related to abortion such as that of the American Public Health Association,[39] which endorsed liberalization of state abortion laws. The guidelines of these organizations were designed in part to aid legislators in formulating state bills.

Not all state laws were modified as a result of legislative reform, however. Abortion statutes in Wisconsin, Texas, and the District of Columbia were ruled unconstitutional by federal district courts, and the Texas law was one of two challenges that resulted in the landmark U.S. Supreme Court ruling.

While abortion reform progressed at the state level, the Federal Government was certainly aware of abortion as a serious national concern. The Government, through the National Institute of Child Health and Human Development and the National Institute of Mental Health, sponsored a workshop on abortion as a public health and mental health problem.[40] A second workshop was held in December 1969, with the following objectives:

1. To review background information including research and relevant methodology;
2. To identify important research needed; and
3. To suggest avenues for approaching various research topics.[41]

The conference was concerned with complications of abortion, both physiological and psychological, the relationship between abortion and contraception, and socioeconomic consequences of induced abortion.[42]

In response to a need for collecting abortion statistics and monitoring the extent of abortion services in the United States, the National Center for Disease Control has established an abortion surveillance program[43] that periodically issues abortion surveillance reports.[44]

The flurry of activity related to abortion at various levels of government and through private channels was effective in liberalizing, or having declared invalid by the courts, the abortion laws of many states. By January 1, 1972, abortion services were widely available in Oregon, Alaska, Hawaii, New York, Washington, and the District of Columbia.[45] The status of the state abortion laws, Table 8-3, varied widely between the various states, however. The result was a wide disparity in the availability of local abortion services, which often had the effect of compelling women to seek abortions outside their state of residence. New York, probably more than any other state, was the destination of many women who sought to obtain an abortion when they were barred from doing so in their own state.

While national attention was increasingly directed at the abortion problem, and with the liberalization of abortion laws in various states through either legislative or judicial channels, national public opinion on abortion changed dramatically.

Blake[46] surveyed public opinion polls during the 1960s based on five Gallup polls taken between 1962 and 1969, and on the 1965 National Fertility

Table 8-3

Major Categories of Abortion Law United States—January 1, 1972

Major Categories of State Abortion Laws	States Having Similar Abortion Laws
I. Abortion allowed only when necessary to preserve the life of the pregnant woman	Arizona, Connecticut, Florida, Idaho, Illinois[1], Indiana, Iowa[2], Kentucky, Louisiana[3], Maine, Michigan, Minnesota, Missouri, Montana, Nebraska, Nevada, New Hampshire, North Dakota, Ohio, Oklahoma, Rhode Island, South Dakota, Tennessee, Utah, Vermont, West Virginia, Wyoming
II. Indications for legal abortion include threats to the pregnant woman's life and forcible rape	Mississippi
III. "Unlawful" or "unjustifiable" abortions are prohibited	Massachusetts[4], New Jersey[4], Pennsylvania
IV. Abortions allowed when continuation of the pregnancy threatens the woman's life or health	Alabama, District of Columbia
V. American Law Institute Model Abortion Law; "A licensed physician is justified in terminating a pregnancy if he believes that there is substantial risk that continuance of the pregnancy would gravely impair the physical or mental health of the mother or that the child would be born with grave physical or mental defect, or that the pregnancy resulted from rape, incest or other felonious intercourse"	Arkansas, California (does not include fetal deformity), Colorado, Delaware, Kansas, Maryland (does not include incest), New Mexico, North Carolina, South Carolina, Virginia
VI. Abortion law based on the May 1968 recommendations of the American College of Obstetricians and Gynecologists. Allows abortion when the pregnancy resulted from felonious intercourse, and when there is risk that continuance of the pregnancy would impair the physical or mental health of the mother. "In determining whether or not there is substantial risk (to the woman's physical or mental health), account may be taken of the mother's total environment, actual or reasonably foreseeable"	Oregon
VII. No legal restriction on reasons for which an abortion may be obtained prior to viability of the fetus	Alaska, Hawaii, New York, Washington
VIII. Legal restrictions on reasons for which an abortion may be obtained were invalidated by court decision	Georgia, Texas, Wisconsin[5]

1. A Federal District Court decision, Doe vs. Scott, 321 F. Supp. 1385 (N.D. Ill., Jan. 29, 1971), holding the Illinois abortion statute unconstitutional has been stayed pending appeal in the United States Supreme Court.

Table 8-3 (cont.)

2. In State vs. Dunklebarger, the Iowa statute which is couched in terms of saving the life ot the woman, has been interpreted to suggest that preservation of health is sufficient. 221 N.W. 592 (Iowa, 1928).

3. Although the Louisiana abortion statute does not contain an express exception to the "crime of abortion" the Louisiana Medical Practice Act authorizes the Medical Board to suspend or institute court proceedings to revoke a doctor's certificate to practice medicine in the state when the doctor has procured or aided or abetted in the procuring of an abortion "unless done for the relief of a woman whose life appears imperiled after due consultation with another licensed physician." La. Rev. Stat. Ann. 37:1261.

4. The statutory terms have been interpreted to permit abortion to save the woman's life or to prevent serious impairment of physical or mental health (Com. v. Wheeler, 53 N,E, 2d 4 (Mass. 1944) and as justified to preserve the mother's life (Gleitman v. Cosgrove, 227 A. 2d 689 (N.J. 1967).

5. The abortion law of several other states have been ruled unconstitutional by lower state trial courts; however, these decisions are binding only in the jurisdiction in which the decision was rendered.

Source: Center for Disease Control, *Abortion Surveillance Report, 1971*, December 1972.

Study.[47] Her analysis indicated that few Americans disapproved of induced abortion to save the life of the pregnant women. Fewer approved of abortion to avoid the birth of a deformed child, and, over time, from 1960 to 1970, possible deformity of the child became somewhat more acceptable as an indication for abortion. By the end of the 1960s, about 25 percent of those questioned disapproved of an abortion for possible child deformity, whereas only 13 percent disapproved of an abortion to save the life of the mother. About two-thirds of those responding to the question, according to Blake, disapproved of an abortion for reasons of economic hardship, a decline from surveys conducted earlier in the decade but still a substantial segment of the population expressing disapproval of abortion on these grounds. Abortion at the request of the pregnant woman met with still further opposition.

However, Blake found considerable variation in the extent of disapproval of abortion for various indications depending on the respondents' religion, age, sex, and socioeconomic status. Disapproval of abortion has declined most among the most highly educated, for example, between 1960 and 1970. She also found some surprising results such as increased disapproval of abortion among lower-class non-Catholics throughout the 1960s, increased disapproval among females as compared to males for abortion on economic indications and for abortion on request, and a higher than expected level of disapproval among young respondents. Acceptance of all indications for induced abortion increased during the decade among Catholics.

Rising public opinion in favor of increased liberalization of abortion laws in England[48] preceded the passage of the Abortion Act. Yet the effect of such opinion on those in Parliament was difficult to measure. Similarly, in the United States the effects of public opinion on abortion reform, either in the legislatures or in the courts, is difficult to determine. It is equally difficult to differentiate the effects of other influences. Most certainly, pressure from special interest organizations on both sides of the issues, as well as the personal beliefs of policymakers, were important factors. The rising tide of public opinion in support of abortion reform, based on the Blake analysis, was not all that overwhelming during the 1960s, and support for completely unrestricted access to abortion services by those responding represented only a minority.[49]

An analysis of attitudes toward abortion from the 1965 National Fertility Study[50] yielded the following conclusions:

1. Married women in the United States, according to the survey results in late 1965, overwhelmingly favored an abortion to save the life of the pregnant women, were evenly divided in the case of rape or fetal deformity, and were generally opposed to abortion for unmarried women, for women who simply do not want more children, and for women who cannot afford another child;
2. Older women were more tolerant of abortion than younger women;
3. Attitudes toward abortion vary widely, depending on the level of education of the woman questioned with more educated women generally favoring abortion more frequently than less educated women;
4. Non-white women were less favorable toward abortion than white women, even controlling for educational levels; many other factors appeared to be related to attitudes on abortion including size of place of residence, income, occupation, fertility, and attitudes toward contraception and sterilization.

In June 1972, Planned Parenthood/World Population commissioned a Gallup survey on attitudes toward abortion.[51] Of those asked if the decision to have an abortion should be made solely by the woman and her physician, sixty-four percent agreed that it should. This was an increase of seven percentage points compared to a similar survey in January of the same year and indicated a substantial shift in public opinion attitudes toward less restrictive abortion laws from surveys conducted during the 1960s. Furthermore, of those who disagreed that abortion should be a decision between the pregnant woman and her physician, very few found abortion unacceptable regardless of the indication. Clearly, substantial changes in public attitudes toward abortion occurred during the early 1970s, either paralleling or closely following the changes in abortion laws of a number of states.

Finally, before directing attention to the evolution of abortion policymaking in specific states, mention must be made of the Report of the President's Commission on Population Growth and the American Future.[52] The Commission dealt with numerous issues related to population in the United States, and the report included the following recommendations on abortion:

1. With the admonition that abortion not be considered a primary means of fertility control, the Commission recommended that state laws restricting

abortion be liberalized along the lines of the New York State statute, such abortions to be performed on request by duly licensed physicians under conditions of medical safety;
2. That federal, state, and local governments make funds available to support abortion services in states with liberalized statutes;
3. That abortion be specifically included in comprehensive health insurance benefits, both public and private.[53]

The Commission's report represented one of the most powerful statements issued by a United States Government source in support of virtually unrestricted access to abortion services and preceded by less than one year the Supreme Court's ruling.

Clearly, the movement toward reform of abortion laws at the state level, national public opinion, and governmental concern over abortion at the Federal level gained considerable momentum during the first two years of the 1970s. But reform efforts slowly met with success in a number of states even before the groundswell that marked the 1970s. The evolution of abortion policymaking within specific states is discussed next, after which attention is directed toward the Supreme Court's decision and its implications for abortion policymaking by the individual states.

The Evolution of Abortion Laws
in Selected States

The first significant liberalization of a state abortion law occurred in Colorado in 1967. The political evolution of the new law's enactment was described by Droegemueller et al.:[54]

In Colorado, the 1861 territorial law remained unchanged until April 25, 1967, when Colorado became the first state in the Union to enact a modernized abortion law. The new law was presented to the Colorado Legislature only once, and that was in the 1967 session. Two years before, a law which would permit welfare workers to give birth control information to relief clients at their own request had been voted down after debates and demonstrations packed with passion. There was adequate debate on the abortion bill, and except for assertions that Colorado would become the abortion Mecca of the county, little emotion was evoked in the arguments . . . Organized medicine took no part in the action.

Individual legislators of both parties, interested lay groups, and individual physicians worked for liberalizing the law . . . there was little organized opposition by any church group to the abortion law . . . The bill passed the House of Representatives, 44 for, 20 against, one representative being absent. The law requires that the patient herself initiate the request for abortion. No hospital and no physician is required to perform or be a party to any abortion.

The Colorado law allowed abortion under the following conditions:

1. The abortion must be performed in an accredited hospital;
2. Three physicians in each hospital constitute an abortion approval board, and all must agree that the abortion is necessary.
3. The abortion must be required because continuance of the pregnancy would result in the death or serious physical or mental impairment of the pregnant woman, or would result in the birth of a child with grave physical deformities or mental retardation.[55]

The results of the first year of the Colorado law indicated that most abortions were performed in Denver, that interpretation of appropriate psychiatric indications varied from facility to facility, and that abortions were probably equally available to all women in the state without regard to socioeconomic status. Of the 407 abortions that were performed during the first year, nearly seventy-five percent were performed for psychiatric indications.[56]

Public opinion before and after the change in the Colorado law showed a significant liberalization in voter attitudes. The first survey was taken in September 1966, and the second in September 1968. The principal findings of the surveys were:

1. Respondents were more willing to discuss abortion with almost anyone in the second survey;
2. Only 25 percent in the second survey said they would actively oppose an organization working to make abortions easier to obtain through medical channels, as compared to 31 percent in the first survey; and
3. The percentage opposing abortions declined over time for each of the indications that were specified in the two surveys.[57]

The initial response to the change in the Colorado law was slow. Most of the hospitals that initially began to provide services under the new law's guidelines were in Denver; elsewhere in the state abortions were difficult to obtain. However, this situation improved with time. The Colorado Medical Society put out guidelines interpreting the law and stressing that no physician in the state is required to perform abortions and that restraint should be exercised in accepting out-of-state patients.[58]

North Carolina and California both adopted abortion statutes during 1967 that were similar to the Colorado law, although the California law excludes fetal deformity as an indication.

The efforts to change the California law began in 1961 and reached fruition in June, 1967. The statute became effective on November 8, 1967, and in addition to the indications and guidelines contained in the Colorado law, required that a licensed physician perform the abortion in a hospital accredited by the Joint Commission on Accreditation of Hospitals after approval by a committee of the hospital's physicians. There was no residency requirement for obtaining abortions.[59]

The abortion statute of California was further liberalized by a ruling of the California Supreme Court in 1969 which proclaimed a woman's right to terminate an unwanted pregnancy.[60]

Although the effects of changes in these laws are often difficult to measure, decreases in both septic abortions and maternal mortality have been noted in California[61] and in New York City[62] after changes in these states' laws. Georgia was one of the earliest states in the nation to liberalize its abortion law. The evolution of this law has been described by Jain and Gooch[63] in a monograph that presents a detailed account of the political events leading to the legislative action on a reform abortion statute. The statute included the following provisions:

1. One of the following indications for abortion is required—a) the continuation of the pregnancy would endanger the life of the pregnant woman or would seriously and permanently injure her health; b) the fetus would very likely be born with a grave, permanent, and irremediable medical or physical defect; or c) the pregnancy resulted from rape.
2. The woman must certify that she is a resident of the State of Georgia;
3. The physician must also concur that the woman is a resident of Georgia;
4. Two additional physicans must agree that an abortion is necessary;
5. The abortion must be performed in a hospital that is licensed by the State and accredited by the Joint Commission on the Accreditation of Hospitals.

As a result of their review of the political processes that led to the passage of the reform Georgia abortion statute, Jain and Gooch[64] made the following observations:

1. A major factor in passage of the statute was the character of its legislative sponsors and the strategic positions they held;
2. While several of the most vocal opponents to the proposed legislation were Roman Catholics, there is only a small Catholic population in Georgia, and the church took no official position on the bill;
3. A major focus of those drafting the bill was to protect the State's physicians who might recommend an abortion. Thus, the legislators were, in large part, able to avoid the more emotional issues that were often the subject of bitter debate in other state legislatures;
4. In both houses of the legislature, the proponents of the bill arranged to have the votes taken when all favorable legislators were present.

The Georgia reform bill, then, became law through a well ordered series of legislative events without bitter and divisive debate within the State. The law, however, was far from the sweeping reform of such a state as New York. In fact, from April 1968 through June 1970, only 461 legal therapeutic abortions were performed in hospitals in Georgia, and most of these were performed in Atlanta.[65] Yet, a movement toward reform of an 1876 abortion law was successful in achieving substantial liberalization without bitter opposition and through the usual legislative channels.

Perhaps no other state has received as much attention as the result of its attempts at abortion reform than New York. Governor Nelson Rockefeller had appointed a commission to study the abortion statutes of that State. Alan Guttmacher, a member of that Commission and leading proponent of abortion reform for many years, has described the workings of the Commission:[66]

In December, 1968, I was appointed to Governor Rockefeller's 11-member Commission which had been formed to examine the abortion statute of New York State and to make recommendations for change. When the Governor convened the commission, he said, "I am not asking whether New York's abortion law should be changed, I am asking how it should be changed." The Commission was made up of a minister, a priest, a rabbi, three professors of law, three physicians, a poetess, and the president of a large Black woman's organization. There were four Catholics, four Protestants, and three Jews. The commission met every two weeks for more than three months. It was apparent that three members wanted no change in the old law despite the Governor's charge, two wished abortion removed entirely from the criminal code, and six advocated the enactment of the A.L.I. model with further liberalization: the majority report—approved 8 to 3—added legal abortion on request for any mother of four children. My proposal of adding a clause to permit abortion on request for any woman 40 years or older was voted down—this was April, 1969.

Guttmacher's narrative of the institution of New York's revised abortion statute continued:[67]

On April 10, 1970, the New York State Legislature amended the State Penal Code, permitting licensed physicians to provide abortion services for any consenting woman less than 24 weeks pregnant. The law specifies no restrictions on place of residence, age, marital status, or consent of spouse, if married, and it makes no restrictions as to the type of facility where abortions might be performed. After 142 years of one of the most restrictive abortion statutes—allowing abortions only when necessary to preserve the life of the mother—New York suddenly had the most liberal abortion law in the world.

The New York State Legislature in 1969 had flatly rejected the bill produced by the Governor's Commission—basically the A.L.I. model plus permissible abortion on request for any woman with four or more children. Those of us in favor of reform hoped in 1970 that we could somehow put through a modified A.L.I. bill. We knew of the "radical" bill sponsored by Constance Cook, an upstate legislator, but had no hope for its passage. Much to everyone's surprise, however, it passed the House by a modest majority. When it came before the Senate there was a tie vote and an expectation that the speaker would break the tie with his negative vote since he was a strong opponent of abortion reform. However, a senator from an upstate Catholic county broke the tie by changing his negative vote to an affirmative one. The bill was to become law July 1, less than 3 months later.

The medical community was in a state of shock, not from opposition, but from total surprise. There were dire prophecies that all existing medical facilities would be dangerously overtaxed by a nationwide demand for abortion. But the New York City Department of Health began to ready the facilities of the 15 municipal hospitals, and the mayor appropriated an extra three million dollars to fund the new abortion service. In recognition of the financial potential, several proprietary hospitals were converted into abortoria. The voluntary hospitals agreed to do their part and some arranged to perform abortions on both an inpatient and an outpatient basis. Some physicians began to prepare their private offices for abortions and others advocated free-standing clinics with built-in safety factors such as blood available for transfusion, cardiac arrest equipment, quick access to a back-up hospital, counselling before and after the operation, and performance of abortion only by specialists in obstetrics and gynecology.

When July 1 arrived, the City Board of Health had not yet established its own standards for abortion services and did not do so until September 17. On that day the New York City Board of Health issued regulations outlawing private office abortions within New York City. They agreed that abortions could be performed in accredited hospitals and their outpatient departments. Also permitted were abortions in licensed free-standing abortion clinics which could meet certain enunciated standards regarding factors such as the size of the operating room, the availability of resuscitating equipment, and the availability of blood; furthermore, abortion of a pregnancy beyond 12 weeks could not be performed in such a free-standing clinic.

Remarkably, the response to the change in the New York abortion statute was effective and swift in meeting the resulting requests for services. The State's new abortion law did not impose any residency requirements, nor did it specify the type of facility in which the procedures could be performed. However, the New York City Board of Health enacted Article 42 of the New York City Health Codes which specified certain restrictions on who could perform abortions and on the facilities in which the abortions were provided. (Figure 8-1.) These health codes were to be models for other jurisdictions in the country and were designed in part to eliminate the use of private physician's offices for legal abortion services while encouraging the use of out-patient facilities to ensure that sufficient resources would be available to respond to the demand for services.[68]

During the first year after enactment of the law, approximately 164,300 legal abortions were performed in New York City of which about forty percent were performed on residents of the city, and twenty-seven percent of these were financed through Medicaid.[69]

The state of Washington liberalized its abortion law through a referendum on November 3, 1970. Previous to the referendum, an abortion reform bill was introduced in the legislature in 1969. The bill was not reported out of committee but was reintroduced in 1970. A referendum provision was added to the bill before it was approved.

The abortion referendum question was voted upon by more people than any other issue on the ballot,[70] and the abortion reform bill was approved by 56.5 percent of the voters. The bill leaves the abortion decision up to the woman and

INTRODUCTORY NOTES

Article 42 was enacted by resolution of the Board of Health adopted on _____ 1970 to provide public health standards of care in the performance of abortions, with proper regard for the health, safety and well-being of the patient. This article requires that abortions be performed only by physicians operating in a place or facility where there is qualified supervision in obstetrics or surgery, and where equipment, staff and facilities are provided to handle hemorrhage, shock, cardiac arrest and other emergencies, as well as to apply aseptic procedures. The article further protects the health of the patient by providing that abortions performed on women pregnant 12 weeks or less may be performed on an ambulatory basis: that pregnancies of longer duration or those involving medical, surgical, gynecological, or psychiatric conditions, or complications occurring during or after the abortion, require inpatient facilities. The article also requires that family planning services should be made available to patients.

42.03 Requirements and standards
    An abortion shall be performed in an abortion service operated in accordance with the provisions of this article and related provisions of this Code.

42.13 Transportation facilities for affiliated service
    An affiliated abortion service shall have immediately available organized transportation facilities capable of insuring that a patient requiring emergency care at the hospital with which such service is affiliated will be transported to such hospital within the total transport time of ten minutes.

42.21 Operating facilities
    (a) An unaffiliated abortion service or an abortion service located in a hospital shall have available on its premises a standard operating room capable of accommodating abdominal as well as vaginal surgical procedures. An affiliated abortion service shall include in its affiliation agreement provision for the use of a standard operating room in the treatment of its patients requiring care on an inpatient basis.
    (b) For abortions specified in Section 42.33 (c), existing outpatient operating facilities may be utilized or new outpatient operating facilities created, if the policies established by the physician in charge of the abortion service and the patient load warrant. If it is found necessary to add to existing outpatient operating facilities, a standard sized treatment room may be converted to an operating facility.
    (c) All rooms in which abortions are performed shall be adequately equipped, supplied and staffed and shall include the following in addition to the instruments and equipment needed for the performance of abortions:
        (1) Anesthesia equipment and such other equipment as is necessary to treat patients for hemorrhage, shock, cardiac arrest, and other emergencies.
        (2) In an unaffiliated abortion service or an abortion service located in a hospital, an adequate supply of drugs, compatible whole blood, blood fractions, blood concentrates, plasma expanders, and parenteral fluids immediately available at all times with appropriate refrigeration equipment therefor; in an affiliated abortion service an adequate supply of drugs, plasma expanders and parenteral fluids shall be available at all times with appropriate refrigeration equipment therefor:
        (3) Dressing room and scrub-up facilities which are suitably located;
        (4) A utility room with facilities for sterilization of bedpan and enema equipment;
        (5) A utility room with facilities for sterlization of supplies, except in an abortion service which receives sterile supplies from a central supply service.
    (d) The operating facilities and equipment shall be constructed and maintained so as to be free from sanitary hazards and safety hazards likely to cause a fire or explosion.

42.29 Staff; social service
    An abortion service shall have a social service unit available to serve its patients adequately.

Figure 8-1. Health Codes on Abortion of the City of New York (Excerpts)

her physician, subject to the restrictions that the abortion, except in an emergency, be performed in an approved facility to women who are residents of Washington and who are not more than seventeen weeks pregnant. The woman must have the consent of her husband if she is married, and of her parents if she is under 18 years of age.[71]

During the first full year of abortion services under the reform law, over 12,000 abortions were performed in Washington, of which 33 percent were under age nineteen and the majority were not currently married. Of those women obtaining abortions, 70 percent were not using contraception.[72]

Not all of the numerous other court cases, legislative bills, and referenda provided support for liberalization of the state abortion laws, however. A number of states conducted referenda on abortion issues during the fall 1972 elections, only a few months before the United States Supreme Court was to issue its ruling on two challenges to state abortion laws.

A proposal to permit abortion at the request of the pregnant woman, provided the pregnancy was less than twenty weeks gestation and that the procedure was performed in a licensed facility by a licensed physician, was defeated in Michigan. Of those voting on the proposal, 61 percent opposed and 39 percent approved of the proposal. However, the Michigan Court of Appeals, on August 23, 1972, ruled the state's law unconstitutional in the first trimester of pregnancy. In North Dakota, a proposal to permit abortions in licensed hospitals for residents of the State was opposed by 77 percent of the voters.[73]

In Massachusetts, voters were asked to reply to the question, "Should the representative of this district be instructed to vote for the repeal of the abortion law of the Commonwealth?" Of those voting on this question, fifty-six percent supported repeal of the law and forty-four percent voted no.[74] Interestingly, the Massachusetts law is vague, and under its provisions abortions have been performed for a number of years.[75]

These are not, of course, the only states in which legislative and judicial activity related to abortion was occurring during the sixties and early seventies. Hundreds, perhaps thousands, of court cases and proposed bills challenged restrictive laws or challenged provisions of reform laws after they were passed by various legislatures. Even to begin to review all of these bills and court cases would be a monumental task beyond the scope of this book. However, the review of selected states provides some idea of the approaches that were chosen by the proponents of abortion reform.

The culmination of the reform effort, the years of debate and litigation, was the 1973 decision on abortion by the United States Supreme Court. The focus of the discussion is next directed toward this decision.

The U.S. Supreme Court Decision

On January 22, 1973, the United States Supreme Court issued a landmark decision on the appeals of challenges to the Texas and Georgia state abortion statutes. The Court, in an opinion delivered by Mr. Justice Blackmun, declared the abortion statutes of these two states to be unconstitutional and, by so doing, assured the legal right of women throughout the country to obtain abortions with very few restrictions. This section reviews the Court's decision and some of its implications.

The Court found that the right to privacy, assured in the Fourteenth Amendment to the Constitution, is violated by abortion statutes such as those in Texas and Georgia. The opinion of the Court read in part as follows:

This right of privacy, whether it be founded in the Fourteenth Amendment's concept of personal liberty and restrictions upon state action, as we feel it is, or, as the District Court determined, in the Ninth Amendment's reservation of rights to the people, is broad enough to encompass a woman's decision whether or not to terminate her pregnancy. The detriment that the State would impose upon the pregnant woman by denying this choice altogether is apparent. Specific and direct harm medically diagnosable even in early pregnancy may be involved. Maternity, or additional offspring, may force upon the woman a distressful life and future. Psychological harm may be imminent. Mental and physical health may be taxed by child care. There is also the distress, for all concerned, associated with the unwanted child, and there is the problem of bringing a child into a family already unable, psychologically and otherwise, to care for it.[76]

These words were central to the Court's judgment. However, the Court did not accept these arguments as assuring the right of a woman to terminate a pregnancy at any time, in any way, or for any reason. The Court further found that:

... the Court's decisions recognizing a right of privacy also acknowledge that some state regulation in areas protected by that right is appropriate ... a state may properly assert important interests in safeguarding health, in maintaining medical standards, and in protecting potential life. At some point in pregnancy, these respective interests become sufficiently compelling to sustain regulation of the factors that govern the abortion decision. The privacy right involved, therefore, cannot be said to be absolute. In fact, it is not clear to us that the claim ... that one has an unlimited right to do with one's body as one pleases bears a close relationship to the right of privacy previously articulated in the Court's decisions. The Court has refused to recognize an unlimited right of this kind in the past.[77]

Thus, the Court raised the question as to when the State's interest in the health of the pregnant woman, and presumably its authority to regulate and restrict abortion services, begins. In the discussion of this issue, the decision continued:

With respect to the State's importance and legitimate interest in the health of the mother, the compelling point, in the light of present medical knowledge, is at approximately the end of the first trimester. This is so because of the now established medical fact ... that until the end of the first trimester mortality in abortion is less than mortality in normal childbirth. It follows that, from and after this point, a State may regulate the abortion procedure to the extent that the regulation reasonably relates to the preservation and protection of maternal health. Examples of permissible state regulation in this area are requirements as to the qualifications of the person who is to perform the abortion; as to the licensure of that person, as to the facility in which the procedure is to be performed, that is, whether it must be a hospital or may be a clinic or some other place of less-than-hospital status; as to the licensing of the facility; and the like.

This means, on the other hand, that, for the period of pregnancy prior to this "compelling" point, the attending physician, in consultation with his patient, is free to determine, without regulation by the State, that in his medical judgement the patient's pregnancy should be terminated. If that decision is reached, the judgement may be effectuated by an abortion free of interference by the State.

With respect to the State's important and legitimate interest in potential life, the "compelling" point is at viability. This is so because the fetus then presumably has the capability of meaningful life outside the mother's womb. State regulation protective of fetal life after viability thus has both logical and biological justifications. If the State is interested in protecting fetal life after viability, it may go so far as to proscribe abortion during that period except when it is necessary to preserve the life or health of the mother.[78]

The Court's decision, then, established the following guidelines for providing abortion services as pertain to the State's rights to regulate or prohibit such services:

1. Until approximately the end of the first trimester, the abortion decision and its effectuation must be left to the medical judgement of the pregnant woman's attending physician;
2. After the first trimester, the State may regulate abortion services only in such ways that are reasonably related to maternal health;
3. For the stage of pregnancy subsequent to viability, the State may regulate or even proscribe abortion except where necessary for the preservation of the life or health of the pregnant woman.

And so, in a decision that must rank as one of the most important in the history of the nation, the United States Supreme Court declared that the states cannot prohibit abortion, with certain restrictions. The implications of this decision for state policymakers is the subject of the remainder of this chapter.

Initially a differentiation must be established between the right of a woman to obtain an abortion, as implied in the Court's decision, and the availability of abortion services. The Court did not directly deal with the latter issue.

Providing abortion services on a national scale requires a level of medical services which does not tax the medical resources of this nation.[79] These services could be provided directly by public agencies, perhaps in concert with the provision of family planning services. They are also, and have traditionally primarily been, provided independently of governmental authority by private agencies such as Planned Parenthood, and by physicians in private practice.

It remains for policymakers at the state and local levels to determine the extent to which public agencies will directly provide abortion services. Within the context of the Supreme Court decision, it would be entirely consistent with established public policy to provide abortion services as a component of comprehensive medical and family planning services; however, many local authorities may prefer to encourage the provision of abortion services through other channels for a variety of reasons. The extent to which governmental agencies are obliged to provide direct abortion services, to ensure the availability of abortion services through any channels that exist within a community, and to finance through public welfare authorities such services for any women who request, but are unable to afford, an abortion are among the numerous issues that must be clarified in light of the Court's decision. Indeed, litigation and legislative activity subsequent to the Court's decision may continue for some time.

For abortion services not directly provided by public agencies, the extent to which health departments can regulate abortion practice must be considered by policymakers. Health departments have, for a long time, been regulating the practice of medicine to varying degrees, depending on the locality and on state and local statutes. This regulation has often tended to be indirect, however, with the department operating under regulations and laws which more directly control medical practice.[80] The extent to which these regulations can be extended in view of the Court's decision is not yet entirely clear, although the authority of the states to regulate the practice of medicine for the protection of the citizens is assured by the U.S. Constitution. The Court's decision on abortion would indicate that any regulation of abortion services must not be designed to—and indeed must not in any way—prohibit the provision of such services.

Further clarification of the extent of acceptable regulation will require additional time, and the most useful guideline for state policymakers that can be provided is to be aware of changes in local regulation of abortion services. This regulation will certainly be more extensive beyond the first trimester of pregnancy, however.

The local health codes of the City of New York probably provide the most useful guidelines for the regulation of abortion services. These guidelines, presented earlier, prohibit abortions in physicians' offices and allow abortions in other facilities, with certain qualifications. The New York City codes seem to have functioned well.[81]

Finally, where direct regulation is not possible, policymakers should consider issuing recommendations or other guidelines which will promote abortion services that conform to accepted medical practice. These guidelines could include the specification of facility and manpower restrictions for abortion services, the encouragement of contraceptive services and all forms of counselling, and the provision of referral for women requiring other medical or social assistance. The creation of a cooperative environment between officials and the providers of services is the most useful approach to promoting guidelines. With a cooperative effort, the guidelines will ensure the best possible medical care for women obtaining abortions without compromising conformance with the Supreme Court decrees.

State and local policymakers have available to them, in working toward such guidelines, many resources including medical societies, educational institutions, financial institutions, and medical care facilities. The experiences of other jurisdictions and individuals in providing abortion services as reflected in the literature or through personal contact can also be helpful. All of these resources should be utilized.

Beyond the regulation of abortion services, numerous issues must be considered. Among the most important of these is the provision of family planning services including contraceptive assistance, sterilization, and other related services. General medical services, aid for infertility problems, health, child care, social welfare aid, and other services also should be provided. In fact, to promote the general welfare, abortion services should be provided in an atmosphere that considers the woman's other needs.

Contraception is especially important in connection with abortion services, since an important objective of public policy, achieved in part through the provision of contraceptive services, should be a reduction in the number of women requiring an abortion, and especially in the number who require more than one abortion.[82] This is especially important since the long term medical and psychological effects of induced abortion remain to be determined.[83]

Abortion services, then, should be integrated with other medical services. This can be achieved directly by providing abortions along with other services, or indirectly by making available in a community all services and allowing the woman to seek out herself those services which she requires. Both approaches, but especially the latter approach, benefit considerably from public education efforts.

Education about abortion can assume many forms and will not be dealt with in depth here. However, it is of considerable importance that women be actively encouraged to seek abortion early in pregnancy if they do not desire to continue the pregnancy. The Supreme Court has recognized the substantial increase in mortality and morbidity, as well as in cost, from abortions performed after twelve weeks gestation.[84] The increase in risk[85] and costs[86] associated with late abortions are worth emphasizing, since they are substantial.

The collection of health statistics is a function of health departments that is unlikely to be challenged as an obstacle to the provision of abortion services under the Supreme Court's guidelines. Useful information is already available from such activities and the monitoring of abortion services in the United States can be expected to be of even greater importance as the number of abortions increases. Policymakers must consider the nature and extent of their participation in such activities at the local and state levels and their participation in national efforts at collecting abortion statistics.[87]

Financing of abortion services, also, is of increasing importance to policy-makers as the number of abortions increases. Third party payments for abortion services are likely to increase, and the provision of financial resources for women unable to afford to pay themselves will probably be required to the extent that such funds are provided for other medical services.

Even before the Court's decision, coverage of abortion services for women who could not afford such services was increasingly included in governmental financing of medical services.[88] It seems unlikely, under the Court's ruling, that financial assistance could be denied for abortion services if they are provided for other medical services. Hopefully, financing of family planning services will also be promoted, especially in view of the relatively low cost for such services as compared to abortion services or maternity costs.[89]

Conclusions

Abortion as a method of fertility control has been traced from ancient times to the present. In the United States, the 1973 decision of the Supreme Court represented a dramatic national liberalization of this country's abortion laws, placing the U.S. among those nations with virtually unrestricted abortion laws. The provision of abortion services so that abortion will be accessible to every woman who seeks to terminate a pregnancy, in conformity with the Court's ruling, should be accomplished without placing unreasonable demands on the health care delivery system.

For the policymaker at the state and local level, consideration of abortion as part of an overall population policy does not end with the Supreme Court's ruling; rather, for many the ruling marks the beginning of a much needed rethinking. Those formulating policy now have an opportunity to determine how abortion should relate to other services without having to answer the question of whether or not services are legal and without having to anticipate legislative or judicial changes in the law. While challenges to the Court's ruling are likely to continue for some time, the Supreme Court has sustained the ruling in February, 1973,[90] and the 1973 decisions remain the law of the land.

Of extreme importance in dealing with the situation that now faces the nation with regard to abortion are public education, the provision of contraceptive services, and the regulation and financing of the practice of abortion in conformity with the Court's ruling. Education and provision of contraception cannot be overemphasized. They offer, for policymakers faced with providing abortions on a nearly unrestricted basis, an opportunity for decreasing the need for women to seek abortions which will benefit the individual woman and society.

In viewing the evolution of abortion in the world and in the United States, one is struck by how widespread the practice was throughout time and across cultures. One is also struck by the rapid and dramatic developments in the United States in the 1960s and 1970s. One can only hope that these developments will be used as a constructive force to improve the life of our present and future population.

Notes

1. C. Tietze and S. Lewit, "Abortion," *Scientific American*, 220: 21-27, 1969.

2. C.S. Ford, "Control of Conception in Cross-cultural Perspective," *Annals New York Academy of Sciences*, 54: 763-768, 1952.

3. M. Nag, "Factors Affecting Human Fertility in Non-industrial Societies: A Cross-cultural Study," *Yale University Publications in Anthropology*, 66, 1962.

4. Ibid.

5. C.S. Ford, "A Comparative Study of Human Reproduction," *Yale University Publications in Anthropology*, 32, 1945.

6. L.S.B. Leakey, "Some Notes on the Masai of Kenya Colony," *Journal of the Royal Anthropological Institute*, 60: 185-210, 1930.

7. A.M. Carr-Saunders, *The Population Problem* (Oxford: Oxford University Press, 1922).

8. M. Nag, op. cit.

9. K. Davis and J. Blake, "Social Structure and Fertility: An Analytical Framework," *Economic Development and Cultural Change*, 4: 211-235, 1956.

10. C. Tietze, "Induced Abortion as a Method of Fertility Control," in S.J. Behrman, L. Corsa, Jr., and R. Freedman, *Fertility and Family Planning: A World View* (Ann Arbor: University of Michigan Press, 1969), pp. 311-337.

11. G. Geijerstam, "Fertility Control by Induced Abortion," in E. Diczfalvsy and U. Borell, *Nobel Symposium 15: Control of Human Fertility* (Stockholm: Almquist and Wiksell, 1971), pp. 219-237.

12. R. Roemer, "Laws of the World," in R. Hall (ed.), *Abortion in a Changing World* (New York: Columbia University Press, 1970).

13. R. Roemer, "Abortion Law: The Approaches of Different Nations," *American Journal of Public Health*, 57: 1906-1922, 1967.

14. A.R. Omran, "Abortion in the Demographic Transition," in National Academy of Sciences, *Rapid Population Growth* (Baltimore: Johns Hopkins Press, 1971).

15. K. Hindell and M. Simms, *Abortion Law Reformed* (London: Peter Owen, 1971).

16. Ibid., p. 71.

17. Ibid., p. 75.

18. C. Tietze, "Abortion Laws and Practices in Europe," *Advances in Planned Parenthood*, 5: 194-212, 1969.

19. P. Diggory, J. Peel, and M. Potts, "Preliminary Assessment of the 1967 Abortion Act in Practice," *Lancet*, February 7, 1970, pp. 287-292.

20. *The Registrar General's Statistical Review of England and Wales for the Year 1969: Supplement on Abortion* (London: Her Majesty's Stationary Office), p. 1.

21. Ibid., p. 2.

22. Y. Koya, "A Study of Induced Abortion in Japan and its Significance," *Milbank Memorial Fund Quarterly*, 32: 282-293, 1954.

23. C. Tietze, *Scientific American*, op. cit.

24. Y. Koya, op. cit.

25. R. Roemer, "Abortion Law Reform and Repeal: Legislative and Judicial Developments," *American Journal of Public Health*, 61: 500-509, 1971.

26. H. David, *Family Planning and Abortion in the Socialist Countries of Central and Eastern Europe* (New York: The Population Council, 1970).

27. R. Roemer, op. cit.

28. M. Requena, "The Problem of Induced Abortion in Latin America," *Demography*, 5: 785-799, 1968.

29. M. Requena, "Social and Economic Correlates of Induced Abortion in Santiago, Chile," *Demography* 2: 33-49, 1965.

30. D.M. Heer, "Abortion, Contraception, and Population Policy in the Soviet Union," *Demography* 2: 531-539, 1965.

31. E.A. Duffy, *The Effects of Changes in the State Abortion Laws* (Washington, D.C.: U.S. Department of Health, Education and Welfare, Government Printing Office, 1971), PHS Publication no. 2165.

32. Ibid., p. 2.

33. M.S. Calderone (ed.), *Abortion in the United States* (New York: Hoeber-Harper, 1958).

34. C.L. Erhardt, C. Tietze, and F.G. Nelson, "United States: Therapeutic Abortion in New York City," *Studies in Family Planning*, 51: 8-9, 1970.

35. R.E. Hall, "Therapeutic Abortion, Sterilization, and Contraception," *American Journal of Obstetrics and Gynecology*, 91: 518-532, 1965.

36. Tietze, *Scientific American*, op. cit.

37. American Law Institute, *Abortion* (Philadelphia, 1962).

38. American College of Obstetricians and Gynecologists, "Statement on Therapeutic Abortion," Newsletter 12(6), 1968.

39. American Public Health Association, "Statement on Abortion," *American Journal of Public Health*, 61: 396, 1971.

40. M.B. Beck, S.H. Newman, and S. Lewit, "Abortion: A National Public and Mental Health Problem—Past, Present, and Proposed Research," *American Journal of Public Health*, 59: 2131-2143, 1969.

41. S. Newman, "Abortion, Obtained and Denied: Research Approaches," *Studies in Family Planning*, 53: 1-8, 1970.

42. C.W. Tyler, Jr., J.D. Asher, and M.G. Freeman, "Induced Abortion and Family Planning: Gynecological Aspects," in Proceedings of the Workshop on Abortion Obtained and Denied: Research Approaches, in *Abortion and Family*

Planning sec. 3, M.B. Beck and S. Lewit (eds.) (Philadelphia: William F. Fell Printing Co., 1971), pp. 113-130.

43. C.W. Tyler, Jr., J.P. Bourne, S.B. Conger, and J.B. Kahn, "Reporting and Surveillance of Legal Abortions in the United States, 1970," in S. Lewit (ed.), *Abortion Techniques and Services* (Amsterdam: Excerpt Medica, 1972).

44. Center for Disease Control, *Abortion Surveillance Report, 1971*, December 1972.

45. Ibid.

46. J. Blake, "Abortion and Public Opinion: The 1960-1970 Decade," *Science*, 171: 540-548, 1971.

47. C.F. Westoff, F.C Moore, and N.B. Ryder, "The Structure of Attitudes Toward Abortion," *Milbank Memorial Fund Quarterly*, 47: 11-37, 1969.

48. T.F. Rodger, "Attitudes Toward Abortion," *American Journal of Psychiatry*, 125: 116-120, 1968.

49. J. Blake, op. cit.

50. C.F. Westoff, et al., op. cit.

51. R. Pomeroy, and L.C. Landman, "Public Opinion Trends: Elective Abortion and Birth Control Service to Teenagers," *Family Planning Perspectives*, 4: 44-55, 1973.

52. *Report of the President's Commission on Population Growth and the American Future* (Washington: Government Printing Office, 1972).

53. Ibid.

54. Reprinted from W. Droegemueller, E.S. Taylor, and V.E. Drose, "The First Year of Experience in Colorado with the New Abortion Law," *American Journal of Obstetrics and Gynecology* 103: 694-702, 1969.

55. Ibid.

56. Ibid.

57. J.C. Cobb, "Abortion in Colorado 1967-1969, Changing Attitudes and Practices Since the New Law," *Advances in Planned Parenthood*, 5: 186-189, 1967.

58. A. Heller and H.G. Whittington, "The Colorado Story: Denver General Hospital Experience With the Change in the Law on Therapeutic Abortion," *American Journal of Psychiatry*, 125: 809-816, 1968.

59. K.P. Russell and E.W. Jackson, "Therapeutic Abortion in California," *American Journal of Obstetrics and Gynecology*, 105: 757-763, 1969.

60. S. Goldsmith, L. Potts, L. Green, and R. Miller, "Counselling and Referral for Legal Abortion in California's Bay Area," *Family Planning Perspectives*, 2(3): 14-19, 1970.

61. P. Goldstein and G. Steward, "Trends in Therapeutic Abortion in San Francisco," *American Journal of Public Health*, 62: 695-699, 1972.

62. J.J. Rovinsky, "Abortion in New York City," *American Journal of Obstetrics and Gynecology*, 38: 333, 1971.

63. S.C. Jain and L.F. Gooch, *Georgia Abortion Act 1968* (Chapel Hill: University of North Carolina, 1972).

64. Ibid.

65. R.W. Rochat, C.W. Tyler, Jr., and A.K. Schoenbucher, "An Epidemiological Analysis of Abortion in Georgia," *American Journal of Public Health*, 61: 543-552, 1971.

66. A.F. Guttmacher, "The Genesis of Liberalized Abortion in New York City: A Personal Insight," *Case Western Reserve Law Review* 23: 756-778, 1972.

67. Ibid.

68. J. Patker and F. Nelson, "Abortion in New York City: The First Nine Months," *Family Planning Perspectives*, 3(3): 5-12, 1971.

69. Ibid.

70. M.H. Redford and E.K. Marcuse, *Legal Abortion in Washington State* (Seattle: Battelle Memorial Institute, 1973).

71. Ibid.

72. Ibid.

73. Planned Parenthood-World Population, "Referenda on Abortion Laws Held in November," *Family Planning/Population Reporter*, 2(1): 6, 1973.

74. Ibid.

75. Massachusetts Department of Public Health, "Abortion Services in Massachusetts," *New England Journal of Medicine*, 288: 686-687, 1973.

76. United States Supreme Court: Docket 70-18, Roe vs. Wade; Docket 70-40, Doe vs. Bolton, January 1973.

77. Ibid.

78. Ibid.

79. S.J. Williams, and E.N. McIntosh. "National Resource Requirements for Abortion Services," *American Journal of Public Health*, in press.

80. W.J. Curran, "The Legal Authority of Health Departments to Regulate Abortion Practice," *American Journal of Public Health*, 61: 621-626, 1971.

81. A. Patker, op. cit.

82. J.J. Rovinsky, "Abortion Recidivism," *American Journal of Obstetrics and Gynecology*, 39: 649-659, 1972.

83. World Health Organization, Technical Report Series, no. 442, 1970.

84. United States Supreme Court, op. cit.

85. C. Tietze and S. Lewit, "Joint Program for the Study of Abortion (JPSA): Early Medical Complications of Legal Abortion," *Studies in Family Planning*, 3(6): 97-122, 1972.

86. S. Williams, op. cit.

87. C.W. Tyler, Jr., J.P. Bourne, S.B. Conger, and J.B. Kahn, op. cit.

88. H.M. Wallace, H. Goldstein, E.M. Gold, and A.C. Ogelsby, "A Study of Title 19 Coverage of Abortion," *American Journal of Public Health*, 62: 1116-1122, 1972.

89. C. Muller and F.S. Jaffe, "Financing Fertility Related Health Services in the United States, 1972-1978: A Preliminary Projection," *Family Planning Perspectives*, 4(1): 6-19.

90. Planned Parenthood-World Population, *Family Planning/Population Reporter*, 2: 25, 1973.

9

Moral Priorities and State Population Policy

David N. Carter*

State Population Policy: An Expression of Individual Moral Priorities

It is clear that states presently play a significant role in establishing a nationwide response to the issues of population growth and distribution. State governments are responsible for policies and programs in a number of areas that relate in complex ways to the development of state and regional population characteristics. It is also clear that with the advent of revenue sharing and probable massive federal incentives for state land use planning the role of the states in establishing the makeup and characteristics of the population in the United States will increase in importance in the immediate future. It is the point of this chapter that establishing the characteristics and makeup of population at the state and ultimately at the national level involves much more than simple response to empirical data (if indeed such a response and value-free data are ever available). The work of states in the population field involves value judgments of state legislators and administrators, public and private interest groups, and individual citizens. It is thus important that all these groups understand the role of the ethical issues in establishing population policy and in carrying it out through various state programs.

As many chapters in this book have demonstrated, states have always played a major role in population policy either through programs which attempt directly to influence and control population growth, density of settlement or settlement patterns, or through policies and programs which, although responding to other issues more directly, still strongly affect population growth and settlement patterns within state boundaries, in contiguous states and even in some noncontiguous states.[1] Lurking behind most population policy utterances, however, and certainly influencing the content and emphasis of individual programs designed to carry out the policy, is the value commitment of the policymaker and program administrator. Reference is not being made here to individual or political loyalties, though the influence of those on program formation is certainly strong and will be considered briefly in the second section of this chapter. What are being brought under scrutiny here are the beliefs of policymakers about such things as the purposes of the state, desirable sorts of

*Regional Planner, Massachusetts Department of Community Affairs.

people for a state, and the benefits of a strong family structure to the stability of the state.

Many observers of state politics might argue that these sorts of considerations only rarely influence program decisions, that they are too esoteric—the kinds of things that politicians discuss after they have lost elections. Other observers and even politicians might argue that such considerations ought not be part of policies or program decisions. They are, it is argued, part of the inner, private person which the politician does not readily yield to the public. Moreover, it might be maintained, policymakers should not attempt to impose their own values on programs which may affect so many different people with different sets of values. Thus, policymakers at the state level are often reluctant to examine the ethical priorities that they bring to any question, let alone the issue of population policy. Ethical discussions are equated with religion and this, of course, draws everyone into the constitutional realm of free choice. A politician or administrator often maintains publicly that he does not inject his own values into a decision, but rather attempts merely to respond to the issues and to the will of the people. Lower level bureaucrats, planners, economists and the like with a smattering of sociology in their background will often call it unprofessional to be raising personal value questions in the midst of program decisions.[2]

All these protestations notwithstanding, it will be maintained that personal value priorities do significantly influence population policy and program decisions. Population policy utterances are usually quite general, even ambiguous. Official proclamations about the need to stabilize population, promote contraceptive services, or encourage the formation of new towns usually say very little. The enactment of these policies requires specific programs on the part of state government, and only when a cluster of programs is attached to a policy utterance does that policy begin to have some meaning. It will be maintained in this chapter that program specificity, the kinds of programs chosen to enact policy and the emphases in those programs may very much be captive of the personal values of state politicians and administrators. The ethical role of the politician is not simply balancing a number of group interests, loyalties, and values which are all competing for attention and power, as might be inferred from Callahan.[3] The role of the politician usually involves shaping these competing interests and values by the values which he or she brings to a decision. Many legitimate but competing values and interests are often excluded from the decision process at the outset because of the value priorities of the decision-maker. Value priorities often play a major role in the decision to enact specific programs and in the direction, positive or negative according to the value point of view of the reviewer, in which policy moves. This is especially true for the sensitive case of the population issue, in which programs involving fertility, mortality, migration, and distribution of wealth are dependent upon complex data sources and individual personalities and preferences. Attempts to quantify data or to limit the issues are often strongly influenced by the moral presuppositions of the quantifier or the individual setting the limits.[4]

Two contrasting sets of individual moral priorities offer clear examples of the influence that personal values can have on public policy decisions—in these cases state population policy. First of all, let a state commissioner of public health be postulated who believes, as a basis for state fertility policy, that individual women should have freedom to control their own fertility and that the state, where feasible, should support this freedom. Let it further be postulated that the commissioner is somewhat concerned about the actual fiscal costs of "unwanted" or "excess" pregnancy to the state, but that a far stronger concern—indeed one which often even overshadows his desire to preserve freedom and autonomy for individual women—is a belief that the family structure must be maintained and strengthened as a way of encouraging order, stability, and responsibility in the state. This does not really represent belief in a certain moral principle, as will be the case in the second set of examples, but rather a belief that something will be of value[5] in maintaining the general quality and stability of the moral life in the state. For the purposes of this discussion, however, these kinds of values will be mixed.

If this set of values is strongly adhered to by the commissioner, one could expect to see some characteristic emphases in the programs that the commissioner considers and authorizes. Family planning services—contraceptives and counseling—would be offered in connection with maternal and child health care. The commissioner might support some free-standing clinics, but the emphasis would be upon the maternal and child health setting. Advocates of the primacy of individual freedom and believers in a crisis in contraceptive services would probably decry this arrangement because of a reduced emphasis on contraceptive services *per se*—especially in the case of unmarried and childless women. The commissioner, however, might maintain that in a situation of scarce family planning resources, he has decided to place his emphasis on the family—on providing family units with manageable numbers of offspring. He might mention his belief that the physician and staff who have delivered a mother's child and served her and her family's needs as conscientiously as possible before and after birth are probably the most effective individuals to broach the subject of family planning.

A commissioner with the value structure outlined might offer contraceptive and abortion services to adolescents because of a marked rise in adolescent illegitimacy in the state. The commissioner would probably, however, insist that wherever possible the parents be brought into the situation at state sponsored facilities, because the family setting and the support of the rest of the family are the best resources, he believes, to help the adolescent through a problem time. Believers in the primacy of the rights of all individuals would be upset at the possible invasion of the privacy of the adolescent, but the commissioner's own value orientation would result in the abortion services made available through parental consent.

By contrast, let a second commissioner of public health be postulated, who also affirmed a state role in helping those women who wish to control their fertility. In place of the value on strengthening families, the overarching value of this commissioner, however, is a belief that the more morally desirable citizens of the state are those who are financially capable—those who hold jobs, pay taxes, etc. This commissioner might believe that it is the responsibility of state government to encourage this type of citizen to settle and reproduce in the state and to discourage settlement and reproduction by those who are financially less capable. The fertility regulation programs instituted by a commissioner with these value priorities would probably be located among lower-income residents of the state. Free-standing family planning clinics would probably be found in great numbers in urban areas with high concentrations of welfare recipients. Though such programs would not be mandated by the value priorities of the commissioner in this second example, nevertheless, the practice of encouraging sterilization among the adolescent children of lower-income and welfare families, such as recently came to light in several instances in the South, might be found acceptable to a commissioner with the value priorities in this second example.

For the second set of contrasting examples, in which value priorities can be seen to have an effect upon population policy decisions, let two governors be cases in point. The first governor holds to some sort of loosely defined utilitarian doctrine of the purposes of the state—the sort held by many individuals in public life—that the state as a governing unit is to provide the greatest amount of well-being for the largest number of people within its borders.[6] Overarching and outweighing this loosely defined utilitarianism is a strong commitment on the part of this governor to social justice and even to reparations for victims in the state of past social, political, and economic injustice.[7]

Faced with dwindling land, water, and energy resources and rapidly growing pollution levels, this governor makes a proclamation that the state should slow its rate of population growth and strive for a zero growth rate.[8] If a governor with social justice/reparations moral priorities announced a policy of eventual zero population growth, his moral priorities would probably cause him to join this policy to a cluster of other policies for resource allocation to make certain that disadvantaged residents of the state suffered less than the average citizen as growth rate cutbacks were implemented. The governor might announce concomitantly a policy encouraging the construction of elderly housing throughout the state. He might pledge the state bonding authority for mortgage and rent supplements for low- and moderate-income residents of the state. Legislation might be introduced by his permitting an override of local zoning if a not-for-profit or limited-dividend corporation wanted to construct a low- and moderate-income housing development and was denied permission by local officials. The governor might also encourage a graduated income tax during the time that his population policy was to take effect, if his state did not already have such a tax scheme.

On the other hand, a governor with a different set of moral priorities might implement entirely different programs as a result of a zero population growth policy proclamation. In this last example, let the assumption be that the governor holds to the same loosely defined utilitarian goals for a state as in the earlier example, but overarching and often outweighing this goal is a belief that individual free will and entrepreneureal skills, to the degree that they do not deny standard property rights and personal rights of others,[9] ought to be protected and encouraged by state government.

A governor with this libertarian priority might encourage cities and towns to place general moratoria on the construction of multifamily housing and (if the legislature could be convinced) would include, in the state's zoning enabling law, broad encouragement of exclusionary zoning, through a liberal interpretation of flood plain categories[10] and the use of multiacre, minimum lot sizes. Such a governor would probably look favorably upon *any* community which set an absolute growth limit for itself by the year 2000. This governor would be less likely than the earlier example to ask through his programs administrators whether communities which established multifamily dwelling moratoria already had a certain percentage of low- and moderate-income and elderly housing. He would be less likely than the governor considered earlier to examine the median incomes of communities which set absolute growth rates for themselves and to demand that such communities, if their median income is high, provide housing for larger numbers of low- and moderate-income families as these communities move toward their eventual growth goals. A governor with the individual entrepreneur priority would doubtless try to keep the welfare payment rates low and not concern himself to any extent with corporate participation in unemployment compensation. In times of economic severity this would make the state less attractive to possible low-income in-migrants and encourage out-migration by those unable to earn a living wage.

In these four cases, essentially neutral or ambiguous population policy decisions—the provision of family planning services and the encouragement of zero population growth—can find expression in markedly different population programs, depending to a significant extent on the value commitments of the state politician or administrator. Potter's position in relation to arguments for optimum population levels finds its further expression in these examples.[11] Potter states that the level of optimum population depends upon how the individual who has established the optimum defines "the good life" or the "well-being" which that optimum population level is designed to guarantee. Optimum population theory has been inadequate to date, he maintains, because it has been a captive mainly of economists who have reduced well-being to a narrow economic common denominator. He believes that optimum population theory really ought to entail a broader ethical concern for justice—a concern that attempts to establish a baseline of expectations—which treats all men and their desires (economic, social, environmental, or whatever) as equal. No intellectual machinery—least of all in the social or natural sciences—has yet been devised to relate all the legitimate desires of men and to establish upon the basis of this relationship a "most favorable" population level.[12] Thus most arguments for population optima are usually shaped by such things as one's own standard of living or desire for certain kind of life companion.

In the much simpler examples presented above, the type of programs chosen to carry out enunciated state population policy have been seen to have the possibility of significant relation to the value priorities of state officials. Most population policy proposals are just as ambiguous as discussions of optimum population levels. They are often captive of limited personal value considerations and equally lacking in the quality of justice found when the interests and needs of all citizen groups are properly represented.

Ethical Accountability In Carrying
Out State Population Policy

It is not constitutionally possible, nor is it probably desirable, to specify in detail what sort of personal value priorities politicians must bring to the task of enacting population policy, though it is fairly certain that individual value priorities have a marked effect on the harm or benefit of programs. Public office ought not be limited to individuals of certain detailed moral persuasions, because no detailed set of moral principles can be relied upon infallibly at this point as the best foundation for public policymaking. It should be possible, however, to set policy through programs such that at least the rights and interests and former exploitation of various population groups can be recognized and blatant favoritism can be eliminated from policymaking. "A baseline of expectations" about the responsiveness of programs to needs of all groups would seem to be a reasonable requirement for all state population policies. The presence of this baseline of expectations shall be referred to in this section as ethical accountability of policies and programs.

The next issues to be approached in this chapter are the kinds of controls which state policymakers may place upon their program decisions to strengthen the ethical accountability of those programs in relation to constituents and, to look at the discussion from the other side, what sort of specificity state residents ought to require when population policy is stated to encourage strengthened accountability. This discussion must be attempted because whether they desire to or not, state officials continually make decisions about population related programs, direct and indirect, which reflect one set of value priorities or another. There is no such thing as a nondecision on these matters. The lack of a direct decision by a state policymaker simply means that a set of prevailing factors and prevailing value priorities move into the vacuum and determine the type and emphasis of programs.

Some helpful directions toward this ethical accountability on state population policy may be derived from one of the important subfields of ethical analysis—critical ethics or metaethics. Metaethical criteria " . . . provide us with reasons, or a set of procedures, for preferring one moral judgment over another."[13] Normative ethics, the other major subfield of the discipline of ethics, describes what things are right or wrong, good or bad, according to certain criteria. However, as has been seen from the above discussion, in regard to one or more programs chosen to give substance to a given policy, radical differences may exist on which set of programs is right, which wrong, depending upon the set of normative ethical criteria adhered to by the politician or program administrator. Therefore, it is necessary to establish some basic standards for determining which set of normative ethical criteria is more adequate than the others. This is the role of metaethics. It is perhaps asking too much to be able to specify which set of normative ethical criteria ought to be used by state population policymakers, and, as noted, there are legitimate differences concerning which set of normative criteria are best for given programs. A public official may, however, establish a basic minimum of ethical accountability in population policymaking by attempting to include metaethical criteria in decision processes—that is, some means of deciding whether the ethical priorities being used in the decision are reasonable and adequate.

There is increasing agreement among ethicists that the adequacy of normative ethical criteria may be judged by the degree to which they satisfy three, metaethical criteria: knowledge of and inclusion of the facts appropriate to the occasion; impartiality with respect to one's own interests and passions; and vivid imagination of how others are affected by one's actions.[14] In the case of policy analysis, these three criteria can provide a useful ethical framework to be included in policy and program decisions and when seriously considered will provide some measure of ethical accountability in the population policy/program process.

How might these three criteria specifically be made part of the decision process for state population policy and programs? "Knowledge of the facts" obviously requires an adequate data base upon which to establish program decisions. As simple as this demand appears, anyone who has been associated with decisions related to state population policy—either population-affecting or population-responsive—realizes that it is a formidable request. Of all the essentials lacking for adequate decision-making on any basis in state government, one of the most prominent is the lack of adequate data. Part of the cause of this is sheer incompetence of state agencies and personnel. The case of the department of commerce in one of the more urbanized New England states is a clear example of this first cause. The department keeps no records of industry starts, inquiries, or departures in the state. Standard procedure for this department when preparing its annual report is to send a lower-grade staff member to the morgues of the larger newspapers around the state to search out articles on industrial activity. The department's reports, projections, etc., are based solely upon this haphazard search.

There are, of course, other problems endemic to the kind of data being sought. Data on land use trends—one of the most important population-related factors in a state—can be rendered useless because of the time involved in survey, assembly and processing. To survey land uses throughout even a small state may require as much as two years. Meanwhile, because large parcels of land can change uses quite rapidly—especially along highways, recreation areas, etc.—the data may be woefully outdated by the time they are gathered into a comprehensive, state-wide picture, and trends based upon the present land uses may be far different for particular areas than trends based upon uses at the time the data were collected.

Third, as touched upon earlier, the adequacy of the data gathered is always affected by the person collecting the data, by his own value priorities, by the language of the questions asked, etc. Many politicians claim to rely upon polls by various private organizations to provide them with the necessary feedback for policymaking and program design. It is clear, however, that as unbiased as polls pretend or desire to be, their results and conclusions can still be strongly influenced by the moral priorities or personal preferences of the pollsters. A simple difference such as framing a question in a positive or negative form ("Is your city overpopulated in relation to available resources?," "Is the population size of your city appropriate to available resources?") can significantly influence the outcome of the poll. Shoddy polling procedures or misrepresentation of the data only add to the initial difficulty. A businessman's association interested in research and development firms in one of the larger Massachusetts communities took a poll on preferred uses by the business community for an urban renewal area in the community. The poll was widely publicized as having been given to 123 businesses and industries in the affected area of the city. The resounding percentages in favor of research and development were stated to be a clear mandate from the business community. Unfortunately, what was not stated was that although the questionnaire had been given to 123 companies, only twenty-three had responded, and a number of those had much to gain from the growth in research and development industries in the area. The bias of the organization which had commissioned the poll resulted in a rather crass manipulation of the polling procedure.

Nevertheless, these difficulties in gathering adequate data for population policy decisions in no way obviate the need for this concern in the decision process. The comprehensiveness of the collection *and* use of relevant data in decision procedures for population policy and programs need to be upgraded. This seems rather obvious, but in practice it is something that must be affirmed again and again. One cannot hope to approach ethical accountability in population policy without a far more informed response than a simple gut reaction to issues for which programs are being designed.

The second metaethical criterion (impartiality with respect to one's own passions and interests) may find expression through a number of important vehicles, as state population policy and program decisions are made. The first thing that a politician making population policy and program decisions might do with respect to these standards is to democratize a decision process. Citizen participation, the watchword, at least on paper,[15] of many Great Society programs ought not be discarded with the advent of the New Federalism. Effective citizen participation in decisions on programs is always necessary because of the question of personal and political loyalties, i.e., passions and interests, unconsidered to this point. Value priorities preclude *a priori* adequate representation of certain rights and interests in decisions about population policy. A decision that individuals who are not economically self-supporting are undesirable residents for a state may result, in the mind of a state administrator, in the diminution of the rights of such individuals to raise families from the very outset of consideration of any program to limit fertility throughout the state. It may be one of the givens for certain administrators that the fertility of such individuals should be strongly curtailed. Personal and political loyalties preclude other equally valid rights and interests of individuals which ought to have been represented in a decision process. A politician is usually pointedly more lenient or receptive to members of his own party with whom dealings have gone on for a number of years or one of his constituents who has worked for him faithfully than with other individuals. Moreover, the influence of campaign financing upon the decision-making of politicians is inescapable. Even for the politician who scrupulously avoids corruption, the simple issue of access is of considerable importance. As former Lt. Governor Simon of Illinois has said on a number of occasions:

If someone donates a thousand dollars to a campaign which I win, and I return to my office at the end of the day with a list of fourteen phone calls that must be returned, of which that contributor's is one, you know that I will not make all fourteen calls, you know that I may make only one, and you know whose call I will return.[16]

Thus, individual loyalties are a powerful influence also for honest politicians. This may mean that even a politician whose list of moral priorities is headed by social justice cannot be absolutely certain that his program decisions adhere to that ethical priority. He may be unknowingly blinded by personal or political loyalties to the extent that moral priorities that he would like to see carried out in his program decisions are actually not represented in those decisions at all.[17]

Part of the answer is, therefore, to place the decision process under the public spotlight—to open it up to input from a number of different citizen groups. This may mean the establishment of citizen task forces, whose recommendations will clearly be present in the initial program decisions with regard to population policy. This sort of citizen participation confronts two problems which are being discussed under the heading of the need for impartiality with respect to one's own passions and interests: the shaping of decisions by personal loyalties, commitments, and value priorities and the usual exclusion of the interests and value priorities of others who may be significantly affected by the policies and programs but who normally have no access to the decision.

Citizen participation must mean more, of course, than simply institutionalizing the input from citizen groups which already have significant informal access to program decision-makers. The administrative branch of Massachusetts state government has been going through a period of reorganization for the last two years in order to place the three hundred-odd departments of state government under ten cabinet level secretaries, responsible directly to the governor. Each secretary was to introduce legislation specifying how the departments and functions assigned to his or her jurisdiction would be interrelated, reorganized, or phased out. This second phase of reorganization would have provided an excellent opportunity for each secretary to assemble representative citizen task forces to advise him or her on the manner in which various departments of state government should be reorganized. One secretary out of ten, the Secretary of Environmental Affairs, took this opportunity. He established seven citizen task forces to advise him on the reorganized relationship of the departments and duties assigned to his office. Unfortunately, the task force members were not representative of a number of citizen groups to whom adequate environmental services would be significant. There were no representatives from community groups in the urban core area, whose need for open space and better recreational facilities is overwhelming. Only one representative from any minority group was found among the total membership of all seven task forces, and that one individual was from an income level and residential setting such that she was not immediately faced with the day-to-day environmental problems of most other minority group members. Meanwhile, strongly evident in membership on all task forces were bankers, corporate lawyers, state officials, university professors and their research assistants, private consultant groups, and suburb-based environmental organizations. The input from all these member groups and professions was certainly important but one could hardly say that the membership reflected balanced or representative citizen participation.

In order to ensure impartiality in population policy and program decisions, citizen participation should be ongoing. This means that feedback and evaluation need to be constant and to receive high priority among program elements. What is needed is not simply the normal reporting process from program officials at various levels that things are going well but some means of receiving feedback from a client population on the effectiveness of a program—i.e. how well it meets their needs and value priorities. It is surprising how rarely this takes place, even in the event of multimillion dollar programs which strongly influence state population characteristics. The kind of evaluation required from U.S. Department of Housing and Urban Development (HUD) for state regional planning programs is a clear example. Regional planning programs may involve many significant population related actions for various subsections of a state. Population projections, economic development, solid waste disposal, and acquisition of open space are some of the normal concerns. In carrying out these programs HUD has specified rather elaborate citizen participation programs, affirmative action hiring programs and special emphases on minority participation. It is standard procedure in yearly progress reports to HUD to indicate that the goals have been met, whether there is any real truth to the contention or not. It is assumed at the state level—with some degree of certitude, based upon past experience—that the reports are never read and thus the glowing accounts of citizen participation and minority representation will never be questioned. In the case of this particular program the emphasis is on getting the money from HUD. Once those funds have been delivered, no further check for accountability is required than the reports of the managers who receive and spend the funds.

To the politician charged with ultimate responsibility for decisions in population programs, citizen participation can be a cumbersome and frustrating exercise. The priorities and concerns of individuals affected by state programs are often far different from those of the policymaker and from those the policymaker believes the client population holds as he enters the decision process. The emphases of individual citizens might seem quite trivial to the individual charged with responsibility for an entire program. Much time might be spent arguing over the furnishing of outpatient clinics for abortion cases, when the administrator needs to know which services will be provided, which cut, given budget limitations. Nevertheless, this is precisely the kind of ethical procedure that a politician or program administrator ought to go through if he is striving to maintain his own value impartiality in a program decision—i.e. if he is striving for ethical accountability. It is an important way to reintroduce the interests and value priorities of various groups which the politician's own value priorities and personal and political loyalties may have screened out of the decision procedure.

Citizen participation is, of course, not the total answer to bringing ethical accountability to state population programs. In addition to knowledge of the facts and impartiality, the one remaining standard which needs to be built into population decisions is the attempt vividly to imagine how others might be affected by one's actions. That is to say, the policymaker should attempt to take the programs which he or she is advocating, programs which are a result, among other things, of personal moral priorities and imagine how a client population might be affected by these program decisions. This is the reverse side of the metaethical criterion which was just considered: impartiality with respect to one's own interests and passions, through citizen participation mechanisms.

The need for this third criterion is quite evident. In the same way that the accountability of individual practices can be vitiated by inadequate value systems which do not take into consideration the rights and needs of all societal groups, so the accountability of group actions can be eclipsed by inadequate group values and political loyalties. The majority input from citizens on a particular population issue is often not enough either because the policymaker cannot hear and understand it accurately or because the majority opinion is wrong and exploitative in relation to some minority group. As Tribe has said much more simply, there may always be the difference between what the people want and what they should want.[18] The shared racial values of United States citizens—indeed the dominant racial expressions of U.S. citizenry—have often been totally unacceptable from an ethical point of view, both domestically and internationally. The majority American attitude which allows Blacks to be treated, even if no longer always designated, as "niggers" found its ready transfer during recent American adventures in Asia into the characterization of Vietnamese as "gooks" and the characterization of Koreans as "slickie boys." Only a majority tolerance of less than human status for Asian peoples would have allowed the wholesale killing of Asian peoples by Americans to go on for so many years with only minority opposition. Thus state population policies need to be evaluated by a standard more reliable than citizen participation alone. The administrator or politician must attempt vividly to imagine the effect of state programs on client populations. To put this same concern another way, state population programs must devote a great deal of time and energy to maintaining the dignity of the client populations.

The importance of this concern for dignity in population programs is presented quite clearly in a chapter, "The Prevalence of Bastards," in William Ryan's *Blaming the Victims*.[19] Ryan describes initially his work as a consultant to a program intended to encourage young unmarried mothers to complete their education and get a job. "The staff workers were middle class and white; the clients, poor and black." He reports that the staff members, instead of discussing how the clients might cope with neglectful slum landlords, the penurious welfare department, and the development of neighborhood preventive programs centering on sex education and contraceptive services, spent their time discussing the strange sexual mores of the lower class black girl, and how to "motivate" clients to get themselves educated, employed, and "off welfare." Needless to say, the success of this program was not overwhelming.

Ryan lists the usual myths concerning black unwed mothers: that they are sexually wanton, much more active than middle class white women; that they would not accept contraceptive services even if they were offered; that they would rather live on the welfare dole than get real jobs; that they are far more accepting of illegitimacy than higher class, white families. He argues persuasively that none of these stereotypes is true, but that if they are used to characterize the client population and thus deny them the dignity they deserve as human beings, the result is exploitative and ineffective programs. A quote from Adelaide Hill and Frederick Jaffe goes right to the point. After presenting figures indicating that the poor are indeed desirous of contraceptive services, they state:

This does not mean that *any* kind of program will work automatically. If the program is proffered with racist overtones, if it is coupled with constant threats to sterilize unmarried mothers on welfare, if it is presented as a punitive means of reducing relief costs, and if the mere request for birth control is taken as *prima facie* evidence that there's a "man in the house," thus jeopardizing the woman's eligibility for public assistance, the response is likely to be negligent.[20]

Vividly imagining how others will be affected by one's program decisions and responding to that vision are, of course, difficult elements to include in the population policy process. They are indeed the reverse side of democratizing a decision process. One must hear, understand, and act upon the needs of the client group as expressed through input procedure. Roderick Firth has described this as one of the characteristics of an ideal moral judge,[21] but how to carry such a generalized description over into the world of day to day political decisions on population programs is extremely problematic. Suffice it to say, in this initial analysis, that vividly imagining how others will be affected—concern for the dignity of the client population—requires something which is anathema to many state decision-makers. It requires humility on the part of the state policymaker. The desire for strong state control of a policy and close adherence to the regulations published by the administrator must be sacrificed to a significant extent to the expressed desires and needs of client populations. Administrators in many areas of state policy will argue that such humility is a capitulation which weakens the effectiveness of policymaking and programs. If programs are run for their own sake, regardless of their effect on client population, this may be true. Since, however, state population programs, among others, are designed to serve client populations, a strong measure of such "capitulation" is necessary. It is necessary from the point of view of the effectiveness of the program and also from the position of the main issue here under discussion—the ethical accountability of state population policies.

There is yet a final way by which politicians and program administrators can attempt to bring ethical accountability to state population policy. It encompasses and displays the three metaethical criteria so far considered. This final way is at one and the same time a standard for policymaking which should be offered by every state politician and a standard which should be demanded by the voters of a state. This is the element of specificity in policymaking. State population policymakers should offer program specificity—they should be willing to designate along with neutral policy statements how those policies will find enactment in particular programs. In this way they indicate a willingness to make known their own value priorities to the voting public. They indicate the degree to which the three criteria for ethical accountability have been an integral part of the program decision procedure. Voters, on the other hand, should demand this same program specificity in relation to any state population policy and in certain general programs. In this way voters require that value priorities, which may, as has been seen, play such an important role in determining how policy statements will actually be carried out, be rendered explicit by politicians. This is .the sort of thing, of course, which many state politicians would like to avoid. There is nothing more desirable than stating policy that receives support from all sides of the value spectrum. In such a case individuals take their own value priorities and read them into the policy statement or program outline, so that specific programs are established which fit their priorities. Political comfort cannot be equated with ethical accountability, however. A clear example of the way that value priorities can be clearly specified in the establishment of policy and programs is found in two recent proposals for commissions to regulate development on Martha's Vineyard, the island off the coast of Cape Cod in Massachusetts. The first bill, the one that smacks of the usual political ambiguity is one proposed by the Commonwealth of Massachusetts.[22] The second bill, which attempts to establish the same kind of regulation, was introduced before the United States Senate by Senator Edward Kennedy.[23]

Both bills attempt to do the same thing. They recognize that runaway development on the Vineyard (in the case of the Kennedy bill, also on Nantucket and the other off-Cape islands) will destroy the beauty of the picturesque island for all concerned—both year-round residents and summer visitors. Both state that the regulation of development is done in behalf of the "health, safety, morals, and general welfare" of the island residents—the catch-all public purpose phrase behind most state zoning enabling laws.[24] Both pieces of legislation establish commissions made up primarily of local residents to formulate and administer the regulatory procedures. There is (beyond the much greater workability of the Kennedy bill) one significant difference between the two pieces of proposed legislation, however. The Kennedy bill reveals clearly some of the moral priorities of the individuals involved in drafting the bill. The Massachusetts bill is characteristically mute at this point. Martha's Vineyard is, of course, known as the playground of the wealthy, although average, working citizens can spend an enjoyable time there and some modestly priced housing is available for year-round residents. The question which must be raised with respect to any attempt to limit development on that island is whether this regulation is an attempt by the wealthy summer residents to keep poorer year-round residents and less affluent recreation-seekers from using the island. The Kennedy bill seems to indicate not, because it contains definite provisions to establish a commission and a fund to construct moderately priced housing on the island, concomitant with the decisions to restrict severely the uses of certain parcels of land on the island. Certainly the problems of securing water, energy, and the disposal of wastes dictate that development limits must be placed upon the island. However, the Kennedy bill seems still to provide for the availability of the resources of this island to all income groups. It seems to parallel one of the earliest examples from this article: a policy proclamation of zero population growth as screened through a lively concern for social justice. The Massachusetts bill contains no specific provisions, and it is anyone's guess what value priorities were at work in its formulation and what value priorities will be active if it is enacted and its regulatory mechanisms are established.

In summary, this chapter has attempted briefly to examine the role of personal value priorities in the making of state population policy and the design of state population programs. It seems clear that personal value priorities of politicians and administrators do play an important role in determining the meaning of usually ambiguous policies, as programs are chosen to enact these policies. Personal value priorities further may determine the emphases of specific programs. As a result of this, the need for politicians and administrators to maintain ethical accountability in state population policies and programs was discussed. Ethical accountability has been understood to express itself in policymaking through three important metaethical criteria: knowledge of the facts, impartiality through suppression of one's personal loyalties and passions, and vivid imagination of how others are affected by the program decisions one makes. Politicians and administrators who realize the impact of their own value commitments in population policies and programs and wish to be ethically accountable to the whole of their constituents and to specific client populations which will be affected by programs may attempt to employ these standards in the decision-making on population policy through better data collection and use, the democratization of population policy and program decisions, and special concern for the dignity of the client population on all policies and programs. The bias, injustice, or unrepresentativeness which may result from the dominant role of politicians' value priorities may be lessened when such standards are employed. Finally, it has been maintained that state politicians ought to make their value priorities known in their population policy by specifying particular programs that will be employed to carry out these policies. Voters, on the other hand, ought to demand this program specificity in order to determine whether population policy and broad programs will indeed be ethically accountable.

Notes

1. See especially the chapters by Tabors and Cook.

2. An interesting discussion of the value/technology interrelationship is found in part II of an article by Alvin Toffler, "Value Impact Forecaster—A Profession of the Future," in Kurk Baier and Nicholas Rescher, *Values and the Future* (New York: Macmillan Company, 1969), pp. 5-12. Toffler highlights a paper by Theodore J. Gordon, Director of Advance Space Stations and Planetary Systems, Douglas Aircraft Company, in which the question of whether values precede technology (Weber), or technology comes first (Marx), is "sidestepped" by an argument that both are part of a loop that includes research and planning.

3. Daniel Callahan, *Ethics and Population Limitation*, An Occasional Paper of the Population Council (New York, 1971), p. 4.

4. See, for example, Jay Forrester, *Urban Dynamics* (Cambridge: MIT Press, 1969). Forrester's modelling for urban futures often seems to be dependent upon some particular stated and unstated desires about the kinds of activities and people that ought to be part of a future urban environment.

5. For a discussion of this distinction, see Baier and Rescher, op. cit., pp. 33-67.

6. See generally John Stuart Mill, *Utilitarianism* (New York: E.P. Dutton and Company, Inc., Everyman's Library, 1951 ed.); Richard Brandt, *Ethical Theory* (Englewood Cliffs, New Jersey: Prentice-Hall, Inc., 1959), pp. 253-258, 380-391; and William Frankena, *Ethics* (Englewood Cliffs, N.J.: Prentice-Hall, Inc., 1963), pp. 29-46, for informative discussions of the principles of utilitarianism.

7. These strong, overarching commitments might correspond to the *prima facie* duties developed by Ross in his classic work, *The Right and the Good* (Oxford: The Oxford University Press, 1967). In Chapter 2, Ross defines a *prima facie* duty as those which are " . . . more or less incumbent on me according to the circumstances of the case." (p. 19). A *prima facie* duty is an act which appears at face value to be required in a situation, but whose requiredness may be modified from time to time, given the appearance of other *prima facie* duties in a situation. Included in his list of duties are, among others, promise-keeping and reparations. The nature of the commitment in this example might correspond to Ross's *prima facie* duties. The specific content of these commitments, i.e., the normative characteristics, would have to be further established.

8. In order to address itself to these conditions, the Hawaii Legislature, in its most recent session, established a State Commission on Population and the Hawaiian Future. (Act 204/1973)

The example holds some striking similarities to the policy statements and program developments of Governor Thomas McCall of Oregon. For a number of years McCall has encouraged visitors not to settle in Oregon. "Visit but don't stay," was his watchword. Now the governor's office is beginning to investigate programs to actively discourage further settlement in the state.

9. Such theories in ethical discourse fall under the general heading of Libertarianism. The classic writing in this field is John Locke's, *Second Treatise on Moral Discourse*. Interesting recent developments in this branch of philosophy are found in a soon to be published treatise by Robert Nozick of Harvard University, *Anarchy, State, and Utopia*.

10. A recent proposed revision of the Massachusetts State Zoning Enabling Law by the Urban Affairs Committee of the Massachusetts Legislature proposed that flood plain include areas which are not subject to seasonal flooding or part of a watershed area but which serve as a wildlife habitat. A city council or town meeting bent upon exclusionary zoning would find such a broad category quite useful.

11. Ralph Potter, "Alternative Approaches to Optimum Population Theory," in Philip Wogaman (ed.), *The Population Crisis and Moral Responsibility* (Washington, D.C.: Public Affairs Press, 1973), pp. 17-37.

12. For a similar argument in relation to arguments for survival see Callahan, ibid., "Population and Human Survival," pp. 46-61.

189

13. Arthur Dyck, "Population Policies and Ethical Acceptability," in Howard M. Barh, Bruce A. Chadwick, and Darwin L. Thomas (eds.), *Population, Resources and the Future; Non-Malthusian Perspectives* (Provo, Utah: Brigham Young University Press, 1972), pp. 301-326. (Thanks are due Professor Dyck for discussing the three metaethical criteria used in this chapter to provide a base for analysis of ethical accountability.)

14. See Brandt, op. cit., pp. 7-10, 11, for a further discussion of metaethical criteria.

One ought not maintain that these three criteria satisfy every ethicists' or everyone else's standards that a normative ethical judgment must meet before it can be declared adequate and rational. Neither do these criteria necessarily fulfill the other major role of metaethical criteria, describing what ethical terms mean (i.e., what does it mean to say that something is "good"?; is one person simply recommending it to another, is he ascribing some special unique quality to it, or what?).

15. Richard F. Babcock and Fred P. Bosselman, "Citizen Participation: A Suburban Suggestion for the Central City," *Law and Contemporary Problems*, 32: 220-231, Spring 1967.

16. Paul Simon, quotation from lecture given in connection with a seminar on policymaking in state government, sponsored by the Kennedy Institute of Politics, Harvard University, February 1973.

17. For a fuller explication of the relationship of personal loyalties to ethical decision making, see Ralph Potter, *War and Moral Discourse* (Philadelphia: John Knox Press, 1969), chapters 1-5.

18. Laurence H. Tribe, "Technology Assessment and the Fourth Discontinuity: The Limits of Instrumental Rationality," *Southern California Law Review*, 46(3): 656, 657, June 1973.

19. William Ryan, *Blaming the Victim* (New York: Random House, 1971), pp. 86-111.

20. Ibid., p. 111.

21. See Baier, Kurt. *The Moral Point of View* (Ithaca, New York: Cornell University Press, 1958); Brandt, op. cit.; Firth, Roderick, "Ethical Absolutism and the Ideal Observer," *Philosophical and Phenomenological Research* 12: 317-345, 1952; and Mandelbaum, Maurice, *The Phenomonology of Moral Experience* (Glencoe, Illinois: The Free Press, 1955).

22. H7479, Massachusetts House of Representatives, 1973 legislative session.

23. S. 1929, 93rd Congress, 1st session, "The Nantucket Sound Islands Trust."

24. Regulation in both bills does not occur through the normal zoning process but through limitations on development permits that may be issued; nevertheless, the relationship with usual zoning procedure is quite strong.

Part III:
The Structure of Policymaking

10 The Politics of Population Policy: Lessons for the Population Pros

John S. Ames*

The immediate impetus for my contribution to this work on state population policy comes from my recent participation in a conference on state population policy sponsored by the Population Council. I had inferred from the pre-conference publicity that this was to be an action-oriented conference, and that the Population Council was willing to listen to proposals for population policy-making from the various New England states and to fund the best of them immediately. I was disappointed in these respects. The conference plodded for two days, discussing at a studied distance the various aspects of the population issue in New England. Ideal policies were proposed, but no attempt was made to take the political context seriously. No funds were forthcoming from the Population Council. They simply wanted to rub elbows with state politicians to see whether it was worth their time to get involved in domestic population issues. (Note: At present the Population Council spends a good deal of its resources on international population issues, but very little on U.S. programs.)

Apparently, part of the difficulty with the conference was that it was conceived, planned, and administered by regional academics and professionals in the population field from the Population Council. State leaders were not consulted on the actual content and direction of the program, only asked to fill slots on the schedule. But the difficulty with the conference also seemed to go much deeper than this. Though politicians and population professionals are both intimately concerned with the population issue, the two groups seem to come at the issue from entirely different perspectives and to look for different results as a product of their consideration. Population professionals—demographers, sociologists, administrators of the Population Council, etc.—seem to concentrate on a very precise articulation of the problem. Indeed, this articulation seems quite often to be the goal of their deliberations. Politicians on the other hand usually want their discussions to result in the formulation of some sort of realistic policy. There is, of course, room for articulation of the problem, but the goal of the political process is normally enactment of policy and programs.

I don't believe that at the Population Council conference the politicians and the population professionals were fully aware that they had differing goals. There were, of course, some trivial actions on the part of the population

---

*Assistant Minority Leader, Massachusetts House of Representatives; member, Executive Committee of the National Society of State Legislators.

professionals that served to alienate them at the start from the politicians. The infantile cheering and catcalls for the "good guys" and the "bad guys" during the showing of the U.S. Population Commission movie and the subsequent debate were certainly counterproductive. Many of the politicians saw this as an indication that the population professionals were on the whole unwilling to consider any other position than their own. Statements such as "I have always believed that the American family stands foursquare in the way of progress," made by apparently one of the leading lights in the professional population field, also did not help. Statements such as this indicate a real lack of awareness of and sensitivity to the point of view of the majority of people who will be affected by population policy recommendations. As I indicated, however, the real problem was that population pros and the politicians were not aware that they had differing agendas. The population pros had a sort of ideal list of actions that it would be advantageous for every state to consider; the politicians came with a knowledge of existing conditions in their states and wanted to consider some real, concrete steps that could be taken immediately in the area of population policy. It would have been helpful had the Population Council provided someone who could have served as a catalyst between the two groups. Such a person would have to have had a keen knowledge not only of academic concerns but also of political process. Unfortunately, no such catalytic person was present, and consequently the two groups never really engaged one another meaningfully.

My reactions in this chapter are thus most immediately affected by my participation in the Population Council Conference. I am quickly led, however, to broader considerations based on wider contacts. The sum total of my experience with academic population professionals causes me to think that there are a number of key features about the governing process of which population pros are only dimly aware. Population pros ought to have a clearer understanding of the policymaking process at the state level before they make recommendations for policy to politicians.

The Politics of the Population Issue

What I am going to say will of necessity have as a base Massachusetts politics, but I don't think that some of the problems that we face in Massachusetts when we consider the politics of the population issue are really so different from other states or even from the nation as a whole. Though, as I shall indicate below, different issues require a different time schedule in the various states. At the outset it must be understood that political consideration of any particular issue is significantly different from scientific consideration of the same issue. Scientists (and when one speaks about population I assume he is referring to sociologists, demographers, etc.) tend to look at their specialty with what politicians often call a "point of view of almost unrealistic detachment." For example, to me, as a politician, it is inconceivable that the President's Commission on Population Growth and the American Future and other scientific minds could view the issue of abortion as merely one factor in a policy of birth limitation. The issue of abortion is, in my opinion, one so emotionally charged that it cannot be considered in the same "ball park" as other population limiting factors, such as the availability of contraceptive devices, etc. Yet I think scientific minds—minds, if you will, insulated from the hurly-burly of everyday life—do not place the abortion issue in the unique social and political category to which it belongs.

A politician is very different from a scientist. One of the big areas of difference between the two species is that a scientist, because he or she deals in the protected world of the abstract, never really gets his hands very dirty in the real world. A scientist, academician if you will, for the sake of accuracy and for the sake of the research that he is involved with, never really has to deal with compromise as a tool of his profession. A scientist, again because of the protected environment in which he normally practices his profession, seems—at least to me as a politician—overly cautious about risking an opinion on a situation until the documented data is so irrefutable that for all practical purposes it doesn't make a great deal of difference that he is willing to state an opinion at that time because everybody knows the situation to be true anyway. To say it another way, a scientist tends not to stick his neck out until the data are so unassailable in support of his position, that from a political point of view he can't add very much to the creative edge of a discussion.

I would love to see a scientist come forward and say, "Well, this has a certain probability of occurring and because the issue is so important, I think it a good idea to tell the public about the possibility of its occurrence rather than to wait until it has happened and then say I told you so." What I'm suggesting is that the risk-taking of the scientific community is virtually nil, and that often this does not help those of us in the political arena because what we need to have is at least some support earlier in a decision-process. We often must make up our minds before all the evidence is in. Specifically, in the area of population issues, it is all very fine to say that our environment is deteriorating and that we are going to run out of oil or some such thing, or that we will face an energy crisis if we don't change our policies. It is an entirely different thing to do something before the facts are so irrefutable that, for all practical purposes, we have lost at least some ability to act or to consider some options because we have waited so long.

Naturally, there are also significant weaknesses in the politicians' style of operation. One of the biases of the political community which I find particularly distressing is the fact that when a problem arises, the immediate reaction on the part of the politicians seems to be that a solution can best be achieved by throwing massive amounts of money and technology at the particular problem.

This attitude, needless to say, is reinforced by members of the scientific community that benefit financially from the politicians' desire to solve problems through money and technology. I find, however, a small voice within me, at least, that says: "Another way to do meaningful problem-solving is to look at the attitudes of people. It is these attitudes which all too often make the bed in which we find ourselves lying in the 20th century." My particular field has been, over the last few years, natural resources; and I am discouraged when, too often, I find my colleagues and I voting for things which involve the expenditures of large amounts of money and the application of large amounts of technology, when possibly and probably another solution could be better achieved by changing the attitudes of the people.[1]

Specifically in relation to the issue of population, I think one of the strongest political factors militating against a meaningful approach to action lies in the system of government that exists in this country today. The system is based on the federalist concept with numerous strong, or at least theoretically strong, more or less independent states. What arises when an issue such as population is approached on a state by state basis, is a tremendous problem—a problem which results from the economics of any state government. In the New England context it is almost laughable, if it were not so bad, to see a state such as Maine which has a large amount of open space—a large potential for recreation and agriculture—trying desperately to attract an industrial base, presumably similar to that which Massachusetts or Connecticut or other urbanized states now have, in order to achieve some sort of economic parity in the New England context. Anybody coming from Massachusetts or Connecticut could easily point to their own experience and say to Maine: "Look, don't make the mistakes we did. Don't try to settle your land and develop your economy the way that we did, because we made some terrible blunders." But Maine, even if Massachusetts or Connecticut did say this to Maine, has no incentive to listen. A flourishing paper mill will bring dollars into a depressed area much more efficiently than a series of farms will. The country as a whole may have a tremendous stake in a clean, unpolluted shoreline for the state of Maine. Yet Maine as an individual state may have much less of a stake in preserving its shoreline—at least for the short run.

It is an unfortunate fact of economic reality that the advantage of a set as a whole is almost never the advantage of a particular subset of that whole. The country as a whole benefits tremendously by the citrus groves that exist in California and Florida, but economically speaking, those citrus groves would bring more to their owners if they were turned into subdivisions. Therefore, it is not to the benefit of the subset, namely, the citrus grove owner, to preserve his land in citrus, whereas the country as a whole has a tremendous stake in seeing that he does. Obviously, politicians, when they are considering problems such as this, tend, because they are creatures that are spawned every two years, to adopt the short-run solution. The incentive for a state politician to become a state's man in the big-picture context of that word is very very small. I know of two

Massachusetts State Representatives that were defeated in the last election that was held because they felt that the abortion issue was of concern only to a potential mother and her doctor, and not that of the state's involvement.[2]

A final problem that often arises in the politicians' style of operation is related to the first. When, for example politicians consider the population issue, they use a yardstick which, although it has been used for a hundred years or so in this country, may not be the best one in this day and age. That yardstick is one of economics—the dollars and cents yardstick to any particular issue, unadorned cost-benefit or cost-effective analysis. If however, instead of asking whether or not a particular project would yield increased revenues to a particular state or municipality, politicians were to ask whether this contemplated project would have adverse effects in terms of energy or resource consumption, they might get an entirely different picture. But the yardstick of energy or resource consumption is not used. Benefits and costs are calculated only according to the crudest of economic measures. Items which cannot be neatly quantified—the cost of disrupting an old and established neighborhood, the benefit of a park-open space area to a densely-settled community, etc.—are often left out of the calculus as long as a proposal will broaden the tax base of a particular community.

It is clear that both the scientific endeavor and the political endeavor have operating limitations, and that the participants in both these fields exhibit characteristic personal weaknesses which heighten the limitations of their fields. Since, however, state population policy is under discussion (basically, the political contest of the population issue), and one would assume that demographers, sociologists, psychologists, and philosophers in the population field would hope that their work would have some relevance to policymaking, I would suggest that the scientists are going to have to learn something of the rules, procedures, and sensitivities of the process of government. Politicians are not interested primarily in discussing an idea in the abstract but in trying to take effective action when those ideas concern people of their political jurisdictions. One would hope that at least eventually the professional populationists would be interested in effective action and thus would begin to ask themselves what might be some of the most promising ways to meet, in the political arena, the issues that they discuss in the abstract.

When one considers population growth and the factors affecting population growth at the state level, one theoretically has a number of approaches from which to choose, if he believes that his state has problems relating to the density or numbers of its citizens. At the Population Council conference the population pros urged the politicians to take direct action. They concerned themselves with factors directly related to fertility—the availability of contraceptive devices, availability of counseling services for the newly married, availability of abortion clinics, and all those other direct factors which, taken as a group, have the possibility of limiting the size of any particular population. They urged the politicians to be brave in facing public opposition to some of these proposals and to be comforted by the knowledge that their hearts were pure, their cause right, and that there were a number of people "out there" who would support them if they were outspoken and forthright, even if those people disagreed with some of the particular forms of direct action. They brought out one of their type of politicians from a Midwestern state who had been successful in the direct action approach.

If the professional population academicians had done some of their homework in the field of state policymaking, however, they would have known that what occurs in one state cannot necessarily be applied successfully to other states, at the same point in time, no matter how brave a politician might wish to be. They might have realized that precedent alone is so weak an argument, that what passes in one state one year might not be applicable in that *same* state the next year. In addition, the population pros might have realized that there are a number of ways to approach the population issue, depending on the political climate and history of the state and on the desired comprehensiveness of the program, which might be more effective than a direct attack upon fertility.

In fact, I would suggest that there is an alternative way of considering population growth and the factors surrounding it which is not a direct attack on fertility, but which in a political context is probably more effective and more closely fits the complex nature of population problems as they appear in the states. I suggest that in a political setting one ought to work with issues that, while apparently bearing only an incidental relationship to population growth, serve as a very valuable fulcrum with which population policies might be moved, if they are addressed sensitively and expertly.

One such fulcrum issue is land use and land use policies. Notice here that, from a strictly political point of view, one does not have to use the word *population* and its emotional overtones, at least for Massachusetts—i.e., population = birth control = abortion. One can bypass these emotionally-charged terms and achieve the same or a more comprehensive policy in the area of population growth. By concentrating on land use, one asks the question: "We have a finite amount of land on which we can settle, grow our food, raise our children, transport ourselves. . . . How will we handle that land, what are we doing with it now, and what will that use mean in the years to come?" It seems obvious to me that even the most superficial consideration of land use raises all the questions of population policy, and in fact goes somewhat further than a consideration of merely the numbers game surrounding population policy without running afoul of what possibly is a rather limited and obviously emotionally charged area.

If, for example, by sensitive study of land use policies, it is determined that a town such as Easton, Massachusetts can support—because of its ecological, sociological, economic potential—a population of only 50,000 people, the question which normally, logically follows is: "What are we going to do about this theoretical maximum that our land and our surroundings can support?" The answer, it would seem to me, is: "We are going to start to adopt policies—zoning, open space, housing codes—which when fully implemented will leave us with only those numbers of people we have determined we can handle." Notice in a situation like this, we are not putting the cart before the horse. We are asking before we consider any policy which would limit population growth: "How many people can this land of ours, this finite resource of ours, handle?" What follows then, obviously, is in a political sense a much more defensible decision. We are not deciding arbitrarily that we want to have fewer people, but we are deciding that we want to have fewer people *because of* a very definite set of reasons. How we achieve those fewer people is not directly addressed by a land use policy, but it follows as night the day that if land can handle only so many people, we must as a society consider methods to achieve that allowable growth in a *well-planned* manner. I emphasize the word "well-planned" because I think that is the key: the well-planned maximum.

Now there are other so-called fulcrum issues which, considered in a sensitive way, would have similar effects on population policy. We are just beginning to hear something about the American work ethic and how leisure time affects our lifestyle. This, whether people realize it or not, is the type of question which, when looked into in sufficient depth, will lead us to question the viability of the numbers of people that inhabit our country and our planet. People in general, and politicians as the mirror image of the larger population, tend to be linear thinkers. By that I mean that they tend to think of solutions as proceeding in a very direct cause-and-effect sequence. When Dr. Donella Meadows talks about non-linear, multi-loop feedback systems, she isn't really talking about the way decisions normally are arrived at—the way decisions are normally arrived at in the political arena. This is not to say that the world does not work by means of numerous interlocking social and economic systems, but merely that people do not think that way. And strange as it may seem, when the subject of population is considered by scientific minds, they do not really seem to think in other than a linear fashion. If one is to limit population, the traditional scientific wisdom seems to be to increase the availability of birth control devices, abortion clinics, etc. Yet, as I have discussed above, this may not be the best way of doing it. The fulcrum issues, which the conventional wisdom tells us lie outside of the population issue as we normally consider it, may be more effective in doing something about the numbers of people in our country and on our planet than a direct, frontal assault on procreation *per se.*

We could go on to discuss a host of remaining fulcrum issues, but I hope that my point has been made. Population pros ought to study the art of policy-making at the state level very carefully. They need to become more adept at reading a political climate and picking among alternative policies and proposals ones which will achieve the same effect as a direct attack on an issue.

In addition, population pros ought to ask themselves which proposals most effectively fit the complexity of the issue that they are addressing. Is a direct attack upon fertility really the most effective way to meet the population issue in its broadest scope? The Supreme Court has decided that the abortion laws in Texas and Georgia (and thus by example, the abortion laws of most of the states) must be liberalized. Admittedly, the implementation of this decision involves an extended battle in the years to come, but the all important legal framework has been established. Birthrates continue to decline nationwide. Fertility in the near future may become a non-issue. By no means, however, will all the states' population problems have been solved. Migration into the more desirable coastal states and certain Midwestern states will continue to be an important growth factor that must be faced by many state politicians. The on-going problem of our outrageous standard of living will make even small population increments significant burdens for many states. The uncontrolled housing policies in states such as Massachusetts, which allow too many people to settle in the wrong places, will continue to face politicians in this state as a population issue. Politicians will have to grapple with the long-range population issue through land use controls and transportation policies. In that process, politicians can use the help of population pros who have taken a long-range view of their own issue, and who are aware of the fine points of the art of making public policy. Hopefully, academics will not leave the population issue simply because their short-range objective of fertility decline may have been achieved. If they have studied the issues carefully and have looked for ways to take effective action, they will remain as significant participants in the policymaking process.

Notes

1. Specifically, cleaning up air and water is all well and good, but politicians seem to want to achieve these goals by throwing technology at the particular problems. Possibly a much better solution could be found if politicians realized that changed consumption styles for everyone would eliminate the *cause* of air and water pollution problems. Therefore, I think that money spent in schools, educating the generations to come, might very well, in the long run, prove to be a better solution to problems than the more direct approach of applying technology. This, of course, is particularly applicable in the population area. If public/personal attitudes towards numbers of children in a family and consumption within that family were to change, then many of the so-called solutions to the population problem would no longer be necessary because the people would have taken upon themselves a lifestyle which in and of itself would reduce the numbers of people on this planet.

2. Another example of a statesman who was defeated because he put long-term considerations before local pressures was Msg. Mimie Pitaro. Representative Pitaro was not defeated on an abortion stand but because of his acceptance of the state's racial imbalance law and thus bussing as a remedy for imbalance. His district did not tolerate a "statesman-like approach" to this emotionally-charged subject.

11

Impact of Federal Revenue-Sharing on the Subsidized Family Planning Service Level in Massachusetts

David R. Weir, Jr.*

1. General Introduction

During the 1960s, the Federal Government greatly expanded its program of categorical (specific) grants-in-aid to state and local governments and private non-profit organizations to provide specific kinds of social services to the needy. Today, under the Nixon administration policy of revenue-sharing, many of these categorical grant programs will either be eliminated in favor of no-strings-attached grants to state and local governments (general revenue-sharing) or consolidated into more broadly categorized block grants to be allocated to state and local governments (special revenue-sharing). The avowed purpose of this "New Federalism" is to eliminate the red tape, delays, and confusing guidelines associated with the administration of these programs by the huge federal bureaucracy and to facilitate the provision of social services by the governmental organizations which are more in touch with the needs of the indigent in particular areas. However, there is substantial evidence that the actual purpose of Federal revenue-sharing is to reduce the overall level of Federally subsidized social services both through the elimination of Federal bureaucracies and through a reduction in the overall cash flow to state and local governments and private agencies.

The purpose of this study is to assess the anticipated impact of revenue-sharing on the provision of a specific social service, family planning, in a specific area, Massachusetts. Family planning services are educational, social (counseling, follow-up) and medical services which enable a couple to plan the number and spacing of their offspring by preventing unwanted conception. The psychological, social, and health benefits of this service are substantial. But these services also have significant economic and noneconomic costs. Providing modern family planning services is estimated to cost on the average $66[1] per patient per year. In addition, family planning services have political costs to those who sponsor them because they are preventive, and therefore less essential than curative services, and because they are controversial, primarily on religious grounds.

The study will be organized, as follows. The next (second) section is designed

Reprinted with the permission of the Alfred P. Sloan School of Management, Massachusetts Institute of Technology.

*Candidate for the M.C.P., Harvard University.

to familiarize the reader with family planning services, and will be devoted to a definition of terms to be used throughout the study, a discussion of the benefits of family planning services, an examination of family planning usage patterns, and a discussion of the need for and provision of subsidized family planning services in the United States.

The third section will be devoted to an analysis of the subsidized family planning system in Massachusetts. A set of input variables, categorized as actors, contexts, ideologies, and laws, rules, and regulations, will be related to an output variable, the subsidized service level (number of patients served annually) in the State. The relation between an input variable and the output variable will then be defined in terms of the influence of the input variable on the output variable relative to the input variables' potential influence on the output variable. Thus, this section will provide a framework for policy analysis which can be used to estimate the impact of Federal revenue-sharing on the output of the system.

The final two sections will include a detailed description of Federal revenue-sharing in relation to Federal grants and reimbursements for family planning services (section 4) and the assessment of the impact of Federal revenue-sharing on the subsidized family planning service level in Massachusetts (section 5).

2. An Introduction to Family Planning Services in the United States

Definition of Terms

Family Planning Services. Family planning services are voluntarily accepted educational, social, and medical services designed to provide fertile couples with the knowledge and means to control the number and spacing of their offspring. Educational and social family planning services include family life and human sexuality education, and counseling, outreach, and follow-up activities concerning the nature and availability of family planning medical services. Family planning medical services[2] include a medical and surgical history, a physical examination, laboratory testing, consultation, medical treatment, prescription of drugs and contraceptive supplies, and medical referral where needed. More specifically, the physical examination includes: thyroid palpation; inspection and palpation of breasts and auxiliary glands; articulation of heart and lungs; blood pressure; weight; abdominal examination; pelvic, including speculum, bimanval, rectovaginal examinations; and extremities. The laboratory test includes: hematocrat or hemoglobin; urinalysis; Papanicoulaou smear. Optional laboratory tests include: VD testing; pregnancy testing; and sickle cell screening. An active family planning patient receives all medical services at least twice a year, except for laboratory testing, which is done once a year.

Family Planning Projects. A family planning project is thus an organization which provides family planning services on a voluntary basis. At a minimum, these services would include medical services, including the prescription of methods and the provision of supplies. Most family planning projects are comprehensive, however, in that they would provide educational and social family planning services, as well as the medical services. A subsidized family planning project provides family planning services to the medically indigent through specific grants from public or private sources and through government reimbursement for services payments to third parties, such as private physicians and hospitals.

Methods of Contraception. The principal methods of easily reversible contraception, any one of which might be prescribed as a part of family planning medical services, are as follows (failure rates in parentheses): Pill (4 percent); IUD (7 percent); condom (16 percent); diaphragm (18 percent); withdrawal (21 percent); rhythm (28 percent); and foam (29 percent).[3] The two most effective developments in contraceptive technology, the Pill and the IUD, both introduced in the 1960s are also the most recent developments.

The Pill is a unique method of contraception in that it is not connected with the sex act in any way. All the user need do is to remember to take one tablet each day, and she obtains almost 100 percent assurance of complete protection. However, the Pill, which works by preventing ovulation, has side-effects which can include: high blood pressure; bloated feelings; weight-gaining; depression; sore breasts; and sporadic bleeding. There is also an increased, though minimal (.006 percent for women over 35, .003 percent for women under 35),[4] risk of blood clots, and some possibility of an increased risk of cancer.

The other recent development in contraceptive technology, the IUD, or inter-uterine device, consists of a polyethylene, plastic, or stainless steel device which is inserted in the uterus by the physician or nurse. The IUD, thus, has the disadvantage, not incurred by the use of the Pill, that it must be inserted and checked to see that it is in place. Also, although advances have been made, it is difficult for women who have not borne a child to use the IUD, since dilation of the cervix is involved. On the other hand, unlike the Pill, there is no need to remember anything, once the IUD is in place. In common with the Pill, the IUD has the disadvantage of side-effects, for some users, which include expelling and unusually heavy menstruation.

Older methods of reversible contraception include the condom and the diaphragm. While having the disadvantages, relative to the Pill and the IUD, of limiting pleasure and being less effective, the condom and the diaphragm have the advantages, relative to the more modern methods, of being easy to use and having minimal side-effects. These advantages are especially held by the condom, which, being just a rubberized sheath used by the male to contain his ejaculation, requires no medical supervision or prescription for use. The diaphragm, used by the female, requires fitting, but then, with spermicidal jelly, can be used without medical supervision. Foam, another method used by the female to contain the male ejaculation, is less effective than the diaphragm.

Older reversible methods not requiring artificial instruments include withdrawal or *coitus interruptus* and the rhythm method. Both these methods are relatively ineffective due, in the case of coitus interruptus, to difficulty in proper timing of the withdrawal, and, in the case of the rhythm method, to the unpredictability of ovulation, which makes it difficult for the woman to determine when she is "safe."

A more drastic method of contraception is sterilization, which, however, in many cases, is not reversible. The vasectomy for men can be easily performed under a local anesthetic by a physician in his office. The operation consists of tying off the *vas deferens* tubes through which the testes are supplied with sperm. This eliminates sperm from the male's ejaculation, but does not limit his sex drive or his ability to have an orgasm. Estimates of the reversibility of this operation range from 30 to 50 percent.[5] Sterilization for women involves a similar, though more complex, operation, in which the oviducts or Fallopian tubes, through which eggs are carried from the ovary to the uterus are sealed off. The more antique version of this operation involves an incision through the abdomen, and requires hospitalization for five days. A more recent but less available version, laproscopic sterilization, involving a much smaller abdominal incision, does not require overnight hospitalization.

The Subsidized Family Planning Service Level. The subsidized family planning service level is defined as the number of patients with family income below 150 percent of poverty level annually provided with subsidized family planning services within a certain geographical area. This subsidized family planning service level will be used as the basic output measure throughout this study. While the service level is a quantitative instrument, it can be used to measure the quality of the services provided through estimates of the proportion of patients receiving comprehensive—social, educational, and medical—services vs. the proportion of patients receiving only medical services. In Massachusetts, for example, it is estimated that 59 percent of the subsidized service level consists of comprehensive services, while the remaining 41 percent consists of medical services only (total service level is 56,000; see Table 11-7).

The Benefits of Family Planning Services

Voluntary family planning services, especially the more effective modern methods, significantly increase the amount of control obtainable by a couple over the number and spacing of their offspring. From the use of this control can flow a number of substantial benefits including greater maternal and child health, greater economic, social and psychological strength for the family, and the prevention of illegitimacy. In terms of maternal health, family planning can help prevent dangerous pregnancies. In terms of child health, family planning can prevent high fertility which is related to high infant mortality, and mental retardation. In one study, for example, fourth and subsequent births were found to account for 29 percent of all yearly live births, but 45 percent of all infant deaths and mentally retarded infants.[6] In terms of the economic, social, and mental health of the family, voluntary family planning enables the couple to have children when they are ready for them, and when they can afford to raise them. Thus, the tragedies of illegitimacy, economic dependency and the unwanted child can be avoided.

The recent Supreme Court decisions in *Roe v. Wade* and *Doe v. Bolton* on January 22, 1973[7] invalidated all restrictions on freedom of abortion during the first thirteen weeks of pregnancy. This decision greatly enhanced abortion as an alternative to family planning for preventing unwanted births. Prior to the decision almost all of the states had prohibited abortion on demand. However, abortion remains a much more drastic means of preventing birth—medically, psychologically, and economically ($200 or more per operation)[8]—and, hence, it appears that family planning will continue to carry the main burden of preventing unwanted births for at least the near term future.

Usage Patterns

Overall Usage of Contraceptives. In 1970, 84.1 percent of all married couples, in which the wife was less than 45, had used a method of contraception at least once. This, represented a slight increase from 1965, when the figure was 82.9 percent. (See Table 11-1.)

Among younger couples (wife < 30) in 1970 the proportion of contracepting couples was higher (88.3 percent) than among older couples (wife 30-44). From 1965 to 1970, the proportion of younger couples who had ever used contraception increased from 84.8 percent to 88.3 percent, while the proportion of older couples ever contracepting decreased slightly from 81.7 percent to 80.4 percent. (See Table 11-1.)

Usage by Contraceptive Type. Between 1965 and 1970, there was a substantial increase, from 37.2 percent to 57.9 percent, in the proportion of married couple contraceptors who were using the modern, more effective methods of contraception—the Pill, sterilization, and the IUD—and a corresponding decline, from 62.8 percent to 42.1 percent, in the proportions using the older, less effective methods—the condom, foam, the rhythm method, the diaphragm, and the douche. This trend towards greater usage of the more modern methods occurred

Table 11-1
Percent of U.S. Married Couples Who Have Ever Used Contraception, Analyzed
by Age and Year (1965 and 1970)

	All Couples (Wife < 45)		Younger Couples (Wife < 30)		Older Couples (Wife 30-44)	
	1965	1970	1965	1970	1965	1970
Ever Used	82.9%	84.1%	84.8%	88.3%	81.7%	80.4%
Never Used	17.1	15.9	15.2	11.7	18.3	19.6
(Number of Respondents)	(4,810)	(5,884)	(1,918)	(2,743)	(2,892)	(3,141)

Source: 1965 and 1970 National Fertility Studies, as reported in: Charles F. Westoff, "The Modernization of U.S. Contraceptive Practice," *Family Planning Perspectives* (July 1972), p. 9. Reprinted with permission from Family Planning Perspectives, Vol. 4, No. 3, 1972, and Dr. Charles F. Westoff.

among younger couples (49.2 percent to 64.8 percent), as well as among older couples (29.6 percent to 51.7 percent). (See Table 11-2.)

In 1970, the most popular contraceptive method was the Pill, which was used by over six million women, representing 34.2 percent of all married couples. The proportion of all couples using the Pill was considerably higher among younger couples (49.4 percent) than older couples (20.6 percent). In fact, in further contrast to the younger couples, among older couples sterilization (25.2 percent) was a more popular method of contraception than the Pill (20.6 percent). The IUD, was the least used modern method among all couples (7.4 percent) and among older couples (5.9 percent), but not among younger couples (9.2 percent). (See Table 11-2.)

Of the older methods, the condom was the most popular method in 1970 among all couples (14.2 percent) and among younger couples (11.4 percent) and older couples (16.6 percent). Foam was the second most popular method among younger couples (8.0 percent), while the rhythm method was the second most popular older method among both older couples (8.3 percent) and all couples (6.4 percent). (See Table 11-2.)

The Need for Subsidized Services

Since 1967, the Federal Government has been making an increasingly substantial effort to subsidize the provision of family planning services to low income women, who might not otherwise have access to these services. Low income women are defined in the HEW "Five Year Plan For Family Planning Services and Population Research Programs," published in 1971, as those with family incomes below the 150 percent of poverty level sliding income scale. (See Table 11-3.)

Table 11-2

Percent of U.S. Married[a] Couples Using Various Methods of Contraception, Analyzed by Age and Year (1965 and 1970)

	All Couples (Wife < 45)		Younger Couples (Wife < 30)		Older Couples (Wife 30-44)	
	1965	1970	1965	1970	1965	1970
Modern Methods	37.2	57.9	49.2	64.8	29.6	51.7
Pill[b]	23.9	34.2	41.4	49.4	12.8	20.6
Sterilization[c]	12.1	16.3	6.1	6.2	16.0	25.2
Wife	7.0	8.5	3.2	3.2	9.5	13.1
Husband	5.1	7.8	2.9	3.0	6.5	12.1
IUD[d]	1.2	7.4	1.7	9.2	0.8	5.9
Older Methods	62.8	42.1	50.8	35.2	70.4	48.3
Condom[e]	21.9	14.2	19.2	11.4	23.7	16.6
Foam	3.3	6.1	4.8	8.0	2.3	4.3
Rhythm	10.9	6.4	7.5	4.2	13.0	8.3
Diaphragm[f]	9.9	5.7	6.2	3.5	12.3	7.6
Douche	5.2	3.2	4.8	2.3	5.5	4.1
Withdrawal	4.0	2.1	2.3	1.7	5.1	2.5
Other[g]	7.6	4.4	6.0	4.1	8.5	4.9
(Number of Respondents)	(3,032)	(3,810)	(1,215)	(1,800)	(1,817)	(2,010)

[a]Who were currently living together.

[b]Includes combination with any other method.

[c]Surgically sterilized at least partly for contraceptive reasons.

[d]Includes combination with any other method except Pill.

[e]Includes combination with any other method except Pill, IUD, or Diaphragm.

[f]Includes combination with any other method except Pill or IUD.

[g]Includes other multiple as well as single methods and a small percentage of unreported methods.

Source: 1965 and 1970 Fertility Studies, as reported in: Charles Westoff, "The Modernization of U.S. Contraceptive Practice," *Family Planning Perspectives* (July 1972), p. 11. Reprinted with permission from *Family Planning Perspectives*, Vol. 4, No. 3, 1972, and Dr. Charles F. Westoff.

Using the number of women estimated from Census data to fall below the 150 percent of poverty level cut-off, as a starting point, the HEW "Five Year Plan" makes various deductions to derive estimates of women in need over a twelve month period. These deductions include subtracting the 15-17 year old cohort, on the assumption that "those above 18 not exposed to pregnancy will offset those below 18 who are." From this sub-total, a 13 percent reduction is made for those sterile to yield a second sub-total. Finally, from the second

Table 11-3

Federal Income Criteria For Subsidized Family Planning Services Non-Farm Income Cut-Offs for 150% of Poverty Level, 1969

Number of Family Members	Income Cut-Off
1 Member (Under age 65)	$2,832
2 Members (Head under age 65)	3,622
3 Members (Head under age 65)	4,358
4 Members (Head under age 65)	5,582
5 Members (Head under age 65)	6,579
6 Members (Head under age 65)	7,382
7 or more Members	9,051

Source: *Current Population Reports*, Series P-60, No. 76, December 16, 1970, Table L, p. 18 in *Report of the Secretary of Health, Education, and Welfare Submitting Five Year Plan for Family Planning Services and Population Research Programs* (Washington, 1971), p. F-12.

sub-total, a 14 percent reduction is made for those pregnant or trying to conceive.[9]

Using this technique, the DHEW Five Year Plan made estimates and projections of the need for subsidized services, during Fiscal Years, 1971-1975 arriving at a projected need figure of 6.6 million women in 1975. (See Table 11-4.)

The Provision of Subsidized Services

The provision of these subsidized services has been made primarily through Federal project grants to state and voluntary agencies. In providing these grants,

Table 11-4

Projected Need for Subsidized Family Planning Services, Fiscal Years, 1971-1975 (000,000)

Fiscal Year	Estimated Need
1971	6.1
1972	6.2
1973	6.3
1974	6.4
1975	6.6

Source: *Report of the Secretary of Health, Education, and Welfare, Submitting Five Year Plan for Family Planning Services and Population Research Programs* (Washington, D.C., 1971), p. 369.

the Federal government has never required more than a 25 percent local matching share, and most Federal funds currently provided require only 10 percent local matching. The level of Federal aid for family planning has grown sixteen-fold since the Federal government initiated significant appropriations for subsidized family services, from $11.3 million in Fiscal Year 1967 to $182.6 million in Fiscal Year 1973. For Fiscal Year 1974, however, the level of Federal funding was reduced to $176 million. Indications, are that by Fiscal Year 1975 the project grant system will be phased out in favor of third-party reimbursement for service payments through Medicaid or National Health Insurance.[10] From 1967 to 1972, the rate per patients served in Federal dollars, has increased from $16 to $57. This increase in rate per patient reflects inflation and the increased provision of the modern contraceptives, such as the IUD and the Pill, which require greater medical supervision. At the current rate of $57 in Federal dollars per patient, it would require $376 million to serve the estimated 6.6 million women in need in 1975, the end of the DHEW Five Year Plan. These rates, it should be noted, are rough estimates. (See Table 11-5.)

The effect of this Federal funding effort since 1967 has been dramatic. The estimated number of low income women served has risen from 0.7 million in 1967 to 2.6 million in 1972, while the percentage of met need has increased from 12.1 percent to 42.6 percent during the same period. (See Table 11-6.)

3. The Subsidized Family Planning System in Massachusetts

The Massachusetts subsidized family planning system centers on the activities of private doctors and non-sectarian private hospitals (except Boston

Table 11-5
Federal Expenditures for Family Planning Services, Fiscal Years 1967-1973

Fiscal Year	Total Amount	Approx. No. of Patients Served	Amount Per Patient Served
1967	$11.3 million	.7	$16
1968	16.0 million	.9	17
1969	34.3 million	1.1	31
1970	55.3 million	1.4	40
1971	80.3 million	1.9	42
1972	148.6 million	2.6	57
1973 (estimated)	182.6 million		
1974 (budgeted)	176.0 million		

Source: Jeannie I. Rosoff, "The Future of Federal Support for Family Planning Services and Population Research," *Family Planning Perspectives*, (Winter, 1973) pp. 8-10. Reprinted with permission from *Family Planning Perspectives*, Vol. 5, No. 1, 1973.

Table 11-6
Met Need for Subsidized Services Fiscal Years, 1967-1972

	FY 1967	FY 1968	FY 1969	FY 1970	FY 1971	FY 1972	FY 1973	FY 1974	FY 1975
Patients Served†	.7	.9	1.1	1.4	1.9	2.6			
Projected Need‡	5.8*	5.9*	6.0	6.0*	6.1	6.2	6.3	6.4	6.6
% Met Need	12.1	15.3	18.3	23.3	31.1	42.6			

*Est. from trend of available data. † Approximate. ‡Below 150% of poverty level.
Sources:
Patients-Served: Planned-Parenthood World-Population, Center for Family Planning Program Development, "Data and Analyses for 1973 Revision of DHEW Five-Year Plan for Family Planning Services," in Jeannie I. Rosoff, "The Future of Federal Support for Family Planning Services and Population Research," *Family Planning Perspectives* (Winter, 1973), p. 8.
Projected Need: *Report of the Secretary of Health, Education, and Welfare Submitting Five Year Plan for Family Planning Services and Population Research Programs* (Washington, 1971), p. 369.

City Hospital) and a group of voluntary public and non-profit private agencies in obtaining and utilizing Federal Government funds to provide free family planning services to low income women in the state. For the private doctors, who serve an estimated 23,000 or 41 percent of the 56,000 low income family planning patients in the State (see Table 11-7), the procedure for obtaining Federal funds is fairly simple. He obtains from the state a Medicaid (Title XIX of the Social Security Act) vendor number. Then he bills the state for reimbursable family planning expenses allowable under the Federal and state regulations governing reimbursement under Title XIX of the Social Security Act. For the voluntary agencies, obtaining and utilizing Federal funds is a much more difficult proposition, since most of their income comes from project grants which must be negotiated with the Region I Office of the National Center For Family Planning Services, and since they must put together comprehensive programs including not only medical services but educational and social services, as well.

The Analytical Approach

In the analysis which follows, the Massachusetts subsidized family planning system will be structured in terms of a set of interacting input variables which together produce a service level, the output variable. The input variables will be categorized under the headings of actors, contexts (relatively slow-changing variables), laws, rules, and regulations, and ideologies. Within these categories, each variable will be further classified as either increasing or restraining with respect to the output variable. An increasing variable will be defined as a factor which is judged to be largely fulfilling its potential for positively influencing the service level. A restraining variable will be defined as an element which is judged to be largely not fulfilling its potential for positively influencing the service level. Within the increasing and restraining classifications in each category, the variables will be rank-ordered by the degree to which they have fulfilled (increasing) or not fulfilled (restraining) their potential for positively influencing the service level. Thus, the analysis will yield several prioritized sets of policy options for leveraging the output of the system, with the most priority being accorded to the first-ranked restraining variables, and the least priority being accorded to the first-ranked increasing variables.

*The Output Variable: The Subsidized
Family Planning Service Level*

In 1972, 56,000 low income women, or 49 percent of the estimated 114,000 such women in need, were supplied with subsidized family planning services in Massachusetts. This 1972 level represented an almost eight-fold increase from the 1968 level of 7,318. As a result of this increase, Massachusetts now ranks third among the New England States in terms of percent of met need. (See Table 11-7.)

23,000 patients, or 41 percent of the subsidized service level, are provided

Table 11-7
Federally Subsidized Family Services in New England Fiscal Year 1972*

State	Women in Need Over 12 Month Period (below 150% of Poverty Level)	Organized Programs	Private Physicians	Total	% Met Need
Total	255,000	73,000	51,000	12,400	49%
R.I.	26,000	14,000	5,000	19,000	73
Conn.	50,000	15,000	10,000	25,000	50
Mass.	114,000	33,000	23,000	56,000	49
Me.	34,000	6,500	7,000	13,500	40
Vt.	13,000	2,000	2,700	4,700	36
N.H.	17,000	2,500	3,500	6,000	35

*Need and service figures are rough approximations.
Source: Center for Family Planning Program Development, Planned Parenthood-World Population, "Laws and Policies on Contraception, Sterilization, Abortion, Family Planning Services, and Medical Care for Minors, New England States." Mimeo (November 1972), Table 5.

with medical services only through private doctors and non-sectarian hospitals who may be reimbursed by the joint State/Federal (50 percent/50 percent) Medicaid program. 33,000, or 59 percent of the service level, however, are provided with social, educational, and medical services through eleven organized programs supported primarily by Federal categorical grants. (See Tables 11-7, 11-8.)

Input Variables

Increasing Variables: *Congress.* The Federal Congress has been, by far, the most important positive influence on the subsidized family planning service level in Massachusetts. From a level of 7,318 patients in 1958, the total number of patients served has risen to 56,000 in Fiscal Year 1972, largely as a result of Federal funds authorized under legislation passed by the National Congress. 23,000 or 41 percent of the Fiscal Year 1972 total of 56,000 patients, are being served through private physicians and hospitals, who, to some extent, are reimbursed for these services through the state-administered Medicaid program, as third party providers. (See Table 11-7.) The State Medicaid program is 50 percent funded by the Federal Government under Congressional legislation establishing Title XIX of the Social Security Act in 1966. Services for the 33,000 patients, or 59 percent of the subsidized patient load in the State, who are served by the eleven comprehensive family planning projects, are provided through categorical grants to these projects. These categorical grants are block

Table 11-8
Federally-Funded Family Planning Projects in Mass.: Budget and Annual Patient Loads, Fiscal Year, 1972

Project	Federal Share Funds	Local Share Funds	Approx. Annual Patient Load
Berkshire County	$ 128,874	$ 15,445	500
Boston	711,748	131,529	19,500
Brockton	99,346	46,110	1,500
Cambridge	126,000	31,475	1,000
Fall River	69,180	23,719	850
Holyoke	83,083	10,800	650
Lowell	125,000	35,680	2,500
North Shore	180,000	77,251	1,500
Somerville	57,808	14,546	1,000
Springfield	173,630	53,831	2,000
Worcester	247,060	59,616	2,000
Total	$1,875,729	$500,002	33,000

Source: Federally-Funded Family Planning Project Proposals.

amounts provided on an annual basis from the regional offices of Federal agencies. Currently ten of the eleven comprehensive projects in the State are being supplied with funds authorized under Title X of the Public Health Service Act, which was passed by Congress in 1970. The eleventh project is being supplied under Title II of the Economic Opportunity Act, as amended in 1967. Title X requires only a 10 percent local matching share, while Title II requires a 20 percent matching share. The local share under both these Titles can be "soft," that is in terms of such non-out-of-pocket items as volunteer time or space for which rent is not paid. This is in contrast to "hard" matching required under Title V of the Social Security Act (as amended in 1967)—a funding vehicle previously used to finance family planning projects in the State. "Hard" matching must include more liquid items such as cash, rents, or salaries. The total amount of Federal monies provided to the eleven comprehensive projects in Fiscal Year 1973 under Titles X and II was approximately $1.9 million, which was matched by a total local budget of approximately $.5 million. By far, the largest project, financially, was Boston with approximately $700,000 in Federal share, about $130,000 in local share, and an annual patient load of about 20,000 patients. The smallest project was Fall River, with about $70,000 in Federal funds, approximately $24,000 in local share, and an annual patient load of approximately 850 patients. With Boston included, the average patient load per project was 3,000 patients. Without Boston, the average patient load per project was about 1,350. (See Table 11-8.)

Besides Title XIX, Federal monies for the purchase of services are also available to the State under Title IV-A of the Social Security Act, as amended in 1967. Until the last six months of Fiscal Year 1973, the State had not complied with the mandatory requirement to provide family planning services as a condition of receiving IV-A monies for social services, which are administered by the State. However, in October, 1972, the Department of Health, Education, and Welfare revised the IV-A regulations to include a 1 percent penalty against the entire State IV-A allocation from the Federal Government ($69.5 million in Fiscal Year 1973), as well as a 90 percent Federal matching share vs. the previous share of 75 percent. These changes, principally the penalty, have led the State to use $220,000 in Federal/State IV-A funds to purchase family planning services during the last half of Fiscal Year 1973.[11]

The Supreme Court. The Supreme Court has played an important role in making subsidized family planning feasible in Massachusetts by declaring unconstitutional State laws against family planning which the State Government, itself, would not rescind. The most important Supreme Court decisions have been *Griswold v. Connecticut*, 381, U.S. 479 (1965) in which prohibitions against the sales of contraceptives to married couples were abrogated, and *Eisenstadt v. Baird*, 405 U.S. 438 (1972) in which prohibitions against the sale of contraceptives to unmarried couples were abrogated.

The President. Both Presidents Johnson and President Nixon have supported Federal assistance for the provision of subsidized family planning services. President Johnson conceived and helped push through Congress the Economic Opportunity Act, under Title II of which funds were provided for initiating more than half of the current family planning projects in the State. President Nixon supported the Family Planning Services and Population Research Act of 1970 (PL 91-572), which created Title X of the Public Health Services Act, under which all but one of the eleven current subsidized family planning projects are now being funded.

The support which these Presidents have given to subsidized family planning services is significant because of the lack of such support from Presidents in the past, and also because the President has powerful tools for obstructing the allocation of appropriations by Congress through using the Office of Management and the Budget to freeze the appropriations. Recently, for example, it was announced that the Department of Health, Education, and Welfare was going to spend only $26.6 billion of the $28.6 billion appropriated by Congress for social services in Fiscal Year 1974.[12]

Under Federal revenue-sharing, President Nixon is now taking drastic steps not only to reduce the level of Federal assistance for social services, but also to place the disposal of this assistance much more at the discretion of state and local governments. Both these trends have depressing implications for the subsidized family planning service level in Massachusetts, since 59 percent of this level is financed through specific Federal categorical grants. (See Table 11-7.)

The Federal Bureaucracy. The federal bureaucracy plays an important role in setting the program and eligibility requirements for Federal assistance and in deciding which areas and which programs should receive categorical grants. Thus, last October, the Social Services Administration of the Department of Health, Education, and Welfare stimulated the use by the State of its Title IV-A (Social Security Act) budget for family planning services by revising the IV-A regulations to include a significant penalty for the non-provision of such services. More recently the Social Services Administration has proposed to remove the penalty provision which would probably lead to the decline of IV-A services in the State. The bureaucracy has similar kinds of authority with respect to the provision of categorical grants. These grants were until recently less available to Massachusetts than to other areas, because of the more restrictive laws in that State.

In summary, the Federal Government has been by far the most important positive influence on the subsidized family planning service level in the State. Without the Federal initiative, this service level would be very low. Hence, the threat to the categorical grants posed by revenue-sharing has serious implications for the maintenance of the service level.

Concerned Citizens Groups. The main impetus behind the creation of more than half of the current Federally-funded organized programs over the past three years came from Federally-funded (Office of Economic Opportunity) anti-poverty programs. These groups saw family planning project grants as a means of expanding their anti-poverty services and as a means of continuing their community services in the face of declining anti-poverty appropriations from the Federal Congress. Model Cities programs have had a financial as well as a community action effect in the projects they have helped sponsor, since they have been able to use Federal funds allocated to them as the local matching share for Federal family planning grants.

Besides anti-poverty groups, the impetuses behind other projects have been: coalitions of business and professional people, a family service organization, and the Planned Parenthood League of Massachusetts.

The concerned citizens' groups have taken the responsibility for hiring executive directors and other staff, obtaining facilities, arranging for doctors' and hospital services and obtaining local share matching requirements. With the transfer of most of project grant funding to Title X of the Public Health Services Act, local matching requirements have been reduced to 10 percent vs. 20 percent for Title V of the Social Security Act and Title II of the Economic Opportunity Act. However, in practice, more than a 10 percent match is usually provided and this requires the cooperation of an "in-kind" provider, usually a hospital. In several cases, Planned-Parenthood, as well as the concerned citizens groups, themselves, have provided "seed money" ($1,000-$5,000) to get a program started. One concerned citizens' group provides an annual cash budget of $7,000, but availability of this kind of private money is rare. Planned Parenthood has an annual budget of $220,000, but only 22 percent of this is available for the provision of services.

Consumers. Medically indigent women have acted as both an initiating and a sustaining force of family planning projects. In the more than half of the projects where Community Action and Model Cities groups initiated the projects, consumer groups played the majority role in getting the projects started. Consumers continue to play an important role on the boards of all the projects, and in providing the demand for the services offered. At most projects the demand has expanded to exceed the supply. It is important to note, however, that among consumers participating in the administration of family planning projects, the interest is not so much in family planning services per se as in family planning services as part of a comprehensive social and medical services package.

The Project Directors. The directors of the eleven established projects have performed a great service in maintaining and expanding the programs started by the concerned citizens' groups. At relatively low salaries (most $13,000 or less), they have supervised the provision of social, educational, training, and medical services, paid the bills, kept records of patients served, and, in many cases, expanded the patient load.

In addition, they have formed an association, the Massachusetts Association of Family Planning Program Directors, which meets monthly to discuss matters of mutual concern. These meetings focus mainly on funding policy and the activities of other state-wide organizations, such as Planned Parenthood and the State Government. With the anticipated decline of project grant funds over the next three years, and the fragmentation of the funding system between state and local agencies, the Project directors have been considering incorporation. Incorporation would enable them to act with one voice in influencing state and local policy, and to serve, with limited liability, as a joint grantee for funding purposes. In April of this year [1973], the project association served as a joint grantee for a $81,000 Department of Community Affairs contract to provide family services to public housing patients through the end of Fiscal Year 1973. But without corporate status, the full responsibility for handling the finances of this project had to be taken by one of the projects rather than by the Association, as a whole.

Private Doctors. The estimate of 23,000 low income women served by private physicians must be considered a "soft" statistic, since it is based on a national estimate by Planned Parenthood—World Population of the proportion of women below 150 percent of poverty obtaining care from private physicians. (See Table 11-7.) Nevertheless, even given an over-estimate of as much as 20 percent, the doctors would still be serving more than half as many patients as the 33,000 served by the organized programs. (See Table 11-7.) Some of these doctors are reimbursed for this service through Title XIX funds.

The service provided by the doctors may be lacking in two respects. First, it may not include the social, educational, and training services provided by the organized programs. Second, private doctors are not as accessible to low income patients as organized programs, since they need more paying patients, while organized programs can afford to go where the low income patients are. If Federal project grants are eliminated, then the organized programs will be jeopardized, and the inadequate services of private doctors may be all that is left to provide family planning services to the low income women in the State.

Private Non-Sectarian Hospitals. Like the doctors, the non-sectarian hospitals have played a small role in the initiating of most Federal projects, but an essential role in establishing them, since the provision of modern family planning services requires hospital laboratory tests and trained medical personnel, who are often associated with hospitals. The reluctance of these hospitals to initiate subsidized family planning programs seems to derive from a reluctance to accept the controls of a government program, and a fear of becoming dependent on the uncertain Federal dollar. Yet, unlike the sectarian and city (except Boston) hospitals, in most cases, they see the provision of family planning services as a positive course of action, and, hence, are willing to cooperate with Federal programs, once the organizational efforts have been initiated by concerned citizens' groups. Furthermore, the in-kind local matching share is in almost all cases provided entirely by these hospitals, six of which actually serve as the grantee for family planning projects.

Planned Parenthood League of Massachusetts. The Planned Parenthood League of Massachusetts (PPLM) complements the role of the Federal projects by providing information and referral to these projects and to private physicians and other clinics. PPLM also provides training and education, including an extensive college sex education program. Finally, the League provides a small amount of seed funds and financial assistance to organized Federal and non-Federal programs. In 1972, Planned Parenthood's budget of $221,515 was divided as follows: initiation and support of medical services (22%), development (17%), education and training (15%), public information (13%), colleges (11%), information and referral (9%), seminars (9%), library and speakers (4%).[13]

Restraining Variables: *The State Government.* During the last half of Fiscal Year 1973, the State Government has made an about-face, and for the first time provided State funds for family planning services. Three state agencies, the Department of Public Welfare, the Department of Community Affairs, and the Office of the Children have asked for proposals to provide family planning services through joint State/Federal (Title IV-A) funds. So far, an estimated $220,000 in contracts have been signed, $175,000 by Welfare and $145,000 by Community Affairs. The Welfare contracts are to provide expanded services, including initial visits and re-visits, through reimbursement of services not currently paid for under Title X (project grants) or Title XIX (Medicaid). The Community Affairs contracts are for the provision of initial visits to new patients in public housing, and require sign-offs by tenants' organizations and local housing authorities. The Office of the Children contracts would be to provide expanded services to minors. If all these contracts are performed, it is estimated that an additional 3,000-5,000 patients could be added to the service level in the State in Fiscal Year 1973. Most contracts are with Title X projects.

The major impetuses behind this historic subsidization of family planning services by the State of Massachusetts were changes in the Federal regulations governing the disbursement of IV-A monies to the states and the unspent State IV-A fund to match IV-A monies. The changes in the IV-A regulations, made in November, 1972, provided for a 1 percent penalty against the entire IV-A budget for the State ($69.5 million in Fiscal Year 1973) if family planning services were not provided. These regulations also provided for a special 90 percent federal matching to state funds used for family planning services vs. 75 percent for other services.[14] The second impetus was the failure of a committee of human services agencies to spend a discretionary fund of 7.5 million dollars, designated by the Legislature to be spent for IV-A eligible expansion services at the discretion of the committee. $2.5 million of the $10 million is State funds and $5.6 million Federal IV-A funds. Thus, the pressure of the penalty clause in the IV-A regulations and the need to spend the expansion pool money plus the opportunity of utilizing the special 90 percent/10 percent matching for family planning services, led the expansion pool committee to make expansion pool funds available for family planning services in the last half of Fiscal Year 1973.

The State Government must still be considered a restraining variable in subsidized family planning matters, however, since it has far from fulfilled its potential as a provider of family planning services, and is unlikely to do so in the near term future. First, the Legislature it should be noted, has never appropriated funds specifically for family planning, and, in the past, line items for family services were carefully examined and sub-items for family planning services extracted. The disposition of the Legislature is not likely to change in the near future, since Massachusetts is a predominately Roman Catholic state, and the Church hierarchy in the State, strongly disapproves of artificial contraception.

Secondly, the proposed revisions in the IV-A regulations plus the anticipated reduction in the total IV-A budget make it extremely unlikely that the State will provide IV-A funds for family planning services in Fiscal Year 1974. The proposed revisions would restrict eligibility and remove the penalty clause which made the State provide family planning services. The reduction in the State IV-A budget as a result of Federal revenue-sharing may be as much as 50 percent.

Thirdly, the State bureaucracy continues to impede the provision of subsidized family planning services in several ways. Complicated documentation forms must be filled out in addition to regular medical history forms. These forms are unnecessarily complex and are not standardized between the several state agencies. Another way in which the State bureaucracy holds back family planning is through not spending earmarked Federal family planning grants (under Title V of the Social Security Act) for family planning. These funds which require no local matching share have been provided at the level of $128,000 a year since Fiscal Year 1971. Yet during these years the planning staff which has theoretically absorbed these funds has declined from four to one (and the remaining employee has not been paid since last July). Finally, the State bureaucrats have formed a Consortium whose main goal seems to be trying to compete with the Project Directors Association for recognition rather than to further the provision of subsidized family planning services in the State. Recently, for example, they set out to obtain funds for a State Plan which would duplicate a planning effort already under way under the auspices of the Project Director's Association.

The Catholic Church. The official Catholic position on contraception, as outlined in Pope Paul's 1968 encyclical, *Humanae Vitae*, is that only the rhythm method is permitted to Catholics. There has been widespread disagreement with this directive in the Catholic community throughout the world, but the Church in Massachusetts seems to have taken the conservative side of the issue. Statements by Archibishop Medeiros, *The Pilot*, the Archdiocese newspaper, and the Massachusetts Catholic Conference, the Church lobbying organization, and the refusal of Catholic hospitals to prescribe contraception other than the rhythm method, all indicate that in Massachusetts the Church has tended to act according to the letter of the encyclical.

More vigorous opposition of the Church to legalized abortion in the state has probably tended to stiffen the Church's stand against family planning since abortion is also a life preventing device.

The actions of the Church on contraception must be an important factor in the State legislature's unwillingness to appropriate funds for family planning, since a majority of the electorate of the state is Catholic. The teachings of the Church do not seem to have prevented Catholics from using artificial contraceptives, however, since the consumer response to the family planning projects has been strong.

The Contexts

Contraceptive Technology. The 1960s witnessed great advances in contraceptive technology with the introduction on a large scale of the significantly more effective "modern" methods of contraception, the Pill, the IUD, and sterilization—together used by almost 60 percent of all U.S. contracepting married couples in 1970. (See Table 11-2.) Important as these advances have been, they require expensive medical supervision in order to be provided. Sterilization can cost up to $200,[15] but, of course, being a one shot operation, involves a much lower annual cost. The provision of the Pill and the IUD is estimated to cost $66 per person on an annual basis.[16] Thus, to provide the estimated 6.6 million non-sterilized women in need in 1975, (see Table 11-4) with modern contraception would cost approximately $436 million.

The cost of modern contraceptive care plus the side-effects of the Pill and the IUD point to the need for less expensive, less organically disruptive contraceptives. The ideal contraceptive would be something like a pill that required no medical supervision, cost five cents, had no side-effects and needed to be taken only once a month by either male or female. Unfortunately, as a recent article in *Science* said "the news about birth control (technology) is that there is no news."[17] No radical research breakthroughs which might lead to something approaching the ideal contraceptive described above is anticipated for at least fifteen years. Improvements will be confined to variations of the current methods.

Hence, the factor of contraceptive technology must be considered a context or slow-changing variable for purposes of this study.

Input Variables: Laws, Rules, and
Regulations[18]

Increasing Variables. The increasing variables in this section consist of the regulations governing the disbursement of funds under various Federal laws. Upon publication, these regulations are printed in *The Federal Register*, and refer to programs funded under various titles of the United States Code. The regulations are, of course, interpreted by those administering them, and it is in their interpreted sense that they are presented here.

Title X Regulations (Public Health Service Act). Family planning services in Massachusetts are now primarily funded under Title X of the Public Health Service Act, promulgated in 1970. The regulations associated with this legislation are fairly restrictive. However, in practice, these regulations are not strictly enforced. In practice, one finds that in Region I, the principal qualifications for funding are, first, that a workable program be demonstrated, and, a somewhat distant second, that the program serve an area of demonstrated need. A workable program means adequate staff to provide medical and social services (counseling, out-reach, and follow-up), hospital back-up and facilities. A line item budget and an estimate of patients served is also required. Accountability is primarily in terms of overall expenses and an estimate of patients served. These accounts need not be detailed. Cost per visit or re-visit is not required, only line item expenses and an estimate of all patients served. Documentation of patients served by any kind of eligibility criteria is not required since Title X regulations do not specify income requirements. However, 150 percent of the poverty level is the criterion used in most studies. (See Table 11-3.)

The relatively low priority of the need criteria at the moment is probably a function of the newness of the family planning programs in the State, most of which did not get started until after 1970. This is not to say that programs have not been placed in areas of unmet need or that service of needy persons is not required. Rather the point is that the emphasis has been on establishing a set of working programs rather than on meeting all the need in the State.

Title IV-A Regulations (Social Security Act). Title IV-A of the Social Security Act was amended in 1967 in order to make mandatory the provision of medical family planning services under state social service plans financed through Title IV-A monies. Services could be provided not only to current AFDC recipients, but to potential recipients, as well. In spite of the mandatory provision, and a 3-1 Federal/State matching provision, Massachusetts did not provide any medical family planning services under its IV-A Social Services plan until the last four months of Fiscal Year 1973.

The funding of family planning through IV-A in the past four months of Fiscal Year 1973, has been prompted by the revision of the IV-A regulations in

October, 1972. Most important of these revisions was the imposition of a penalty equal to 1 percent of the total IV-A Federal budget for the state (set at $69.5 million in Fiscal Year 1973 and Fiscal Year 1974), if medical family services were not provided. In addition, the Federal matching share was increased to 90 percent (a provision of HR1). These revisions plus an unspent "expansion pool" has led to the expenditure of $220,000 for family planning services by the State during the last four months of Fiscal Year 1973.

Revisions in the IV-A regulations, proposed in February of this year, could radically alter the availability of IV-A funds for family planning. Among the new restrictions would be elimination of the ability of private groups to donate the local share, and restriction of the potential recipient income to 133 1/3 percent of the current state assistance payment level. Most important, the regulations would limit services to potential AFDC (Aid to Families With Dependent Children) recipients whose problem could be corrected within six months. Since it takes nine months for gestation, family planning cannot avoid a birth within the specified period of time, and, hence, potential recipients would not be eligible for family planning services at all.

Finally, the State implementation of IV-A funded family planning programs has created new problems for the providers in that a detailed eligibility form must be filled out by each recipient and kept by the provider in case of auditing. Only a summary form totaling patients served need be sent to the funding agency (currently either Welfare or the Department of Community Affairs), however, for reimbursement. The rates set by Welfare ($60 for an initial visit and $41 for a re-visit) and Community Affairs ($75 for an initial visit) have been extremely liberal, however, and are significantly above the actual costs of participating projects.

Title II Regulations (Economic Opportunity Act). Under Title II, approximately $126,000 in project grants is supplied to the Cambridge project for the provision of medical, social, and educational services. Title II regulations governing project grants are similar to Title X regulations, having the dual criterion of a workable program and a medically indigent population. However, there seems to have been more emphasis by the Region I office of the Office of Economic Opportunity, which administers the Title II grants, on providing family planning services to hard core poverty areas than in the case of the Title X grants.

Title V Regulations (Social Security Act). The regulations governing Title V of the Social Security Act have little bearing on the family planning service level in the State. Although $128,000 has been provided to the State in each of the past two years in formula grants (no state matching required) earmarked either for the provision of family planning services or for the planning of these services, very little of this money has been used for these purposes. Project grants are no longer provided to programs in the State under Title V.

Restraining Variables: *Medical Profession Standards.* The cost of family planning services may be kept unnecessarily high due to the medical profession's requirement that doctors and hospitals be involved in the provision of the more effective "modern" contraceptives. These professional services amount to more than half of the cost of comprehensive family planning service programs. It is questionable whether doctor and hospital (laboratory tests) services are needed in every case. In Thailand, to give a contrast, these services are used on a referral basis, and most contraceptives, including the Pill and the IUD, are dispensed by a nurse practitioner using a check list.[19] If a similar practice could be instituted in the United States, the cost of family planning services could be greatly reduced.

State Laws. With the *Griswold v. Connecticut*, 381, U.S. 479 (1965) and *Eisenstadt v. Baird*, 405 U.S. 438 (1972) decisions of the United States Supreme Court, the only laws restricting the provision of family planning services in Massachusetts are in regard to minors. Physicians cannot currently provide family planning services to minors without parental consent. This creates an unnecessary barrier to the provision of these services, especially considering that 28 percent of nevermarried young women 15-19 have had sexual intercourse (the proportion rises from 14 percent at age 15 to 46 percent by age 19).[20] Bills filed for the 1973 Session of the General Court by Representatives Wetmore and Matenso would remove these restrictions, but there seems little chance of passage given the controversiality of family planning in the State.

Input Variables: Ideologies

Increasing Variables: *The Human Rights and Welfare Ideology.* This ideology has underlaid all the major Federal legislation under which subsidized family projects have been funded. The provision of such services has been justified on the grounds of equal access to medical services, the prevention of poverty, the prevention of illegitimacy, and maternal and child health. A tenet of this ideology, held more typically by Democratic administrations under whom most family planning legislation has been passed, is that the Federal Government should act to aid the indigent directly rather than through the states. This belief underlies the categorical grants which have enabled local groups to create family planning projects in Massachusetts in the face of inaction by the State.

The Environmentalist and Population Control Ideology. Concern about widespread population has existed at least since the publication of Malthus' *An Essay on the Principle of Population* in 1798, in which the author saw famine as a major check on population due to the tendency of the population to grow faster than the food supply.[21]

Much of the same kind of theme is being sounded today by environmentalists and population experts—that the combination of overpopulation, consumption of finite resources, and pollution are going to lead to widespread starvation in the near future. In the *Limits to Growth*, the modern sequel to Malthus' *Essay*, a group of MIT management scientists have even made a computerized forecast of a major population collapse around the year 2100.[22] The need for stabilizing population and economic growth has received increasing publicity through the media and such organizations as Zero Population Growth and the Sierra Club. The international nature of the problem was recognized at the U.N. Conference on the Environment held in Stockholm in July 1972.

Women's Rights Ideologies. Women's rights groups have greatly proliferated in the past several years. These organizations, such as NOW (National Organization For Women) tend to see the ability of a woman to control her own fertility, whether through family planning or abortion, as a basic human right. These organizations have supported subsidized family planning services and have been in the forefront of the movement for abortion law reform. Doubtless the women's rights ideology has been and will continue to be a powerful support of subsidized family planning services, although involvement in women's rights is a luxury that can be afforded only by middle class women.

Anti-Poor And Racist Ideologies. The most controversial aspect of family planning lies in its being supported by anti-humanists and racists as a means of reducing the population of the poor and minorities. Though this kind of support for family planning is extremely limited, it has the effect of raising serious questions in the minds of minority groups about the motives behind subsidized family planning for low income women. The association of family planning with population control by birth control advocates further amplifies the issue of motives behind the subsidized family planning program. These questions might be answered by stressing the individual and family benefits of family planning, which are already accessible to the middle and upper income populations.

Restraining Variables: *The Catholic Ideology.* Pope Paul's 1968 encyclical, *Humanae Vitae*, which proscribes artificial contraception to Catholics, has evoked increasing and widespread dissent in the Catholic community.[23] There is a feeling among segments of Catholic theologians and groups of Bishops that Catholics have the right to dissent from official teaching when there seem to be sufficient reasons to do so. It seemly likely that with the growth of the environmentalists and overpopulation ideology that the dissent from the teaching of *Humanae Vitae* will increase.

The Federalist Ideology. The federalist ideology, more associated with the Republican than the Democratic party, advocates Federal revenue-sharing with the state governments rather than direct aid to localities. Revenue-sharing in lieu of categorical grants to localities would severely hinder subsidized family planning in Massachusetts, since the state government gives little support to subsidized family planning services. Federal revenue-sharing will be considered in more detail in sections 4 and 5.

Summary: Priorities for Policy Development

The purpose of the systems analysis described in the previous chapter was to develop a framework for policy analysis relative to the subsidized family planning service level in Massachusetts. This analysis identified the input variables with the greatest potential for change in a direction which would positively influence the output variable. These variables, thus, represent the top priority focuses for the development of policy to leverage the service output. The following list summarizes in rank-order these priorities. Greatest priority was accorded to restraining variables and least priority to increasing variables.

Actors

1. The State Government
2. The Catholic Church
3. The Planned Parenthood League of Massachusetts
4. Private non-Sectarian Hospitals
5. Private Doctors
6. Family Planning Project Directors
7. Consumers
8. Concerned Citizens Groups
9. The Federal Government

Laws, Rules and Regulations

1. Medical Professional Standard
2. State Laws
3. Title V Regulations (Social Security Act)
4. Title II Regulations (Economic Opportunity Act)
5. Title IV-A Regulations (Social Security Act)
6. Title X Regulations (Public Health Services Act)

Ideologies

1. The Catholic Ideology
2. The Federalist Ideology
3. The Environmentalist and Population Control Ideology
4. The Human Rights and Welfare Ideology

It will be noted that the anti-poor and racist ideology has been left out of the list, since it is not an appropriate policy consideration.

While the above list indicates priorities for policy development, there remains the question of whether effective policies can be developed within a short term planning horizon. This question will be addressed in the conclusions where the ability of the system to respond to the loss of categorical grants as a result of the implementation of Federal revenue-sharing will be considered.

4. Federal Revenue-Sharing and Categorical Grants for Family Planning Services

The domestic program of the second-term Nixon administration can best be described by the much abused term, "revenue-sharing." As originally proposed by Presidents Kennedy and Johnson's Chief Economic Advisor, Professor Walter Heller, revenue-sharing meant the disbursement of budget *surpluses* by the Federal Government to state and local governments on an unrestricted basis to help them pay for general government expenses, such as police and fire protection and sanitation services. These funds would be derived from a fixed percentage of Federal income and, hence, would increase with the expansion of the Federal tax base.[24]

Under President Nixon, in his second term, however, revenue-sharing has taken on quite a different cast than that envisaged by Dr. Heller. Under the slogan of a "New Federalism," revenue-sharing is being used as a means of not only dismantling sections of the Federal bureaucracy, such as the Office of Economic Opportunity, but also of actually reducing the amount of Federal assistance provided to states and localities. In Fiscal Year 1974, the first year of revenue-sharing, for example, the total of the amount of Federal assistance will decline to $44.8 million from $45 million in Fiscal 1973. Just to have maintained the level of the previous fiscal year in Fiscal Year 1974 in the face of inflation would have required an assistance level of $46.5 billion.[25] Thus, instead of the "bonus" envisaged by Presidential advisor Heller in the 1960s, revenue-sharing in the 1970s will mean a decline in Federal aid to state and local governments.

Federal revenue-sharing under President Nixon actually includes two programs: general revenue-sharing and special revenue-sharing. General revenue-sharing, which has already been implemented under the State and Local Assistance Act passed by Congress in 1972, involves the transfer to state and local governments of largely unrestricted funds on a formula basis. In the case of states, these funds can be used for any legal expenditure except matching Federal grants. In the case of county and municipal governments, the use of these funds is restricted to "high priority expenditures," which are, however, broadly defined. These "high priority" local expenditures include: maintenance and operating expenses for public safety (including law enforcement, fire protection and building code enforcement); environmental protection (including sewage disposal, sanitation, and pollution abatement); public transportation (including transit systems and roads); health; recreation; libraries; social services for the poor and aged; and financial administration. Either of two formulas, whichever provides the largest amount, is used to allocate funds to States: a five factor formula considering population, urbanized population, population weighted inversely for per capita income, income tax collections, and general tax effort; or a three factor formula which considers population, general tax effort, and per capita income. Allocations to local governments are based on the three factor formula, only. Although, both state and local governments can use revenue-sharing funds to reduce taxes, these formulas ensure that by so doing they will reduce general revenue-sharing funds allocated to them in future years.[26] Local governments cannot use general revenue-sharing dollars to pay for education, or general administration expenses or to match Federal grants. However, they can substitute these funds for other programs now paid for out of local funds. The total amount allocated to states and localities under general revenue-sharing over the five year period, Fiscal Year 1973-Fiscal Year 1977 will be $30.2 billion, distributed annually as follows:

Table 11-9
Projected Total U.S. General Revenue-Sharing Allocations, Fiscal Years 1973-1977 ($000,000,000)

1973	$6.8
1974	6.0
1975	6.2
1976	6.3
1977	4.9

Source: *The Boston Globe*, February 19, 1973, p. 8.

Although the authority of the principal funding vehicle for categorical grants for comprehensive family planning projects, Title X of the Public Health Services Act, is to be renewed by Congress for Fiscal Year, 1974, the best current information is that the Nixon administration will seek to dismantle this grant program the following year.[27] In addition, it is thought that family planning services will not be included in any consolidated block grants under special revenue-sharing.

Hence, it appears that under the policy of Federal revenue-sharing, the categorical grants for family planning will suffer the same fate as the Office of Economic Opportunity poverty programs, and be eliminated as a specific category in the Federal assistance program in favor of largely unrestricted grants to state and local governments. Being a controversial and a preventative rather than curative service, it is most unlikely that family planning services will be provided out of general or special revenue-sharing funds allocated to the state and local governments in Massachusetts. This point of view is reinforced by the response to a questionnaire sent out last fall by the Senate Sub-committee on Intergovernmental Relations (chaired by Senator Edmund Muskie) to over 2,300 cities and towns across the United States, ranging in size from 10,000 to 100,000.[28] The results of this survey indicated that very few municipalities would channel general revenue-sharing funds into social services for the poor or elderly or other forms of recurring expenditures. With respect to special revenue-sharing, past experience has indicated that the option to provide family planning services out of comprehensive grants such as Maternal and Infant Care Grants, is usually not taken. It was this experience which was one of the principal impetuses behind the development of the specific categorical grants for family planning services.

Thus, the consequence of Federal revenue-sharing for subsidized family planning services in Massachusetts appears to be the complete loss of approximately $1.9 million in categorical grants within the next two years.

5. Conclusions

The Reduction in Federal Assistance

As was explained in the previous section, the probable consequence of the implementation of Federal revenue-sharing is that the $1.9 million in specific categorical grants (see Table 11-8) currently utilized by private non-profit agencies to provide subsidized family planning services to approximately 33,000 low income women in Massachusetts will be eliminated within the next two years. As was also explained in the previous chapter, it is unlikely that this loss in funds will be compensated for by the usage of unrestricted (general revenue-sharing) or block grant (special revenue-sharing) revenue-sharing funds for the provision of family planning services by state or local governments because of the low priority they assign to family planning services.

Before the future role of the Federal Government in the Massachusetts subsidized family planning system can be adequately assessed, however, the compensating effect of the recent strengthening of the joint Federal/State third-party payment mechanism must be evaluated.

The two principal Federal means for reimbursement for services to a third-party provider are Titles IV-A and XIX of the Social Security Act. Both these methods of financing are State-administered and have the disadvantage over the Federally-administered categorical grant program (Title X of the Public Health Services Act) that the State requires strict documentation of the eligibility of the patients served. These would impose a heavy administrative burden on comprehensive family planning projects deprived of categorical grants. Another disadvantage of the State-administered reimbursement programs is the lag in payments, which makes it difficult for programs trying to expand services to maintain an adequate cash flow.

The recent revisions in the Title IV-A and Title XIX regulations[29] have strengthened these Titles as a source of funds for family planning in Massachusetts. The State share has been reduced to 10 percent from 25 percent for IV-A and from 50 percent for Title XIX. The provision of family planning services has been made mandatory under Title XIX, and a 1 percent penalty, applied against the entire Federal share ($69.5 million in Fiscal Year 1974) has been required if the services are not adequately provided under the State's Title IV-A program.

If Title IV-A funds were to be provided in significant amounts for family planning services as a result of these current regulations, the projects could be maintained with these funds. Under Title IV-A, all aspects of the comprehensive projects can be supported: medical services (except those reimbursable under Medicaid), social and educational services, and administrative costs. Furthermore, the income eligibility criterion for Title IV-A is considerably broader ($7,000 for a family of four)[30] than the 150 percent of poverty level criterion for the Title X categorical grants ($5,582 for a family of four; see Table 11-3). However, the probability of more Title IV-A funds ($220,000 was provided during the last half of Fiscal Year 1973 as a result of the penalty provision) being supplied by the State in Fiscal Year 1974 is extremely low. Not only will proposed revisions in regulations eliminate the penalty provision and reduce the eligibility, but they may also eliminate family planning altogether by prohibiting services to those who have a condition which cannot be remedied within six months.[31] Furthermore, there is a prospect that the total Federal share of the IV-A budget may be reduced to as low as $30 million (from $69.5 million in Fiscal 1973).[32] The combined effect of these two events will almost certainly be to eliminate family planning as a State social service in Fiscal Year 1974.

Thus, it appears that Title XIX or some form of national health insurance will become the main support of family planning services with the demise of the categorical grants within the next two years. The effect of this event will be to reduce both the quantity and quality of subsidized family planning services in the State. The quality will be affected because the income eligibility for Title XIX reimbursement is lower ($4,176 for a family of four)[33] than for Title X ($5,582 for a family of four), and because the Medicaid providers (doctors and hospitals) are less accessible than the projects which have been located for the purpose of serving the medically indigent. It is doubtful that the 90 percent Federal share will have any effect since the providers are already fully reimbursed by the State/Federal Medicaid program for family planning services. The quality of subsidized services will be reduced since under Title XIX only medical services can be reimbursed, and with the loss of the categorical grants the comprehensive projects would not be able to survive, assuming all the other variables in the system remained constant. Before drawing final conclusions, however, this assumption of *ceteris paribus* must be carefully examined.

The Potential Of The System To Compensate
For The Reduction In Federal Assistance

The systems analysis exercise indicated that the variables with the greatest potential for change in a direction which would positively influence the subsidized family planning service level are as follows:

Actors

1. The State Government
2. The Catholic Church
3. Planned Parenthood League of Massachusetts

Laws, Rules, and Regulations

1. Medical Profession Standards
2. State Laws

Ideologies

1. The Catholic Ideology
2. The Federalist Ideology

These variables, then, are the logical focuses for the development of programs to leverage the service level so as to compensate for the depressing effect of the reduction of Federal assistance under the policy of revenue-sharing. However, at this point, a distinction must be made between the concept of potential for change and the concept of potential for effective, implementable program development in the short run, e.g., within the next two years. We will find that while the potential for change is great, the potential for the development of programs to fully compensate for the reduction in Federal assistance is low, in the short run.

The State Government. Under severe attack from tax payer organizations (e.g., Mass Action) already, it is doubtful that the State government will supply more of a controversial, preventative service such as family planning than it currently does, unless forced to by Federal penalties, as in the case of IV-A monies. At present it appears that the Federal penalities for non-provision of family planning services under Title IV-A will be eliminated and the total amount of IV-A monies available to the State under IV-A drastically reduced. Hence, it is likely that the service provided by the State under the joint Federal/State IV-A program will practically disappear.

Most of the 33,000 patients served by the comprehensive projects will probably be absorbed by the Title XIX system of private physician and hospital providers. But some of these patients will be lost to the system due to the stricter eligibility requirements of Title XIX and the more limited access to XIX providers in comparison to the comprehensive projects.

The Catholic Church. There is a great ferment going on in the Catholic Church concerning artificial contraception. It is estimated that up to 40 percent of the Church hierarchy now favors the use of artificial contraception.[34] However, the hierarchy in Massachusetts has followed the letter of Pope Paul's 1968 Encyclical, *Humanae Vitae*, and officially rejects the use of artificial contraception as immoral. It is unlikely, therefore, that the Church in Massachusetts will change its official position in the short run. Thus, the provision of contraceptive services in the State will remain officially controversial.

Planned Parenthood League of Massachusetts. Planned Parenthood League of Massachusetts remains the most potent single source of private funds in the State, with an annual budget in 1972 of $221,515.[35] However, the role which it plays, which is largely educational and informational, has become compatible, with the establishment of the Federal comprehensive projects and the growth of public awareness of the value and availability of family planning services. If Planned Parenthood's budget could be diverted to the categorically-funded projects, these funds might enable these projects to survive the loss of the categorical grants, and continue, albeit on a more limited basis, to provide accessible comprehensive services to the areas which they now serve. However, Planned Parenthood is too careful of its role as the leading private family planning organization in the State to simply turn over a significant portion of its funds to largely publicly-funded projects. Thus, it is likely that PPLM will continue to expand its informational and educational programs, as it is now doing with its college and teenage sex education programs.

Medical Profession Standards. Medical profession standards, as has been shown, contribute to the high cost of medical family planning services. If doctors could be used less and nurses and paraprofessionals more, the cost of family planning services could be significantly reduced, since doctors salaries are by far the highest of any of the staff members. However, in spite of skyrocketing medical costs, it is doubtful that such powerful and conservative organizations as the AMA will allow such changes to occur very quickly.

State Laws. The State Law prohibiting the allocation of contraceptives to minors without the consent of their parents is unlikely to be revised in this session of the General Court. Although several bills have been submitted proposing such revisions, family planning is still too controversial an issue in the State for many

State legislators to stick their necks out to support such bills. As has been pointed out, all previous changes in State laws were through abrogation by Supreme Court decisions.

The Catholic Ideology. Ideologies, being founded on values, change more slowly than the other categories of variables. The Catholic ideology with respect to artificial contraception is under severe questioning within the hierarchy of the Church. Nevertheless, Pope Paul, having taken a strong stand against it in his 1968 encyclical *Humanae Vitae*, is unlikely to change his position in the near term. Without his support, it is unlikely that the official position of the Church will change.

The Federalist Ideology. The Federalist ideology has probably reached the peak of its influence, since, with such programs as revenue-sharing now in effect, it is now in the hazardous phase of being translated into programs. Nevertheless, until these programs have been fully implemented, it is likely that the concept of federalism, initiated by such diverse public figures as Nelson Rockefeller and Prof. Walter Heller, will retain its appeal.

Hence, it must be concluded that in the near term, e.g., the remainder of the Nixon administration, it is unlikely that there is enough realizable potential for effective, implementable program development in the Massachusetts subsidized family planning system for it to fully compensate for the depressing effect of the anticipated loss of Federal categorical grants in the systems service level.

The Net Impact Of Federal Revenue-Sharing
on the Subsidized Family Planning Service
Level in Massachusetts

In conclusion, the anticipated net impact of Federal revenue-sharing on the subsidized family planning service level in Massachusetts will be to quantitatively and qualitatively depress this level. Under revenue-sharing the categorical grants supporting the comprehensive service family planning projects which currently provide 59 percent of the subsidized family planning services in the State, will be phased out. Many of the patients served by these projects may be absorbed by the joint State/Federal Medical Assistance program. However, many of these patients will be lost to the subsidized family planning system because of the more restrictive eligibility requirements of the Medical Assistance program and the more limited access to this program by the medically indigent. In addition, the loss of the categorically-funded comprehensive projects will reduce the quality of the subsidized family services provided in the State, since the Medical Assistance program provides only medical services, while the comprehensive projects provide social and educational services as well as medical services.

It should be borne in mind that this study has examined Federal policy at a time of rapid transition. While at this point in time, it is believed that the conclusions reached are valid, it is possible that near-term events not now clearly visible could change the conclusions of the study. For example, the passage of National health insurance legislation might provide greater support for family planning services than the current State/Federal Medical Assistance program. Hence, future research on the subsidized family planning service level in Massachusetts could profitably be directed at monitoring the critical variable of Federal social service policy.

Notes

1. Westinghouse Population Center, *Cost Study Of A Sample of the National Center for Family Planning Services* (Columbia, Maryland, 1972), p. 71.

2. Committee on Terminology of the National Family Planning Forum, "A Family Planning Glossary," *Family Planning Perspectives*, Vol. 4 (July 1972), pp. 34-35.

3. Leslie A. and Charles F. Westoff, *From Now to Zero: Fertility, Contraception, and Abortion In America* (Boston, 1968), p. 69.

4. Ibid., p. 93.

5. Ibid., p. 55.

6. "Family Planning Services and Population Research Act of 1970 (PL 91-572)—Legislative History," *United States Code, Congressional and Administrative News 91st Congress, Second Session 1973* (St. Paul, Minn., 1971), p. 5070.

7. *Family Planning/Population Reporter*, Vol. 2 (February 1973), pp. 1, 3-5.

8. Westoff, *From Now to Zero*, p. 143.

9. *Report of The Secretary of Health, Education, and Welfare Submitting Five-Year Plan For Family Planning Services And Population Research Programs* (Washington, 1971), p. 350.

10. Jeannie I. Rosoff, "Introduction of New Legislation to Extend the Family Planning Services and Population Research Act (Title X)," *Planned Parenthood-World Population Memorandum* (April 9, 1973), pp. 1-2.

11. Personal communication with personnel at Departments of Community Affairs and Public Welfare, Commonwealth of Massachusetts, April 1973.

12. *The Boston Globe*, April 5, 1973.

13. Planned Parenthood League of Massachusetts, *PPLM Reports* (March 1973), p. 6.

14. Jeannie I. Rosoff, "Proposed Regulations To Restrict Current Title IV-A Social Service Programs," *Planned Parenthood-World Population Memorandum* (February 16, 1973), p. 3.

15. Westoff, *From Now to Zero*, p. 55.

16. Westinghouse Population Center, *Cost Study*, p. 71.

17. Jean L. Marx, "Birth Control: Current Technology, Future Prospects," *Science* Vol. 179 (March 23, 1973), pp. 1222-1224.

18. See appropriate sections of the Federal Register.

19. Conversation with John C. Snyder, Professor of Population and Public Health, School of Public Health, March 30, 1973.

20. John F. Kantner and Melvin Zelnick, "Contraception and Pregnancy: Experience of Young Unmarried Women in the United States," *Family Planning Perspectives*, Vol. 5.

21. Thomas Malthus, *First Essay On Population*, 1798 (New York, 1966), p. 140.

22. Donella H. Meadows, Denis L. Meadows, Jorgen Randers, William W. Behrens, *The Limits To Growth* (New York, 1972), p. 132.

23. Charles E. Curran, "New Catholic Hospital Code," *Family Planning Prospectives*, Vol. 4 (July 1972), pp. 7-8.

24. *The Boston Globe*, February 19, 1973, p. 8.

25. Ibid., p. 1.

26. "General Revenue-Sharing," *The Advocate For Human Services*, Vol. 2 (February 28, 1973), p. 1.

27. Rosoff, "Introduction of New Legislation," pp. 1-2.

28. "General Revenue-Sharing: Status Report," *Focus on Voluntarism* (Spring, 1973), p. 7.

29. Rosoff, "Proposed Regulations," p. 3.

30. Miles Mahoney, "Request for Proposals for Child Care and/or Family Planning Services to Public Housing Authorities," *Department of Community Affairs Memorandum* (March 1970), p. 3.

31. Rosoff, "Proposed Regulations," p. 2.

32. Communications with personnel, Social Services Unit, Massachusetts Department of Public Welfare, March 1973.

33. Massachusetts Law Reform Institute, *Using Medicaid* (Boston, 1971), p. 5.

34. Curran, "New Catholic Code," pp. 7-8.

35. Planned Parenthood League of Massachusetts, *PPLM Reports* (March 1973), p. 6.

Acknowledgments

The author wishes to thank the following individuals who, by enabling him to participate in the activities of the Massachusetts subsidized family planning system, made possible a substantial amount of the research that went into this study.

Mrs. Edna Smith, Director
The Boston Family Planning Project

Mrs. Phyliss Brown, Director
The North Shore Family Planning Project

Mrs. Donna Morse, Director
The Lowell Family Planning Project

Mr. William Daniel, Director
The Central Massachusetts Family Planning Project

Mr. Clyde Younger, Director, Region I Office
The National Center for Family Planning Services

Mrs. Martha Davis Dean, Assistant Commissioner For
    Social Services
The Massachusetts Department of Public Welfare

Ms. Patty Joffe, Social Services Unit
The Massachusetts Department of Public Welfare

12 Attitudes Towards Population Growth and Planning in a New Hampshire Town

David R. Weir, Jr.*

Recently, in the southern New Hampshire town of Peterborough, a public opinion survey revealed that most of the town's citizens had a strong preference for a limited population growth rate and for more control over the distribution of residential and commercial growth within the town. Heretofore, it had appeared that growth was unqualifiedly welcome in this scenic area, but now that rapid growth has started to make its appearance, it appears that the region's residents are starting to have doubts about its benefits.

Peterborough is a rural community of about 4,000 persons, which is located at the intersection of a north-south State Highway and an east-west U.S. highway, about seventy-five miles northwest of Boston. The town is situated in a scenic area along the Contoocook River, a northward-flowing tributary of the Merrimack. A chain of mountains borders the town in the East, and Mount Monadnock, highest mountain in southern New Hampshire, dominates the view in the West. Most of the thirty-six square miles of the town outside of the village is covered with forest vegetation, broken occasionally by scattered fields, farms, and housing developments.

In the past twenty years, the agricultural sector of the town's economy has virtually disappeared, and the principal sources of income are now light industry, retail and service enterprises, and industrial and residential construction. According to the 1970 Census reports, the community is somewhat more prosperous than average. In that year, the median family income was $10,719, compared to $9,698 for the State of New Hampshire, and $9,590 for the United States as a whole. The percentage of the town's families with incomes below the non-farm poverty level ($3,743 for a non-farm family of four) was 3.4 percent in 1970, compared to 6.7 percent for the State of New Hampshire and 10.7 percent for the United States as a whole.

The opinion survey on attitudes towards future growth was conducted in the fall of 1972 by the Peterborough Planning Board with the help of a voluntary group of citizens. The impetus for the survey was the Board's desire to generate support for a professional planning effort to provide guidelines for controlling the mushrooming residential and commercial growth that was beginning to affect the town. The Planning Board and the citizens' group prepared a six page legal-sized questionnaire on attitudes towards growth in general; residential,

*Candidate for the M.C.P., Harvard University.

commercial, and industrial growth; and open space land use. After revisions based on several public hearings, the questionnaire was handed out to all voters leaving the town's only polling place on National Election Day, November 7, 1973. Eligible non-voters and non-resident taxpayers were mailed questionnaires. Collection boxes were set up at the town hall and at all town banks. By the close of the survey, the second week in December, 1017 questionnaires had been returned, representing about 25 percent of the town. Of these, 939, or 33 percent of the checklist, were registered voters.

While the survey was not conducted in a scientific manner, the subsequent strong approval by the March town meeting of proposals based on positions strongly endorsed in the survey, including the appropriation of $30,000 for a professional planning study, suggested that its findings were indeed valid. Furthermore, the amateur status of the survey served to limit its expense to the town to the costs of mailing questionnaires to non-voters and non-resident taxpayers and mimeographing the questionnaires on the town mimeograph machine. Through the student affiliation of one summer resident volunteer, the questionnaires were keypunched and tabulated free of charge by the Information Processing Center at The Massachusetts Institute of Technology. Miscellaneous expenses of the survey were paid from an environmental internship stipend granted to the same student volunteer by the Massachusetts Audubon Society.

The results of the survey revealed strong preferences by the townspeople for a slight rate of population growth and for greater use by the town of volunteer and professional planning assistance to control the distribution of future growth. Furthermore, not only were these preferences deep, they were also broadly based across demographic subcategories. The analysis of attitudes towards future population growth revealed that about three-quarters of the sample preferred the average growth rate of the 1960-70 decade (100 people per year) or less. And about half of these, or almost a third of the total sample, preferred no future growth at all or a negative growth rate. Only about a fifth of the respondents preferred a higher rate of growth than that of the previous decade. When examined by demographic subcategories, including age, sex, marital status, number of children under eighteen living at home, and length of time lived in Peterborough, the growth preferences were consistent with those of the total sample. Thus, in summary, in the fall of 1972, the town of Peterborough as a whole and many subgroups within the community expressed a strong preference for maintaining a gradual growth rate. (See Table 12-1.)

The results of the survey also revealed strong support in the Peterborough community for the use of volunteer and professional planning assistance by the town government. About three-quarters of the respondents favored the use of such assistance by the town, while only about one-fifth opposed it. As with the preference for a limited rate of population growth, the level of support for the use of planning assistance was consistent across a variety of demographic subcategories, including age, sex, marital status, number of children under eighteen living at home, and years lived in Peterborough. (See Table 12-2.)

Table 12-1
Population Growth Rate Preferences in the Town of Peterborough

	No Growth or Decrease	Slight Growth, (100 per year) No Growth or Decrease	Moderate Growth (200 per year) or Unlimited Growth	Size of Sample ( )
	%	%	%	
Total	31	76	18	(1017)
Age				
30 or less	38	82	14	(117)
31-60	29	75	18	(499)
Over 60	32	77	19	(325)
Sex				
Male	29	73	21	(484)
Female	34	80	15	(502)
Marital Status				
Single	43	84	13	(111)
Married	29	76	18	(748)
Wid./Div.	34	74	22	(125)
No. of Child. under 18 Living at Home				
None	33	77	18	(648)
One	27	78	19	(107)
Two	28	82	12	(108)
Three or more	26	66	23	(105)
Years in Peterborough				
0-1	32	80	14	(103)
1-5	29	73	20	(230)
5-10	28	80	17	(169)
10-20	37	76	18	(141)
Over 20	33	79	17	(347)

Question: How would you like to see Peterborough's population change?
Decrease
Stay the same
Slight growth (100 people per year)
Moderate growth (200 people per year)
Unlimited growth

In summary, the town of Peterborough, in the Monadnock region of southern New Hampshire, has indicated, through a recent public opinion poll, that it would prefer a limited rate of population growth and the use of planning assistance to guide the spatial distribution of what growth does occur. Possibly,

Table 12-2
Endorsement of Use of Volunteer and Professional Planning Assistance by the Town

	Endorsed %	Opposed %	Sample Size ( )
Total	76	17	(1017)
Age			
30 or less	82	12	(147)
31-60	77	17	(499)
Over 60	76	17	(325)
Sex			
Male	78	18	(484)
Female	76	16	(502)
Marital Status			
Single	77	14	(111)
Married	78	17	(748)
Wid./Div.	74	17	(125)
No. of Child. under 18 Living at Home			
None	75	19	(648)
One	84	12	(107)
Two	82	14	(108)
Three or more	77	16	(105)
Years in Peterborough			
0-1	84	13	(103)
1-5	84	12	(230)
5-10	80	13	(169)
10-20	72	21	(141)
Over 20	70	23	(347)

Question: Should the town seek volunteer and professional planning assistance as a guide to orderly growth?

the results of this poll may indicate a trend towards greater support of planning for growth in this rapidly-growing area of southern New Hampshire.

13

Determinants of Legislative Voting Behavior on Population Policy: An Analysis of the Massachusetts House of Representatives in 1970 and 1971

Maris A. Vinovskis
R. Marshall Jones
Thomas New*

Despite our increased awareness of the importance of political decision-making in determining population policy in this country, almost no empirical work has been done to investigate the nature of legislative voting behavior on population issues. The few attempts to analyze voting behavior on population policy in the legislatures have been limited by their inability to obtain detailed data on the socioeconomic characteristics of the legislators or their constituents. In addition, as most of these studies have relied on statistical techniques such as cross-tabulation rather than multiple regression analysis, it has been very difficult to ascertain the relative importance of various factors in accounting for the voting patterns of legislators on population policy.

In order to begin to remedy these deficiencies, we have analyzed the Massachusetts House of Representatives in two different legislative sessions—1970 and 1971. We were able to obtain considerable socioeconomic data on each state representative as well as on his constituents so that we could analyze the determinants of voting behavior on population policy in more detail than previous studies. Furthermore, by utilizing multiple regression techniques of analysis we were better able to evaluate the relative importance of each factor in accounting for differences in the voting patterns of the legislators on population issues.

Population Policy in Massachusetts before 1970

Massachusetts enacted legislation against contraceptives in 1879 in a law entitled, "An Act Concerning Offenses Against Chastity, Morality, and Decency." Though there was some opposition to its passage, the law was enacted

We would like to gratefully acknowledge financial support for computer time for this project from the Harvard Population Center and the Research Committee of the Graduate School of the University of Wisconsin.

*Maris A. Vinovskis is Assistant Professor of History, University of Wisconsin, and a Rockefeller Fellow in the History of the Family Project at the American Antiquarian Society and Clark University. R. Marshall Jones and Thomas New were students of Mr. Vinovskis and aided in the research reported in this chapter.

without any great difficulty. As in many other states, this law reflected the efforts of Anthony Comstock and his supporters who had successfully lobbied for similar legislation at the national level six years earlier. It was not until 1966 that this law was fundamentally altered by the Massachusetts legislature.[1]

Legislative and judicial efforts in the early 20th century in Massachusetts to modify the anti-contraceptive aspects of the law failed. However, by the 1930s the Massachusetts Birth Control League felt that public opinion and state policy had sufficiently shifted so that clinics could now be opened to provide contraceptive services. But in 1937 the police raided the Salem center and arrested four of the individuals working there at the time. The defendents were found guilty in the district court and that decision was later upheld by the Massachusetts Supreme Court in *Commonwealth v. Gardner.* The court's broad prohibition against contraceptives forced birth-control advocates to seek redress through legislative channels.[2]

As there was little expectation that the Massachusetts legislature would repeal the 1879 law, a group that organized itself as the Massachusetts Mother's Health Council attempted to bring this issue before the public whom they felt would be more sympathetic to changing the law. In 1940 they initiated the process for a referendum by collecting 43,000 certified signatures—almost twice as many as required by law.

As anticipated, the Massachusetts legislature rejected the proposed liberalization of the law and the matter went before the public in November 1942. The voters rejected the attempt to liberalize the birth control legislation by a vote of 683,059 (58 percent of votes cast) to 495,964 (42 percent of the votes cast).[3]

Despite the defeats in both the legislature and in the referendum, proponents of the liberalization of the law felt that they had not been given an adequate opportunity for passage of their bill as many voters (17.6 percent) had cast blank ballots on the referendum—presumably because they did not understand the issue. Therefore, the group, now renamed the Planned Parenthood League of Massachusetts, decided to bring the matter before the public again in a referendum in 1948 (Massachusetts requires a six-year interval between referendum attempts). This time a more intensive effort was undertaken to educate the public and to reduce the number of blanks cast on the assumption that voters who had previously cast blanks would now support revision of the birth control law.

The results of the referendum were similar to those six years earlier—1,085,350 voters opposed the proposal (57 percent of the votes) and 806,829 supported it (43 percent of the votes cast). Though the percentage of blanks had been reduced from 17.6 percent to 12.2 percent, the decrease in blanks was apparently rather evenly split between the two positions.[4]

During the battles in the legislature, the votes on birth control legislation found a division along party lines with the Republicans supporting the liberalization of the law and the Democrats opposing it. The debates were very heated and spokesmen for the Catholic Church openly opposed any changes in the existing contraceptive laws.

Though some members of the Planned Parenthood League of Massachusetts wanted to bring the issue before the public once more in 1954 in a referendum, the idea was now opposed by the Republican Party which had blamed the heavy Catholic turnout during the 1948 referendum for their gubernatorial defeat. In addition, Planned Parenthood itself was gradually moving away from political activity in order to concentrate its efforts on educating the public. As a result, no major challenge to the existing birth control laws was launched at that time.[5]

In 1965 the advocates of the liberalization of the birth control laws felt that the time had come for another attempt in the legislature. The Catholic Church was no longer adamant in opposing changes in the anti-contraceptive statute. In addition, a number of leading Catholics in medicine now supported changing the present law. Furthermore, the recent Supreme Court decision invalidating Connecticut's strict anti-contraceptive law provided encouragement for another try in the Massachusetts legislature.

Despite the signs of a shift in the attitudes on the issue of contraception among legislators and the general public, the effort failed in the House by a 119 to 97 vote. The continued opposition was not due to hostility toward any changes in the existing law, but rather to this particular bill, which did not provide adequate safeguards for the morality of young people in the eyes of many of the Catholic legislators. Again the vote was along party lines with 89 percent of the Republicans favoring the bill and 75 percent of the Democrats opposing it in the House.

In the 1966 legislative session another effort was made to change the law. The new bill (H. 2965) added provisions to minimize the possibility of contraceptive devices becoming available to young people by outlawing such merchandising techniques as vending machines for the sale of contraceptives. However, this modification was not enough and the House amended the bill by limiting it only to married women. The amended bill then passed 136-80 in the House and 29-11 in the Senate. Again the vote followed party lines to some degree as 92 percent of the Republicans in the House supported it while only 51 percent of the Democrats endorsed it.[6]

With the passage of this bill, future efforts to liberalize population policy in the Massachusetts legislature would now be focused on the attempts to allow unmarried women access to contraceptives or to the liberalization of the existing abortion laws.

Characteristics of the Massachusetts Legislature

It would be impossible to understand or explain the voting behavior of any group of legislators without some knowledge of the social, economic, religious, and political backgrounds the legislators bring to their work. Equally important would be some understanding of the social, economic, religious and political characteristics of the constituencies the legislators represent.

The Massachusetts House of Representatives consists of 240 members elected every two years. However, the constituencies actually number only 170 units, as Massachusetts has many multi-member districts.

Though Massachusetts has a very competitive two-party system for major state offices such as governor or attorney general, the legislature is predominantly Democratic.[7] In 1970 Democrats held 72 percent of the seats in the House and 75 percent in 1971. Despite the intense competition at the state-wide level between Democrats and Republicans, there is relatively little competition for legislative seats. Of the 210 members of the House who ran for re-election in 1970, approximately 60 percent were either unopposed or did not face a close primary or final election contest.

There are major social, economic and religious differences between the Republican and Democratic legislators. In a study of the 1964 state representatives, Sheldon Goldman found that Republican state representatives tended to be better educated than Democrats though both groups are, on the whole, well-educated. Furthermore, he found a higher proportion of Republicans than Democrats coming from middle or upper-class backgrounds.[8]

The major difference between the Democratic and Republican legislators is their religious affiliation. While the total legislature is predominantly Catholic, with approximately 75 percent being Catholic in 1970 and 77 percent in 1971, a greater percentage of Democrats are Catholic than are Republicans.

Republican legislators tend to represent constituents whose socioeconomic status is higher than those generally represented by Democrats. In addition, Republican constituencies are concentrated more in rural and suburban areas while Democratic constituencies tend to be located in urban areas.

Table 13-1
Religious Affiliation of Massachusetts State Representatives by Political Party in 1970 and 1971

| | 1970 | |
	Republicans	Democrats
Catholic	34.33%	90.59%
Non-Catholic	65.67%	9.41%
	(*n*=67)	(*n*=170)

| | 1971 | |
	Republicans	Democrats
Catholic	33.33%	91.62%
Non-Catholic	66.67%	8.38%
	(*n*=60)	(*n*=179)

The variety of social, economic, and religious differences among Republican and Democratic state representatives and their constituents makes it difficult to determine the relative importance of each factor when analyzing the legislative behavior of the representatives. On the question of voting behavior on population issues being examined here, one cannot be certain whether a birth control bill is opposed by a legislator because he happens to be a Democrat, a Catholic, or a representative of an urban constituency which tends to have a higher concentration of Catholics than the state as a whole. It is only when the various potential influencing factors are studied by regression analysis that we can begin to ascertain the relative importance of each of these factors in accounting for the pattern of legislative voting on population policy.

Variables Used for the Multiple Regression Analysis

We will examine the pattern of voting behavior on population policy in the Massachusetts House of Representatives in two different sessions—1970 and 1971. Information on voting behavior, personal characteristics of the legislators, and the nature of their constituents was obtained for 237 state representatives in 1970 and for 239 in 1971. However, as our index of liberalism on population policy required that a member voted on all three bills, the number of legislators used in the final regression runs was 193 in 1970 and 178 in 1971.[9] The variables used in our analysis are presented in Table 13-2.

Indices of liberalism on population policy were constructed for 1970 and 1971 on the basis of three roll-call votes in each session. The votes in each session were selected because they reflected three different aspects of population policy and could be scaled to reflect the relative liberalism of the legislators on that issue. The three roll-call votes used in each session were as follows:

1. A bill to make contraceptive devices and information available to unmarried women.
2. A bill to create a commission to study the issue of abortion reform.
3. A bill to abolish the crime of abortion in Massachusetts.

None of these bills were successful in either of the sessions. The attempt to make contraceptive devices or information available to unmarried women was defeated in the House by a vote of 142-81 in 1970 and 116-105 in 1971.[10] An effort to create a commission to study the issue of abortion was defeated by a margin of 127-94 in 1970 and 163-68 in 1971.[11] Finally, the attempt to abolish the crime of abortion failed by a vote of 184-32 in 1970 and 205-29 in 1971.[12]

Initially a scale of zero to three was constructed on population policy by assigning a value of one if the legislator favored a liberalization of the law and zero if he opposed it on each of the three roll-call votes. Thus, an overall index of zero indicates an opposition to liberalization of population policy on all three bills, whereas an index of three indicates support of all three bills.

However, this index is based on the arbitrary assumption that the intervals of the scale (zero to one, one to two, etc.) are equal in terms of reflecting the degree of liberalism of the members. In order to minimize this problem and to make the results more comparable over time, the index was weighted for each representative by taking into account the number of legislators in each category of that index. The index numbers were spaced along a scale at a distance from each other equal to one-half the number of legislators in any one category plus one-half the number of legislators in the preceding category. In other words, if the total number of legislators were arranged along a line by each category (all the legislators in category zero followed by all of those in category one, etc.), then the scale points would fall on that line at the midpoints of each category. In the final regression runs, this weighted index was used though there was very little change introduced as the two indices are highly correlated (.99 in 1970 and .97 in 1971).[13]

In order to understand the interaction of personal considerations and constituent influence in determining the voting patterns of the Massachusetts state representatives, data was gathered on the characteristics of each legislator and his district. Four personal characteristics of each legislator were ascertained—party affiliation, age of member, religious affiliation, and an index of liberalism on other legislative matters as measured by the percentage of times they voted with the recommendations of the Americans for Democratic Action (not including ADA recommendations on population policy). In addition, four characteristics of each of the legislative districts was recorded—median educa-

Table 13-2
Variables Used in Multiple Regression Analysis

I. Population Policy of Legislators

Y — Index of liberalism on population issues

II. Characteristics of the Legislators

X_1 — Party affiliation (0 = Republican, 1 = Democrat)

X_2 — Age

X_3 — Religion (0 = Non-Catholic, 1 = Catholic)

X_4 — Percentage of times voting with the recommendations of the Americans for Democratic Action

III. Characteristics of the Legislative Districts

X_5 — Median educational level of the population 25 years old and over

X_6 — Percentage of voters who are registered Republicans

X_7 — Median income of families

X_8 — Population density

tional level of the population twenty-five years old and over, percentage of the voters who are registered Republicans, median income of families, and the population density.

Statistical Procedures Employed

Most studies of the determinants of legislative voting behavior rely on a cross-tabulation of a particular vote or group of votes against some categorical characteristics of the legislators involved. Yet this method is of limited utility because one is often condensing interval scale data into broad categories, and it is very difficult to ascertain the relative importance of several different variables at the same time.

Though some cross-tabulation analysis was carried out in order to obtain the weights for the indices of liberalism on population policy, most of this study is based on multiple regression analysis. Multiple regression analysis allows one to study the linear relationship between any one of the independent variables, X_1 to X_8, and a dependent variable, Y, while taking into consideration the effect of each of the remaining independent variables on the dependent variable. The underlying mathematical procedure is the use of the linear least-squares method which produces the smallest possible residual between the predicted value of the dependent variable from the regression equation and its actual value. An additional advantage of multiple regression analysis is that it also minimizes any problems due to ratio correlation.[14]

There is always the danger that two or more of the independent variables will be highly correlated with each other. As multiple regression analysis is based on the assumption that no linear dependence exists between the explanatory variables, the existence of multicollinearity among the variables would invalidate our results. Therefore, care was taken not to include any independent variables which were highly correlated with each other.[15]

In an effort to test the relative contribution of each independent variable to the explanation of the index of liberalism on population policy, a series of stepwise regressions were run with each of the independent variables individually omitted, while the remaining variables were regressed against the index of liberalism on population issues. The resultant changes in R^2 due to the omission of each independent variable gives us another indication of the relative importance of these variables in accounting for differentials in the index of liberalism on population policy among the state representatives.

Results

The means and standard deviations of the variables for each session are displayed in Table 13-3.

Table 13-3
Means and Standard Deviations of Variables

	1970		1971	
	Mean	Standard Deviation	Mean	Standard Deviation
Index of liberalism on population issues	49.53	26.23	49.45	26.45
Party affiliation	.72	.45	.78	.42
Age	46.81	10.78	44.48	12.15
Religion	.76	.43	.79	.41
Percentage of times voting with the recommendations of the Americans for Democratic Action	43.03	23.74	44.07	29.96
Median educational level of the population 25 years old and over	11.39	1.47	11.29	1.51
Percentage of voters who are registered Republicans	21.11	11.35	20.66	10.49
Median income of families	6520.2	1293.6	6421.6	1229.5
Population density	5354.0	5331.8	5482.1	5359.5

A preliminary analysis of the relationships between the index of liberalism on population policy and the independent variables was based on simple correlation coefficients. The results for the 1970 and 1971 sessions indicated a positive correlation between the index of liberalism on population issues and the index of liberalism on other legislative votes, the educational level of the district, the percentage of voters who are registered Republicans, and the median income of families in that area. The correlation coefficients were negative between the index of liberalism on population policy and whether a legislator is a Democrat, whether he is a Catholic, his age, and the population density of his district.

Though the correlation coefficients are useful in establishing the relationship between any two variables, they are handicapped by the fact that the relationship may really be caused by a third factor which has not been considered. In addition, as most of the independent variables are also correlated with each other, it is difficult to ascertain the relative importance of each one of them in accounting for the differences among the state representatives in their voting behavior on population policies. To minimize these problems we used multiple regression analysis. Regression equations were calculated for 1970 and 1971 in the form:

Table 13-4
Correlation Coefficients Between the Index of Liberalism on Population Issues and the Independent Variables

	1970	1971
Party affiliation	−.474	−.393
Age	−.226	−.335
Religion	−.680	−.547
Percentage of times voting with the recommendations of the Americans for Democratic Action	.700	.638
Median educational level of the population 25 years old and over	.326	.302
Percentage of voters who are registered Republicans	.449	.414
Median income of families	.505	.480
Population density	−.262	−.268

$$Y = a + b_1 Y_1 + b_2 Y_2 + b_3 Y_3 + b_4 Y_4 + b_5 Y_5 + b_6 Y_6 + b_7 Y_7 + b_8 Y_8$$

where Y is the index of liberalism on population policy, a is a constant, $X_1 \ldots X_8$ are independent variables, and $b_1 \ldots b_8$ are the regression coefficients.

The results of the regression equations for the 1970 and 1971 sessions are summarized below in Table 13-5.

Table 13-5
Regression Coefficients

	1970	1971
Party affiliation	−1.9973	−4.1411
Age	−.1054	−.1351
Religion	−21.7743	−16.2439
Percentage of times voting with the recommendations of the Americans for Democratic Action	.4711	.3920
Median educational level of the population 25 years old and over	−.6842	1.6867
Percentage of voters who are registered Republicans	.1517	.0469
Median income of families	.0018	.0024
Population density	−.0005	−.0005
Constant	48.0212	21.3823

Though the regression coefficients indicate the effect of each of the independent variables on the dependent one, it is impossible to evaluate the relative importance of each variable on the basis of regression coefficients by themselves as the independent variables are measured in different units. Therefore, it is necessary to use the standardized regression coefficients (beta coefficients), as they do indicate the relative importance of the independent variables.

Table 13-6
Beta Coefficients

	1970	1971
Party affiliation	−.0343	−.0655
Age	−.0443	−.0620
Religion	−.3547**	−.2523**
Percentage of times voting with the recommendations of the Americans for Democratic Action	.4263**	.4440**
Median educational level of the population 25 years old and over	−.0383	.0965
Percentage of voters who are registered Republicans	.0656	.0186
Median income of families	.0867	.1107
Population density	−.1017*	−.0927

** = significant at the .01 level
 * = significant at the .05 level

The beta coefficients indicate a very similar pattern to the correlation coefficients in terms of the direction of the relationships. The index of liberalism on legislative issues, the percentage of voters who are registered Republicans, and the median income of families was positively related to the index of liberalism on population policy. Whether a legislator was a Democrat, whether he was a Catholic, his age, and the population density of his district were negatively related to the index of liberalism on population policy and the educational level of the legislator's district in 1970 and a positive relationship in 1971.

Besides indicating the direction of the relationships, beta coefficients also give us an idea of the relative ability of the independent variables to account for differences among state representatives on the index of liberalism on population policy. The two best predictors are the religious affiliation of the legislator and the index of liberalism on other legislative issues. Compared to those two factors, the rest of the independent variables are relatively weak, with only population density being significant at the .05 level in 1970.

We can also examine changes in R^2 when each of the independent variables are removed while the rest of them remain in the regression equation in order to obtain another indication of the relative significance of the independent variables.

Table 13-7
Change in R^2 Due to Removal of Each Variable from Regression Equation While the Rest of the Variables are Retained

Variables Removed	Change in R^2	
	1970	1971
Party affiliation	.0013	.0002
Age	.0003	−.0003
Religion	−.0659	−.0304
Percentage of times voting with the recommendations of the Americans for Democratic Action	−.1006	−.1288
Median educational level of the population 25 years old and over	.0010	−.0035
Percentage of voters who are registered Republicans	−.0002	.0024
Median income of families	−.0019	−.0037
Population density	−.0054	−.0033
Characteristics of the legislators ($X_1, X_2, X_3,$ and X_4)	−.3388	−.2992
Characteristics of the legislative district ($X_5, X_6, X_7,$ and X_8)	−.0170	−.0317
R^2 with all variables in the equation	.6379	.5628

In most instances there is a loss in R^2 when any independent variable is removed. However, in five of the sixteen instances there is an increase in R^2 due to the fact that the loss in R^2 caused by the removal of that variable is more than made up by the gain in an additional degree of freedom in calculating the regression equation.

The results of this analysis confirm our earlier findings—only the religious affiliation of the legislator and his index of liberalism on other legislative matters are very important. In addition, we can ascertain the relative importance of the personal characteristics of the legislators and the characteristics of their districts by removing each set of variables from the regression equation while keeping the other one. The loss in R^2 indicates that the personal characteristics of the state representatives is much more important in accounting for differences in the index of liberalism on population policy than the characteristics of their constituents.

In addition to our use of correlation coefficients, beta coefficients, and changes in R^2, we also need to look at the overall effectiveness of the resultant regression equations in explaining the dependent variable. Probably the most useful measure of this is R^2—the ratio between the variance of the dependent variable explained by the independent variables and the total variance of the dependent variable. Thus, if the independent variables perfectly predict the values of the dependent variable, R^2 would be equal to one. On the other hand, if the independent variables have no relationship to the dependent variable and therefore are not helpful in predicting values of the dependent variable, R^2 would be equal to zero.

For the 1970 legislative session, R^2 is .6379. That is, approximately 64 percent of the variance in the index of liberalism on population policy can be explained by the eight independent variables we have used. The explanatory ability of the same eight variables in the 1971 session was .5628.

Discussion of Results

The results of this inquiry are not surprising in terms of the direction of the relationships for Massachusetts. As we anticipated, Democratic, Catholic, and older legislators tended to be less liberal on population issues. Similarly, legislators representing more urban areas, which have a higher concentration of a Catholic population in Massachusetts than the rural areas, are also less liberal. On the other hand, state representatives who usually vote liberal on other legislative issues also tend to vote more liberally on population policy. Also, representatives from districts which are more Republican or have higher family incomes tend to vote more liberally on population issues. The relationship of the educational level of the constituents to the voting behavior of its legislators was mixed—negative for the 1970 session and positive in the 1971 session.

Though the direction of the relationships was expected, the strengths of the various factors was somewhat surprising. Personal characteristics were very important in explaining differences in the voting behavior on population issues among the state representatives but the characteristics of their constituents had relatively little ability to account for these voting patterns. Perhaps this is an indication that these population issues before the Massachusetts House of Representatives did not arouse much public interest in 1970 and 1971. An examination of the major state newspapers at the time did not suggest strong public agitation on these bills.

Much of the discussion of population policy in Massachusetts has stressed that Democratic and Catholic legislators tended to be more hostile to the liberalization of the existing state laws on birth-control and abortion issues—especially as more Democratic legislators were Catholic than their Republican counterparts. However, our analysis suggests that party affiliation is not a very good predictor of liberalism on population policy in Massachusetts once we take into account the influence of other personal and constituent factors. Religious affiliation, on the other hand, is an important determinant of the degree of liberalism on these population questions.

Interestingly, the single most important factor in predicting a legislator's vote on population policy was his index of liberalism on other legislative issues. This suggests that a state representative's own basic attitudes on legislative matters plays a very important role in determining how he will approach the population issues placed before him in the House.

As personal considerations play such a large role in determining the votes of state representatives on population policy, we might wonder how easily and accurately can the average voter ascertain the attitude of prospective legislators on these issues. Before the November 1970 election, the Massachusetts League of Women Voters asked all candidates for state representative eight policy questions—including two relating to population issues:[16]

1. Are you in favor of more liberal birth control laws?
2. Would you support changes in the present abortion laws to make them more liberal?

We wanted to see how accurately the replies to these questions reflected the subsequent voting behavior of the state representatives who were elected to the House. As the questions on population policy asked by the Massachusetts League of Women Voters were quite general, we did not anticipate perfect agreement between the replies of these candidates for office and their later votes on these issues. However, we would expect a reasonably close relationship for most legislators if indeed candidates for office are generally forthright with their constituents.

Table 13-8

Comparison of Answers by Candidates for the Massachusetts House of Representatives to League of Women Voters Question on Liberalization of the Birth Control Law and Their Subsequent Vote in the House on Liberalization of That Law in 1971

| | | In Favor of Liberalization | | |
	Yes	No	Qualified Answer	No Reply
Vote on Liberalization — Yes	89.87%	31.25%	50.00%	16.67%
Vote on Liberalization — No	10.13%	68.75%	50.00%	83.33%
	(n=79)	(n=16)	(n=16)	(n=108)

The results in Table 13-8 suggest that legislators who indicated a clear preference on liberalization of the birth control laws generally voted the same way in the House—particularly those who indicated a preference toward the liberalization of the law. Thus, approximately 90 percent of those who said they favored a liberalization of the birth control laws voted to liberalize them though only 69 percent who said they were against liberalization actually voted against the bill. But the most striking fact is that one derives a very distorted image of the attitudes of prospective legislators on this issue by looking only at the 43 percent of the state representatives who expressed a clear preference on this subject. On the basis of the answers to the questionnaire, we would anticipate 83 percent support for liberalization of the birth control law. In fact, however, only 47 percent of the legislators finally supported liberalization of the law when it reached them on the floor of the House. The reason for this disparity is quite obvious from the results in Table 13-8. Over 80 percent of those who did not reply to the questionnaires subsequently voted against the liberalization of the birth control law. In other words, voters get an inaccurate overall impression of attitudes on liberalization of birth control laws because so many of the candidates for state representative who opposed liberalization did not reply to the questionnaire. On the other hand, the questionnaire generally did reflect accurately the subsequent voting behavior of those candidates who expressed a clear preference on liberalization of the existing birth control laws.

Table 13-9

Comparison of Answers by Candidates for the Massachusetts House of Representatives to League of Women Voters Question on Liberalization of the Abortion Law and Their Subsequent Vote in the House on Liberalization of That Law in 1971

| | | In Favor of Liberalization | | |
	Yes	No	Qualified Answer	No Reply
Vote on Liberalization — Yes	43.14%	0%	12.90%	3.33%
No	56.86%	100.0%	87.10%	96.77%
	(n=51)	(n=25)	(n=31)	(n=124)

When we perform a similar analysis on the replies to the abortion question, the results are generally the same. These successful candidates for state representative usually voted the same way they indicated on the questionnaire—though on the abortion issue a much smaller percentage of those who said they favored liberalization actually voted for this bill than on the birth control issue. Perhaps this reflects the fact that many legislators who said they favored liberalization of the present abortion law did not agree with the degree of change proposed by the 1971 bill before them.

As before, most of those who did not reply to this question voted against liberalization of the abortion law. Thus, voters again received an incorrect impression of the overall degree of support for liberalization of the abortion law on the basis of the replies to the Massachusetts League of Women Voters questionnaire.

There are several tentative conclusions one might draw about the usefulness of pre-election policy questionnaires in giving voters an indication of the policy preferences of candidates for the legislature. In terms of those replying to the questionnaire, the results are generally a good reflection of thier subsequent voting behavior. Perhaps the questionnaire might be somewhat improved by being more exact in specifying how the laws are to be changed, but this might in turn encourage even more prospective legislators to avoid answering these questions as some of them may not have had ample opportunity to study the specific proposed provisions of any particular bill. The real weakness in the use of these questionnaires is that so many candidates for state representative did not answer them. The only ultimate solution is that voters will have to react much more negatively to any candidate for political office who refuses to clearly state their views on policy issues before the election.

Conclusion

In this essay we have tried to explore some of the determinants of voting behavior on population policy by the Massachusetts state representatives in 1970 and 1971. Our findings have suggested that the personal characteristics of legislators rather than the characteristics of their constituents are the best predictors of their degree of liberalism on population policy. In addition, we found that of the four personal characteristics we analyzed, the two most important were a legislator's religious affiliation and his index of liberalism on other legislative matters. Finally, our analysis of the effectiveness of pre-election policy questionnaires to all candidates suggested their usefulness—particularly if we could eliminate the large number of non-replies in the future.

Before we really understand the determinants of legislative behavior on population policy, much more work will have to be done at both the state and national levels. Whether the results for the Massachusetts House of Representatives for the 1970 and 1971 sessions are limited to only that state and that particular time period cannot be ascertained without detailed studies of other areas. In addition, much more effort should be made in future studies to obtain data from legislators on their perception of the nature of the population problem and how their specific views affect their legislative behavior.

Notes

1. Carol F. Brooks, "The Early History of the Anti-Contraceptive Laws in Massachusetts and Connecticut," *American Quarterly*, 18 (1966), 3-23.

2. For a very useful analysis of the relationship between the judicial and the legislative process in the changes in birth control legislation in the United States, see C. Thomas Dienes, *Law, Politics, and Birth Control* (Urbana, Ill.: University of Illinois Press, 1972). The book also has a very good summary of developments in Massachusetts on the birth control issue.

3. For a good discussion of the attempts to change the birth control laws during these years, see John R. Rodman, "Trying to Reform the Birth Control Law: A Study in Massachusetts Politics," (Unpublished thesis, Government 225, Harvard University, 1955).

4. Ibid.

5. Ibid.

6. On the 1965 and 1966 efforts in the Massachusetts legislature, see Dienes, op. cit., pp. 200-209.

7. There are several good analyses of Massachusetts politics that can be used. Among them are Murray Levin and George Blackwood, *The Compleat Politician: Political Strategy in Massachusetts* (New York: Bobbs Merrill, 1962); Edgar Litt, *The Political Cultures of Massachusetts* (Cambridge, Mass.: MIT Press, 1965); Philip Coulter and Glen Gordon, *Voting Behavior in Massachusetts: Explorations in Political Ecology* (Amherst, Mass.: University of Massachusetts Press, 1967).

8. Sheldon Goldman, *Roll Call Behavior in the Massachusetts House of Representatives: A Test of Selected Hypotheses* (Amherst, Mass.: University of Massachusetts Press, 1968), 17-38.

9. The exclusion of legislators who did not vote on all three bills probably did not distort our results, as there did not appear to be any systematic attempt on behalf of the state representatives to avoid being recorded on these issues.

10. Roll-call vote number 63 on H. 520 in 1970; roll-call vote number 262 on H. 1231 in 1971.

11. Roll-call vote number 53 on resolve by Representative Fishman in 1970; roll-call vote number 85 on H. 4089 in 1971.

12. Roll-call vote number 52 on H. 1113 in 1970; roll-call vote number 83 on H. 3680 in 1971.

13. We are indebted to Professor Allan G. Bogue for suggesting to us the standardization of the index of liberalism on population policy on a 100 point scale. For a detailed discussion of the problem of comparing scaled indices of legislative voting behavior in different sessions, see Aage R. Clausen, "Measurement Identity in the Longitudinal Analysis of Legislative Voting," *The American Political Science Review*, 61 (1967), 1020-1035.

14. N.R. Draper and H. Smith, *Applied Regression Analysis* (New York: Wiley, 1966); William L. Hays, *Statistics* (New York: Holt, Rinehart and Winston, 1963), pp. 490-577; Edwin Kuh and John R. Meyer, "Correlation and Regression Estimates When the Data are Ratios," *Econometrica*, 23 (1955), 400-416.

15. J. Johnston, *Econometric Methods* 2nd ed. (New York: McGraw Hill,

1972), pp. 159-168; Hubert M. Blalock, Jr., "Correlated Independent Variables: The Problem of Multicollinearity," *Social Forces*, 62 (1963), 233-238.

16. League of Women Voters of Massachusetts, "A Voter's Guide for Nov. 3," supplement in the *Boston Globe* (October 20, 1970), pp. 1-24.

14 Family Planning Policy Development in North Carolina: Weak Tea

One of the most dramatic and rapid shifts ever to occur in U.S. public policy has been the transition since 1959 from a stated position that the government should take no action to provide support for family planning programs in this country or abroad to the development of an affirmative federal policy. This policy, backed by a substantial budget and a detailed program plan, contains the specific goal of offering effective family planning services by 1975 "to all Americans who want them but cannot afford them,"[1] as well as a far-reaching and expanding program of assistance to other countries in the areas of population and family planning.[2] While numerous authors have commented on this shift and a few articles have, at least tentatively, attempted to analyze it,[3] there has as yet been no definitive study of family planning and population policy development at the national level. Such an analysis, although urgently needed, represents a large and complex task. This article describes a much more modest study of the development of family planning policy on the county level in the state of North Carolina. The study was conducted, however, in the belief that it could illuminate some more general aspects of family planning—if not for the country as a whole, at least for many states in the South.

Affirmative policies and effective programs on regional, state and local levels are needed to implement federal policies and to attain national goals. Thus, about 20 percent of the medically indigent women estimated to be "in need" were reported as being served by organized family planning programs in the United States in 1969.[4] The federal policies were the same everywhere, but variations in unmet need were considerable among regions, states and counties, ranging from no services reported at all, to more than 90 percent reported served. A study of policy development in North Carolina seemed particularly appropriate because there was a long history of public involvement in the provision of family planning services to the indigent, there existed an official governor's committee on family planning (comprising the principal public and private agencies in the state administering family planning service and research

Reprinted with permission from *Family Planning Perspectives*, vol. 4, no. 2, 1972, p. 47. The article was originally adapted from "Family Planning in North Carolina: The Politics of a Lukewarm Issue," Monograph 17, Carolina Population Center, University of North Carolina at Chapel Hill, 1972.

*Research Advisor for the Population Council in Colombia.

programs), an international center for the study of population had been formed at the University of North Carolina and the state health department had a family planning policy and program. Nevertheless, the individual counties still enjoyed considerable autonomy to decide what kind of and how much family planning— if any—they would offer (thus permitting the investigator to study and compare policy processes in a variety of local settings).

Family Planning in North Carolina

As early as 1932, the North Carolina Conference for Social Service and the State Board of Charities and Public Welfare adopted resolutions favoring birth control,[5] and in the same year the state's first birth control clinic was opened, under private auspices.[6]

In 1937, the State Health Department for the first time officially sponsored a birth control program in order to:

1. Reduce the high infant death rate and the loss of mothers' lives,
2. Curb the high birthrate among dependent families and create an awareness of the importance of proper spacing of all future children of the state as the prerequisite for healthful and happy family life,
3. Endeavor to increase the birthrate among the physically fit, and the financially and intellectually competent.[7]

From the outset, the birth control program in North Carolina was organized under medical auspices, although there is evidence to suggest that the underlying aims related more to "eugenics" than health as usually defined:

We have undertaken in the Bureau to give assistance to those organizations, particularly to the women's organizations and the welfare groups in the state, in an effort leading toward adopting a positive breeding of better family children, more of them, and the curbing of the breeding of the undesirables.

We adopted this on the understanding that it is a public health enterprise, because there is no other means except organized medical societies to put over the program . . . The program was ready to be launched by a group of welfare officers. We took the ground that it was a dangerous procedure for a group of laymen to handle, and therefore we are holding this program in medical channels, as we are interested in the medical indications.[8]

The local health officers decided whether initiation of a birth control program was "advisable." If the local health officer considered initiation of a birth control program to be "advisable," he was required to obtain the approval of the local medical society: "Approval by local practitioners has been insisted upon by the State Health Department before inauguration of the program"; and it was indicated that "no attempt has been made to make the service available to great numbers."[9]

It seems reasonable, in light of the innovativeness of the program and the constraints operating, to characterize the early record as successful, as did a report which stated that, by 1940, 75 percent of the 81 public health units offered the service,[10] and that approximately four percent of the "eligible" group of underprivileged women had been served in the areas covered.[11] This early momentum of family planning activity was not, however, maintained. The level of services, as reported to the State Board of Health, remained relatively stable from 1948 to 1952, with about 4,000 family planning visits recorded annually, and thereafter generally declined, until by 1960 only 2,000 visits were recorded—a level only slightly higher than that reported for 1939. Beginning in 1961, with the advent of the oral contraceptive, the reported level of services again rose significantly: For 1967, there were 27,360 patient visits reported, a 14-fold increase over the 1960 figure.[12]

Despite North Carolina's pioneering role in the initiation of family planning programs and the significant increase in services reported during the 1960s, the state has not maintained a superior standing in relation to other states. A national study of subsidized family planning needs and services showed that, for the year ending June 30, 1968, North Carolina ranked twenty-first among all 50 states in provision of services to the medically indigent (serving 13 percent of women "in need" compared to 14 percent for the country as a whole).[13] A resurvey at the end of 1969, 18 months later, showed that North Carolina's relative position had slipped even further, tying Minnesota for twenty-third place among the states—serving 14 percent of those in need, compared to 20 percent reported served by organized programs in the nation[14] as a whole.

At first blush, it is reasonable to question the utility of a study of family planning policy development in this state in the 1960s, when the issue was 'decided' three decades earlier. After 1960, a number of new factors arose which required that family planning policy be considered de novo in that decade. Among these factors were: the development of effective coitus-independent methods of contraception; the increased availability of federal funding (particularly in the latter half of the decade); increased awareness by health, welfare and antipoverty agencies of the association of excess fertility with a variety of social problems;[15] and a changing sociocultural milieu, permitting freer discussion about and services directed toward problems related to human sexuality.

As a result, the policy questions of whether to upgrade, reinvigorate or broaden existing programs were perceived at the local level largely as new issues. Early efforts had been concentrated almost entirely within health departments, and funds had not been earmarked specifically for family planning, so that little awareness of the programs existed outside the departments of health and social services. In the 1960s—and particularly during the second half of the decade—this situation changed. Partially as a response to the increased availability of federal funds, partially because of increased awareness among professionals and increased demand for services from the medically indigent, local governments in some counties were pressed to provide what were, for them, relatively large appropriations for the programs. New agencies, particularly the local Community Action Programs, began to become involved. Consequently, family planning for the medically indigent during the second half of the 1960s enjoyed more visibility among policy markers in the state of North Carolina than it ever had before.

Methodology

Leverage Points. The concept of "leverage points" in a policy-making system is predicated on the uneven distribution of involvement in the policy process, which allows the analyst to "focus on a delimited number of persons."[16] "However, the success of such an approach depends on one's capacity to identify this core group of persons."[17] Leverage points differ between and among systems, but illustrative examples are the influence of a particular institution, the role attached to a particular officeholder (subjectively and objectively) or the effect a private individual may have in a policy-making system. However, for the purpose of this study of policy process, the assumption will be made, after Gergen[18] and others,[19] "that the subunits of greatest importance are individual persons rather than organizations or institutions, and that a thorough understanding of public policy will ultimately depend on knowledge of individual participants."[20]

In connection with the effect of system size on leverage points, it has been asserted that "one fact that does emerge consistently is that of a general positive relationship between the size of the city or community and the number of influentials."[21] This correlation has important ramifications in terms of the scope and feasibility of this study, for it seems reasonable to expect that the number of individuals exerting leverage on a given social policy issue in most North Carolina counties would not be large in view of the relatively small populations of the counties. A corollary expectation would be that the important actors in the policy process might be identified more easily than would be the case in larger communities. In considering the policy issue of county family planning programs for the medically indigent in North Carolina, the local directors of health, community action programs, and social services as well as the members of their respective boards and of the boards of county commissioners represent potential leverage points in the system. It was therefore decided to begin to identify the important actors in the policy process by means of this decisional and positional approach, which then could be supplemented by including in the research informal (or other formal) leaders identified by reputation in the initial contact with the core group.

In view of the hypothesized central importance of the individual policy-maker in the process under study, his values, perceptions, expectations, and behavior relating to a given issue all merit the attention of the researcher. For the investigation of these parameters a methodological tool capable of producing a high information yield on different levels and from different aspects of the respondent's involvement is required. A flexible and widely used instrument which comes closest to meeting these criteria is the face-to-face interview.

Interview. The "focused interview"[22] was felt to be the most appropriate form of face-to-face interview for several reasons.[23]

1. Sufficient general knowledge about the policy process involved was available to allow the formulation of a set of propositions which provided the necessary areas of focus.

2. This approach, in contradistinction to the structured interview, does not list a set of questions to be asked each respondent in a given order, but allows considerable freedom for the interviewer to adapt the order, phrasing, and follow-up of questions in light of the responses. As a result, the direction of the interview can be structured according to the respondent's perceptions, thereby reducing the risk of giving artificial saliance to a particular subject or point of view.

3. The focused interview allows the interviewer to probe potentially interesting areas at greater depth than in the standard interview and to follow up unanticipated responses.

4. This type of interview was expected to yield a richer lode of data because of its flexibility and apparent suitability for use with individuals occupying important positions.

Each person interviewed was given a clear description of the study. The interviewer was identified as a physician graduate student in the School of Public Health at the state university; the stated objective of the interview was to contribute to a study of how family planning programs developed in the counties of the state; and the anonymity of the interviewee was emphasized. In addition, each interviewee was told that the study had the support of the Governor's Committee on Population and the Family, which was interested both in learning more about the county programs and in possible ways of assisting them if such were desired.

A stratified sample of 10 counties was chosen for study on the basis of 10 geographic, demographic and health variables. These were: region, population size, racial composition, rural-urban status, proportion of families in poverty status; infant mortality rates; illegitimacy ratios; public assistance cases per 1,000 population; crude birthrate; and the percentage of unmet need for family planning services.[24] The first five criteria are geographic, demographic or economic; the latter five were chosen because of their perceived relevance to family planning. In general, an effort was made to match counties on the basis of the first five criteria, and contrast them with the family planning criteria. Counties which had been intensively or recently studied were excluded. A deliberate effort was made to include counties which had programs funded by the Office of Economic Opportunity (OEO) (two were chosen); those which had particularly successful or unsuccessful programs (as judged by proportion of unmet need); and those displaying other characteristics which might be expected to effect the policy process. No effort was made randomly to select a representative sample of counties. However, the sample included counties from the mountains to the coast, comprising a mixture of urban and rural, affluent and poor, large and small in size and population.

Most of the data were gathered from September through December of 1969, during which time the author was in the field almost continuously. Follow-up to complete the data collection took place during the first three months of 1970. The author spent an average of seven days in each county interviewing each of the principal policy makers, as judged by position, reputation and power to make decisions affecting county policy in the area under investigation. In each county, the chairman of the board of county commissioners, the director of social services, the health director and the director of the community action agency were interviewed, except for three individuals who had relocated. Altogether, 94 persons were interviewed, including various other members of these agencies, four presidents of the county medical societies, four county managers, four chairmen or members of welfare boards, social workers, newsmen, hospital and health administrators and ministers.

The study was described to each person interviewed: The interviewer identified himself as a physician graduate student at the state university school of public health; the object of the interview was to contribute to a study of how family planning programs developed; anonymity was guaranteed.

Interviews averaged about one hour in length, although seven took more than two hours, and six were completed in less than 15 minutes. The author was given free access to the minutes of meetings, copies of letters, program statistics, budgets and press clippings. Only two respondents appeared hostile, and a half-dozen others seemed somewhat suspicious about the purpose of the interview, despite all attempts to reassure them. Second interviews were held with seven respondents, and in one case a third interview was arranged.

A wealth of detailed data was collected, constituting 10 separate case studies of the policy process in North Carolina counties. In the reports which follow, the counties' actual names are disguised to protect the anonymity of respondents.

1. Bypass County

Prior to 1967 there was no family planning program in Bypass County. The part-time health director took no initiative in organizing this type of service, and the department of social services had concentrated its efforts on arranging sterilization operations for welfare recipients. The board of county commissioners had never discussed family planning at any of its meetings, much less appropriated funds to provide services. The chairman, who was also chairman of the board of health, when asked about the county program (which had already been in operation for two years) replied: "I don't know anything about it and I've never discussed it with anyone else . . . [W]e normally leave things like that up to department heads."

The county's family planning program was organized as the result of efforts by the local community action agency and, more specifically, by its dynamic director, who was a native of the county, had been active in local politics and possessed a deep understanding of the people and their problems. This initiative was welcomed by the department of social services.

The projected program was opposed, however, by some segments of the medical profession, who were concerned with arrangements regarding remuneration for clinical services and who feared that private patients would be recruited. The county medical society requested that payment be made on a fee-for-service basis to a rotating panel of private physicians. Eventually, it was agreed that only one physician, paid on an hourly basis, would be hired to man the clinic. The physicians favored the provision of family planning services to the indigent population, but were concerned over the means to be employed. The president of the medical society credited the physicians and the health department with initiating the program, but this was not corroborated by other data sources. Indeed, the program almost foundered at its inception over the payment question, as its OEO federal funding depended on local physician cooperation.

In 1967, the social services department earmarked the necessary matching funds, the OEO grant was made to the community action agency, a staff of four was employed, clinic services were provided at the health department and an energetic outreach effort was launched to recruit and follow up patients. In 1969, a full-time outreach director was added to the staff, and later another clinic was located in a distant part of the county (which stretches for one hundred miles). Some transportation was provided for patients, clinics were held in the evening and the staff fostered a friendly and informal atmosphere in the clinic sessions—all of which helped the program's reputation.

The results were successful. Nearly four in 10 of the population estimated to be in need of services were apparently reached in the first two years of operation, the drop-out rate was estimated at 24 percent and the program had contacted 2,300 women and had 600 active patients. Those members of the board of county commissioners who were aware of the program favored it as a way of reducing the welfare rolls; it was also approved by the board of health. However, there are no data to suggest that either body ever formally considered the question of family planning. Aside from the social service department's decision to provide matching funds, the policy process appears essentially to have bypassed the local decision-making channels by virtue of its outside funding source. Since the board of commissioners was required to sanction the activities of the community action agency, it could be said to have provided de facto approval of a policy to organize a public family planning program.

2. Token County

Token County's health department was, until the late 1960s, one of the few in the state which provided no family planning services, and which had no maternal and child health program. Despite the relative affluence of this urban county, the department was understaffed and poorly funded; the full-time health director had a difficult time providing the few personal health services which were offered. Many local physicians were hostile to "government medicine," under which rubric the health department was placed. In addition, some physicians displayed considerable resentment toward public assistance recipients, as well as fear that public health programs might recruit private patients.

It has been estimated that in excess of 3,450 women in the county need subsidized family planning services,[25] and this was recognized in 1967 by a former chairman of the board of social services, the directors of health and social services and a former chairman of the board of county commissioners. The former welfare head, a dynamic and community-minded woman, stirred the interest of the others and, as a result, a meeting was arranged in early 1968 with the county medical society, to seek its cooperation in starting a family planning program. In a very heated exchange, some members of the medical society expressed opposition to providing subsidized family planning services to the medically indigent, although 60 percent of them voted for providing services if they could be organized on a fee-for-service basis in physicians' private offices, rather than in a health department clinic. The county commissioners, who favored a family planning program as a means of reducing welfare expenditures, appropriated $500 to allow 15 public assistance recipients to receive family planning services on a "experimental" basis. This funding was later described as "tokenism" by the president of the medical society, who stated that family planning will be provided for the poor only when it is energetically advocated by the society or some other agency. He cited excessive workloads and lack of interest as the main reasons why physicians were unlikely to provide leadership. Another local physician stated that the society had never successfully dealt with any community health problem.

Later in 1968, the local community action agency presented a well-documented brief recommending a family planning program to the county commissioners, the medical society and the health department. It was received with apparent interest, but no action ensued, probably because there was considerable opposition to the poverty agency on the part of the commissioners and other elements in the community.

The department of social services filed a report on the experimental program after one year, and it was refunded at the same level; no evaluation was carried out as far as is known. The county administration remained sorely pressed for funds, with low revenues (one of the lowest property tax rates in the state), and very heavy demands for funds due to the rapid growth of the county population. The board of commissioners, elected on a platform opposing a tax increase, appropriated funds only for services it considered essential; family planning was "way down on the list" of priorities, according to the county manager. As a result, Token County, although large, populous and relatively affluent, continued to limit family planning services to 15 women of the more than 3,450 in need. The policy process in this case is clear-cut, with formal deliberations on the part of the county commissioners and the appropriation of earmarked funds to provide services to a specified, token number of women.

3. Thrust County

The chairman of the board of social services was said to have shown "annoyance" whenever it was reported to him that a woman receiving Aid to Families with Dependent Children (AFDC) had become pregnant; he was reported, as a result, to have led the drive which culminated in 1964 in the establishment of a public family planning program. The board had been told of the active involvement of the social services department in the family planning program in Mecklenburg County, which was reported to have stemmed rising welfare costs. This information apparently influenced policy making in Thrust County, for early in 1963, the director of social services suggested to the health director that such a program be initiated. The health director, at first skeptical, mulled over the proposal for about 18 months before presenting it to the board of health. Although not as enthusiastic as the board of social services, according to the health director, the health board approved a family planning program, and the plan was presented to the board of county commissioners with a cost-benefit analysis derived from the Mecklenburg experience, showing how the number of public assistance recipients and the cost of services relating to pregnancies among the indigent would be reduced if welfare clients lowered their fertility. The commissioners endorsed the program as an economy move, appropriated $4,000 for supplies and ever since have given it high priority, according to all of the individuals interviewed.

The program began in May 1964, and was later incorporated into the outpatient services of the three local hospitals. By the middle of 1968, it was estimated to be providing services to nearly three in 10 of those considered to be in need,[26] ranking as one of the most successful programs in the state. Budget requests for the program have never been questioned (although they had risen by 1969 to approximately $9,000 a year for drugs alone) and a quarterly report of the program results is presented to the commissioners by the health director.

It is difficult to judge the amount of opposition to the program. In 1968, the local newspaper carried several "scare" articles about the side effects of oral contraceptives, and during that summer there was a drop in the demand for services. This was attributed by the health department to black militants "stirring up" opposition in the housing developments. It was reported that visiting public health nurses were followed and patients watched, with the result that patients told the nurses to go away when they came to call. Similarly, the local director of the community action program reported that "the poor black sees family planning as the white man's way of keeping his numbers down." He stated that the health department was resented because over the years blacks had not been treated with dignity there. The data indicated that both individual and institutional racism did exist among the white establishment, although respondents agreed that race relations had improved in recent years. However, the health department turned down offers of assistance from the community action program and other antipoverty organizations, on the stated grounds that "going house-to-house" might hurt the program. Indigenous community workers from the community action agency, being drawn from the black poverty group and having experience and expertise in working in the ghetto, might have been expected to provide valuable assistance, both in terms of patient recruitment and community relations, since approximately 75 percent of the program participants were black.

The health department received no calls or letters expressing opposition to the program, but occasional complaints did come from medical practitioners regarding private patients availing themselves of the program services. It is not, of course, possible to measure in any exact way the effect of the various sources of opposition, but the respondents considered only the black militant opposition "significant." After the summer of 1968, participation in the program again increased (see Table 14-1). In view of this, and of the success of the program compared to other counties in the state, it seems doubtful that the opposition had a major effect on participation.

In Thrust County policy making relating to the public family planning program proceeded in an orderly way through the expected steps and channels.

4. Distaff County

Until 1967, the only birth control assistance supported by public policy for the poor of this isolated, mountain community was half-payment by the county commissioners of "usual and customary fees" for sterilization procedures. Two individuals, however, had sought for a number of years to develop a family planning program in the county. One was a busy, community-minded general practitioner and the other, a member of the board of health, who had served as chairman of the board of the local community action program and later became

Table 14-1

Estimated Number and Percent of Women in Need* of Subsidized Family Planning Services Who Were Active Patients in 10 North Carolina County Family Planning Programs in FY 1968 and 1969-1970

County	Estimated Population in Need	Number of Active Participants† 1969-1970	Percent of Target Population Served FY 1968*	1969-1970	Amount of Funding	Source of Funding
Bypass	1,614	608‡	23	37	$25,764	OEO
Token	3,454	16	0	0.5	500	county commissioners
Thrust	4,892	2,004	28	41	9,000§	county commissioners
Distaff	1,235	25	0	2	200	women's club
Backdoor	4,019	427	5	10	na	Welfare and health departments, and CAA
Lonestar	633	162	39	26	na	county commissioners; health department
Cauldron	3,827	291‡	7	8	na	welfare department
Catchon	1,122	308	7	28	20,500	OEO
Switch	930	59‡	6	6	na	health department
Acton	5,233	1,086‡	17	21	12,000**	DHEW Maternity and Infant Care Project

*Office of Economic Opportunity, *Need for Subsidized Family Planning Services: United States, Each State and County, 1968*, U.S. Government Printing Office, Washington, D.C., 1969, pp. 118-122.

†As estimated from data collected by the author from September 1969 through March 1970.

‡*Annual Public Health Reports:* County Form, Local Health Division, N.C. State Board of Health, Raleigh, N.C., 1969.

§ Drugs Only.

**Estimated.

na=not available.

chairman of the board of county commissioners. In early 1967, a local women's club elected a new president, a woman active in community affairs. According to the respondents, the family planning program became her two-year project as president. She helped marshal all of the agencies and individuals who were in favor of it. Through the local community action agency, a proposal was submitted to the OEO, but was turned down. However, the women's club donated $200, and with the services of the physician and his private nurse, technical assistance from the state board of health and equipment from the county health department, a program was launched in July 1967.

There was no significant opposition to the program but, as described by the physician involved, there was "a certain passivity about it." The county commissioners apparently favored it, but did not appropriate funds; the board of health, according to its chairman, was neither "for it nor against it," and claimed it was a state program; the health department gave what support it could, but had no health director and was grossly understaffed; finally, local physicians were said to have been opposed to most public health activities. Initially, public health nurses from two adjacent counties in the three-county health district attended the fortnightly clinic sessions. However, with an average attendance of only three patients per clinic, these were soon taken over by the lone public health nurse in Distaff County. This lady, a Roman Catholic, was initially opposed to the program, but later, according to physicians, was "all for it."

Respondents attributed the failure of the program to attract more patients to lack of outreach personnel, and lack of transportation to the single clinic location. The clinic charge of one dollar per visit might also have been a deterrent, but there may well have been a problem of motivation, as the respondents suggested, especially since these poor white mountain people are not accustomed to attending health department clinics, as are southern blacks. They apparently combine a fear of physicians with a distaste for "charity clinics," and were reported to resist change because of lack of education and intrinsic stubbornness. (If few were on welfare, this may also have contributed to the "passivity" attributed to the county commissioners.) The women are reported frequently to shun prenatal care and present themselves only at the time of delivery. Family planning may represent a 'delicate' subject to them. It was suggested that husbands may harbor fears that contraception would affect their sex lives, and that fundamentalist religious beliefs may account for some of the resistance to family planning. It seems clear, however, that part of the lack of success in Distaff County must have been due to the relative lack of availability and accessibility of services, both physically and psychologically.

The policy-making process in Distaff County circumvented the usual channels, and was stimulated by two individuals, neither of whom occupied a position in local government or a public agency.

5. Backdoor County

Before 1961, the health department made family planning services available to a small number of patients. The health director, wishing to develop an organized family planning program, enlisted the support of the director of social services. A family planning clinic was finally established in the health department in December 1961; it offered oral contraceptives and was operated by a state health department physician.

The health director, reportedly fearful of opposition from the board of county commissioners and the community at large, decided to use the "backdoor approach": approval of the commissioners and board of health was not sought, but the program was endorsed by the local medical society. A small but increasing number of patients enrolled over the years, but the program was handicapped from 1966 to 1969, during which time there was no health director. In addition, respondents cited, as an obstacle to the program's success, the requirement that each patient obtain certification by the department of social services; this often necessitated two trips to the county seat. Two other major problems were reported: lack of transportation in a large and predominantly rural county and the orientation of the health department towards the black population. Backdoor County has a predominantly white population, and six out of 10 of all residents are poor. The health department took the position that those who could pay for private medical service should do so; in practice, this resulted in more ready acceptance of blacks for family planning services than whites, although far more whites were in need.

A new dynamism and spirit of cooperation pervaded the family planning program after a new and energetic health director arrived in February 1969. Within a short time the social services certification requirement was scrapped, patients were screened by the health department, eligibility requirements were liberalized, the community action agency provided clinic personnel and transportation for approximately 40 percent of the clinic load, and, even more important, mounted an extensive outreach program. The department of social services actively referred patients, worked closely with the health department on follow-up and provided funds for the purchase of contraceptive supplies.

The county commissioners, however, remained on the periphery of the policy-making process despite the program's reinvigoration and the commissioners' desire to reduce welfare expenditures. When interviewed the chairman said he did not even know that there was a program, much less by whom it was operated or how it was funded. The chairman of the board of health stated, "I don't keep up with it." He attended only two meetings of the board in that year. Local government appeared preoccupied with the dilemma posed by the need for more revenue, on the one hand, and its reluctance to raise the relatively low property tax rate, on the other. The policy to provide family planning services to the medically indigent developed without the participation of the formal policy-making bodies, if not in spite of their apathy. The program continued to be supported by both the general appropriations to the health department and funds designated for the purchase of contraceptive supplies. However, it was never the subject of debate by policy makers, and no resolutions or discussions are recorded in the minutes of their meetings. The program continued to improve in terms of size and effectiveness as a result of the high level of cooperation between the health, social service and antipoverty agencies.

6. Lonestar County

This geographically large county has a small population, its 8,000 residents are almost equally divided between whites and blacks and a 1964 study indicated that 60 percent of the people were from families earning less than $3,000 per year.[27] The health director was also responsible for two other, more populous counties; he paid Lonestar County two-hour visits twice weekly. As a result, the nursing supervisor actually functioned as health director, and it was she who in 1964 attended a family planning workshop conducted in the state capital, and returned to Lonestar County determined to start a family planning program. During the preceding four years, family planning services had been provided to an average of five patients per year. The nursing supervisor enlisted the support of the board of county commissioners, the board of health and the ministerial association. Offers of assistance also came from the county's only physician and from the state board of health.

The program began in 1964. Health department budget funds were used to purchase contraceptive supplies, with the approval of the commissioners, who were eager to reduce welfare expenditures and illegitimacy in the county. Half of the respondents said that the program was accorded a "high" priority, the other half reported it had "low" priority. Perhaps this was because the commissioners favored the program but were unable or unwilling to provide adequate financial support. The department of social services reported that it gave "enthusiastic" support, but both its director and the nursing supervisor spoke of the "lack of motivation" on the part of those in need, and it was reported that coercive measures (such as implicit and explicit threats to withdraw welfare) had been used in some cases.

The family planning program was able by 1969 to recruit about one-quarter of the population in need of services, a much better record than obtained in the state as a whole.[28] Respondents said the program was handicapped by lack of outreach, unavailability of transportation for long-distance travel and some resistance to family planning because of religious objections, ignorance, fears relating to sexuality and, in a few cases, the issue of black genocide. The program director said that although a few patients left the program because of the genocide question, most of these returned. The bad publicity resulting from a serious illness, attributed by a patient in 1966 to her contraceptive method, is thought to have had a greater adverse effect on the program. Poor whites are thought to have been unwilling in the past to participate in a "black" program, although they comprised 15 percent of the 1969 patient caseload.

In this county a program was organized principally as a result of the efforts of the public health nursing supervisor, who stimulated the policy process.

7. Cauldron County

Cauldron County is the most densely populated county in the state, with a relatively large population and small land area. It is urban, prosperous and nearly three-fourths of the residents are white. For 25 years, condoms and foam were sold at cost by the health department to a few patients, but there was no family planning program of any size prior to February 1964. A new director of social services, upon her arrival in the community in September 1962, began a campaign to organize a program to provide family planning services to the bulk of the indigent population. The board of social services was approached with a cost-benefit analysis of such a program and supported it. However, opposition was reported from the medical society and especially from a few physicians who held that the intrauterine contraceptive was an abortifacient. Contributing to the opposition was the traditional antipathy between the many conservative medical practitioners and the department of social services, which was under almost continuous fire in the local press. In addition, some physician respondents expressed concern about the possible loss of private patients. The opposition culminated in a confrontation between the director of social services and a leading local physician, with the former refusing to abandon the program or the plan to use intrauterine devices.

As a result of the efforts of the director of social services, contraceptive supplies were included in the departmental budget, although this was not brought to the attention of the board of county commissioners in order to avoid possible opposition. The budget was approved, but no mention of family planning appears in the minutes of the meeting. Several respondents said that the county commissioners subsequently supported the family planning program as an effective way to reduce welfare expenditures. The board of health was apparently not involved in the policy process (although the services were provided in a health department maternity clinic), perhaps because of the reported lack of interest in family planning on the part of the health director.

The program met with modest success at its downtown location, serving some eight percent of the need by 1969. However, about 85 percent of its patients were black, although poor whites outnumber poor blacks in the community. The program was said to have suffered from lack of health department funds and personnel; another factor may have been that there was no special family planning clinic; rather, the service was part of a general maternity service. Physician opposition to the intrauterine device continued, and for some time a patient could only be fitted after being seen by a psychiatrist. For one year after the program clinician had a heart attack, no new patients were enrolled. The health director stated that the program was not being promoted energetically because of fears that the limited personnel might be "swamped."

The clinic was relocated in August 1969 to the hospital, which is situated several miles away from the downtown area and a similar distance from the poor neighborhoods. The move was supported by the physicians and the hospital board, since the clinic was needed to enable the hospital to mount a successful obstetrics residency program. The departments of health and social services opposed the move because the location was inaccessible to the poor, physically and psychologically, and the hospital insisted on charging all family planning patients at regular clinic rates. The hospital administration insisted that this policy would not act as a deterrent and was necessary to preserve uniformity among outpatient clinics, maintain an advantageous bargaining position vis-à-vis the department of social services regarding fees to be paid, and to obtain information on patients who might receive inpatient services in the future. It claimed that it did not intend to pursue collection "strenuously."

For a short time after the clinic was moved attendance remained constant, although the patients became noticeably better dressed and the proportion of white patients was said to have increased. (The 1969 OEO county study, however, reported a marked reduction in patients from seven percent served in FY 1968 to 4.4 percent served in 1969—after the move.[29]) About one-sixth of the patients paid the five-dollar clinic fee, but most did not go to the appointment desk in order to avoid the payment question. Several physician interviewees voiced fears about lack of cooperation from the obstetricians, many of whom were said to be apathetic. Initially, physician attendance was reasonably good, and the program benefited from the efforts of a capable senior resident and the efficient public health nurses who assisted in the clinic operation. The move ended the opposition to the intrauterine device and many patients were fitted.

8. Catchon County

This rural, poor county is large in size but small in population, which is about half black and half white. There are only four physicians in the county (one of whom is the part-time health director) and two public health nurses. Until January 1967, the only family planning activity was the distribution of foam to patients visiting the health department, and an occasional prescription for oral contraceptives. For a number of years, however, the board of commissioners had appropriated funds for the surgical sterilization of about 30 poor women per year.

A local tricounty community action agency proposal to start a federally financed family planning program was supported by the health department but opposed by the county commissioners, the department of social services and local farmers, and was not backed by the physicians. However, with assistance from the state health department, a small independent program was started in the local health department, funded by $250 earmarked by the county commissioners in the 1967-68 budget; this action apparently was catalyzed by the antipoverty agency's proposal. Meanwhile, the community action agency received an OEO grant and started a program in two adjacent counties. This program began to look more attractive to the county commissioners as they saw federal funds committed on a large scale. Thus, in July 1967, Catchon County decided to join the federal program. As a result, approximately $20,000 became available for the county, which hired a full-time family planning director (an experienced and capable public health nurse), a part-time clerk and two part-time aides. The program in Catchon County exceeded the accomplishments of the two other counties in the project by serving nearly one-third of the estimated population in need in the first two years of operation. It enjoyed the support of the county commissioners and complete cooperation from the health department, where it was physically housed. The department of social services, which apparently resented the community action agency and was described by several respondents as having alienated their clients, was reported to be uncooperative. The department complained that family planning program personnel were recommending applicants for public assistance whom it wanted to discourage, apparently even in genuine cases of dire need. By 1970, only three percent of the clients enrolled by the family planning program were welfare recipients, supporting the contention that little effort had been made to refer women receiving public assistance. There was minor opposition from two ministers worried that the program might encourage promiscuity, from a druggist who felt his business was being affected and from the health director, who generally favored the program but expressed the opinion that too many private patients were taking advantage of it. However, the program director believed that only the lack of cooperation from the department of social services hurt the program.

The community action agency director and the health director persuaded the commissioners to double the family planning budget (to $500) for FY 1969, but the program remained handicapped by lack of space, physician-time and transportation. However, all interviewees were unanimous that there would have been little or no activity in this area without the initiative of the community action agency. Equally doubtful was the ability of the county to continue to fund a program of this scope and effectiveness if federal funds were no longer available. The program personnel and earmarked funds were cited as the prime reasons for the success of the program.

This county illustrates the way in which an outside funding source can affect policy making in the area of family planning for the indigent.

9. Switch County

Switch County is semirural and more affluent than most mountain counties; the population is small and 94 percent white. The health department had supplied contraceptive jellies and foam since the early post-World War II period, but the service was on a very small scale. During the 1950s, the director of social services was known throughout the state for her strenuous espousal of sterilization as the "one effective method" of family limitation. Many recipients of public assistance were sterilized. Although this woman left in 1960, there remained a strong sentiment in favor of sterilization, and several respondents stated their belief that local government was "shackled" because there was no state legislation permitting compulsory sterilization of welfare recipients after they had borne a given number of children. The part-time health director indicated that he also advocated sterilization, and personally performed more of these operations than all other local physicians combined.

No organized family planning program was established in the county until January 1966. This was attributed to a lack of enthusiasm by the health director for contraception (as opposed to sterilization). None of the respondents could account for his apparent change of heart in 1966, but it is clear that this was a key element in the policy process. From early 1966 on, the health director, along with other physicians, promoted the program. It also received support and referrals from the department of social services. However, family planning was not discussed at meetings of the board of county commissioners, nor were funds appropriated for the program. At first, it was supported by funds generated by other health department activities, but in 1968 the commissioners took over this source of revenue and the small-scale program was supported from the health department budget. Clinics were held monthly, and as of 1969 less than 10 percent of women in need had been enrolled. The health director, however, did not believe that there was much unmet need, and no major emphasis was placed on patient recruitment, in part because there were only three public health nurses in the entire county. Because of opposition from some physicians concerned about losing private patients, it was decided to avoid publicity about clinic dates and hours. At the behest of the local pharmacists, the health director instituted financial screening of patients who received oral contraceptives at less than the retail price.

10. Acton County

About four in 10 of the residents of this populous and urban county lived below the poverty line as of 1969. Before 1964, the health department had a very limited family planning program based on the diaphragm, but a more extensive program was aggressively advocated by a new health director in late 1963. His initiative received strong support from the local obstetricians, who were concerned about the paucity of prenatal care and high illegitimacy and birthrates among the medically indigent population. The board of county commissioners, eager to reduce welfare expenditures, also supported the program. Technical assistance from the state board of health was provided to start the clinic operation and, in 1965, Acton County was asked (probably because of its large and active health department) if it wished to be one of three counties in the state to participate in a federal model Maternal and Infant Care program. From 1965, approximately $80,000 per year was received for this program, with roughly one-third spent on family planning (although this was earmarked only after 1967). As a result, a large family planning program was built, with over 1,000 active patients in 1970—about one in five of those in need.

There was little opposition to the family planning program: One physician, who dispensed drugs, asked the health department to stop serving private patients. There was some apparently racist criticism of the entire Maternal and Infant Care program on the grounds that it provided too many services to the "lazy." This came about because homemakers were assigned to help pregnant black women. Articles in the local newspaper indicated that there was a strong current of antiwelfare and racist sentiment in the county generally, and offers of help in family planning patient recruitment from the local community action agency were refused by the health department, which viewed it with great hostility.

The county commissioners were enthusiastic about the family planning program, but the chairman said that it would founder if the federal and state funding were lost. The program received strong support from the department of social services, and the county medical society favored it, according to its president. There is no public record of resolutions relating specifically to family planning by the board of health or the board of commissioners.

The Major Findings

Despite the subtle, complex, diffuse and idiosyncratic nature of the processes studied, eleven major findings emerged:

1. The policy-making process relating to public family planning programs was dominated in all 10 counties by one or two individuals, or a single agency.

2. County commissioners supported family planning programs mainly because of their desire to reduce welfare expenditures.

3. The policy makers did not perceive any organized opposition to family planning programs for the indigent.

4. Significant opposition did come from the medical profession, as a result of disapproval of the means, although not the goals of the program. That is, they favored publicly funded birth control service for the poor, but wanted it to be provided in private doctors' offices on a fee-for-service basis.

5. The key constraints were: lack of leadership from health departments, opposition from the medical profession, lack of salience of the issue for policy makers, lack of expertise inherent in the county system of government and lack of funds and personnel.

6. Respondents perceived the most important needs of their family planning programs to be publicity, additional funds, outreach and transportation, in that order.

7. In general, the issue studied appeared to be of relatively low salience for

policy makers (the boards of health, boards of county commissioners and the health directors).

8. There was general agreement among policy makers that public family planning programs were desirable.

9. The availability of federal funds had important implications for policy making, especially by enabling poor counties to overcome local indifference or opposition and organize extensive programs.

10. Policy decisions regarding family planning programs were not recorded in the minutes of the meetings of boards of commissioners or boards of health.

11. The majority of the counties studied did not have defined program objectives or effective evaluation procedures.

Leadership

Leadership was a key factor in policy development. In nine of the 10 counties a single individual or agency appears to have been instrumental in the policy-making process. Only 11 individuals or groups were identified as having played key roles, and these were very diverse—the president of a women's club, the community action agencies, a new director of social services, a new health director, the chairman of the board of social services. Important parts were played by a number of other individuals and groups. The presence of these few key actors, however, appears to have been a *sufficient condition* for the generation of a decision to provide at least some family planning services, given the other elements present in the system. On the other hand, the presence of the other actors appears to represent a *necessary but not sufficient condition* for the policy-making process.

How could such an apparently disproportionate role have been played in the policy-making process by so few individuals, in a society generally characterized by the pluralistic approach to decision making?

This appears to have been possible because family planning for the indigent is a lesser issue of the type decided by professional personnel rather than top community leaders, where the "sums of money involved are often minor in comparison with total expenditures for all services in the community, and top policy decision is usually not required to allow these activities to proceed."[30]

Health Directors

A striking finding was the lack of strong leadership in the policy-making process provided by most departments of health. Of the 10 counties, only one had a strong, full-time director who had served continuously from the beginning of the family planning program. The four health directors considered to be most effective, in terms of the family planning program as well as from a more general evaluation of their overall functioning, were all full-time health department employees. On the other hand, three of the five directors judged to be less effective in their jobs were part-time health department employees.

A second interesting finding was that all three of the part-time health directors spontaneously expressed concern that private patients might take advantage of the family planning program, and one personally screened the patients to make sure that this did not occur. None of the full-time directors articulated similar opinions. The part-time physicians, affiliated with their colleagues in full-time private practice in a social and professional system centered around the local medical society, were affected in their public health roles by the attitudes of their medical conferrees.

Directors of Social Services

Eight of the 10 welfare directors were judged to accord family planning for the indigent a high priority (compared to four out of nine health directors and one of the 10 county commission chairmen). This group was considered by the investigator to have a greater appreciation of the relationships between family planning, health, poverty, and welfare dependency than any other group interviewed, with the exception of community action agency directors. However, directors of social services are not in as strategic a position as health directors to influence family planning policy making, because they lack formal responsibility for family planning (which is considered to be a health department prerogative), are unable to provide services directly and have lacked directly available funding sources.

The County Commissioners

The study produced data showing that county commissioners support family planning services primarily in an effort to reduce welfare expenditures. However, chairmen of boards of county commissioners frequently cited other objectives, too, such as "the betterment of the community," "to reduce poverty," "to reduce illegitimacy" and "to improve the life of the poor."

Commissioners' attitudes appeared to vary widely, from those whose approach was compounded of a compassionate and humanitarian wish to see individuals break the poverty cycle to those who were ideologically opposed to public assistance for the needy. At least eight of the 10 counties studied had been appropriating funds for the sterilization of welfare recipients before their new or reinvigorated family planning programs started.

Racism

It was not possible meaningfully to quantify the racist sentiments encountered. However, the significance of such tendencies was overshadowed by another finding: *Discriminatory attitudes seem to be directed toward all of the disadvantaged, public assistance population, regardless of color.* Thus, one of the two county commission chairmen who were unsympathetic to the AFDC program stated: "Too many unwed mothers are having children—mostly poor whites and colored people. That's where you run into the welfare problem—the state and the federal government says you must take care of them. We're trying to hold some of that down." (The county was one of six in the state which were being sued for refusing to provide the local contribution for a federal work incentive program.) In the county where the greatest repository of sentiment in favor of compulsory sterilization laws was found among respondents, the black population comprised only six percent of the county total.

Two of the 10 chairmen interviewed made overtly racist remarks. (One chairman made joking reference to the holder of a responsible county office as a "white man's nigger.") However, no chairman made remarks which could even remotely be construed to indicate attitudes favoring family planning as a strategy to achieve race genocide. In three counties, however, respondents mentioned isolated instances in which members of the black community had suggested that the family planning program constituted an effort on the part of the white people to perpetrate race genocide on blacks. In most cases such sentiments were attributed to a small number of political activists, very occasionally to a family planning patient. Seven of the respondents were black, including a physician in each of the counties where there were any black medical practitioners.

Opposition from the Medical Profession

Although all respondents claimed that there was no organized opposition to the public family planning program, the data reflected serious resistance from the organized medical profession. In eight of the 10 counties respondents reported that the private physicians feared that the program was recruiting private patients, and objected to it. While this position was generally held by a minority of practitioners, in several counties significant opposition arose either from the county medical society or from a group of private physicians. Only in one county was the program considered by the author to have received enthusiastic support from the local medical society; in no case was a program initiated due to the efforts of such a body.

Paradoxically, interviews with 18 physicians and all other respondents produced unequivocal evidence that the overwhelming majority of physicians favored fertility limitation on the part of the medically indigent and supported making available means to achieve this goal. The opposition of the medical profession to family planning programs relates to *means*, not *ends*: Many physicians tended to view health department activities as "government medicine" or "socialized medicine." They feared losing private patients and were preoccupied with the fee-for-service system of remuneration, and the traditional entrepreneurial doctor-patient relationship. The result of these diametrically opposed attitudes was ambivalence: Physicians favored family planning for the indigent because of a variety of medical, social and political concerns; however, physicians as a "guild" opposed programs organized under public auspices. Ironically, the opposition of the profession was overcome in a few counties by the political support of those forces whose main concern was welfare and taxes.

Community Action Agencies

A significant finding was the effect of community action agencies as an intervening variable between county resources and the policy process. All the counties studied had such agencies, but their size, program thrust and effectiveness varied greatly. However, these agencies did represent access to considerable quantities of federal funds earmarked for family planning services to the poor. In two of the four poor counties studied, there were no family planning programs until the community action agency organized them. It was asserted by the director of the antipoverty agency in one of these counties that the task would have been much more difficult if there had already been an ineffective or token health department program in operation.

Family Planning Program Effectiveness

Table 14-1 illustrates the relative success of the 10 county programs studied, in terms of their effectiveness in enrolling as active patients the estimated population in need. As can be seen from this table, the effectiveness of the programs, according to the measure being applied, varied greatly, from less than 10 percent to more than 40 percent served of those in need.

The affluence of a county and its identification as rural or urban did not serve as useful indicators of the likelihood that it would have an effective family planning program. The availability of outside funds was seen to be of considerable importance in three of the most effective counties (Bypass, Thrust and Switch). Some of the other more important influences appeared to be the presence of dynamic leadership, extent of opposition, awareness of need, the caliber of professional personnel, the attitude of the county commissioners and the degree of coordination between individuals and agencies, and the part played by chance appeared to be large in a number of counties. Of all these factors, the most critical appeared to be the presence of committed, dynamic individuals who could provide the necessary leadership.

Salience of the Issue to Policy Makers

Family planning did not arouse a major controversy in any of the communities studied. In no case had family planning for the indigent been an issue in an election campaign, nor had the issue *per se* been especially newsworthy in the 10 counties. Overall, in the seven counties with a local newspaper, there was more favorable than unfavorable publicity, as judged from the clippings on file, but in no case did it appear to constitute an issue of major public concern. In only two of the 10 counties was it found that county commissioners had made public statements on the subject of family planning programs for the indigent; in both cases their comments had been favorable.

The salience of public family planning programs was found to vary considerably: One county commission chairman was completely unaware of the program; two others were believed to have been unable to make well-informed statements on the subject; and six others offered a "low profile." None of the 10 counties was found to have gone on public record, in the form of a resolution in the minutes of commissioners' meetings, as having made a policy decision either in favor of or in opposition to such a program. In four counties, the subject reportedly had never been discussed at a commissioners' meeting. In part, this reflected the generally casual way in which local government is conducted, rather than a deliberate effort to avoid going on record as supporting a program concerned with human sexuality. None of the officials interviewed suggested that they were reticent to act because the program was "controversial." On the other hand, in none of the counties was the appropriate proportion of personnel time charged against family planning activities, so that the commissioners (and the health and social service directors) had no way of assessing how much was actually being expended on such programs.

Since all county commissioners interviewed stated that there was no organized opposition to family planning, it was clear from both the interviews and the county appropriations that education, roads, attracting new industry, public assistance and health programs other than family planning all ranked higher in priority than family planning. County commissioners are part-time government officials, usually with little training for their task, so that priorities tend to be inherited from previous administrations, or set by current expediencies, rather than worked out on the basis of well-documented needs and demands. In particular, because of the short-fall of revenue as compared to needed expenditures, county commissioners tend not to consider new programs unless they are forced to do so by local demand or by the state or federal governments.

Lack of Policy Definition

The data showed that policy to provide family planning to the indigent was largely ill-defined. In only three counties had a need estimate been made, based on reliable data, and in only one of the three had a rough time-frame been worked out for reaching the target. The findings were almost identical in the area of evaluation. Three programs were considered to be undertaking creditable evaluation, two of which were administered by community action agencies. The third was in a health department program. The latter case, however, can probably be cited as the exception proving the rule that health department programs lack goal-definition, specified objectives and scientific evaluation.

About the Policy-Making Process

Two conclusions about the policy-making process appear to be warranted:

1. The prime prerequisite for a policy to start or reinvigorate a family planning program appeared to be that one or several individuals, or an agency or agencies, energetically promote such action and provide sufficient impetus and leadership to stimulate other important actors in the policy process.

2. The degree of success achieved in the *implementation* of this policy, i.e., the organization of an effective program, appeared to depend on another set of variables, chief among which was the availability of funds. (It is likely that success in stimulating a policy decision in favor of initiating a program depended in part on the probability of funds being available for the program.)

Reliability

The study was based primarily on a single set of interviews conducted by the investigator, with the following advantages and disadvantages:

In the early stages of research on a topic, a maximum amount of information can be generated in a minimum of time. Perhaps the major shortcoming of this approach has to do with the issue of reliability, or the degree of variation in behavior caused by inconsistencies in the measurement. For the majority of such studies, there is no way of determining the extent to which observations reflect either simple inconsistencies in the measuring device or temporary and fluctuating behaviors on the part of the individual being studied.[31]

The problem of reliability was addressed in several ways. First, there was a consistent effort made to triangulate the data; that is, conclusions on a given point were drawn only on the basis of several interviewees' responses and whenever possible from corroborating data such as the minutes of meetings,

282

budget appropriations, and press clippings. Second, the interview guide was standardized to the extent possible using the focused interview approach so as to make interviews maximally comparable. Third, the pretest, by virtue of the practice it afforded, gave the interviewer an opportunity to develop a relatively standardized interviewing style. It seems probable that the interviewer's skill increased during the field work proper, but this was not perceived to alter the findings in any discernible way. Fourth, extensive notes were recorded during each interview and were later typed in order to provide a direct record of the interchange. Finally, the problem of reconciling the findings of a number of field workers did not arise as all the data were collected by the interviewer.

Validity

The problem of investigator bias looms large in a study of policy-making such as this, where the researcher functions as the basic research instrument. It has been stated that "If the face-to-face interview is to be relied on as a primary source of data, there is no ultimate solution to the problem of bias."[32] An attempt was made to minimize this bias by stressing the anonymity of the respondent and by describing the study in terms of its importance, the backing it had from prestigious sources, and the goal of collecting information of practical value to the counties of North Carolina. One example of the effect of the interviewer's obvious interest in family planning was that judging from the rest of the data, nine of the respondents appeared to exaggerate the role they had played in policy-making. However, it is not possible to gauge the effect of the interviewer being a non-Southerner, a physician, and associated with an academic institution. There was, however, a strong conviction that essentially similar findings would be found by another investigator.

New York City and North Carolina

A number of striking differences are apparent when the process involved in the policy decision to initiate family planning services in New York City's tax-supported municipal hospitals in 1958[33] is compared to the process studied in North Carolina more than a decade later. In both cases there was no legal impediment to provision of these services. In North Carolina a permissive climate prevailed for policy making as a result of substantial agreement among policy makers regarding the need, while in New York the issue was political and divisive. Of course, the differences in the two processes are heavily influenced by the turnabout in national policy which occurred over the decade—a change which the successful outcome of the New York City controversy certainly helped to bring about. Nevertheless, some of the significant basic differences in the two processes still seem instructive. For example, in New York:

1. The proponents of family planning services devised carefully thought out strategies, whereas in North Carolina policies seldom if ever grew out of well-organized planning.

2. There had been in New York a "total and effective ban on any contraceptive information or service being given to anyone,"[34] and the commissioner of hospitals had assured physicians who wanted to fight the ban that, "You can't fight the Archdiocese."[35] There was no comparable level of opposition to the provision of contraceptive service in the North Carolina counties.

3. The crucial period in which the policy issue was debated publicly and vigorously in New York can be accurately pinpointed to a period of only two months. In the North Carolina counties respondents were often vague about the time a decision was made or a program begun, and in many cases were wrong by a matter of years.

4. Finally, in New York there was a well-developed awareness, among proponents and opponents alike, that they were dealing with an important issue, one for which it was considered worthwhile becoming involved in a bruising public fight. In none of the North Carolina counties studied did the issue achieve anything like this degree of controversiality, visibility and importance. For the most part, it was considered briefly and casually only by those groups and individuals who might have been expected to be involved in the policy process.

In North Carolina, the only opposition of significance came from the medical profession. In one case, this opposition did have a major effect on the scope of the family planning program and the method of delivery of services. In another case, a disagreement regarding physician remuneration came close to preventing the program from being launched. However, more often the apathy, lack of interest and dearth of leadership among the physicians simply made it more difficult to obtain appropriate policy decisions or to operate the resulting programs optimally. At any rate, the extent of their opposition was dwarfed by the magnitude of the official Roman Catholic opposition to birth control in the public hospitals of New York. In the latter case, given the controversiality of the issue and the extent of the resources at the command of the opposing sides in New York, the dynamics of the policy process appear logical and appropriate. On the other hand, when the sociopolitical climate regarding family planning for the indigent in North Carolina is considered, it is not surprising to see that the issue produced a good deal less public debate, and the policy process characterized by less urgency and dynamism—left to the few who felt strongly about the subject. In North Carolina, there was usually no need carefully to plot strategy, to build a forceful coalition of groups in favor or to engage in an extensive program of public education. The decision to provide such services could be, and therefore was, made without fanfare or public debate, in contrast with the New York situation.

Such an easy victory, however, may have its price. New York City was reported in 1969 to have nearly 100 family planning clinics, established in virtually all the health department centers and municipal hospitals, and in many of the voluntary hospitals, in Planned Parenthood and antipoverty settings, and to be serving nearly 120,000 patients[36]—two-thirds of its estimated need.[37] In the same year, North Carolina was reported to be serving a total of less than 32,000 patients—only 14 percent of its estimated need.[38] *Indeed, the North Carolina study emphasizes the need to accept with great caution statements regarding lack of opposition.* Moreover, support regarding the ends involved in a policy issue may be emasculated by a disagreement over appropriate means. To sum up, support or opposition stems from a complex amalgam of human motivations, two of which are likely to be apathy and ambivalence.

Conclusions

In most of the counties studied, the major support for family planning for the medically indigent came from individuals or agencies interested in reducing poverty itself (usually the community action agencies), or in reducing the costs of supporting the poor (usually the welfare departments). Most opposition came from private physicians, who feared the introduction of family planning programs as another step towards the imposition of "government medicine." Because the issue of family planning did not generally have great salience, either among its supporters or its opponents, it was often possible for a single strongly motivated individual or agency (usually from outside the principal local power structure—the board of county commissioners) to stimulate initiation of a family planning program. This was especially true if the interested individual or agency could mobilize a significant amount of outside funding for the program. Whereas nonsalience may be an aid to program *initiation*, it appears to be a decided drawback to program *implementation* and *expansion*, the North Carolina experience would indicate, since the nation's family planning programs as a whole advanced from serving 14 percent of the need as of June 30, 1968 to 20 percent as of December 31, 1969; while North Carolina, which initiated some services in the early 1930s, moved from 13 percent served in mid-1968 to 14 percent served by the end of 1969. "Keeping the pot boiling," of course, may result in nothing ever being accomplished, but if the issue remains always lukewarm, it is probable that only token programs will be implemented, and even the enlarged availability of federal funding may not be taken advantage of by local communities.

Notes

1. Richard M. Nixon, Presidential Message on Population and Family Planning, July 18, 1969; *Report of the Secretary of Health, Education, and*

285

Welfare Submitting Five-Year Plan for Family Planning Services and Population Research Programs, October, 1971, as prepared for the Special Subcommittee on Human Resources of the Senate Committee on Labor and Public Welfare, (Washington, D.C.: Government Printing Office, 1971).

2. Agency for International Development, *Population Program Assistance* (Washington, D.C.: Government Printing Office, 1971).

3. E.g., L. Corsa, Jr., M.D., "United States: Public Policy Programs in Family Planning," *Studies in Family Planning* 27:1, 1968. F.S. Jaffe, "Family Planning, Public Policy and Intervention Strategy," *Journal of Social Issues*, 23:145, 1967; J.I. Rosoff, "Washington Memoranda," Planned Parenthood-World Population, Washington, D.C., 1966-1972 (mimeo), for a running account of national public policy developments.

4. J.G. Dryfoos, F.S. Jaffe, D.R. Weintraub, J.P. Cobb and C.J. Bernsohn, "Eighteen Months Later: Family Planning Services in the United States, 1969," *Family Planning Perspectives*, 3 (2):29, 1971.

5. F.R. Pratt, "Programs for Public Health Nurses in Birth Control Work," *American Journal of Public Health*, 30:1097, 1940.

6. R. Norton, M.D., "A Health Department Birth Control Program," *American Journal of Public Health*, 29:254, 1939.

7. F.R. Pratt, 1940, op. cit.

8. G.M. Cooper, M.D., *Transactions of the Medical Society of the State of North Carolina*, 85:729, 1938.

9. R. Norton, M.D., 1939, op. cit., pp. 254-255.

10. G.M. Cooper, M.D., F.R. Pratt and M. Hagood, "Four Years of Contraception as a Public Health Service in North Carolina," *American Journal of Public Health*, 31:1249, 1941.

11. Ibid., p. 1252.

12. H.E. Bill, M.D., "North Carolina Public Health Department Family Planning Program: Historical Background," N.C. State Board of Health, 1968 (mimeo), p. 8.

13. Office of Economic Opportunity (OEO), *Need for Subsidized Family Planning Services: United States, Each State and County, 1968* (Washington, D.C.: Government Printing Office, 1969), p. 11.

14. J.G. Dryfoos, et al., 1971, op. cit., p. 38.

15. A.A. Campbell, "The Role of Family Planning in the Reduction of Poverty," *Journal of Marriage and the Family*, 30:236, 1968.

16. Kenneth J. Gergen, "Assessing the Leverage Points in the Process of Policy Formation," in *Study of Policy Formation*, p. 181.

17. Ibid.

18. Ibid., p. 182.

19. See those scholars listed in *Studies in Family Planning*, no. 16 (Jan., 1967), p. 12.

20. Gergen, op. cit., p. 182.

21. Ibid., p. 192.

22. Robert K. Merton, M. Fiske, and P.L. Kendall, *The Focused Interview* (New York: Free Press, 1956).

23. Gergen, "Methodology in the Study of Policy Formation," p. 222.

24. OEO, 1969, op. cit., pp. 118-122.

25. Ibid., p. 118.

26. Ibid.

27. M.P. Brooks, *The Dimensions of Poverty in North Carolina*, Monograph no. 1, N.C. Fund (Durham, N.C., 1964).

28. J.G. Dryfoos, et al., 1971, op. cit.

29. OEO, *Need for Subsidized Family Planning Services: United States, Each State and County, 1969* (Washington, D.C. Government Printing Office, 1972).

30. F. Hunter, *Community Power Structure* (Chapel Hill: University of North Carolina Press, 1953), p. 226.

31. Gergen, "Methodology in the Study of Policy Formation," p. 210.

32. Ibid.

33. *The Anatomy of a Victory: A Panel Discussion of a Public Controversy*, Planned Parenthood Federation of America (New York, 1959).

34. Ibid., p. 3.

35. Ibid., p. 4.

36. Planned Parenthood of New York City, "Family Planning in New York City: Recommendations for Action," *Family Planning Perspectives*, 2 (4):25, 1970.

37. OEO, 1969, op. cit., pp. 114-115.

38. J.G. Dryfoos, et al., 1971, op. cit., pp. 38 and 40.

15 Legislating Population Policy

John R. Bermingham*

Preparation, preparation, preparation—it is impossible to over-stress the importance of good preparatory work to ensure the passage of any sort of legislation. The field of population policy is no exception.

But don't fail to start because of poor preparation! Time can be short, and the opportunity for good preparatory work simply may not be available. Start anyway. A poorly prepared legislative effort generally fails, but it does pave the way for good preparatory work for the next general session. And, who knows?—poorly prepared legislation sometimes passes.

Please be my guest! Feel free to use the legislative process as a raucous sounding board and vehicle for public education. While some proposals have maximum chance of passage if they are moved along very quietly, others are bound to stir controversy and, often, the more the pot is stirred the better the chance of success. After all, like it or not, and dull and backward as the legislative process often seems to an outsider, the legislature is the focal point of all social and economic pressures in the state. Shout, scream, be dignified, be subtle—choose your mode to fit your need, but never forget that this is the forum for exchanging ideas, and this is the stage where action can occur. Legislators can act their roles and can often be of tremendous assistance in dramatizing the needs of special interest groups. An articulate, well-informed, interested legislator will certainly do this for constituents interested in population matters.

Having laid down these basic principals, now consider what is meant by "population policy." To those for whom these words are written the term "population policy" will have a fairly clear meaning. The area of expertise of the average legislator, however, is in some field other than population, and he will probably not have the foggiest notion of what is meant by the words, "population policy," so that the use of that terminology should be discouraged. No state has adopted a comprehensive population policy; no state has even made the attempt! What has happened and what is happening, however, is the piecemeal adoption of legislation on a variety of subjects such as:

abortion	insurance
adoptions	land use

---

*Assistant to the Governor, State of Colorado, for Environmental Affairs and State Planning.

budgets	prophylactics
clinics	special commissions
education	statistics
family planning	sterilization
governmental structure	tax law changes

A comprehensive population policy would contain either a single, integrated enactment or a series of integrated enactments covering most, if not all, of these subjects, and the pervasive theme would be an endeavor to achieve a better overall society in the future—children who are wanted children, people who are healthy people, and population growth and distribution that does not overtax the environment, social mechanisms, and public facilities.

The field is simply too big, too complex, and too charged with emotions to lend itself to comprehensive legislation covering all these elements, but times are clearly ripe for a one-step-at-a-time approach in every state of the country. Which brings us back to preparation. In the following pages, I have outlined what I believe are the necessary prerequisites for legislating new population policies.

1. Bring together a relatively small group of interested, knowledgeable, and articulate individuals and reach a decision as to what you wish to accomplish. Then make sure that you have lines of communication with the friendly groups that are most likely to be affected by the proposed legislation. For a family planning act this means private physicians, public hospitals, welfare workers, and so forth. A bill dealing with insurance or tax-law changes will obviously require an entirely different set of specialists. The main point to be remembered at this stage is that it is impossible for one person to write a bill. Any bill of significance will affect a large web of interests, and the proponents should foresee the effect on each strand in order to keep the stumbling blocks at a minimum.

2. Actual drafting of language can commence once the substance of the proposal has been agreed upon. (Incidentally, the proponents may wish to include alternatives or fall-back positions which also need to be drafted.) A friendly legislator can take the proposal to the legislative drafting office, and the draft should then be brought back and circulated among all the interested proponents. Then comes the "nit-picking," "fine tuning"—call it what you will—and this process may run through several drafts before the proponents are in fairly general agreement as to the form of the legislation.

It is important in this step to think ahead and foresee the objections that opponents to the legislation are likely to raise. Wherever possible avoid using terminology that is unnecessary for the accomplishment of the main purpose of the bill, but which would be sure to generate strident opposition if included. Perhaps it is just a euphemism, but "family planning" is certainly much easier to sell than "birth control."

3. The factual arguments in support of the bill and also the rebuttal to

opponents' contentions should be extremely well prepared, both in summary one-page form and in depth. Legislators are always harried, and they will become very impatient with a proposal that cannot be stated, explained, and justified in a few short sentences. At the same time, however, any legislator's support and confidence will evaporate immediately if proponents cannot back up and support their proposal with hard facts. Population proposals are not uppermost in the minds of most legislators. Most legislators are probably inclined to go along with population proposals, but support will melt quickly in the face of opposition unless their arguments can be countered promptly and quickly. Be prepared. A handful of legislators need to be fully informed.

4. Witnesses can make or break a bill at a committee hearing. Select them with care. Actual case histories and live witnesses can be very effective; avoid rambling monotones; and remember, one articulate conservative person from the lower class with direct first-hand experiences will be tremendously effective, whereas an ivory tower or League of Women Voter type—no matter how cogent the testimony—may merely serve to certify to the legislators that the proposal is just some liberal cause that should not be passed.

5. Lobbying will be essential, but the amount and nature of the lobbying that may be needed is as varied as the nature of the proposals and the dispositions of the legislators. Lobbying is necessary because legislatures never have time to consider and pass all the bills that are presented. It is only the bills that are pushed and nursed along that have any real hope of final passage.

With luck, and if the proposal is not too difficult or controversial, the entire lobbying effort can be performed by one interested legislator. The legislator will introduce the bill, talk to his colleagues at appropriate moments, and guide it through the legislative process like a guardian angel.

Legislators recognize lobbying as being a very positive and constructive part of the legislative process, so lobbyists can expect to be well received—initially. Lobbyists who are insensitive to legislators' busy time schedules, who are argumentative, abrasive, uninformed, long-winded, lacking in candor, untrustworthy, and so forth, might just as well spend their time elsewhere. A good lobbyist, on the other hand, will not be bashful, will ask for advice and help from other lobbyists, will be accurate, straightforward, and to the point, and will never, never, never mislead. Friendly legislators who are working with the proponents of the measure can be tremendously helpful in advising on the selection of lobbyists.

6. Fund raising may or may not be necessary. Each case and each state is different. Hopefully the lobbying can be done on a volunteer basis, but this is not always possible. Promotional materials may be necessary as well as mailings, either directly to legislators or, more likely, to stir up the troops in the field.

7. Look for allies. County commissioners and their lobbyists, for example, can be extremely helpful in securing the passage of a family planning act because they can see the direct relationship between such an act and their county welfare

rolls. Police officials occasionally can be helpful for the same reason. Support from medical societies, church groups, environmental organizations, and the like should certainly be solicited and made known, and often groups such as these can be very helpful in stimulating letters to legislators. Obtaining strong statements of support from prominent individuals whose daily experience gives them a firsthand knowledge of the problem will also be impressive, be it the head of a general hospital with respect to abortion law, or the head of an insurance agency with respect to health insurance coverage.

8. The news media can be extremely helpful with respect to controversial issues such as abortion, sterilization, and tax-law changes that favor the two-child family, but will be totally disinterested in the designation of one state agency to handle all federal funding programs or the creation of a state agency to collect statistics. Where the matter is controversial, the press is likely to be sympathetic and with forethought a series of news items can be generated and released at appropriate intervals. Where possible, lobby the county commissioners to take a public stand, lobby the governing boards of the state health department and the state welfare department to take a stand; occasionally a mayor can be persuaded to take a public position. Background support such as this makes it easier for a legislator to vote "aye" on a controversial proposal.

9. Technical strategy must be prepared by the interested legislators. Does one try to get many sponsors or rely on one sponsor? When should the bill be introduced? What arrangements can be made to have the bill sent to a friendly committee? What motions should be made in committee? Should the bill start in the House of in the Senate? What legislative tricks can be used or guarded against?

By way of example, the first "liberal" abortion law was passed by Colorado in 1967. The bill had passed the House and was on its way to the Senate where it was facing a certain death. The presiding officer of the Senate, who assigns bills to committee, was a Catholic who had publicly declared that he was opposed to the bill and that he would send the bill to a committee that had a Catholic chairman who was equally opposed to the bill. The bill was saved, however, by persuading a friendly clerical staff person in the basement of the Capitol to drag her feet on the technical processing of the measure that is required of all bills as they move from one house to another. Then, when the presiding officer was out of the Capitol for a couple of hours, a signal went down to the basement, the bill came up, the President Pro Tem assigned the bill to a friendly committee and once again it was on the move. Preparation, preparation, preparation. . . .

Since preparation is so important in the passage of a piece of legislation and since, also it is so terribly time-consuming, it is very important for persons interested in population proposals to select their proposals with care. Which ones have real significance? Which ones can be used as an icebreaker? Which ones are simply fluff?

Policy declarations, resolutions asking schools and colleges to institute

population and environmental education, creation of citizen advisory commit-
tees and the like—these are just fluff and very little time should be spent on
them. The same can probably be said for tax law changes designed to encourage
two-child families—the two-child family apparently is already here, and state tax
laws have a minor effect on fertility in any event.

On the other hand, the strong effort and battle in Colorado in 1965 for the
adoption of a law permitting welfare workers to dispense birth control
information and supplies very clearly had a solid impact in striking down
governmental inhibitions and red tape. The bill also paved the way for the
abortion legislation in 1967, and passage of that one bill then made it easier for
other states to follow suit. In 1971 the Colorado legislature endeavored to
further liberalize both its family planning act and its abortion law. The abortion
proposal was defeated in the Senate by one vote after an intense fight, but two
days later the nation's then most liberal family planning act breezed through—
everyone said, "This is the way to go!" Bills such as these have truly significant
impact on the population as a whole, and the efforts to pass such bills are truly
worthwhile.

Another extremely important but frequently overlooked area is the matter of
budgeting. All too often persons interested in population matters will feel they
have achieved a tremendous victory in getting legislation on the books that
authorizes state funds to be expended. A year later, however, the monies
actually appropriated are puny or non-existent! Therefore, whenever appropriations are necessary to make a policy effective, it is vitally important to lobby
for the necessary funds. The state health department or whatever agency would
be charged with administering the funds must be persuaded to make a strong
request for adequate funding for the program. Then the staff in the unit that
develops the governor's budget must be persuaded as to the effectiveness of the
program. The staff of the legislative budget unit must be similarly lobbyed, as
well as the senators and representatives in charge of legislative appropriation
recommendations.

My concluding thoughts will be simply a restatement of my opening
thoughts—preparation is the key to being successful in the legislative process but
even if you are not prepared, try anyway—you might "luck out" and you will at
least be preparing yourself for the next year's effort. Remember that state
legislators, generally speaking, enjoy carrying out the public will; they can be
very helpful in dramatizing and solidifying the public will. They claim to be
public servants. Use them accordingly, and good luck!

16 The States as Laboratories

Paul Simon*

Periodically some observer of the political scene notes that there is really not much excuse for having state governments any more. Too often what takes place—and what does not take place—justifies that conclusion.

Not only is the state scene often one of corruption—and my state of Illinois unfortunately has a host of examples in both political parties—there is the other reality that generally little is happening other than simple administration of existing programs. There is a reshuffling of titles and the always-present resolve to "administer this state more effectively" (often by people elected who know nothing about state government), but the lack of substantial program is discouraging. State government much too often is mediocrity triumphant.

Even without effective leadership, there is a rational justification for the existence of states because federal administration of all programs would be unwieldy. In addition, getting rid of the states is a meaningless, theoretical exercise of words because the states are here to stay. Not only are they existing realities, but their budget power, if not their influence, is growing. As I write this, the budget of the state of Illinois is approximately ten times the budget of the nation of Pakistan. To suggest that an entity like Illinois, with an expenditure in excess of $7 billion in a single year, is suddenly going to shrivel and vanish is hardly realistic. The history of state governments to this point suggests further growth of state bureaucracy, and recent education and reapportionment decisions by the U.S. Supreme Court offer additional grants of power to the state governments.

While some academicians suggest that states are an anachronism, others join Professor Samuel L. Beer of Harvard who wrote:

My analysis poses the rude question: what use are the states? . . . Examined by this cold, pragmatic light, without any tinge of nostalgia or rhetoric, the states will, I believe, prove to have great promise as instruments in the further building of a national democracy.[1]

A major justification for state governments unfortunately has been largely unused: its role in experimentation. One of the advantages our federal system can provide is that we can try new ideas at the state level, learn their strengths and weaknesses, and then apply the lessons to the national scene. We need not

---

*Professor of Public Affairs, Sangamon State University.

make national blunders. The population field—and the problems related to it—is one of many areas where this experimentation could take place.

Two examples of what a state can do (unfortunately not recent examples) are in Wisconsin and Nebraska.

The innovator in Wisconsin was Robert M. LaFollette, governor of that state for five years beginning in 1901 until his election to the U.S. Senate. He pushed for primary elections rather than the caucus system which then dominated Wisconsin and the nation. Denounced as "a populistic scheme of a hare-brained demagogue," the primary soon caught on nationally; and despite some weaknesses in it, the primary system is a vast improvement over the caucus operations. LaFollette reformed the tax structure in Wisconsin; and the nation followed. He put some curbs on railroad rate charges and eliminated the free railroad passes to political leaders; the nation followed. As no governor prior to his time, LaFollette took advantage of the university community for consultation and ideas ("The state was not created for the University; the University exists for the state," he told them); the academic-political alignment has been growing in many states since the LaFollette example. He pressed for labor laws which all states and the nation now recognize as essential. Civil service and lobbying reform, conservation, and franchise regulation—all were stamped in some special way with the LaFollette imprint. The laws of every state in the nation have been affected by the LaFollette leadership. Literally every citizen in the United States has had his or her life changed at least in some small way by the leadership of Robert LaFollette as Governor of Wisconsin.

Nebraska offers another example of experimentation, but one not followed so far by other jurisdictions. In large part because of the leadership of U.S. Senator George Norris, who dominated the political scene of that state, Nebraska moved to a unicameral legislative chamber. No other state has done it, but all have discussed it. Even assuming the experiment is a failure—and I do not make that assumption—states must be willing to experiment and fail, so that the nation can learn not only what will work, but what will not work.

There are a few other isolated examples of experimental state leadership, but unfortunately not many. "No-fault" insurance is an example of state leadership. In the correctional field, Peter Bensinger of Illinois caused major improvements and some experiments, and in Massachusetts Jerome Miller headed a movement to rid that state of the traditional "reform school," an experiment still being debated by some as to its merits as this manuscript is being typed.

States ought to do much more experimental work. And the population arena is one of many where states could be providing fifty laboratories for the nation. Here are a few examples of possible research in the population field:

Encourage Population Limitation

While the most recent statistics on birth rates within the United States are encouraging, those most knowledgeable in the field suggest that population growth within the United States will remain a serious potential problem for some time to come. Even if that were not the case, the United States can hardly say to India, Pakistan, and other nations that they ought to exert themselves more to restrain population growth while the United States does almost nothing on the problem within our borders. It is true that our problems, for a variety of cultural and economic reasons, are much less severe. But some Asians and Africans—and some within our borders—are concerned that the cry for reducing population has racist overtones; they say that those of us who are in the economically-dominant white minority see the balance of world numbers shifting more and more to those of color, and so we concern ourselves with population growth. There may be those who see in population growth this particular "specter," but their numbers are few. Most of the concern stems from the knowledge that uncontrolled population growth will place greater and greater demands on agricultural production, regardless of who must be fed. U.S. policy at home should make clear by example to Asians, Africans, and others that we are not simply pointing the finger at others, but are practicing population control at home.

States—or at least a state or two—could pioneer by providing an additional increment in income tax deduction for the first two children. Except for a few in the higher tax brackets, this would not take money away from a family with six children, but would suggest as a state policy that we recognize the desirability of stable population. If the present exemption in State X is $600, then all single persons, all couples with no children, and the first two of any children in a family would be able to deduct $700 per person rather than $600. For example, a family with six children would receive an additional deduction for both parents and for two of their six children, so ordinarily they would benefit. The couple just marrying would be conscious of the fact that state policy encourages not having more than two children and expresses it in concrete terms. And for those who do not pay an income tax, some financial incentives could be worked out; greater assistance on public aid, for the first two children, for example. The impact of an additional $100 deduction for the first two children would hardly be a sufficient financial incentive by itself for couples to have only two children, but it would be a topic of conversation because of the controversy it would stir, and might have a significant psychological impact.

Maybe it would have no impact on birthrates at all. If the trial proved unsuccessful, we would have learned one method of population control that at least under limited circumstances did not have a measurable effect. But it might work. And if a state or two tried it and found that it did, then the nation—and other nations—could follow the example.

Discourage Population Movement
Through Financial Incentive

In almost every nation, a movement of people away from rural areas and small towns to urban centers is taking place at a frightening cost, both socially and economically. While the U.S. economy is able to take this shift more easily than other countries, the irony of this shift is that government policies not only did not cope adequately with it, the policies compounded the evil by encouraging the shift to the urban centers.

In Illinois, for example, the state's population grew by 10.2 percent between 1960 and 1970. Yet in this same period forty-nine of the state's 102 counties lost population.

Vance Packard, in his excellent book, *A Nation of Strangers,*[2] (excellent, perhaps, because I agree with its thesis) suggests that in the process of excessive movement within our nation we have developed many people without roots, people who sometimes solve the resulting emotional problems in socially unacceptable ways. Not only have they lost these roots and what that signifies to them, they have also disposed of the social restraints provided by friends and neighbors and a sense of identification and attachment to a place. Anyone who has served overseas in the Army can verify with concrete examples the validity of the Packard thesis: Tom Smith from a small Missouri community suddenly behaves much differently when he is stationed in Germany, or at least he often does.

If you accept Packard's contention that there is excessive movement within the nation, then there should be some conscious actions by government to discourage some of the movement. But today government does more to move people than to discourage movement.

And even if you do not accept the general theory of the undesirability of much movement, few would challenge the undesirability of the massive movement from rural areas to urban, compounding our problems in both.

What experiments could states try to provide some assistance and stability?

1. *We could provide a per capita tax deduction for all persons living at the same location more than five years.*

Perhaps it could be $10 per person, and those who do not pay an income tax would receive a like amount in a direct grant. The money would make people conscious of a direct cost they would have when they move, and more important, make them conscious of a public policy which discourages too much movement.

Exceptions would probably have to be made for those who must move because of a new highway, urban renewal, or some other project—although a case can be made for avoiding such an exception; it would discourage some projects by increasing the opposition to them, or at least make the projects a little more people-conscious.

Would such a per capita assistance program actually change patterns of movement? No one knows. Even the head of a household with three children who earns $15,000 to $25,000 a year must make a calculation of costs when he considers moving, and to lose $10 per person in his family for five years means a loss of $250—not a huge sum, but not an insignificant one to that person either.

In a state like Illinois the cost of an experiment would be approximately $50 million a year, some of which would return in additional taxes. While that sum may sound high, it is less than 1 percent of our state budget. And the program *might* reduce some of the economic and social costs from the present patterns of movement. If one state tries it and it works, the entire nation would benefit.

2. *We can experiment with tax laws which encourage property maintenance and improvement.*

Deteriorating property causes movement.

There have been some minor experiments with changes in the law which would encourage upkeep and improvement of real estate, but nothing very substantial. Without belaboring the reader with a myriad of details about a complex area, the reality is that most tax laws today relating to property penalize the person who makes improvements.

To those who measure impact of a tax on recipients, most have reached the conclusion that the real estate tax is a regressive tax. The Massachusetts Special Commission to Develop a Master Tax Plan in its report of 1970 called the real estate tax "the most regressive of all those in the entire tax structure" of that state. The reality is that the tax is more regressive than the standard measurements suggest, for the person owning the property may well be a person of more than adequate means, while the people living on his property are not. Those who occupy his real estate may suffer because the owner knows that if he improves his property the taxes will increase.

Here is an old, standard form of taxation where experimentation primarily has been in the means of determining more accurate assessments and improving collecting procedures.

Where is the state that will lead with some experiments which will encourage home maintenance and improvement, and thereby encourage more stable neighborhoods?

3. *An experimental program is needed in which job guarantees are made to all citizens.*

No state could afford to test this statewide, but many states could try it in a county or two.

If Illinois were to say that in Alexander County (population 12,015), and perhaps in one other small county, that we would guarantee everyone eighteen or over a job, through the private sector insofar as possible and where that is not possible with government as the employer of last resort, what would happen?

I mention Alexander County because it illustrates many problems. The population dropped from 16,061 in 1960 to 12,015 in the 1970 census. The largest city in the county is Cairo, which went from a population of 9,348 in the 1960 census to 6,277 in 1970. Cairo is a city you may have heard about, for it has experienced bloodshed and racial strife. The unemployment rate is 13 percent, and one of the reasons for the bloodshed is that whites and blacks in this racially torn town are fighting for the few jobs that exist. (I spent a disproportionately large amount of my time as Lieutenant Governor in the community, or talking with people from Cairo.)

Another reason for the racial unrest is that among the people who have moved are many in the twenty to forty age bracket who ordinarily might be providing reconciling community leadership, but who went to St. Louis, Memphis, Chicago, or elsewhere to get a job. The community suffered in numbers, but perhaps more important, Cairo has been deprived of much of its leadership potential, leadership that could more easily have accommodated change than have some who have remained in the community.

The state would have to announce that only those residing in the community thirty days prior to the proclamation of the program would be eligible in order to stem a flood of new people into the town who would claim eligibility for jobs.

Then programs to encourage local industry would have to be worked out; a small factory might be asked to add ten employees with the understanding that the state would pay one-half the salary of those employees for the first three months of their work. Other incentives to the private sector could be provided. And those who could not be given any position in the private sector could work at nearby state parks, work at child-care centers, work at repairing public housing projects, and other programs. With a little imagination there is no shortage of such potential projects.

If this program were tried, what would happen to the racial tensions in the community? What would happen to the high public aid (welfare) costs? What would happen to the crime rate? What would happen to sales tax receipts which the state would receive from local businesses, indicating the impact on both the state and the business sector? What would happen to income tax revenue to both the state and national governments? Would the exodus from the community continue?

These and many other questions could be answered for the first time anywhere in the nation. I have guesses on the answers, but I don't know, nor does anyone else. But some state ought to be finding the answers.

Many other examples of experiments could be cited, some of them directly—and some indirectly—related to the problem of mobility of population. Should municipalities be given more authority to control population movement? What form should it take? If an increment in state deposits held by a bank (always a sought-after prize) could go to those banks which demonstrate they are extending themselves to provide business-stimulating loans in counties which have shown a population loss, what would happen? Or apply the same standard to the disadvantaged areas of the city; what would happen?

All of these proposals, as well as others which could be mentioned, require a combination of knowledge of state government, ability to work with the legislature, imagination, and political courage. And the last quality is the most important of the four.

It is in the nature of experiments that some will fail, and people who run for election or re-election do not like to be associated in the public mind with failures, particularly if your opponent can run across the state holding television news conferences citing examples of "millions of dollars of your money being thrown down the drain."

The two arguments traditionally used against experimentation by state governments are:

"The legislature won't approve them." The reality: A governor who knows how to work effectively with a legislative body can do it; the governor who uses this excuse is reflecting more on his own competence than on the composition of the legislature.

"States are in such a financial bind that they can't do these things." The reality: States are not in that bad a shape. Some states now have substantial surpluses, because the great demands on their resources no longer are growing rapidly. In most states between 2 and 7 percent of the budget could be used with some flexibility, for experimental purposes. If only 1 percent of a state budget were to be used for experimental programs, there would be major benefits to both the state and nation. There is no state which cannot afford 1 percent for experimental programs.

The lack of political courage is the real roadblock.

And here the reader must realize that governors face a tax-conscious electorate. Too many successful candidates for governor have pointed to "millions of dollars of waste" by their opponents, and have given patently false promises about either lowering taxes or not increasing taxes. Trapped by their own political oratory, they are powerless to lead; they become custodians of state government rather than leaders.

The nation is the loser.

But it need not always be so. Other Robert LaFollettes can arise, governors who are willing to lead in the population field and in other areas.

There are men and women with that kind of potential in every state. Hopefully some of them will emerge.

Notes

1. Paper prepared for the first Toward '76 Conference sponsored by the Center for the Study of Federalism and Federalism Seventy-Six, Inc. Issued by the Center for the Study of Federalism, 1973.

2. Vance Packard, *A Nation of Strangers* (New York: David McKay, 1972).

17

The Need for an Ethical Response to the Report of the Commission on Population Growth and the American Future

Arthur J. Dyck*

One might well harbor the impression that this analysis of the Report of the Commission on Population Growth and the American Future, since it is written by a moralist, will be a moral commentary on a scientific document. Such an expectation with all its appearance of plausibility should be utterly rejected. It is true that I am a moralist; it is true also that my commentary will be moral. But it is not true that the Report of the Commission is a scientific document. Some of its content, whether in the form of facts, is, to be sure, based on scientific research, however soft the data in some cases. The Report, however, is fundamentally a moral document, replete with moral admonitions and its own ideological commitments. It espouses, sometimes explicitly, sometimes implicitly, definite moral ideals and recommends the implementation of these ideals.

The Report has directed its recommendations to policymakers at all levels of government. However, among the various levels of government, the states have the primary resonsibility for the administration of most population-related programs. States administer family planning programs, are responsible for land use and housing policies, and determine types of transportation and transportation patterns within their borders. It is very important, therefore, that state administrators and legislators look closely at the recommendations of the U.S. Commission and understand very clearly the long-range implications of those recommendations. Since the moral presuppositions of the majority of the Commission's members are so important to the substance of their recommendations, the meaning of these value judgments needs to be clarified for state officials.

The Commission gauges population growth and population policies by their effects upon the quality of life, freedom, and justice, and their best realization in our society. In characterizing the Commission's Report as a moral document, I do not intend either to bless or to curse it; rather I wish to maintain that responsible action by state lawmakers and administrators must include as assessment of the Report's understanding of quality of life, freedom, and justice and its recommendations for the best methods to realize these ideals.

*Mary B. Saltonstall Professor of Population Ethics, Harvard University.

Quality of Life

One of the striking features of the Population Commission's Report, particularly for those who must choose between alternative population policies, is that the Commission nowhere directly engages policies that would demand some form of compulsory regulation of fertility behavior. This means that the Commission's arguments against compulsion never become explicit. Nevertheless, it is not too difficult to piece together some of the major reasons why the Commission ignores and rejects compulsion.

To begin with the Population Commission's Report does not see population growth in the United States as a crisis or as leading to a crisis. One important argument against a crisis view of American population growth rests on the observation that birth rates in the United States are low and have been steadily declining from the early 1960s onward. The Commission is very cautious about this downward trend because of the increasing number of young women of reproductive age who are the children of the so-called baby boom. However, despite these cautionary notes in the Commission's Report, current census data show that the downward trend continues, even to the point of falling below the fertility rate required for replacement.[1]

But it is not only the declining rate of population growth that leads the Commission to ignore and reject compulsion. The Population Commission represents a particular ideological point of view within the spectrum of views as to how to understand the nature of population problems and the values associated with fertility behavior. There are three major ideological alternatives that vie for acceptance in debates over population growth and what to do about it. These three major ideological perspectives are represented by what we shall call crisis environmentalists, family planners, and developmentalists. The Population Commission is very solidly in the camp of the family planners, but as we shall see, assimilates some of the concerns of crisis environmentalists, and to a lesser extent, some of the concerns of developmentalists. It is important that policymakers understand that these three perspectives are not mutually exclusive, and that emphasis on one or the other viewpoint makes a considerable difference for the kinds of population policies that are seen as good or desirable. Emphasis on one or the other of these three perspectives also greatly influences the ordering of priorities and consequently, the policies that are adopted. Let us briefly consider here how these ideological perspectives differ from one another.

Crisis environmentalists are focused on the relationship between population growth and the quality of the environment or ecosystem on which the survival of the human race is dependent. These crisis environmentalists differ on what kind of disaster they predict from continued rapid population growth or continued population growth *per se*. Some of them emphasize the limits to food and others emphasize a variety of forms of environmental degradation or resource depletion. All, however, agree that crises can or probably will be caused primarily by population growth.

The early Malthus is a classical representative of this view. A contemporary prophet of environmental doom directly associated with continued population growth, either rapid or slow, is Paul Ehrlich. Very simply for Ehrlich, our environment is sick and the disease is over-population. The remedy for this disease is zero population growth, achieved as rapidly as possible, and using coercive methods as necessary.[2]

Ehrlich's type of analysis sharply curtails and short circuits moral debate regarding the morally best population policies. There is one moral issue, namely survival, nothing less than the survival of the whole human species and of the ecosystem that sustains it. So far as population policy is concerned, it is presumed that one moves from the less publicly unpalatable to the more publicly unpalatable policies whenever it is found that the less objectionable policies are not sufficient to insure zero population growth. Ultimately, then, the most significant moral criterion for judging population policies is their effectiveness in achieving zero population growth.

Whereas crisis environmentalists like Paul Ehrlich focus their concerns around the survival of the whole human species and of the environment necessary to assure this, family planners focus upon the way in which population growth and fertility behavior benefit or harm the family. Of major concern to family planners and to the Population Commission is the existence of unwanted and unplanned pregnancies. Family planners, the Population Commission included, make the assumption—an assumption found in Malthus—that there is a felt need on the part of couples to keep their fertility at roughly those levels necessary to achieve zero population growth.[3] This is not an utterly wild assumption. Hunter-gatherer societies now being very carefully observed definitely achieve and maintain stable, non-growing populations. Furthermore, research by Charles Westoff and others on unwanted and unplanned fertility suggests that the virtual elimination of unwanted and unplanned births would approximate zero population growth for the American population.[4] The family planners, therefore, assume that population policy and programs should be designed to allow people to achieve the fertility levels that they want. They assume that most problems related to population will be met if this goal is attained.

With respect to the family planning position, some questions might well be raised about the reliability of the data on unwanted births and the implications drawn from them, but the Commission is very committed to their validity. Why is this true? One reason has already been indicated: the Commission shares one Malthusian hypothesis, namely, that there is a felt need for small family size that leads to zero population growth. Another equally if not more significant reason is that the Population Commission with its family planning ideology is committed to individual freedom. The Commission very generally seeks to minimize government intervention in American life. Indeed, the Commission Report in its chapter on the use of resources, an area where some would see government regulation as necessary and urgent, issues the following ringing declaration:

Imbedded in our traditions as to what constitutes the American way of life is freedom from public regulation—virtually free use of water; use of uncongested, unregulated roadways; freedom to do as we please with what we own. . . .[5]

In summary, then, the Commission denies the necessity of compulsion to achieve zero growth rates. In opposition to the crisis environmentalists, the Population Commission sees increased rather than diminished procreative freedom for individuals and individual couples as the way to zero population growth. The solution to whatever ills are engendered by population growth or by relatively large families will be achieved once every individual, and every couple of whatever age, marital, or financial status, have totally free access to all available methods of birth control, including sterilization and abortion.

Finally, how do developmentalists view population problems? There are, to be sure, a wide range of population analyses and policy proposals that can be designated as developmental. The discussion here can only be illustrative.

Whereas crisis environmentalists and family planners alike see the goal of population policies as influencing fertility behavior in the direction of reducing birth rates, developmentalists are focused upon the need to respond to the effects of fertility behavior and birth rates. Thus, for example, population policy for developmentalists seeks ways to feed populations, advocates changes in technology that will diminish environmental degradation, and implements efforts to reduce conditions of poverty—such as high infant and maternal mortality, poor health care, insufficient income, unemployment, illiteracy, malnutrition, etc.

The classical developmentalist who challenged the whole Malthusian concept of over-population is Marx. Marx took the view that over-population is a term that is only appropriate in economic systems where workers are exploited. In an economic system where jobs are not guaranteed or where some wages are not living wages, some people are seen as excess population. The answer to this diagnosis of over-population for Marx was a social and economic system in which workers would have full employment opportunities, living wages, and would not be denied their procreative freedom. While Malthus and the family planners and crisis environmentalists who are among his modern followers strive to reduce the number that are to be seated at the banquet table of life, Marx called for an increase in what could be provided at the banquet table as well as a better distribution of the goods available. In this regard Marx has some unlikely allies in the official Roman Catholic views of Popes John XXIII and Paul VI, both of whom emphasized the need for affluent nations more equitably to share their goods and at the same time to assist less affluent nations to achieve higher standards of living.[6] Welfare economists, either Marxist or non-Marxist, share this general concern for raising the standards of living around the world.

Engels did recognize, as do contemporary developmentalists, that space is finite, and that there is the abstract possibility of having too many people on this earth.[7] However, he took the view that Communist societies with their emphasis on planning would have no difficulty in preventing such an eventuality. Developmentalists generally rely very heavily on this same kind of assumption, namely that societies that manage to achieve a reasonably high standard of living for all of their members will have brought about the social conditions that lead to low fertility, i.e., widespread literacy, good communication systems, knowledge about and access to fertility control methods, a high degree of urbanization, and the medical care that minimizes infant and maternal mortality. Developmentalists are conscious of the historical fact that the economically highly developed countries have participated in what is called the demographic transition. This transition involves a shift from high birth rates and high death rates to low birth rates and low death rates. Indeed, some demographers see reasonably good evidence that some of the less affluent developing countries are entering their demographic transition at a more rapid pace than was true of the presently affluent nations.[8] Developmentalists believe that programs designed to increase the welfare of specific populations are the most effective population programs, because increased welfare slows rapid population growth.

Some developmentalists believe that very minimal changes in the welfare of population units—families, villages, or other social groups—such as more education, reduction in infant mortality, better knowledge of nutrition, better health care and the like, would already with or without resort to modern contraceptives greatly reduce birth rates in less affluent nations and among less affluent groups in countries like the United States. It is interesting to note that John Wyon found that in certain areas of India in which the green revolution has increased income and food production, birth rates are going down without increased resort to modern contraceptives.[9] With higher incomes, these Indian villagers are seeking more education for their children, can more readily keep their children alive, and their children in turn, as they seek more goods and more education, are delaying marriage, and hence also delaying and reducing child bearing. Delaying marriage is an extremely important variable in reducing birth rates. It is probably a major reason why even in the United States birth rates continue to decline despite the increasing number of women of reproductive age.

The Population Commission Report, although as we have tried to indicate is of the family planning ideology, tries to assimilate some of the concerns of the crisis environmentalists and the developmentalists. Thus, for example, the Commission takes the view that population growth has the effect of making it more difficult for society to cope with its social problems—problems like environmental degradation, crime, poverty, unemployment, lack of housing, etc. However, the Commission is cautions about making this association between population growth and social problems of the kind referred to. The Report recognizes that none of the problems cited will be solved by achieving zero population growth. What the Commission claims or implies is that the solution to these problems will be made easier by zero population growth. The question the policymakers must answer as he considers the Commission's Report is whether this assumption is true.

To begin with, let us examine the relationship between population levels and environmental degradation. Roger Revelle, of the Harvard Center for Population Studies, has made the following analysis:

The lack of utility of any simple correlation between environmental deterioration and population growth can be demonstrated by calculating the size of the population of the United States which, with the same per capita income and dirty habits as the average U.S. citizen in 1965, would have produced no more pollution than the country experienced in 1940.

Other things being equal, the number of automobiles and the amount of gasoline and paper consumed would have remained about constant over the quarter century if our population had declined from 133 million people in 1940 to 67 million in 1965. To maintain a constant flow of sulfur dioxide in the air from electric power plants, the population would have had to decrease to only 40 million people. Presumably the amount of nitrogen fertilizers would not have increased, if all but 17 million Americans had re-emigrated to the homes of their ancestors. Only 17 million people in the country would use the same amount of nitrogen in 1965 as we used in 1940. The national parks would have remained as uncrowded in 1965 as they were in 1940 if our population during the interval had gone down from 130 million people in 1940 to 30 million people in 1965, instead of going up to 195 million, as, of course, it actually did.

These unlikely speculations emphasize the uncertainties of the relationships between population, gross national product, and the quality of life, of which environmental deterioration is one aspect.[10]

From this analysis we can discern that pollution is a way of life and must be attacked in its own right. Clearly, we cannot accept this way of life as the price of affluence. Wherever environmental deterioration is a *present* danger, the behavior that causes it must be immediately curtailed.

Furthermore, if environmental deterioration is an inevitable byproduct of affluence, and if the Population Commission is correct in assuming that affluence will rise as zero population growth is achieved, then zero population growth will bring about more rather than less environmental deterioration unless, of course, the habits that go with our current forms of affluence are changed. Hence, the views and the recommendations of the Population Commission actually threaten to increase our environmental crisis rather than diminish it.

A state genuinely concerned about environmental degradation will seek ways to curb and/or change current technologies and styles of life that contribute to it. It appears that the U.S. Commission is unwilling to recommend such plans, however, because it is unwilling to introduce government regulation of this kind or any other kind. Its unwillingness cannot be attributed to any claim that environmental deterioration is not a population-related issue. The Commission not only thinks that it is but is also quite willing to make several recommendations, such as money for couples who wish to adopt, permissive abortion laws, day care centers, etc., even though these measures by themselves promise little or nothing for the reduction of birth rates. The Commission does make a number of recommendations for population-related areas even though they will not directly affect fertility. As we shall see in our discussion of freedom, practically all of the recommendations of the Commission are direct attempts to increase freedom, particularly procreative freedom, regardless of how fertility behavior is affected by such increased freedom.

Like the problem of environmental degradation, problems associated with poverty and racial discrimination can for the groups who are most immediately affected be worsened rather than ameliorated. It is not at all clear, for example, that blacks will benefit from stabilizing or decreasing their numbers. The ways in which these and parallel problems of the poor and of minorities are treated by the Population Commission's Report will be discussed when questions of justice are considered. Let us turn now to the Commission's view of freedom.

Freedom

Freedom clearly has top priority in this Report. The attempt to enhance and realize it is the major consideration in deciding which recommendations to make, and which recommendations are good and beneficial. It would appear that the recommendations made in the Report all have the effect of greatly facilitating freedom. Note, for example, the following recommendations: all existing government programs that distribute birth control services and information are to be financed at a much higher rate than presently; minors are to be given complete access, without impediment, to birth control methods and information including sterilization and abortion; abortion is to be freely available to all, and is to be subsidized by the government and/or by health insurance both public and private; child care services are to be available to all; population and sexual education is to be government subsidized and available to all through community organizations, the media, and the schools; for racial minorities and the poor the government is to develop job-training, help finance suburban low and moderate income housing, and reduce the dependence of local governments on property tax. At first blush this is an impressive list of new freedoms. But the list bears careful scrutiny.

The Report recommends considerable extension and increased funding for birth control clinics. The amount recommended for such birth control services is more than ten times what the Commission recommends for maternal health and infant care projects under Title V of the Social Security Act. It is very difficult to see why so much more money is given for birth control services *per se* than for the maternal and infant care projects that include such services. From an ethical point of view, it is highly questionable whether poor people, who have high infant mortality rates and other health problems, are offered nearly as much in the way of free choice when offered birth control clinics as compared with the tremendous gains in freedom and welfare that would come from offering them birth control services along with maternal and infant health services. In the absence of any Commission recommendation of total medical care for everyone, irrespective of means, and in the absence of any plan that would greatly increase the income of the poor, policymakers should recognize that maternal health and infant care projects are a critical high priority item, both from the standpoint of freedom and distributive justice. This developmentalist perspective at least deserved careful scrutiny in the Report.

With one stroke of the pen, minors appear to have been given total reproductive freedom. The Report makes no distinction between minors living at home and those who do not. Nor are upper or lower age limits for minors stated.

Consider what this means. Sexually active individuals of twelve or thirteen could choose whether to use contraceptives, be sterilized, or have an abortion without cost to them and without any necessity that their parents know. There would be no need for discussions of "family planning." That would be a euphemism of another era. Sex is not a familial matter at all; it is an individual matter. That is what the law of the land would teach.

One might ask what has this got to do with the question of freedom? Sterilization and abortion, both available without impediment to minors if the Report is to be followed, are irreversible acts insofar as any of their most undesirable consequences are concerned. What would we think of the proposal that children have the right to decide whether and how long they will go to school or be educated? If children are to be truly free, this right should be granted them. No age limits for granting this right could, of course, be set. However, such a lack of legal guidelines on age is what the Commission is recommending for decisions on sterilization and decisions on abortion. As things now stand, education is compulsory up to a certain age. The arguments for this are that children need education in order to mature and to acquire the skills that will enable them to make choices and to realize their own potential for a satisfying life. This, at least up to the present, we have happily forced upon them. Thus it seems that children cannot decide whether or not to go to school, but they can decide at any age that they will never want any children and be sterilized. State policymakers should seriously examine the moral and logical contradictions in a policy that compels children to acquire the maturation and skills needed to make responsible decisions on the one hand, and yet urges that children be accorded the right to make some of the most momentous and irreversible decisions of their lives with or without parental or other adult guidance.

The recommendations of the Commission regarding minors are not the only way in which some of the most important familial functions are individualized. The pre-eminent consideration that leads the Commission to advocate abortion is not its impact on birth rates, about which the Commission can only speculate, but rather the freedom that it promises for women as individuals. Commissioner Grace Olivarez raises some issues about this notion of freedom that the Commission had an obligation to air and discuss thoroughly. She notes that:

Advocacy by women for legalized abortion on a national scale is so anti-women's liberation and women's freedom that it flys in the face of what some of us are trying to accomplish through the women's movement, namely, equality—equality means an equal sharing of responsibilities *by* and *as* men and women.

With women already bearing the major burden for the reproductive process, men have never had it so good. Women alone must suffer the consequences of an imperfect contraceptive pill—the blood clots, severe headaches, nausea, edema, etc. Women alone endure the cramping and hemorrhaging from an intra-uterine device. No man ever died from an abortion.

A more serious question is the kind of future we all have to look forward to if men are excused either morally or legally from their responsibility for participation in the creation of life. Women should be working to bring men into the camp of responsible parenthood, a responsibility that women have had to shoulder almost alone. Perhaps in our eagerness for equality, we have, in fact, contributed to the existing irresponsible attitude some men have toward their relationship to women and their offspring. Legalized abortion will free those men from worrying about whether they should bear some responsibility for the consequences of sexual experience.[11]

The abortion policy advocated in the Report drives a serious wedge, not only between parent and child, but also between parents.

Permissive abortion laws raise a number of moral issues that are far too readily dismissed by the Report, among them the following: the extent to which abortion is substituted for contraception; the persistence of illegal abortions, even in Eastern European countries, England, Sweden, etc., where the costs and availability of abortion are not supposed to be problems; increased risk of death from legal abortions; increased risk of prematurity and other undesirable consequences of abortion, and a lack of fetal protection, particularly for fetuses used in experimentation.[12] Indeed, the issue of abortion calls attention to a major weakness of the whole report. Nowhere is any weight given to the pedagogical role of the law. This neglected consideration facilitates the kinds of recommendations the Report makes regarding minors, child care facilities, abortion, and sterilization. It contributes to the failure of the Commission to take cognizance of certain evils that accompany permissive abortion laws of the New York variety—the kind of law the Report advocates. In several cases in New York fetuses still living after abortion have been allowed to die, and in several instances physicians knowingly perform abortions on women with fetuses more than twenty-four weeks old. These are not counted as illegal abortions, though in fact they are. The point of citing these instances is that one should not take lightly the warnings of various commissioners regarding the dangers of resort to destructive methods in solving a social problem. The disregard for life in New

York connected with abortion is serious enough to merit more than the lip service given by the Report to the possibility that permissive abortion policies might undermine regard for human life.

Moreover, the family comes in for another jolt. The Report solidly endorses the availability of child care. This recommendation has great potential for good, but also for ill. Combined with the rhetoric of unwanted children, to which a number of the dissenting commissioners object, it is one more way in which parent and child are divorced from one another. Certainly it is not clear whether child care will have this effect. The moral issue is whether or not there is sufficient evidence to assume that universal provision of child care is more beneficial than harmful. The Report is aware that there is no clear demographic justification for these child care centers. Again, however, it seems to be another way to give women and parents more freedom, and freedom in this Report is always good in itself. But the welfare of children and the quality of their development in their earliest years are also questions of freedom. For the maturity of our children and their ability to make choices will depend in large measure on the warmth and security that they experience as infants. How this is best achieved certainly requires much more analysis and documentation than the Report offers.

Clearly, in its recommendations and throughout the Report, the Commission is thinking of freedom as the removal of legal and administrative impediments. In contrast to developmentalists the Report does not give priority to freedom as the ability or power to choose and the conditions that enhance that power. The recommendation to subsidize the poor families who wish to adopt children is a happy exception. The other recommendations made by the Commission on behalf of racial minorities and the poor, although they are in principle designed to enhance freedom, fall considerably short of calling for the conditions that enable people to make reasonably meaningful and satisfying choices about their lives in such matters as housing and jobs. What is necessary to bring these groups into the mainstream of the American economy is at least a matter that requires considerably more attention to the requirements of social justice than is evident in the Report.

Social Justice

The relationship of the Report to the crying need for social justice in this country is a curious one. Throughout the Report there are numerous references to the great need to eliminate the effects of poverty. Furthermore, it is explicitly acknowledged that the birth rates of the poor and minority groups would be reduced by reducing poverty. Thus, for example, the general association of low fertility with better education and better income is cited. The fact that college-educated black women have lower fertility than other college-educated women is not ignored. But what is disappointing is that no recommendation is made that calls upon the state governments or the federal government to develop or implement policies that would deal directly with involuntary poverty. Nowhere are explicit reasons given why the Commission should or should not recommend policies that go considerably further than those the Report recommends for facilitating choices in securing jobs and housing. For example, if population and sex education are to be feasible, many of the schools in which poor people are to attain this education will need to be considerably upgraded. At the same time, a great deal of important job training occurs in schools. Better schools and scholarships for the poor and minority groups would seem to be vital for preparing people for the job market. The most obvious thing that the poor people need is income. It is difficult to see how a Commission concerned with lowering fertility rates as one means to reduce poverty can justify its failure to grapple with the difficult policy issues that surround the debates on guaranteed income, full employment, and the like. These are issues which should have been considered if the Commission had remained close to its stated desires for social justice among the poor. In addition, they may be more effective means of relating to the Commission's emphasis—overdrawn as it is—on the fertility aspect of the population issue. Nevertheless, the family planning ethos that the Commission represents and the Commission's unsympathetic response to the concerns of developmentalists for equity are here all too readily apparent. As one astute black woman has noted,

Even without children my life would still be bad—they're not going to give us what *they* have, the birth control people. They just want us to be a poor version of them only without our children and our faith in God and our tasty fried food, or anything.[13]

These feelings of one poverty-stricken black mother underline the claims for social justice. Within any population policy, attention must be given to these. Not only does justice require it, but lower birth rates, as the developmentalists recognize, are associated with lower infant mortality rates, increased educational and job opportunities, and better health care, particularly for women and children. Direct assaults on the conditions of poverty and the provision of good health care for all must be part of any population policy if such a policy is to be just and effective.

The Commission treats at least one social justice issue more responsibly. It rejects the injustices associated with attempts to influence fertility behavior through positive or negative incentives. The Commission is aware that incentives discriminate against less affluent sectors of any society and penalize the children of parents who fail to respond favorably to an incentive program.[14] In any event, there is no direct evidence that incentives can reduce birth rates and therefore no assurance that any injustices that might be perpetrated through their use would be worth the price.

In summary, let me briefly mention certain priorities of population policy for the states as I see them, and note how the Population Commission has responded to them.

Voluntarism vs. Governmental Compulsion

It should be readily apparent by now that I am in substantial agreement with the Population Commission Report in electing voluntarism and rejecting governmental resort to both compulsory measures and financial incentives designed directly to influence fertility behavior. I concur with the Population Commission that there are weighty reasons, rooted in current population trends and in traditions that value freedom and justice, for rejecting policies involving compulsion and incentives. I would argue, however, that there is an urgent need for some strict government regulation and/or incentives that would change the technologies, products, and behavior that cause environmental degradation. Pollution is a critical problem and solutions to it require governmental intervention now. Lower fertility rates in the absence of changes in pollution habits will not help us and may even hinder us. The Population Commission is misleading on this point.

Strengthening Family Life

Family life in the United States needs strengthening. Individualizing reproductive decisions can just as well favor higher birth rates as it presently favors lower birth rates, depending upon the fashions of the day. Strong family units, as among Jews in this country for example, have been associated with the lowest birth rates of any ethnic or religious group. Furthermore, individualizing sterilizations and abortions has no predictable effects on fertility, but for minors and the families of minors living at home may have some tragic consequences. These consequences, neglected by the Commission's recommendations, should be thoroughly investigated by state population policymakers.

I am not hereby arguing against those recommendations of the Commission favoring increased population and sex education and greater availability of contraceptives and contraceptive information. Rather I have been arguing that the Commission should be more concerned to increase the involvement of parents in sex education and also in the contraceptive choices of their children, particularly the children who are living with their parents. I would defend also the Commission's recommendations to spend government money for research to discover safer and otherwise better contraceptives. As noted, some of the popular contraceptives currently in use, have undesirable side effects.

Moving Toward Stable and
Stationary Population Growth

To argue that the family ought to be strengthened is not to take issue with the Commission regarding the desirability of achieving zero population growth. It seems reasonable to assume that space is limited. If, like the Population Commission, one affirms a goal of eventual zero population growth, an interesting kind of question and potential problem arises. How can any of us be certain that voluntary decisions made by couples will result in the number of children that bring about zero population growth?

The Commission is assuming that individual self-interest in choosing how many children to have will correspond on the average and over time with the interests of a society in having a certain number of people. This view of the correspondence of individual interests and societal interests has been challenged by individuals like Garret Hardin.[15] Hardin has compared the desire to have children with the desire of sheepherders to increase the size of their individual flocks. In a situation where there is a limited amount of grazing land, a society of sheepherders each bent on increasing their herds could not, Hardin contends, rely on voluntary means of curtailing the number of sheep who will graze on the land, and hence voluntarism will lead to overgrazing.

Hardin's analogy is certainly misleading, and probably fallacious. No human group has as many children as it possibly can, not even the celebrated Hutterites. Relatively large families are of great value under special conditions, such as those obtaining in peasant cultures, but in all these cultures family size is definitely limited.[16]

Even if we reject Hardin's view, however, does it follow that voluntarism will lead to zero population growth? At the present, no one can know for certain. The experience of hunter-gatherer societies still in existence in remote areas of the world is that zero population growth can be achieved voluntarily. How applicable this is to modern societies remains to be tested, provided that voluntarism is given an opportunity to work. One reason why voluntarism may succeed is that the interest people have in children may not be primarily a matter of self-interest, whether understood in the Commission's way or in Hardin's way; rather it may be much more an interest in the continuation of one's family and of one's community. Bearing and rearing a child is a contribution to the continuation of one's social group. Indeed, children are obviously needed for the survival of one's group. Where this interest in the future is jeopardized by having too many children, one would expect precisely those who have an interest in the future and the future of a society to want to limit births to the number needed to secure the welfare of their own children.[17]

Social Justice

It is very important to note that seeing one's interest in one's own children as an interest in one's group or society depends upon having some fair share of the goods in that society. Those who are too poor or are for other reasons alienated from any social group could not be expected to conform to the social norms or needs of any group that deprives them or otherwise alienates them. Ultimately, therefore, no population policy can be just in societies where gross inequities are tolerated or perpetrated.

Surely the highest priority for both state and federal governments in this country that directly relates to the fertility behavior of its citizens is social justice, particularly racial justice. The Population Commission knows that lower infant and maternal mortality, better education, economic opportunities, etc., are all associated with lower fertility. The scandalous death rates from malnutrition and lack of health care among the poor and especially among blacks—always much higher than for whites—demands immediate and strong responses both for the sake of justice itself and for the sake of anything that deserves the name family planning. The fundamental necessity to replace a policy of aid to dependent children that impedes rather than encourages family formation also must be squarely faced. The Population Commission has failed to recommend major assaults on these problems.

Population policies can only be morally justified insofar as the total welfare of populations affected by them is enhanced. The welfare of this country requires social justice; it is not enhanced by policies that do nothing substantial to save the lives and spirit of those who suffer from existing racial and economic inequities.

The Report of the U.S. Commission on Population Growth and the American Future is a significant document for anyone concerned with policymaking at the state level. It is a useful attempt, as faulted and ambiguous as it is, to consider the multiple factors that comprise population policies. In responding to the recommendations of the report, state policymakers should consider the interlocking issues presented by the Report but not be mislead by the Report's incomplete consideration of ethical issues. Freedom entails more than the absence of constraints and to use a narrow conception of freedom as a rationale for population policy is, as has been demonstrated, both naive and counterproductive. Second, any population policy not firmly planted in concerns for social justice becomes in itself unjust and a means for perpetuating unjust institutions. The weakness of the Commission's Report in the sphere of social justice cannot be over-emphasized to state policymakers who may wish to respond to the Report.

Notes

1. To achieve zero population growth requires 2.11 children per woman; the estimated average for 1972 is 2.08 children per woman. Given our present levels

of immigration, an average of exactly two children per woman leads to zero population growth; toward the end of 1972, birth rates had fallen below two children per woman.

2. *The Population Bomb* (New York: Ballantine, 1968).

3. For a discussion of the felt-need hypothesis, see A.J. Dyck, "Religious Factors in the Population Problem," in D.R. Cutler (ed.), *The Religious Situation: 1968* (Boston: Beacon Press, 1968), pp. 163-195.

4. Bumpass, L. and C.F. Westoff, "The Perfect Contraceptive Population," *Science*, Vol. 169, 1970.

5. *Population and the American Future*, The Report of the Commission on Population Growth and the American Future (Washington, D.C.: U.S. Government Printing Office, 1972), p. 51.

6. Pope John XXIII, *Mater et Magistra*, 1961, and Pope Paul VI, *Populorum Progressia*, 1967.

7. Engel's letter to Kautsky, February 1, 1881.

8. Kirk, Dudley, "A New Demographic Transition?" in *Rapid Population Growth: Consequences and Policy Implications* (Baltimore: The Johns Hopkins Press, 1971), Vol. II, pp. 123-147.

9. Wyon, J.B. and J.E. Gordon, *The Khanna Study* (Cambridge: Harvard University Press, 1971), pp. 291-314.

10. Revelle, Roger (Testimony), *Effects of Population Growth on Natural Resources and the Environment*. Hearings before the Reuss Subcommittee on Conservation and Natural Resources (Washington, D.C.: U.S. Government Printing Office, 1969).

11. *Population and the American Future*, op. cit., pp. 160-161.

12. The advantages and disadvantages of various abortion policies are thoroughly discussed by John M. Frimis, "Three Schemes of Regulation," in J.T. Noonan, Jr. (ed.) *The Morality of Abortion* (Cambridge: Harvard University Press, 1970), pp. 172-219. Note also the relevant chapters in Hilgers, T.W. and D.J. Horan (eds.), *Abortion and Social Justice* (New York: Sheed and Ward, 1973). Experiments using aborted fetuses in the state of New York since the passage of its more permissive law have involved the transplantation of thymus glands (*JAMA*, March 8, 1971) and keeping cerebral cortex alive up to a total period of nine months (*Science* 173, August 27, 1971), pp. 829-832.

13. Coles, Robert, *Children of Crisis* (Boston: Atlantic-Little, Brown, 1964), pp. 368-369.

14. Veatch, R.M. "Government Incentives: Ethical Issues at Stake" in: J.P. Wogaman (ed.), *The Population Crisis and Moral Responsibility* (Washington, D.C.: Public Affairs Press, 1973).

15. Hardin, Garrett, "The Tragedy of the Commons," *Science* 162, 1969, pp. 1243-1248.

16. See, for example, Wyon and Gordon, op. cit.

17. For a discussion of what policies might be morally justifiable as a last resort should voluntarism fail, and for further details about the kind of interest parents have in their children, see A.J. Dyck, "Population Policy and Ethical

Acceptability," in *Rapid Population Growth: Consequences and Policy Implications*, Vol. II, op. cit.

About the Editors

Elihu Bergman is Assistant Director of the Harvard Center for Population Studies; he received the Ph.D. in political science from the University of North Carolina. He has been with the Ford Foundation, VISTA, Development and Resources Corporation, and the Agency for International Development. His professional specialization has been the management of development programs in the United States and overseas; his major research interest is the political analysis of population policy. Dr. Bergman was an organizer and has served as Executive Secretary of the International Population Policy Consortium. He is a contributor to Richard L. Clinton and R. Kenneth Godwin (eds.), *Research in the Politics of Population* (Lexington Books, 1972) and coeditor (with Peter Bachrach) of *Power and Choice: The Formulation of American Population Policy* (Lexington Books, 1973).

David N. Carter is a regional planner with the Massachusetts Department of Community Affairs; his responsibilities include drafting legislation for county reorganization and regional planning. Mr. Carter is a candidate for the Ph.D. in Religious and Philosophical Ethics at Harvard Divinity School.

Rebecca J. Cook received the B.A. from Barnard College, Columbia University, and the M.P.A. from the John Fitzgerald Kennedy School of Government, Harvard University. Her professional specialization has been the development of public policy in population and environmental affairs. Ms. Cook has been employed by the Smithsonian Institution and the Pearson Commission of the World Bank; she has served as intern and consultant to the Population Council on state population policies.

Richard D. Tabors is Lecturer in City and Regional Planning and Research Associate in Population Studies, Harvard University. He received an interdisciplinary Ph.D. in geography and economics from the Maxwell School, Syracuse University. Dr. Tabors' research has focused on regional planning in Bangladesh and urban/environmental planning in the United States. His previous publications include *The Definition of Multifunctional Planning Regions: A Case Study of East Pakistan* (Harvard Center for Population Studies, 1971).

David R. Weir, Jr. received the M.S. in public management from the Massachusetts Institute of Technology in 1973; he is a candidate for the M.C.P. at Harvard University. His professional experience has included opinion survey research, social services, and land use planning.

Mary Ellen Urann received the A.B. in political science from Wellesley College in 1972. She is a student at Boston University School of Law and a research assistant at the Harvard Center for Population Studies. She has also been employed by the Massachusetts Citizen's Committee on Environmental Affairs, which gathered and coordinated citizen input during the reorganization of the state Executive Office of Environmental Affairs.

DATE DUE

GAYLORD   PRINTED IN U S.A